Life for Us Is What We Make It

Blacks in the Diaspora
Darlene Clark Hine, John McCluskey, Jr., and
David Barry Gaspar

General Editors

Life for Us Is What We Make It

*Building Black Community
in Detroit, 1915–1945*

Richard W. Thomas

Indiana University Press
Bloomington & Indianapolis

The paper used in this publication meets the minimum requirements of American National Standard for Information Sciences—Permanence of Paper for Printed Library Materials, ANSI Z39.48-1984.

Manufactured in the United States of America

Library of Congress Cataloging-in-Publication Data

Thomas, Richard Walter, date.
    Life for us is what we make it : building Black community in
       Detroit, 1915–1945 / Richard W. Thomas.
       p. cm. — (Blacks in the disapora)
    Includes bibliographical references and index.
    ISBN 0-253-35990-2
    1. Afro-Americans—Michigan—Detroit—History—20th century.
  2. Detroit (Mich.)—History. I. Title II. Series
    F574.D49N484 1992
    977.4'3400496073—dc20   91-26518

1 2 3 4 5   96 95 94 93 92

In Memory of my parents,
Walter and Estelle Thomas

CONTENTS

ILLUSTRATIONS

Photographs

Maps

Tables

PREFACE

THE BLACK COMMUNITY BUILDING PROCESS: A CONCEPTIONAL
FRAMEWORK FOR ANALYZING THE BLACK URBAN EXPERIENCE IN
INDUSTRIAL DETROIT, 1915–1945

In 1976, I wrote a Ph.D. dissertation entitled "From Peasant to Proletarian: The Formation and Organization of the Black Industrial Working Class in Detroit." The conceptional framework for that study was based upon the premise that the historical process by which a largely agricultural class was transformed into an industrial working class influenced: the struture of black leadership; internal institutions; and the economic, social and political development of the larger black community. This interpretation held that black industrial workers represented both the key historical factors and the social and economic change within the Detroit black community between 1915 and 1945. These industrial workers created the demand for the goods and services produced by the emerging black professional and business class but restricted by racism to the internal markets of the black community. Furthermore, the political modernization of the black community in Detroit during the 1930s drew support from the same segments of the black community involved in the unionization of the black industrial working class.[1]

In 1985, Joe William Trotter, Jr.'s book *Black Milwaukee: The Making of an Industrial Proletariat* was published. Trotter graciously credited my 1976 study for confirming his interest in proletarianization as a conceptional framework. He went on to say that Peter Gottlieb's work on black migrants in Pittsburgh and my work were the only detailed historical works "that focused on the process of Afro-American, urban industrial, working-class formations"—that our studies "constitute the immediate springboard from which proletarianization" is offered in his work as "an alternative perspective in research on black life in the urban North."[2] According to Trotter only a few studies, including Gottlieb's, Trotter's, and mine, have departed from the traditional historical approaches which focus on ghetto formation as the central theme of the black urban experience. I have since attempted to expand my conceptional framework to include more change factors in what I call "the community building process." I define the community building process as the sum total of the historical efforts of black individuals, institutions, and organizations to survive and progress as a people and to create and sustain a genuine and creative communal presence.

While much of this community building process has evolved within an historical dialectic involving the sheer struggle for survival and progress within a racist society, it has always transcended mere struggle for these admittedly practical and essential goals. At its heart, the black community building process has been driven by the oldest and deepest felt vision of black people in America—the struggle for freedom and equality. Therefore, I see black community building as an approach to the black urban experience in Detroit as much more organic than my previous work. Rather, I see it in the light of Vincent Harding's organic and visionary approach to the black experience in America, what he described as "a comprehensive and organic survey of the black movement toward freedom, of our search and struggle for justice, equality, and self-determination in the United States."[3] The community building process, then, implies an organic approach to understanding the sum total of the historical efforts of blacks in industrial Detroit to survive and progress. Hopefully, the conceptional approach I take in this study will contribute to what Trotter feels is needed in the field, namely, "systematic analyses, in a variety of contexts, of the complex relationship between proletarianization, institutional life, politics, race relations, and particularly, ghetto formation."[4]

Since 1976, I have gradually attempted to broaden my understanding of the black urban experience in industrial Detroit. Through research, teaching, and community involvement connected with my position primarily in the Urban Affairs Programs, I have come to appreciate the need for urban scholars to both generate and contribute to a body of knowledge which, while expanding our understanding of urban life, also commits us to the task of what Kenneth E. Boulding refers to as "human betterment."[5] As I have watched the black community in Detroit suffer through decades of poverty, crime, and violence, I have been forced to search for solutions through both research and practice.[6] My initial interest in the role of the black industrial working class in the growth and development of black Detroit helped clarify for me the active role of workers in that process. However, that understanding was not enough; I needed to pose other questions about the process by which black urban communities build themselves at various stages of their development. What change agents, social and economic forces, institutions, organizations, and choices determined the thrust of the community building process at different points in time? Most importantly, I needed to know how black Detroit survived and progressed during the three difficult decades between 1915 and 1945. Only then could I perhaps contribute to a body of knowledge which would both interest urban scholars and contribute to the survival and progress of the present black community, not only in Detroit but in other similarly situated black communities as well.

This book is about the process of black community building in industrial Detroit between 1915 and 1945, although it begins with community building in the nineteenth century. It focuses upon how industrial workers,

social workers, ministers, politicians, protest leaders, business and professional people, housewives, youth, and a range of community institutions
and organizations all contributed to the process of building a community.
This approach builds upon, but differs from, both the ghetto and the
proletarianization approaches to the black urban experience. It is an
attempt at understanding this experience from a more holistic perspective
rather than from a perspective emanating from one or more dominate
aspects of that experience in industrial America. The more we learn about
the complex nature of the black urban experience in industrial America,
the more we will have to expand and modify our theoretical paradigms.

Certain individuals, classes, institutions, and organizations played key
roles at various stages of the community building process. For instance,
the industrial working class acted as the catalyst for the entire process
beginning with World War I, thus setting in motion the economic and
social transformation of the larger black community. Other classes and
individuals played pivotal roles at other stages of the community building
process. For example, John C. Dancy as Director of the Detroit Urban
League developed desperately needed social programs such as Green
Pastures Camp and established and nurtured valuable networks among
influential black and white resource people, networks which greatly benefited poor black families. In addition, he, along with his staff, contributed
to the stabilization of the black industrial working class (what Trotter
would refer to as the "proletarianization" of the black working class),
which resulted in its gaining a permanent place in industrial Detroit.

During the First World War and the postwar period, the interplay
between black workers and the Detroit Urban League and the latter's
relationship with the white power structure determined the pace of community development. Each stage of the process of community building
required creative responses and adaptations to both internal and external
conditions. Often times, individuals, classes, institutions, and organizations, which had successively shepherded the black community or some
segment of it through one stage of development, were either unable or
unwilling to meet the needs and demands of particular community segments at other stages of community building. Clearly, black churches did
not have the resources or trained personnel to tackle the complex problems
of the migrants as efficiently as the Detroit Urban League. But several
black churches were able to participate in such programs as Negro Health
Week. Yet, black ministers who had patiently built relationships with the
Ford establishment after World War I, which proved so vital to the continual employment of black workers in the Ford plants at that stage of
community building, were unwilling to accept unionization as a viable
next step in the community building process.

Community building also embodied symbiotic relationships between
classes within the black community during certain stages. The black professionals and business class depended for their very survival upon the

black working class. Therefore, it was to their advantage to create organizations like the Booker T. Washington Trade Association and the Housewives League of Detroit to marshal community support for their services and products. While some scholars have interpreted such efforts as designed to benefit only the black middle class, the facts seems to indicate that benefits accrued to the larger community as well via professional and business peoples' support of community institutions.

Weathering the storm during the worst times, or just plain "hanging in there," contributed to community building as well. Of course the struggle against all forms of racial discrimination galvanized the community. Racial discrimination, however, raised the social consciousness of the black community and stimulated black self-help activities. Black politicians of both parties contributed to the community building process by getting blacks to exercise their right to vote. Although the black Democrats eventually carried the day, the black Republicans pioneered black political independence within the black community.

During the 1930s, the black community had to make some really hard choices concerning the future direction of the community building process. One was whether to stay with the party of Lincoln or take a leap of faith with the party of Roosevelt. The other choice, by far the most difficult of the two because of its more local impact, was between two very different strategies of community building: unionization and Ford corporate paternalism. The outcome of this conflict moved the black community to a higher stage of development.

Black community building, therefore, was not a smooth or conflict-free process. It proceeded through much trial and error and not without rancor between its chief builders and benefactors. Notwithstanding these impediments, by 1945, the black community in Detroit developed into one of the major centers of black progress. This study is an attempt to explain the community building process which made such progress possible.

ACKNOWLEDGMENTS

This book would not have been possible without the assistance of many devoted people. Foremost among these precious souls is my wife, June, who quietly but forcefully reminded me to put everything else aside and "finish the book!" and who sacrificed her own scholarly interests to allot me the time to do so.

I will always be grateful to several coworkers in the Urban Affairs Programs at Michigan State University for typing and retyping parts of the manuscript: Barbara Gaffield, Shirley Hoksbergen, Irma Gutierrez, and Marie McNutt who did the bulk of the typing and retyping of one draft. Sally Pratt patiently edited one draft of the manuscript. Mary Breslin was a virtual saint. She not only retyped segments of the book but also caught mistakes made in haste. Fran Fowler worked long hours completing the final draft.

Two graduate students in history, Kyungsik Irene Shim and Njeru Murage, helped with the research in the Urban League Papers for parts of chapter 3. Ms. Shim also worked with Tim Akers in the Labor Archives at Wayne State University. Sobha Ramanand checked and recomputed several tables. With a last minute notice, Bradley J. Davis took time away from his graduate work to redo the maps.

Harry Reed read the entire first draft and made valuable comments. Darlene Hine encouraged me through the revision, with high hopes for the possible contribution of this study to black urban history.

To my friend and Dean of Urban Affairs Programs at Michigan State University, Dr. Joe T. Darden, I owe much. Dean Darden never stopped encouraging to complete the task. He paid for the editing and the maps and allowed me to infringe upon his time when I needed that extra bit of encouragement.

Life for Us Is What We Make It

One

Early Struggles and Community Building

ROOTS OF THE STRUGGLE

As in the history of other oppressed groups and people, the black struggle against injustices helped to lay the foundation for community building. This struggle provided the cohesive and energizing spirit that welded blacks together to form communities whose collective purposes embodied much more than mere reactions to racial oppression. Rather, this struggle kept alive the hope and the vision—the twin engines of the black experience—which for centuries drove black communities, against all odds, toward economic, political, and social betterment. As in other communities, the early struggles laid the foundation for the future community building in black Detroit.

On the eve of World War I, black Detroit wondered about its future. So much had occurred in the past few decades. Opportunities had been gained and lost. Yet Detroit blacks had had success in building some sense of community. Many an old black Detroiter could remember when black people could not vote and black children could not attend public schools.

Blacks educated their children in damp, poorly lit church basements. It was a big victory, therefore, when the first black child walked through the door of one of Detroit's public schools on October 11, 1869.[1] A little over a year later, black men proudly cast their first ballots in the state election.[2] These victories had not come easily to black Detroiters.

In the 1840s, only a sprinkling of blacks could be seen in Detroit; there was nothing close to the complex and dynamic community life that would emerge a hundred years later. Detroit's proximity to Canada made it an ideal city for a terminus of the Underground Railroad. Thousands of fleeing, runaway slaves crossed the Detroit River annually, and as many as forty-three escaped across the river in one night.[3] Consequently, Detroit attracted many runaway slaves. Among these runaways were Thornton and Ruth Blackburn, whose arrest by a local sheriff on behalf of Kentucky slave hunters triggered the first black insurrection in the history of Detroit. In the ensuing struggle, the sheriff lost his life and the Blackburns escaped to Canada.[4] White Detroit was given notice: It was not just dealing with isolated black fugitive slaves disconnected from a protective community; instead, white Detroit officials were up against a black community that extended its protection to include all blacks, free and slave.

Detroit was more than a haven for fugitive slaves. Free blacks found the city more hospitable than the South. For several decades preceding the Civil War, free, skilled blacks from the Virginia cities of Fredericksburg, Richmond, and Petersburg brought their families to Detroit to escape the harsh black codes of their home state.[5] Once in Detroit, these blacks soon discovered the cruel realities of northern racism. They could not vote, they could work only in the most menial jobs, their children could not attend public schools, and they were largely unwelcome in white churches.[6] Yet these few blacks, ragged fugitives and weary but free men and women, determined to brave the worst, rolled up their sleeves, and started building a community.

As in other black communities, the church evolved into the first permanent institution of this new community; it also became the cornerstone of black activities. Church basements were used as black public schools, while chapels were used for both preaching and political gatherings. Blacks also used their churches for recreational purposes.[7] Three churches provided the institutional core of the evolving black community: the Second Baptist Church, established in 1836; the Bethel African Methodist Episcopal Church, founded in 1839; and St. Matthew's Church, founded as a Protestant Episcopal mission in 1846.[8] These churches often promoted congregational divisions within the black community, but they closed ranks when the larger black community faced common problems.

Similar to black churches in other nineteenth-century northern and southern cities, black churches in Detroit were "all-purpose" institutions, serving the overall needs of an exclusively black population. In several pre–Civil War cities, such as Philadelphia, New York, Baltimore, and

Boston, black churches evolved in response to the unwillingness of white churches to address the social and spiritual needs of their black coreligionists.[9] The white churches' rejection forced blacks to develop an institution which became the cornerstone of most northern black urban communities.

Black mutual aid and cultural organizations in Detroit emerged in significant numbers in the 1840s and 1850s, complementing the community building process of black churches. In this regard, the black community in Detroit reflected the community building trend going on in other black urban communities such as New York, Philadelphia, Baltimore, and Charleston between 1820 and 1840.[10]

In the 1840s, Detroit blacks joined a national movement among northern blacks to hold "Negro conventions." Rising job competition from European immigrants and increased racism from native whites forced northern blacks to organize separate institutions and conventions that would speak to their needs.[11] In late October 1843, Detroit blacks hosted the Michigan State Colored Convention. Blacks from around the state swarmed to the city to discuss their political and economic status. The convention denounced the state for depriving blacks of the right to vote. Much like their twentieth-century counterparts, the assembled blacks voiced concern over the lack of employment opportunities for black youth, especially in the manual trades. Much like black conventions in other states, the Detroit convention rejected proposals by radical blacks of the period who advocated black emigration to other countries. Instead, they took the more moderate position that blacks should cultivate good morals, establish moral reform societies, and develop habits of industry, thrift, education, and temperance.[12]

Black state conventions and black newspapers fostered a sense of self-definition throughout black urban communities in the North during the last half of the nineteenth century. Blacks from widely separate communities could meet to discuss and compare strategies for survival. Average working-class blacks could not afford to travel long distances to attend conferences, but they could at least read, or have read to them, stories of how blacks were surviving in other cities. Conventions and newspapers evolved into the first communication and educational networks used for group survival by blacks in the urban North.[13] Such networks kept black Detroiters in touch with the larger black struggles throughout the state and the nation.

In 1850, seven years after they had hosted the black state convention, Detroit blacks, many of whom were fugitive slaves, realized their worst fears: President Fillmore signed into law a new and more enforceable Fugitive Slave Bill. Panic ran rampant throughout the black community. Blacks who had thought they were relatively safe and who had painfully built new lives and established ties in the community now had to abandon homes and possessions in their haste to escape across the Detroit River into Canada. Throughout the next decade, waves of fugitive blacks and their families—some probably free relations of fugitives—fled to Canada. This number increased the Canadian black population from forty thousand in 1850 to close to sixty thousand in 1860.[14]

The new Fugitive Slave Law angered the blacks remaining in Detroit, creating a defiant mood among them. A month after the law went into effect, a crowd of blacks and sympathetic whites rioted over the arrest of a fugitive slave named Giles Rose. As the slave catchers attempted to return Rose to slavery in the South, the rioting crowd grew more furious, necessitating the calling of three companies of troops to prevent violence. Finally, the frightened mayor of Detroit called a mass meeting where a suggestion was made and accepted that Rose's freedom be purchased.[15]

Buying freedom for Detroit's fugitive slaves was far too expensive to be a common practice. More importantly, as historian Benjamin Quarles pointed out: "To most Negroes, outright defiance was a more emotionally satisfying response to the fugitive slaves than flight outside the country or raising money to pay a master."[16] Throughout the North, militant blacks defied the Fugitive Slave Law by holding anti–Fugitive Slave Law meetings and organizing vigilance committees. The latter activity consisted of boarding and lodging fugitive slaves for a period, obtaining food and clothing, giving a little money, providing legal information, and offering protection from constantly roaming kidnappers.[17] Some of these vigilance committees had white members, but, like most of those in Boston and Detroit, they tended to be all black.[18]

One of the largest black vigilance committees was the African-American Mysteries: The Order of the Men of Oppression. Composed of blacks from the United States and Canada, it had a membership numbering in the thousands. The Grand Charter Lodge of the organization was set up in a building on Jefferson Avenue between Bates and Randolph Streets. George de Baptiste and William Lambert, two prominent radical blacks in Detroit, belonged to the organization. The organization sent agents into the South to aid slaves in their escapes, which resulted in the escape of nearly forty thousand slaves.[19]

Helping their black brethren escape slavery became a holy crusade among many northern free blacks. They devised countless methods to subvert the Fugitive Slave Law. One effective method was to use their own "free" papers to help slaves escape. As a Detroit paper stated in an article on the Underground Railroad in Detroit: "This very system of free papers and passes, which was designed by the slave owners to strengthen and secure the 'peculiar institution,' was made an instrument of freedom." A good example, the papers pointed out, was the way in which a certificate owned by George de Baptiste "was used no less than 33 times to aid slaves to escape."[20]

Participation in the Underground Railroad was obviously illegal, but Detroit blacks, like thousands of other northern blacks, deliberately chose to break the law to secure freedom for their southern brethren. White laws had lost their sanctity for these black radicals of the 1850s. The laws of black survival had invalidated all white laws which supported slavery and oppression.

If black Detroiters had any doubts in the 1850s as to the reality of a mounting white racism, they were removed by the Michigan Constitutional Convention and the subsequent popular referendum which granted detribalized Indians the right to vote but refused it to blacks. One of the reasons for denying black males the vote was summed up quite dramatically by one of the many demagogues of the time: "What man would like to see his daughter encircled by one of these sable gentlemen breathing in her ear the soft accents of love?"[21] Blacks would have to wait two decades before casting the ballot, so they had to rethink their strategies for survival. Some moderate Detroit blacks abandoned their traditional opposition to the radical philosophy of emigration. Others assembled in a Detroit home to hear John Brown and Frederick Douglass during the summer of 1859. Brown, five of his men, and fourteen slaves had arrived from Missouri to seek support for their planned insurrection. Brown met with Douglass and several Detroit black leaders at the home of William Webb. Douglass objected to Brown's original plan to raid single plantations until he had assembled about a thousand slaves, with whom he would then "swoop down on the large towns and cities, collecting forces and material as he progressed." According to a newspaper account eleven years later, Brown became angry at Douglass's objection and implied that perhaps Douglass was a coward. Douglass denied the implication and said he would give material aid if he chose not to approve of or participate in the planned insurrection. Local black leader George de Baptiste also objected to the plan, but in its place he proposed a gunpowder plot to blow up fifteen of the largest churches in the South on a fixed Sunday. Brown objected to de Baptiste's plan, arguing that he did not want to shed blood needlessly. De Baptiste still insisted upon radical measures, saying that Brown's plan would fail and cost millions of lives.[22]

The meeting marked a radical change in Detroit blacks' perception of the struggle. They became desperate enough to seriously discuss revolutionary violence against the slave system. Black and white abolitionists had fought against slavery for decades only to see the slavery system ultimately given more enforceable protection by federal law. On a summer day in 1859 in Detroit, the offenses of history sprang up from their seedbed seeking a reckoning. John Brown and his faithful followers went to their deaths soon after, but not without deepening black Detroit's sense of struggle.

On March 6, 1863, barely two months after President Lincoln had declared slaves to be free in the rebellious South and while Detroit blacks were yet celebrating "the day of Jubilee," a white mob, inflamed over the alleged rape of two girls by a black man named William Faulkner, rioted and burned down most of the black community. The predominantly Irish mob attacked men, women, and children, old and young; they killed two blacks and seriously injured many others. Over two hundred blacks lost their homes. Many left Detroit and never returned. After spending years in prison, Faulkner was declared innocent of the charges.[23]

The Detroit riot of 1863 was part of a general anti-black hysteria that existed in several northern cities during the Civil War period. Irish people made up the majority of the anti-black mobs that gathered in these cities. They felt threatened by a war that was being fought to free black slaves who they thought would then come north and compete against them for jobs.

A high level of viciousness characterized these anti-black riots, which claimed the lives of black men, women and children. In some cities white rioters burned black communities to the ground. Blacks in New York suffered the most. Hundreds were run out of town. In one case angry white mobs lynched blacks from lampposts.[24]

The pain of the riot bit deeply into the psyche of black Detroit. They had never felt secure in the city. Too many of them were fugitive slaves, hesitant to put down roots for fear that some ambitious slave catcher would catch them. Thus, the Canadian shoreline beckoned as the ultimate refuge.

The Civil War, however, offered a balm that helped ease the hurt and frustration of the 1863 riot. Young black men had a chance to strike a blow against the much-hated slave system. Black men in Detroit longed to join the battle against the slave holders and to put their patriotism to the test. When black men were finally allowed to enlist in the Union Army, Detroit blacks stood among the first to join up. Fugitive slaves living in Canada returned to Detroit across the river to sign up to fight in the war. In March 1864 black soldiers of the 102nd United States Colored Troops left Detroit to join the Union Army in South Carolina. During nineteen months of service, 1,409 Detroit black soldiers fought in ten bloody battles. At the end of the war, 144 had given their lives to end slavery.[25]

An opportunity to give one's life in a war against black slavery had deep meaning for the black community. Black men had fought in earlier wars, the Revolutionary War, and the War of 1812. Although they would fight in every American war thereafter, the Civil War held special significance: it was the only American war in which the national interest and the survival of blacks as a people hung in the balance together.

BLACK CELEBRATIONS: SYMBOLS OF COMMUNITY
STRUGGLE AND SURVIVAL

For a while, historical events seemed to be favoring blacks, even in the midst of certain enduring hardships. Even the horrible race riots in March of 1863 could not dampen the enthusiasm of Detroit blacks over the Emancipation Proclamation. In January 1863 blacks met in the African

Methodist Church and sang "Blow Ye the Triumph Blow." They then formed a committee to draft resolutions to express their feelings:

> Resolved that we thank God for putting it into the heart of Abraham Lincoln to proclaim liberty to the colored race; because it works benefits not only to four millions of colored men, but to five millions called at [*sic*] the South "poor white trash," who have no education, and their masters, the slave-owners are determined they shall have none, and they are therefore fit only for filibustering, and carrying out the cursed design of the slavery propagandists at [*sic*] the South, and their vile supporters at [*sic*] the North. We believe that slavery makes labor disrespectable, and any country in this state, must necessarily remain under the curse of God, until such evils are removed. We hail the Emancipation as a great good to mankind. We hail it with joyful acclamations, and shall only await the morrow to see more plainly and perfectly developed the idea and principle of the President. May God bless Abraham Lincoln and the people.[26]

Several days later, a mixed crowd of black and white, young and old, rich and poor, packed into a black Baptist Church to celebrate the proclamation.[27]

In 1866, mixed blacks—those with racially mixed ancestry—won the right to vote, a privilege denied the majority of black Detroiters until the fall of 1870. By that time, the Fifteenth Amendment had already been ratified and was part of the federal Constitution; it was fortunate for Michigan blacks that the amendment had been ratified at the federal level, because close to half of Michigan's voters voted against granting blacks the franchise.[28] The Fifteenth Amendment was only the first step in a long, long journey. Winning the right to vote would not bear fruit for the black community as a whole until almost a century later when an increased black population would transform the ballot from a mere electoral token that allowed the black middle class and upper class to pursue their family and class interests into a major force for black political, social, and economic survival.

On October 11, 1869, black children were admitted for the first time to the Detroit Public School System. Providing education for black children had been problematic for the black community since the 1830s. Political and social pressures associated with the Fugitive Slave Laws and the organized struggles of free blacks to secure freedom for their southern brethren constantly destabilized the Detroit black community. The black community, however, still was able to initiate some efforts toward the education of its young. Black churches became black schools during weekdays. In 1839 Detroiters petitioned the state legislature to aid Detroit to establish a separate school for black children in the city. Finally, school officials added an eighth district to the Detroit school system to accommodate black children. This district came under the jurisdiction of the Detroit School Board. The Board appointed black and white teachers to teach in these schools. By 1869 three black schools existed in Detroit with another one under construction.[29]

The post–Civil War spirit led to the opening up of the public schools to black children. In this historic moment, blacks in Detroit, as elsewhere in the country, enjoyed the first fruits of post-Reconstruction racial progress. In March 1875, the icing on the cake came in the form of the Civil Rights Bill. Once again, blacks celebrated their good fortune in mass meetings held on street corners and in churches.[30]

By the 1870s, black celebrations had come to play an increasingly significant role in the Detroit black community. Most of these celebrations arose from the struggles of black people in the new world such as those leading to the independence of Haiti in 1793 and the emancipation of slaves in the British West Indies in 1834. The earliest black history event celebrated was March 5, 1770, the day of the Boston Massacre, in which British troops shot and killed five civilians, including Crispus Attucks, a black. At first, the Boston Massacre was commemorated by many people, with Crispus Attucks being numbered among the martyrs of the massacre. However, that celebration soon gave way to Independence Day, a celebration of the July 4, 1776, adoption of the Declaration of Independence, which was observed mainly by whites. Blacks in Boston resurrected Attucks's martyrdom as a holiday to protest the Dred Scott decision. In 1888, Boston blacks realized their fondest dreams when the state legislature and the city council gave $13,000 to build a Crispus Attucks monument on the Boston Commons. Several generations later, Boston blacks would succeed in having the governor of the state officially designate and proclaim March 5 as "Crispus Attucks Day."[31] Crispus Attucks Day was thus one of the first black celebrations used to develop black community solidarity. As such, it contributed to the community building process in those black communities in which it was celebrated.

Ranked as the most popular and widely held black celebration during the antebellum period was the commemoration of August 1, 1834, the day when an act of Parliament abolishing slavery in the British West Indies became effective. Both blacks and their white abolitionist supporters found it more relevant to celebrate this day than the Fourth of July, which they viewed as a "mockery . . . as long as slavery existed in our country."[32]

August 1, therefore, became a major social event in free black communities. "For racial intermingling in a friendly and relaxed setting," a scholar commented, "no affair could touch an August 1 picnic."[33] Detroit and Canadian blacks, often joined by whites, celebrated August 1 in Windsor and Sandwich, Ontario, Canada. For several decades, Detroit white newspapers reported on these black celebrations. On one such occasion in 1851 the *Detroit Free Press* reported:

> Our colored inhabitants yesterday celebrated the anniversary of emancipation in the British West Indian colonies in good style. Quite a lengthy and showy

procession, headed by a band of music, marched through the streets to the river and crossed to Canada, where speeches and refreshments were the order of the day. Everything we are told was conducted with decorum.[34]

After emancipation of American slaves on January 1, 1863, blacks had two major black holidays to celebrate. Sometimes black Detroiters celebrated the emancipation of American slaves on the same day as their traditional celebration of West Indian emancipation mentioned above. This seemed odd to some white observers. "There is certainly something very incongruous," commented one white reporter, "in the idea of selecting the 1st of August as the anniversary of President Lincoln's proclamation, and going to an obscure village in Canada to celebrate it. However," this reporter concluded, "It is better there than not at all."[35]

Had this white reporter inquired more thoroughly into the annual black celebration, he might have learned that black Detroiters and their Canadian brethren were most probably celebrating both black holidays at the same time because of the convenience of good summer weather. Many blacks also preferred this time of year, particularly September 22, as Slave Emancipation Day because it was on September 22 in 1862 that President Lincoln issued his preliminary proclamation declaring that if the rebel southern states did not surrender by January 1, he would abolish slavery in those states.[36] Even so, as a "historic holiday," according to Quarles, "September 22, despite its more favorable position on the calendar, never really rivaled January 1."[37] Such was certainly the case in Detroit in 1871, where blacks, on January 4, "turned out in large numbers to hear speeches, eat and have fun."[38] Both celebrations would continue well into the twentieth century.

The ratification of the Fifteenth Amendment on March 30, 1870, soon took its place among black holidays and celebrations, if only for a brief time. Black women in some cities celebrated the occasion by wearing "shawls of red, white, and blue." At one ratification celebration in Baltimore, over 10,000 blacks paraded through the streets. Many blacks came to prefer this historic day to the day of emancipation since it was argued that "Lincoln's proclamation only benefitted the slave. Whereas the Fifteenth Amendment benefitted all Negroes."[39]

The majority of Detroit blacks celebrated the ratification day by just incorporating it into the annual August 1 celebration in Canada. Blacks devoted one day of the 1870 celebration to the emancipation of slaves in the British West Indies and another day to the commemoration of the abolition of slavery in the United States and the adoption of the Fifteenth Amendment to the U.S. Constitution. For a while blacks from every social background participated in these annual black celebrations. One particularly observant reporter caught the full color of the 1869 black celebration in Canada: "The 35th anniversary of the emancipation in the West Indian Islands was celebrated yesterday at Sandwich. . . . They came on foot, and on horseback, in fancy carriages, and on tumbledown wagons, gaily dressed and seedy, of all ages and shades of duskiness."[40]

Traditionally, speeches at these celebrations reminded the celebrants that the occasion meant more than eating and having fun. On one occasion, a former Kentucky slave admonished the crowd: "My friends, it is a great mistake to suppose that we came here merely to eat and drink and laugh, and have a good time. Unless, we can do or say something to make each other better men and women in the future, we should have stayed home."[41]

For blacks in Detroit, and other black communities in the United States and Canada, black celebrations helped to create a sense of collective struggle. The white reporter who could not understand why blacks celebrated some of their historic holidays on dates other than those on which the historic events occurred and who could not understand why blacks would want to celebrate such holidays in an "obscure village in Canada" probably never realized the deeper meaning of these holidays for blacks. In all likelihood, he and others never fully understood the symbolic meaning in celebrating the liberation of blacks on the Canadian soil which had been for so long a refuge for fugitive slaves. Canada held an important place in the hearts and souls of black Detroit and would continue to do so for years to come. These black celebrations created an international community among black Americans in Detroit and black Canadians in Sandwich and Windsor in Ontario. But much more than that, these celebrations created and maintained a sense of black peoplehood, connecting the past with the future. In short, black celebrations were among the first cultural representations of black community building in Detroit.

INTERNAL PROBLEMS OF A COMMUNITY IN FLUX

One of the sad ironies of history is that members of a race or nation are often united only when they are oppressed or struggling against some external enemy. Once the victory is in sight, old internal conflicts reemerge. And if they were not there before, they develop. A case in point: Black elites in the 1870s began to be a bit embarrassed by the race-consciousness of the black celebrations. At times, segments of this class expressed little interest in community building; rather, they tended to use their newly-won voting power, along with the help of their white Republican friends, to work their way into white society. Black community-building social activities, therefore, were counterproductive to the black elites' class-building agenda for survival. This is the first of several critical historical junctures in the black community building process where segments of the larger black community embraced diametrically opposed values and strategies for enhancing and empowering the community. This historical juncture became even more critical when certain segments of the black community sought to become "members" of the larger white community at the expense of the black community solidarity. As early as 1871, leading black citizens in Detroit stopped participating in black celebrations such as the commemoration of the Fifteenth Amendment. A couple of years later these black elites approved a resolution recommending that blacks stop celebrating black holidays because such celebrations had the tendency to "perpetuate caste feelings." Instead, these black elites argued, blacks should celebrate only national holidays.[42] These black elites frowned upon the more pronounced "black" celebrations, because they tended to galvanize racial solidarity, which slowed the process of black assimilation. Yet, the real problem was not the celebrations but the pervasive racism, which necessitated that such celebrations be effective modes for building a community to offer protection from such racism.

CLASS BARRIER TO COMMUNITY BUILDING

Segments of the black elites also avoided popular black public dances. They only attended social affairs given by their own clubs. Black elite families, such as the Robert A. Pelhams and the Thaddeus Warsaws, were indistinguishable in their social mannerisms from the white elites, whom they painfully attempted to imitate through their exclusive dinners and teas. Similar class developments occurred in other black communities such as Cleveland and Chicago.[43]

Color reigned supreme among the black elites during this period. They carefully married within their class and color, so much so that others called them "crème de la crème." They refused to open their ranks to any Detroit blacks lower than themselves in the social scale. In one sense, such attitudes and social practices appeared to be incompatible with the fact that the black elite was often in the forefront in the battle against racism and the fact that black upper-class women occasionally engaged in humanitarian work among the urban poor.[44] Yet these apparent contradictions were quite consistent with the exclusive survival agenda of the black elite. By avoiding all black-oriented social activities (except when they needed black community support for some political position) they were able to distance themselves from the "visible" black community, which helped them gain access to white society. The black elite preferred the appellation "Afro-American" over "Negro" because they believed whites preferred the former. By following these social practices, the black elites believed they stood a better chance of integrating into white America. Even the humanitarian work of Detroit's black upper-class ladies was calculated more to keep up with white counterparts than to provide a ladder for the black masses to climb up the black social structure.[45] In fact, they trembled at the thought of association with the black masses.

Members of the Detroit black elite not only looked down their noses at blacks outside their social circle, they also engaged in "victim blaming." They readily joined the white upper class in blaming the problems of the black urban poor upon the group itself. They purposely established social clubs and social networks for the survival of their own class. From the moment the black community obtained the vote, the black elites strategically used it to further their class aims. They became a link between the black community and the then thriving Republican Party. By using their ties—albeit weak—with the black community, the black elites were able to obtain political plums for their sons and daughters. In short, the black elites subordinated the possibility of a political agenda for building up the larger black community to their own class agenda. Katzman paints the picture well:

> In the end, these men and their close circle—all of whom were members of the black elite—would reap the greatest benefits from the black community's stalwart Republicanism. Political participation provided them with an entree into the white community, and they were responsible for making integration the primary articulated goal of black political activity during a period when employment, education, and housing should have been more essential issues for most Detroit blacks. The elite profited most directly by monopolizing nearly all of the patronage that flowed to the black community; little of it filtered down to the lower classes.[46]

In all fairness to the Detroit black elites, they were not alone in their class-based survival orientation. Rather, they had been part of the post-Reconstruction northern black leadership with roots in the antebellum, free-black communities of New York, Chicago, Philadelphia, Washington, D.C., and Baltimore. Their involvement in the abolition movement had developed into close economic and social ties with the white community. These ties tended to encourage a belief in integration as the best possible solution for black people.[47] But the black elite had no intention of working for the integration of *all* black people.

This class bias and exclusiveness on the part of many members of the black elite stemmed from their view of their unique relationship to the larger black community. Most of them did not believe in black community building as an end in itself or in building a sense of black community pride as expressed in black celebrations. Rather, their beliefs and actions tended to reflect a view of community building as a means to an end, that end being the greater integration of their class into white society. Community building as an end in itself would have to wait until white racism forced all classes of blacks to close ranks and unite for their collective survival and progress.

The northern black elitists held to their belief in integration even while white racial attitudes hardened in the South and in the North. Positive change had been rapid and impressive in the 1870s and 1880s. Southern racism decreased for a while and northern cities integrated their schools. Things seemed to be looking up for blacks everywhere. Yet by 1883 the Supreme Court had overturned the U.S. Civil Rights Act of 1875. Soon the traditional white allies of northern blacks would either die off or lose their influence. The black elites of Detroit, however, remained in the saddle for awhile. Notwithstanding the black community's internal political conflicts which prevented sustained unity during the 1870s and 1880s, the 1890s witnessed the greatest black electoral victories that would occur before World War I.[48]

THE NEW BLACK MIDDLE-CLASS STRATEGY FOR BLACK COMMUNITY BUILDING

Industrialization brought in larger numbers of European immigrants. They took jobs away from the black working class and eroded the political influence of the black elite. In 1890 blacks noticed that white politicians like Mayor Hazen S. Pingree had begun to court European immigrant groups rather than blacks.[49] A year earlier in 1889, a local black newspaper, the *Plain Dealer,* had warned its readers of the changing times and of what blacks must do:

> Afro-Americans in every section of the country are forming leagues and societies in which they are discussing the conditions of their race, and methods for its betterment. The recent insults in the North and the outrages in the South are subjects of interest and indignation for every man who has brains enough to appreciate the dangerous trend of public sentiment against a class who are already unfortunate enough. What are the young men of Detroit doing in the matter? Are they indifferent to the fact that race indignities throughout the entire country are becoming more numerous? We have had clubs for dancing and clubs for card playing, and literary clubs, and social clubs, which are all well enough in their way, but the bright young men whom we delight to meet in these social affairs should remember that they are to be the bulwark of safety to their race in the future, and should realize that there is a time for serious consideration as well as social amusement and that time is at hand.[50]

The emerging new black middle class heard this message. By the turn of the century the black upper class had lost its token political leverage in the white community and had little influence within the black community. The new middle class was now at the helm, and not a moment too soon. Survival strategies of the black elites had proven dysfunctional not only for themselves as a class but for the larger black community as well. Integration had never worked as a viable survival strategy for the majority of black Detroiters in the late nineteenth century. Having one's sons or daughters attend white universities, white churches, and fashionable parties could not build and sustain the community to which they belonged by race and history. In hard truth, however, such achievements were mere tokens masquerading as universal race progress. In the end, the harsh hand of time demanded a reckoning. New leadership was needed if blacks were to survive and progress.

In the 1880s, the new black middle class charted the future direction of black Detroit by choosing the path of independent black business development as a mode of community building. Gradually black business people began abandoning the white market for the black market. Southern migrants provided some impetus for this development as they increased the black population. The main impetus, however, resulted from "the aggressiveness and ambition" of the new arrivals. Ambitious southern blacks arriving in Detroit in the 1880s could not help but notice the bustling industries and the ragtag European immigrants flooding through the factory gates. Try as they might, blacks could not obtain jobs in the factories. Many a black worker would watch European immigrants arrive one day without the proverbial "pot to piss in" and before long see the same immigrants climb the occupational ladder to economic security. No wonder a black dishwasher commented in 1891: "First it was de Irish, den it was de Dutch and now it's de Polacks as grinds us down. I s'pose when dey [the Poles] gets like de Irish and stands up for a fair price, some odder strangers'll come over de sea 'nd jine de family and cut us down again."[51] Black professionals, such as lawyers, did little better, being forced to earn their bread and butter in other vocations.[52]

Increasingly, blacks lost ground due to immigrant competition and white racism. The better domestic jobs were reserved for white servants. In 1870 blacks comprised over half of Detroit's barbers (most cut the hair of whites), but by 1910 their numbers had shrunk to a mere 7.3 percent. Competition from Italian immigrants and increasing racial restriction contributed greatly to this decline in black barbers.[53] Katzman points out that, in the early 1890s, possibly as many as 30 percent of the black male workers in Detroit worked regularly or occasionally on the docks. While he claims that no statistics exist indicating changes over time in the racial makeup of the dock workers as a group, he suggests that blacks probably made up a larger percentage of dock workers in the 1870s and 1880s "than they did in the 1890s and the first decade of the twentieth century." According to Katzman, "It is likely that the immigrants who arrived in Detroit after 1890—the Poles and Italians—replaced many blacks on the docks."[54] European immigration met the increasing labor demands of industrializing Detroit, resulting in the marginalization of the black working class. From 1890 to 1910, the overwhelming majority of industrial workers in Detroit were recent immigrants from Europe. In some factories, the entire work force was composed of foreign-born workers. In 1910, only 106 out of 3,750 workers in car and railroad shops of Detroit were native-born white Americans. Many factories in the city hired along ethnic lines only, and some drew their workforce from only one ethnic group. For example, before World War I, the Dodge Brothers hired only Polish workers. As a result, black workers were closed out of these "ethnically organized" factories. In 1890, the brass and ship industries did not employ a single black worker. Out of 5,839 male workers in the tobacco, stove, iron, machine, and shoe industries, only twenty-one workers were black. Conditions remained unchanged a decade later. The entire range of shoe, book, brass, chemical, furniture, gas, iron and steel, machine, stove, tin, tobacco, and wire industries, employing 10,498 males, employed only thirteen black males in 1900. The 1900 census reported only 139 blacks among 36,598 workers in the manufacturing and mechanical operations. By 1910, five years before the demand for black labor hit Detroit industries, only twenty-five black workers could be found among "the 10,000 mostly foreign-born, semiskilled operatives and laborers who worked in Detroit's automobile factories." Black women suffered the same fate as black men. In 1910, black women workers labored in domestic and personal services.[55] In short, from the Civil War to World War I, the vast majority of black workers labored on the margins of Detroit's industrializing economy.

If blacks were going to progress or at least survive until a time when they could do better, they would have to turn inward and develop new strategies for meeting the challenges of the times. Black Detroiters of the 1880s and 1890s had reached an historical crossroad in the community building process. One road led to a continual struggle to integrate into the white mainstream and the other road led to independent black development.

The Detroit black elite chose integration at all costs. Any notion of independent development ran counter to their class ideology and mode of survival. Not so for the emerging new black middle class in Detroit and in other northern areas. What appeared to be a backward step in racial progress to the black elite represented opportunities for achieving racial solidarity for the budding black business class in Detroit.

Composed of skilled artisans such as bakers, coopers, masons, plasterers, along with small-scale entrepreneurs such as lunchroom owners and cigar-store keepers, the new black middle class embodied the spirit of future black survival and progress in Detroit. From the 1880s to about 1910, black middle class entrepreneurs established saloons, hotels, news dealerships, candy stores, funeral homes, groceries, drugstores, moving companies, coal yards, lumber yards, and especially financial and realty agencies. Some overly ambitious black leaders in 1890 made a valiant but abortive attempt to maintain a joint stock company, the Detroit Industrial and Financial Cooperative Association. Authorized to buy and sell houses, and to lend money to the black laboring classes to build houses, the association did not last long.[56]

Confined by residential segregation to the expanding ghetto and excluded from traditional black service jobs dependent on white clients, such as barbering, the new black middle class had no other choice but to choose a strategy of community building based on racial pride, solidarity, and economic independence. Thus, this phase of community building evolved from increasing residential segregation, which produced and sustained key sectors of economic development within the black community. In adopting this strategy, the new black middle class in Detroit was merely responding to the new needs of the increasingly segregated black community. In addition, most of the southern migrants to Detroit after 1900 joined the ranks of the middle class.[57]

Blacks continued to establish large scale economic organizations, but they continued to fail. The time was not yet ripe for such economic activity. The black community needed a larger population base, a self-contained consumer market that could support black business as a vital mode of community building. This condition would soon be met by extensive black migration from the South, which would increase the black population sufficiently to support black business enterprises.[58]

If budding black capitalists had had access to the investment capital of many of the black elite families, such as the Coles, Lamberts, Watsons, and Strakers, who invested in real estate—mainly in white neighborhoods—the internal economic development of the black community would have proceeded at a faster rate. Such wealth channeled into black economic ventures could have created some jobs at a time when European immigrant workers were pushing black workers out of the job market. At the time, however, the black community did not have any solid financial institutions to facilitate such job-generating activities, and, most importantly, the black elite used their wealth primarily to benefit their offspring, who, instead of contributing to the survival and growth of the budding black entrepreneurial effort, opted for "the government payroll."[59]

Notwithstanding the black elites' lack of collective vision and their narrow perspective on the means for black survival—namely integration—black middle-class entrepreneurs by 1900 had abandoned integration as a viable mode of community building. An infusion of new blood from black communities in Michigan's hinterland and the South added a fresh zeal to the black community building process. The new black middle class differed from the old black elite in that they saw themselves as responsible for uplifting "the race." "Although they shared some of the old elite's patronizing attitudes towards the poor and failed at times to understand the life styles of the lower classes," Katzman pointed out that "they appeared more genuinely interested in all blacks than the old elite had been, and they sought to help all who were in need." If any one thing can be pinpointed as the salient philosophy which fueled and directed their efforts of the new middle class, it was their sense of an historical mission and obligation to the larger black community. This was something the black elite neither had nor cared to cultivate. "Unlike the old elite," Katzman continues, "the new black middle class recognized that society imposed a common destiny on all Negroes and that the improvement of their own lives was linked with the advancement of the whole black community."[60]

The new black middle-class clubs reflected this attitude. Unlike the more exclusive black elites, the middle class organized their social clubs with an eye toward uplifting the black community. Most importantly, black middle-class clubs led the way in extending a helping hand to new arrivals, who more often than not were the working poor. One middle-class club organized in 1906 sought to "protect decent girls and to reform fallen women by teaching . . . millinery, dressmaking, and embroidery. . . ." The Christian Industrial Club, founded in 1909, provided housing for working black girls, and the Detroit Women's Council, set up in 1911, helped new arrivals. Whatever their class bias, these clubs formed the core of the new black middle-class movement to build the black community.[61]

By the eve of World War I, the new black middle class in several major urban areas had developed an internal institutional "safety net" for the black community. Rather than waiting for whites to change their racial attitudes, they opted to go it alone if need be. Realizing that the black elite was more interested in socializing with upper-class whites than with blacks of the middle or lower classes, the black middle class created its own internal support system and edged the upper class out of power. Those of the black upper class who wanted to join in the black struggle to build a community were generally welcomed but were not allowed to change the new agenda for black survival and progress, which would remain in the hands of the new black middle class until the 1930s.

Racial solidarity and self-help were, therefore, the philosophical pillars of the new black middle-class mode of community building that emerged between 1870 and 1900. A spirit of black self-help swept the South in the midst of the dismantling of radical reconstruction. Southern middle-class blacks migrating North took this philosophy with them. Once in the North, they and their northern counterparts sustained and nurtured it to fruition. When Booker T. Washington organized the National Negro Business League in 1900 he tapped into a nationwide groundswell of black economic nationalism. To his great credit, Washington provided this groundswell with national organizational form and direction. By 1907 the National Negro Business League had 320 branches throughout the country. Detroit would establish its local league in 1926.[62]

Between 1865 and 1915, the demographic profile of the black community changed dramatically, even while it maintained some characteristic features common to black community formations in industrializing cities. Between 1865 and 1917, the black population in Detroit never went beyond six thousand. The largest percentage of population increase during this period, 59 percent, occurred between 1860 and 1870 but included only about 800 blacks. Such a small number of blacks stood little chance of competing against European immigrants who increased their numbers from 51,000 in 1880 to 156,000 in 1910.[63] During this period, the largest black community was located on the lower east side of the city with Woodward Avenue as the "identifiable western boundary" of black Detroit. Eighty-seven percent of Detroit's blacks lived in an interconnected area on the east side which, since the 1850s, had been identified as the black community. However, this community was characterized by heterogeneous res-

idential patterns.[64] As better-off blacks sought better housing, they tended
to move farther north, leaving the poorer blacks concentrated in the more
densely populated sectors of the black community. From 1910 to 1920,
the black community experienced its most rapid population change in over
a half century. More blacks entered Detroit during this ten year period
than in the previous sixty years.

In 1915, when the *Michigan Manual of Freedmen's Progress* was published, black Detroiters, many of whom were members of the newly emerging middle class, had much of which to be proud. There were lawyers,
doctors, dentists, business people of all sorts, and a nationally renowned
inventor, Elijah McCoy, who had patented fifty inventions relating to
automatic lubrication for machines.[65] As impressive as the middle-class
gains seemed at the time, further community building had been arrested
by the exclusion of black workers from the rapid industrialization that was
changing the face of Detroit. But contrary to Olivier Zunz's contention
that blacks in industrializing Detroit "experienced a settlement process
radically different from that of white ethnic groups, a process which led
to the formation of the ghetto [in which] blacks lived history in reverse,"[66]
the black settlement process involved more than "the formation of a ghetto"
or "living history in reverse." It represented the process of community
building within the racial and economic confines of an industrializing city.
As Katzman comments, "the increase in population wrought great changes
in the black community. Detroit 'black bottom' became literally a city
within a city; the variety and breadth of life and institutions within the
black community could match that of Detroit itself."[67] It was this "variety
and breadth of life and institutions within the black community" that
Olivier Zunz failed to appreciate properly in his interpretation of black
development in industrializing Detroit. The dramatic increase in the black
population set the stage for future black community building, and the
formation of the black industrial working class provided the catalyst for
the next stage of the process.

The historical roots of the black community building process in Detroit
reach back to a time before the middle of the nineteenth century. The
early struggles of former slaves and fugitive slaves against racial discrimination and against recapture by slave holders forged a sense of peoplehood.
As a terminus for the Underground Railroad and sitting just across the
river from Canada, Detroit attracted thousands of runaway slaves. However, those who remained in Detroit, even if they were free, faced racial
discrimination of every type. For several decades they could not vote, and
their children could not attend public schools. But such treatment did not
break their spirits. They established their own schools in their churches.
They joined blacks from other cities in other states and held Negro
Conventions to discuss methods of uplifting black communities. They

participated in the Underground Railway while fully aware of the illegality of such action.

Several black Detroiters had the honor of meeting and hearing John Brown and Frederick Douglass during the summer of 1859. During the Civil War, black Detroiters marched off to fight to end the slave system and free their brethren. In the same year that President Lincoln signed the Emancipation Proclamation, a white mob, of mostly Irish citizens, rioted, and attacked black men, women, and children, killing two men and rendering over two hundred blacks homeless.

In the midst of the racism and hardship, Detroit blacks found time to celebrate. Before the Emancipation Proclamation in 1863, Detroit blacks' major celebrations centered around the emancipation of the British West Indies on August 1, 1834. On this day blacks from Detroit and nearby communities in Canada gathered together and celebrated with songs, speeches, and good food.

As the community grew and developed, it produced classes and divisions reflecting different views of which strategies would best serve the interest of the larger community. The black elite did not always see itself as part of the building process of the larger black community. Oftentimes, it had its own class building agenda. As a result, class barriers impeded the community building process. The new black middle class, however, took up the reins and began charting a new course for the community. While they were not as successful as they would become during and after World War I, with the expansion of the black population, they did develop a self-help philosophy that contributed to the black community building process. The struggles and victories of the nineteenth-century black community in Detroit prepared it for the next stage of community building.

Two

The Demand for Black Labor, Migration, and the Emerging Black Industrial Working Class, 1915–1930

There is undoubtedly a large industrial opportunity for Negroes in Detroit. Since many employers who are already employing Negroes are pleased and are seeking more of them.... We may reasonably expect the Negro worker to gain a permanent hold in the Detroit industries.

George Edmund Haynes,
Negro Newcomers
in Detroit, 1918

BLACK WORKERS AS HISTORIC AGENTS OF CHANGE: MIGRATION AS THEIR RESPONSE TO NORTHERN DEMANDS FOR THEIR LABOR

Since the late 1970s, a few scholars have begun to examine the black urban experience from an historical perspective quite different from the traditional ghetto-formation and ghetto-synthesis approaches reflected in the works of such scholars as Gilbert Osofsky, Allan Spear, David Katzam, Thomas Philpott, Kenneth Kusmer, and James Borchert. Notwithstanding their tremendous contributions to the field of black urban history and the variations among their approaches, all these scholars, as Joe Trotter has pointed out, "place spatial dynamics and some variant of race relations at the center of their work."[1]

In contrast to the aforementioned scholars, Gottlieb, Thomas, and Trotter have placed the formation of the black industrial working class at the center of their work. In 1976, I argued that "black industrial workers represented the single most important occupational class and were the most viable force for social and economic change within the black community between 1915 and 1945."[2] Trotter developed and refined this approach, placing it at the center of his own work. He referred to it as "proletarianization"—as an alternative perspective in research on black life in the urban north.[3]

This chapter uses a community building model. This model adopts a wider perspective than the formation of the black industrial working class (or proletarianization) while maintaining the black working class's central place in the community building process. Although the demand for black labor, migration, and the emerging black industrial working class all contributed to the building of the black community between 1915 and 1930, the emerging black industrial working class played the leading role in this process. In fact, this class constituted the historical catalyst that set in motion the entire community building process during and after the world war. Other agents of change—the Detroit Urban League, key black institutions, and individual churches—assisted in the process. But, at its core, this process of community building would always, however indirectly, be driven by the industrial working class. Black industrial workers formed the major occupational class upon whose back northern black urban communities grew and developed. In Detroit, these workers formed the vital link, the life line, between the black community and the industrializing city. This approach, therefore, does not negate the importance of Trotter's work on proletarianization but, rather, attempts to explore the relationship of proletarianization to other forms of black community building.

World War I and the drying up of the European immigrant-labor pool created the need for a comparably cheap substitute pool of laborers, who could be found in sufficient numbers only in the black South. Long ignored by America's bustling industries, southern black workers now found themselves in great demand; as the value of black labor increased, the black community stood on firmer ground.[4]

By opening up previously unavailable jobs in northern factories and mills, the war-time industrial demand stimulated mass black migration out of the South, disrupting old communities as they left to build new ones. Southern black workers confined to low wages and denigrating plantation labor could protest southern living and working conditions by migrating northward. Migration, therefore, became a major mode of survival for the southern black working class. In the large picture, southern blacks were participating in what Peter Gottlieb describes as a "worldwide country-to-city migration that has paralleled the rise of commercial and industrial economies."[5] The new black middle class in northern cities also benefited from this industrial demand. Black entrepreneurs in Chicago, Cleveland, Detroit, and other northern cities would have failed to develop beyond their pre-war economic status had this large-scale migration northward not occurred.[6]

As influential as northern industrial demand was in broadening blacks' survival options by stimulating migration to the North, southern black workers played a key role by deciding to go north, and this was no easy decision. They often had to reject the advice of leaders who favored remaining in the South. The well-known black leader Booker T. Washington argued that the South was the best place for blacks. Black sociologist Kelly Miller proclaimed that black industrial opportunities could be found in the Black Belt and that the South was the black man's "Land of Goshen." The pro-Washington paper, the *New York Age,* cautioned skilled southern black workers to think carefully before migrating north where skilled jobs were difficult, at best, to get. In one sense this advice was true. While blacks in the South were denied jobs in the newer industries, such as textile and railroad shop occupations, they did find employment in a few unskilled industrial jobs. These so-called Negro jobs were in coal mines, sawmills, turpentine camps, railroad track construction, and steel and iron mills. Some of these "industrial opportunities" were indeed similar to the wide range of industrial jobs available to southern blacks in the North.[7]

Black leaders who opposed the migration had their own personal and class agendas for building and maintaining black communities. These agendas depended on the black masses' remaining passive and following the lead of the black middle and upper classes. But many southern black workers had a different vision. They sensed the need to fashion their own mode of survival quite independent of the local and national black leadership who opposed migration. Determined to go north to seek their "New Jerusalem," southern black workers knew they had to hitch themselves to a new star.

Migration dominated conversation in southern black barbershops and grocery stores. Men gathered to read letters from the North. They would "review all the instances of mistreatment and injustice which fell to the lot of the Negro in the South."[8] In Hattiesburg, Mississippi, blacks talked about nothing but the migration. Throughout the South, when black preachers tried to dissuade their flocks from leaving, the congregations would refuse to attend church services.[9]

Between the fall of 1916 and 1917, Robert Horton, a black barber in Hattiesburg, Mississippi, organized a migration club that recruited close to forty black men and women to migrate to Chicago. This migration club included members of his own family as well. Once in Chicago, Horton and his friends from Hattiesburg began recruiting other friends and relatives to Chicago. They even succeeded in recruiting a minister who had tried to prevent them from leaving the South to resettle in Chicago. Soon the Hattiesburg group, which had started as a migration club in the South, became a transplanted community in the North. As James R. Grossman has pointed out so well, this example "suggests how a grassroots social movement developed despite the opposition of an entrenched regional leadership."[10]

Who would have thought—surely not most black leaders—that black workers had minds of their own, with a keen sense of their own class survival? As one very perceptive Mississippi preacher put it: "The leaders of the race are powerless to prevent his [the southern migrant's] going. They had nothing to do with it, and indeed, all of them, for obvious reasons, are opposed to the exodus."[11]

Even southern white businessmen had a hard time keeping black workers from migrating. So southern black leaders and white businessmen decided to work together. They held conferences on interracial cooperation and worked on cleaning up black working-class areas, among other efforts, in order to persuade black workers to stay home. Clearly, northern industrial demands for southern black labor were hurting the southern economy, yet thousands of southern black workers would not be dissuaded from migrating north. Finally, southern white businessmen and politicians resorted to physical force. White policemen pulled black workers off northbound trains, arrested them en masse at train stations, and intimidated them in every possible manner. Authorities arrested and fined labor agents for recruiting black workers for northern industries. Yet, the labor agents persisted. Oftentimes entire families and groups of neighbors would leave for the North under the instigation and direction of labor agents working for major northern industrial firms. In some cases, labor agents assisted in freeing black sharecroppers from slave-like restrictions on plantations from which they would have never escaped otherwise. Of course, labor agents were paid for their services.[12]

Southern white authorities should have known that such repressive measures would fail in the end. Black workers continued to leave the South. By now, they knew the value of their labor. "The Negro sees clearly that it is to the interest of the southern white capitalist to keep him for his labor," one field researcher commented. "Hence, all the advice about staying in the South . . . he reads backwards."[13]

Thousands of southern black workers, therefore, chose migration over the advice of their leaders, who typically believed black workers were too ignorant to know what was best for them. Modes of survival that benefited the black leadership class seldom met the class needs of black workers. Staying put in the South would have obviously benefited black preachers, businessmen, and professionals. They would have survived—but on the bowed backs of black workers. So the southern black workers, share croppers, and dock hands followed their own vision and fashioned their own modes of survival.

For many southern black workers, the North symbolized the Promised Land. This symbolism, wrote one observer, "infused the (migration) movement with religious fervor expressed in the biblical imagery of flight out of Egypt and going to Canaan."[14] When some southern blacks reached the

North, they exploded with exuberance. One such group of Mississippi blacks took time to hold a prayer meeting "to mark the exact moment of deliverance." As soon as their train reached the middle of an Ohio River bridge, the migrants stopped their watches and "knelt to offer thanks"; after the prayer, they sang the hymn, "I Done Come Out of the Land of Egypt with the Good News."[15]

These southern migrants, who to many black southern and northern leaders were but faceless and poor souls to be guided and taught the ways of urban civilization, were destined to become the catalyst that would set into motion the rapid urbanization of nearly static, black urban communities. As several scholars have pointed out: Had southern black workers decided not to migrate—as indeed they could well have done, since many of their brethren did remain in the South—northern black communities would have stagnated. Most certainly, northern black political development would have suffered another setback. As Martin Kilson has argued:

> The important consequence of this migration was the endowment of thousands of Negroes with the political rights they were forcibly denied in the post-Reconstruction South. Had migration not been feasible for Negroes in this period, doubtless the acquisition of basic political rights and thus the primary stages of political modernization would have been delayed for another half century.[16]

The great black migration, then, was a key factor in the building of northern black urban communities during and after World War I. It was also a major mode of survival for the southern black working class. Northern industrial demand for black labor built only half a bridge; the vision of southern black workers built the other half.

During this period, Detroit ranked as one of the leading northern industrial centers drawing black labor out of the South. Henry Ford's promise of five dollars a day reached black and white workers throughout the South. But it was not only Ford's industrial largess that sent distant workers running to catch the first train or bus en route to Detroit. For several decades before the war, Detroit had been competing with other cities in the Great Lakes region, as well as the rest of the nation, in the population race. Detroit ranked fifteenth in size in the United States in 1860. In 1870 and 1880, it was seventeenth. Both Detroit and Milwaukee had doubled their populations by 1880, numbering 115,000 and 116,000 people, respectively. In 1860 the two cities were running about neck and neck with Detroit numbering 285,704 people and Milwaukee narrowly trailing with 285,315. That same year, Detroit climbed to become the thirteenth largest city in the United States. Yet Detroit was far behind three of her lakeport sister cities. Buffalo and Cleveland could each boast of being one-fourth larger than Detroit. Compared with Chicago, Detroit was barely moving. Chicago's economic structure dominated the Midwest, having siphoned off much of Detroit's regional trade.[17]

Detroit was a coiled spring by 1900. Iron and steel industries formed the city's industrial core in the 1880s. Detroit had the largest railroad car and wheel factory in the nation. Huge stove factories such as the Detroit Stove Company, the Peninsula Stove Company, and the Michigan Stove Company, were major Detroit industries before the turn of the century. These industries were complemented by others that were equally impressive. Parke, Davis and Company, the famous makers of pharmaceutical products, began in Detroit in 1867. By 1910 Parke, Davis and Company contributed significantly to Detroit's economic growth. Well over sixty cigar and chewing tobacco establishments placed Detroit on the map as the largest producer of chewing tobacco in the United States.[18]

Detroit's industrial growth attracted people like a magnet from around the state, the nation, and the world. Though foreign immigrants met a good portion of Detroit's industrial labor needs during this period, workers from rural Michigan supplied much of the labor required for the expanding city.[19]

Although the majority of European immigrants came to work in Detroit's automobile factories, Poles, Lithuanians, Croatians, Slovenians, Sicilians, Hungarians, and others arrived in the city in the 1880s and 1890s to work in the foundries of railroad car and stove factories, on railroads, and in salt works and lumber yards.[20]

By 1910, the auto age had affected every facet of industrial Detroit, transforming and increasing its population and revolutionizing its social, cultural, and political character. Automobile production and the magic and myth of Henry Ford attracted workers from other industrial areas both in and outside the state. Yugoslavs, Finns, and Lithuanians who had worked in the copper mines and lumber camps of Michigan's Upper Peninsula flocked to Detroit in 1914 in pursuit of higher wages in the auto industry. Ukranians and other Slavic Russians left the cold, damp, and dangerous coal mining pits of New York and Pennsylvania for the "pleasanter" work in Detroit's automobile factories. Sicilians, Poles, Bulgarians, and Macedonians all were drawn into Detroit's boom industry.[21]

This automobile boom pushed Detroit ahead in the population race among industrial cities. In 1900, Detroit was the thirteenth largest city in the nation. Ten years later, she climbed to ninth place on the back of the motor car. By 1920 she soared to fourth place among America's great cities. Only the Depression prevented Detroit from pushing Philadelphia out of third place.[22]

Of the seventy-five cities leading in manufacturing industries in 1910, Detroit ranked sixth in plants, sixth in wage earners, and sixth in the value of products. Ten years later Detroit ranked fourth in all these categories. From 1909 to 1914 the number of persons engaged in manufacturing in Detroit increased 26.2 percent, compared to the 7.6 percent increase for the entire country. Capital invested in Detroit increased 55.3 percent, compared to the 23.7 percent increase nationally; and the labor

Table 1

Black and White Population in Detroit, 1910–1930

	1910	1920	1930	Percentage Increase	
				1910–20	1920–30
Black	5,741	40,838	120,066	611.3	194.0
White	459,926	952,065	1,440,141	107.0	51.3
Total population*	465,766	993,678	1,568,662	113.3	57.9

Sources: U.S. Department of Commerce, Bureau of the Census: *Thirteenth Census of the United States, 1910: Population, II, 953; Fourteenth Census of the United States, 1920: Population III, 496; Fifteenth Census of the United States, 1930: Population II, 728.*
*Other non-whites included in total population.

force increased 23.9 percent, compared to a 6.4 percent increase nationally. Two years later, Detroit led the country in percentage of increase in manufacturing.[23]

True enough, the automobile industry was at the core of Detroit's industrial expansion, but the city was a leader in other industrial areas as well. During this period of industrial expansion, particularly in the 1870s, more aluminum was cast in Detroit yearly than in any other city in the world. Detroit led the world in the production of copper, brass, aluminum, malleable iron, and in truck manufacturing. Other industries in the city that ranked high nationally as well as internationally during this period included machine shop products, slaughtering and meat packing, tobacco, pharmaceutical preparation, bakery products, lumber and timber products, stoves and furnaces, clothing, chemicals, and adding machines.[24]

When Detroit's population increased from 283,704 in 1900 to 465,766 in 1910 as a result of the industrial expansion, few blacks were among those who swelled the ranks of the city's workers. But when the population almost doubled in 1920, making Detroit the fourth largest city in the United States,[25] the black population had increased by over 600 percent. Ten years later, when Detroit had close to a million and a half people, the black population had increased to 120,066 (see table 1).

World War I sparked population increases in Detroit as well as in other industrial cities. European immigrants returning home, and later restrictions on European immigration contributed to increases in the black working-class population in the cities.

By September 1915, a large influx of blacks into Detroit had begun. In May, June, and July of 1916, one thousand blacks were arriving in the city every month. The United States Department of Labor estimated that during 1916–17, between 25,000 and 35,000 blacks came to Detroit. The bulk, then, of the black population, which numbered over 40,000 in 1920, had come to the city in one year! This 1916–17 wave, which represented from 63 to 88 percent of the black people in Detroit in 1920, had hardly subsided before the second wave of 1924–25 doubled the 1920 figure, bringing in over 40,000 more blacks. By 1926, 85 percent of the black population had come to Detroit in one decade.[26]

Black migrants came in during two major migration waves: one in 1916–17 in response to the increasing demand for labor, and the other in 1924–25 when the full effect of decreased foreign immigration was felt in the labor market. Both waves resulted from the increase in the value of Detroit's manufacturing products, which was triggered by the rapid industrial expansion of 1914–19. In most cases the flow of black migration was affected by the demand for black labor. For example, the 1920–21 recession that left 17,000 black workers without jobs forced many black workers to migrate to other northern industrial cities or to go back home to the South.[27]

Industrial Detroit was ill-prepared to receive thousands of rural black folk. The shock of adjusting to waves of European immigrants had not yet passed. Now the city found itself inundated with black country folk. But some city fathers, pressed by the labor demands of industry, not only tolerated the influx but encouraged it. Some employers hesitated, maintaining their traditional stance of excluding black workers; but the handwriting on the wall was clear: Detroit's industrial expansion needed all the black labor it could get. So Detroit employers went against precedent and tradition and stationed labor agents in neighboring industrial cities like Cincinnati to woo southern blacks to Detroit; others brought them in themselves by the train carloads. According to a report by the Detroit Urban League in the Spring of 1918, the vast majority of those migrants came from Alabama and Georgia, followed in number by Florida, Arkansas, Mississippi, and Illinois.[28]

The Urban League played a leading role in placing these black migrants. In 1917, the League found work for 10,861 blacks, 80 percent of whom had been in Detroit less than one year. Seventy-five percent had been in the city only six months. Although the first wave of migrants had been primarily single men, by the summer and early fall of 1917, women began to appear in large numbers. Of the 11,000 black migrants the League placed in work during this period over 3,000 were women. Sixty percent of them had arrived during the summer and early fall. The vast majority of these women were forced to work because their husbands' wages were too low to sustain the family. Fortunately, these women had some basic job skills that enabled them to be successful in "any branch of industry where they were given an opportunity". But another group of black women migrants, about 40 percent of the whole, lacked the most basic skills necessary to work in urban jobs. They had come from the backwoods of the South with their husbands who had been recruited by labor agents.

These women had grown up hunting and fishing and going barefoot for most of their lives. Unlike many of the migrants who had lived in southern cities before coming north, these women had never seen a city.[29]

Much as the demand for black male labor was created partially by a shortage of white immigrant industrial labor, a shortage of white female immigrant labor created a demand for black female domestic labor. However, the League could only recommend about 50 percent of these black female immigrants because they lacked basic skills. They would need to be exposed to northern life for at least a year before they could qualify even for domestic work, simply because domestic work in Detroit homes required familiarity with modern kitchen facilities. This problem prompted the League to establish a Domestic Training School to prepare such women for domestic employment in Detroit.[30]

Other changes in the composition of the black migrant stream included an increasing number of both women and children. This indicated that more men were bringing their families with them and that women and children were joining their male relatives who were already in the city. As if trips punctuated with uncertainty were not enough, many migrants fell victim to fake labor agents in the South, who tricked them out of their money by promising them transportation to northern cities and jobs. Migrants fortunate enough to find an honest labor agent who delivered on his promises still had to contend with con artists roaming railroad stations preying on the unwary.[31]

As black southern workers streamed into Detroit, the tradition of excluding blacks from Detroit's industries underwent dramatic changes. Blacks entered a variety of industrial occupations from which they had been previously excluded. At the outbreak of World War I, the industrial status of Detroit blacks had not improved much from that of 1910. A few blacks had found employment in some of industrial laundries, but their numbers were insignificant.[32] A contemporary observer noticed that "where a Negro was found engaged in some occupation outside of personal service even though it be performing the most unskilled and backbreaking labor, he was looked upon as a curiosity."[33] During the late nineteenth century, a large European immigrant population had uprooted Detroit blacks from many of their traditional jobs in bootblacking and barbering. As Detroit became more or less an industrial city, these same immigrants met the demands for unskilled labor. Detroit's labor market favored white workers over black workers regardless of the skill of the latter or their longevity in the city. Black workers discovered that European immigrants could arrive in Detroit without jobs or skills and without a knowledge of English and use white-skin privileges to secure better housing and better jobs than blacks.[34] Only the world war and the postwar restrictions on European immigration saved the day for the black workers waiting in the wings of industrial Detroit. When the demand for unskilled workers of whatever color went sky high, black workers went in with the rest. Thus, the stage was set for the emergence of blacks on an unprecedented scale into the Detroit industrial labor market.

In 1915, blacks were beginning to be hired in large enough numbers to be noticed. A 1920 study of 67 plants pointed out that only five of the 67 plants had employed blacks before 1910, five in 1914, while 56 of them employed blacks after 1915.[35] In April 1917 the Packard Motor Company had 300 blacks on its payroll and was the city's leading employer of black workers. Buhl Malleable Iron Company employed 280 blacks. The Ford Motor Company and the Continental Company each had 200 black workers. In 1919, Ford employed 1,700 black workers out of a total black labor force of about 15,000.[36]

Ford's black hiring policy did not vary much from the general industrial pattern from 1914 to 1919. In January of 1916 the company had only 50 blacks among its 32,702 employees. A year later the figure rose to 136 among 35,411 employees. Three months later black employment jumped to 200. By 1918, Ford employed 1,059 black workers. By 1921, The Ford Motor Company had become the automobile industry's largest employer of blacks, boasting 1,675 black workers on its payroll and employing blacks in "virtually every hourly-rotated classification".[37]

This employment policy made Ford a big hero in the black community, which, in 1920, numbered 40,838 people (see table 1).

Although other Detroit businesses did not employ as many blacks as Ford during this period, they did radically change their racial hiring practices. From 1915 to 1920 certain plants that had had no black workers before the war had work forces composed of 25 to 48 percent black workers. Of 74 such plants in 1920, 46 had work forces that were 10 percent black; seven of them were 30 percent black; and two were 48 percent black. These gains loomed even larger when compared to blacks' national industrial situation in 1910. In 1910 only 183 blacks had jobs in the auto industry throughout the entire country. Ten years later, 8,000 blacks worked in the Detroit auto industry alone. In 1910 only 115 blacks had obtained jobs in brass mills nationally; by 1920, Detroit brass mills had ten times that number. In 1910, a mere 92 blacks worked in the nation's copper foundries; Detroit boasted eight times that number in 1920.[38]

In 1910, Detroit black industrial workers trailed behind Philadelphia, Pittsburgh, Cleveland, and Cincinnati in percentage of total black work force in the manufacturing and mechanical industries. By 1920, these black workers led the field. Detroit black workers also had the lowest percentage of total workers in the low-wage domestic and personal service.[39] Since the manufacturing and mechanical industries represented the growth sectors in the economy, the increasing percentage of the total black work force within these high-wage sectors contributed to the overall economic survival and progress of the black community.

Blacks moved to high-wage industrial sectors in unprecedented numbers and also increased their numbers in the semiskilled and skilled industrial occupations. The automobile and allied industries employed about 50 percent of the black skilled workers in Detroit. In 1910, only eight black semiskilled workers had jobs in the automobile plants, but by 1920 their numbers had increased to 809.[40]

The shift from agricultural, domestic, and personal services occupations to manufacturing and mechanical occupations represented a major occupational advance within the community building process. Black upward mobility within the manufacturing and mechanical sector represented yet another advance. This can be dramatically understood if one imagines a long-term Detroit black resident, who had been confined to low-wage domestic and personal service work, moving not only into previously unobtainable high-wage industrial work but, once there, moving up at least to the semiskilled level.[41] For a recently arrived southern migrant previously confined to southern agricultural work and paid even lower wages than those paid for domestic and personal services in the North, the move into the industrial sector represented even more upward mobility.[42]

One of the major reasons southern black workers came North was to make more money. Berry Gordy, Sr., the late father of Berry Gordy, Jr., who founded Motown, the famous music industry in Detroit, came to Detroit in the 1920s because he felt certain that he "could make big money in Detroit."

> I got up there in Detroit and I saw how things was. I saw a lotta people makin' money! I just kept lookin' 'round to make money. But I liked it so well; I knew if other people were making good money, I was gonna be able to make some. I was reading the paper and it say where the plumbers were making twelve dollars a day and the brick layers and plasterers, too. I could get a job in a blacksmith's shop paying four and a half a day. Well, that's more than I ever made in a regular job during off season down in Georgia. Down there when the crop was in and it was wintertime pay over two dollar a day. So, I just know I could make big money in Detroit.[43]

Not unlike other recent black migrants in Detroit, Gordy, Sr. had a wife and children back home in the South. He had to persuade her to follow him to this industrial Promised Land.

> I wrote for my wife, Bertha, to come up; I was gonna stay here. I told her to sell everything. I meant for her to sell the cows, our home, the chickens, mules, horse, wagon, and buggy, sell everything! But she didn't sell nothin'!! I was lonely, you know. I kept writin', forcin' her to come on up. It was only a month 'fore I could get her here, but it seemed to me like six months! I was so anxious for her to leave Georgia, and I didn't give up on that. So, Bertha came to Detroit. We had some hungry days now, off and on. I struggled on and kept on scufflin' 'til I got goin' where I could kinda make money.[44]

Black workers in Detroit received an average wage of about 54.2 cents per hour compared to 26.5 cents per hour in the South. On the average, the move to Detroit increased southern blacks' wages by 27.7 cents per hour or 104 percent. This increase in money wages did not reflect a similar increase in "real" wages. The cost of living in the south was 22 percent less than in the North. As a result, the real wages in the North were 6.2 cents less than the money wages or 48 cents per hour instead of 54.2. Therefore, the actual increase in wages for blacks in Detroit was not as high as it appeared, despite the increase in real wages of 21.5 cents per hour, or 81 percent.[45]

There could be no doubt about the fact that working in Detroit's factories and mills meant "big bucks" for southern blacks. Many southern migrants, once poor, illiterate sharecroppers, made a little over three dollars a day back home. In Detroit, they made from six to eleven dollars a day. "There are hundreds of Negroes in Detroit," remarked one social worker in 1920, "who are making more money in one day than they made in the South in a week."[46] The lure and promise of high wages pushed many black workers into working longer hours. Some worked so hard and in surroundings so unhealthy, such as those in foundries, that it affected their health.

While money was a major factor influencing southern black migrants' decisions to come North, other factors also played a key role in their decisions to leave family and friends. A survey of 1,000 black heads of families in Detroit conducted in the summer of 1926 revealed a range of reasons why black migrants had come North. Most of these heads of households were laborers and farmers, with few skilled, trade, or professional persons among them. The vast majority of them (741) had come to Detroit for "general better conditions"; 194 had left home for Detroit for "industrial opportunity and advancement"; 102 came to Detroit for "financial improvement"; 25 "wanted a change"; 22 came to Detroit because their families were there; 20 came to visit, "liked the city and stayed"; 20 came because their relatives wanted them to settle in the city; 18 came for "better educational opportunities for their children"; 15 came for "better protection"; 13 came for "social opportunities"; 13 came for "greater freedom"; 7 came for "safety."[47] Clearly, these black heads of households desired a better life for themselves and their families. And it was this quest for a better life that laid the foundation for the community building process.

Migrants tended to be young men between the ages of 18 and 40. But age did not prevent older men from coming to Detroit looking for the much-heralded jobs and high wages in Detroit industries. Large numbers of older black migrants began arriving in the city during the early stages of the migration. Many were sixty years or older and had sold their homes and furniture for transportation to the North. Unfortunately, industries in Detroit as well as in other industrial cities rarely hired men over forty if younger men were available, the only exceptions being in cases of labor scarcity. Employment managers argued that this age discrimination was simply based upon the fact that the heavy work in the industries broke down older men, resulting in high turnover and loss of production time. If these men could not obtain less strenuous work as janitors or porters or did not have relatives in the city to support them, they soon became wards of the city. This older male migrant situation finally compelled the DUL, to suggest that information be circulated in the South explaining that few employment opportunities existed in Detroit for older men.[48]

Higher wages in the manufacturing and mechanical industries tended to attract black workers from Detroit's low-wage occupations, particularly domestic and personal services where black workers received between 24 and 47 cents per hour.[49] Detroit's industrial sector, similar to other northern industrial sectors, had already begun feeding upon the southern agricultural sector's cheap black labor supply and would continue this process until the 1950s. What is often overlooked, however, is that northern industrial sectors fed on both southern agricultural and northern nonindustrial sectors.

High wages in the industrial sector forced the nonindustrial sectors to compete for a scarce labor supply or to employ workers usually not employed in industrial work. These workers tended to be women, the majority of whom were black. From 1910 to 1930 black women comprised the majority of workers employed in the largest and lowest paying non-industrial occupations, such as domestic and personal service. In 1910, 78 percent of all black women in the labor force worked in domestic and personal service, compared to 24 percent of all white women in the labor force. By 1920, while white men, white women, and black men had jobs in the manufacturing and mechanical industries, black women again had the highest percentage, 79.1, of their total work force in domestic and personal service, compared to 19.2 percent for white women. Although the ten years from 1910 to 1920 had been peak years for white and black male and white female industrial workers, black women remained trapped in the lowest paying sectors of Detroit's economy. Ten years later, probably as the result of the Depression's early effects on black workers in general, 88 percent of black women workers remained trapped in domestic and personal service, compared to 24 percent for white women workers.[50]

A few black women had been employed in the factories during acute labor shortages. But these women were let go as soon as the war ended. In spite of this obvious racism and sexism, black women workers made some occupational progress during the period. From 1915 to 1920, black women worked in department stores; in meat-packing houses; in cleaning industries such as laundries and dye houses; in houses; in the cigar industry; in various metal trades such as automobile factories, auto-parts factories, and machine shops; and, in larger numbers, in hotels and restaurants. Black women did manage to break into a few new occupations such as elevator operators, but more than half of the black women in Detroit were still in domestic and personal services jobs in 1940.[51]

In 1916, the DUL and The A. Krolik Garment Company engaged in an experiment to introduce black women to garment work, leading eventually to a work force made up entirely of black women at the factory. The company began training three black women in the routine of the factory so they in turn could train other black women who would comprise the workforce. Soon, other manufacturers expressed interest in all-black-women work forces. By the spring of 1917, the Krolik experiment had become a "successful going concern" employing fifty black women. Earlier in the year, the Buhl Malleable Iron Company, impressed by the Krolik experiment with black women workers began its own experimental program. The company hired black women as coremakers. The women received twelve dollars a week while training. Since the average wage of an experienced coremaker was between fifteen and eighteen dollars a week, these black women were indeed fortunate. Beyond their personal good fortune, these first black women coremakers were pioneering in fields of industrial work traditionally closed to black women. The Buhl Company also hired black women in their shipping room. Of course, these first black women were on display and had to perform well so as to pave the way for those who would follow them. The DUL had carefully engineered the Buhl hiring of black women by taking a few "clean-cut colored girls through the . . . plant" ostensibly on tour with the intention of "giving the Board of Managers an opportunity of seeing some of the better class of colored women".[52]

While a small percentage of women workers managed to obtain industrial jobs, largely as a result of the efforts of the Urban League, the greatest demand for black women's labor remained in the area of domestic work. Skilled black women workers experienced great difficulty obtaining employment in their field of training. In the fall of 1919, a young black woman from Nashville, Tennessee, skilled in the operation of linotype and monotype, was rejected by several companies in the city based upon their claim that the unions would not accept her because of her race. After the DUL's director talked to the manager of one company, explained the difficulty of obtaining jobs for skilled black workers, and then talked to the company's white workers, the woman was accepted. But such outcomes proved rare for the vast majority of skilled black women. Seven years later, a survey revealed that skilled and well-educated black women in Detroit either had to take work far beneath their training and abilities or not work at all.[53]

Industrial Detroit seemed not to be interested in having black women work outside of traditional occupations that reinforced the racial status quo. By 1919, the DUL's Domestic Training School had a model flat set up to train the "green" women arriving from the South to work in Detroit's modern households. Two years later, the League's March report indicated that most of the demand for black women was in general housework. "At this season when employers among women began their spring cleaning," the League director reported, "we are hopeful of increasing this number."

However, a few black women were finding jobs as elevator operators and shop girls. As the demand for black domestic labor increased, the state's Women's Employment Service began cooperating with the League in meeting the need by turning over to them "a goodly number of their calls for domestic service."[54]

This cooperation between the League and the Michigan State Women's Employment Service provided much-needed jobs for black women, many of whom had to work in order to supplement the insufficient wages of their husbands. Black domestic workers, therefore, contributed vital financial support to black families and by extension to the black community. Since black domestics tended to be the mainstay of black churches, their meager wages contributed greatly to the growth and development of those institutions that formed the heart of the community building process in black Detroit and other cities. On the other hand, this cooperation retarded that same process by reinforcing racial and sexual stratification in Detroit's evolving labor market, confining black women to menial occupations such as domestic work regardless of their training and education.

Unbeknownst to themselves and several public and private agencies that facilitated the flow of their labor, black women who were domestic and personal service workers contributed to the industrialization of Detroit by supplying the expanding white middle class with domestic home service as well as by meeting the larger domestic and personal service demands of industrializing and urbanizing Detroit in hotels, office buildings, and eating establishments. They provided this essential labor during a period when the pool of white domestics was drying up as a result of the expansion of employment opportunities for white women in industrialized Detroit. White and black women, given a choice, rejected domestic work for factory, shop, and office work. These nondomestic jobs tended to increase in the rapid industrializing and urbanizing American society of the 20th century. But the trend favored white women over black, regardless of the latter's training or education. So as industrialization and urbanization expanded opportunities for whites, the demand for black domestic labor increased. Black women found themselves meeting a demand for labor at the bottom of the social order, releasing white women from unattractive domestic work to work instead in the offices, shops, and factories of industrializing Detroit.[55]

A decade after the first wave of black immigrants from the South arrived in industrial Detroit, black women were the mainstay of domestic labor in the city. But whenever opportunities arose, they followed their white sisters into nondomestic work in offices as clerks and stenographers. Yet black women continued to be confined largely to domestic and other menial type employment. In 1926, reliable sources estimated that from 2,000 to 3,000 black women worked at various occupations in Detroit. About 506 black women were employed in the laundry industry, including hotels. The next largest category of black women worked in hotels (as maids), restaurants, and related places. Still another group worked in the garment trades and meat-packing houses. The next smallest category of black women worked in stores, office buildings (as elevator operators, maids, and service girls). Teachers, social workers, and skilled industrial workers represented the smallest group of black women workers.[56]

In January of 1930, the League's annual report indicated that the status of employment for black women workers was changing very slowly: "Most of the women have been placed as domestics; however, a goodly number have been referred to the stores and apartment houses as elevator operators and maids; a fairly large group found employment as stenographers, typists, and file clerks in offices."[57] This slow change in the employment status of black women retarded their contribution to the process of black community building, but they compensated for this drag on the community by taking any job that provided support for their families. In fact, the sacrifice of black women in doing menial work proved to be one of the dominant factors in the community building process in black Detroit.

SURVIVING OBSTACLES TO COMMUNITY BUILDING: THE EMERGING
BLACK INDUSTRIAL WORKING CLASS AS THE VITAL LINK BETWEEN
INDUSTRIALIZING DETROIT AND THE BLACK COMMUNITY
BUILDING PROCESS

Despite countless obstacles, in less than a decade many southern black men and women had entered the Detroit labor market and built a reputation as solid and dependable workers. Their wages were not the best but they were much better than those they had received in the South. In a relatively short period of time, many of these workers had become seasoned industrial workers, overcoming pre-industrial, regional, and cultural traditions. They liked the Motor City and while they would go back south to visit friends and relatives, Detroit was in their blood. Obstacles remained to be overcome. Many had not yet been tested by fire. Working and living in industrializing Detroit was still difficult, especially for black workers. Obtaining work was often only the beginning of a long, hard process of "settling in." The black industrial working class was still emerging, not yet fully acclimated to Detroit's urban-industrial culture. They were still on trial. The entire future of black community building hung precariously in the balance.

Although many black workers had demonstrated their ability to perform industrial work, some white employers still harbored concern about the degree of stability among the transplanted southern black working class. During the first couple of years, southern black workers tended to quit work a little too often. This tendency became noticeable at the Ford Motor Company as early as 1918 when 364 black workers out of 1,059 newly hired blacks quit. A year later, 868 black workers out of a total of 1,597 black Ford workers quit.[58]

Contrary to what many employers wanted to believe about southern workers—namely, that they could not adjust to northern industrial modes of work—quitting was one of the ways in which black workers protested hard and demeaning work. Employers in other industrial cities faced the same problems with southern black workers. According to Gottlieb, blacks working in the Pittsburgh mills had "little incentive to become long-term employees. The hot dangerous dead-end work most frequently given to new black workers was not the sort of labor most men stuck to day in and day out, from one year to the next. . . . Men who sought rewards commensurate with their efforts in the furnace shops and rolling mills spurned such employment to try their luck elsewhere."[59] Trotter's work on black industrial workers in Milwaukee reveals similar tendencies among black industrial workers to resist bad working conditions by quitting.[60] Bad working conditions, however, were not the only reasons for high turnover among southern black workers. Many southern blacks, Gottlieb argues, "looked forward to drawing their earnings and quitting their jobs for a while to return to southern homes or to travel about the North visiting friends and relatives or just seeing the sights."[61]

Since they knew the value of their labor in the Detroit labor market, black workers used their labor as leverage to obtain better jobs. Many recently arrived southern black workers were illiterate but not dumb. They went from job to job to find the jobs they felt suited them. They did not always succeed, but they tried anyway. Forrester B. Washington, the first director of the Detroit Urban League, understood some aspects of this working-class behavior when he explained why newly arrived black workers "shifted" from job to job. "Who can blame him for moving about . . . at the beginning in a vain search for the wonderful Detroit factories he had heard about in the South."[62]

But Washington failed to understand how the sudden rise in the industrial demand for black labor raised black workers' social consciousness and encouraged many of them to pick and choose where they wanted to work. Black workers quickly discovered that they often had the upper hand during labor shortages. Northern employers often interpreted frequent quits and labor turnover as the result of southern black workers' pre-industrial background. However black workers became increasingly aware that they could play employers off against one another. Southern black migrants, for example, would work a while in a railroad camp until the first paycheck or until they learned of the chance for higher wages in the steel and construction fields. Then they would leave, taking their labor to the highest bidder. "Those who knew the game," a Labor Department representative explained, "did not even wait to try the work and quarters after their transportation had been paid but struck out at once for 'greener fields.'"[63] Even higher wages often failed to entice black workers to remain "stable."

No wonder executives of northern industry and their employment managers seriously considered national conscription of labor to solve their problem.[64]

Once black workers found satisfying jobs, they became stable workers which contributed to the community building process. Oftentimes, as in Detroit in the 1920s, labor turnover among black industrial workers was related to long distances between home and work. Most blacks worked in plants located great distances from their black neighborhoods. These neighborhoods had been settled by black domestic and service workers who lived close to their work near the business district. But when blacks started working in the industrial sector located in other parts of the city, the problems of travel and distance introduced complications into their lives. If black factory workers could have rented or bought housing near the plants where they worked, this problem would have been solved, but racist landlords effectively hampered efforts to use this alternative.[65]

The lack of adequate housing severely restricted the flow and stability of the migrant population and slowed the emergence of the black industrial working class. As early as 1919, John C. Dancy, Director of the Detroit Urban League, lamented: "there seems to be no letup on the part of colored people in coming into Detroit. In spite of the serious housing problem they are coming in and throwing themselves on the mercy of the people to find space for them." He complained of the practices of General Motors and accused them and DuPont of complicating the problem by bringing in large numbers of migrants. Although some blacks were returning south to escape the Detroit winter, not enough of them were leaving to relieve the housing problem. Despite the housing shortage black workers continued to flock to Detroit. During the fall of 1919, every train pulling in from the South brought "its quota of colored people." Dancy expressed fear that the lack of available houses during the coming winter would result in "an alarming death rate." On several occasions, the league asked for assistance in discouraging black workers from migrating to Detroit. They recommended that newspapers and churches in the South discourage people from migrating to Detroit during the housing crisis. However, discouraging migration was no easy task because, as one observer pointed out, "a great many of these people coming north would rather withstand the rigors of the winter and . . . housing discomforts in the North rather than stay in the South where there is no security from harm and mob violence."[66]

By the spring of 1926, the lack of housing and unemployment in northern industrial cities prompted the National Urban League to send a release to black newspapers informing them of these conditions and advising potential black migrants against migrating at that time unless they already had a job. One black newspaper refused to publish the release, believing that the National Urban League (NUL) was discouraging black migration. As if that misrepresentation was not enough, a white newspaper in South Carolina obtained the release and used it in an editorial discouraging blacks from moving to the North. The NUL had no other choice but to continue the policy since people needed advice, and not sending the release would lead to "larger numbers of colored people in the northern communities which are already overpopulated."[67]

Efforts to stem the tide of southern black migration ignored black migration from other northern industrial cities such as Cleveland. In June of 1922, black workers from Cleveland made up a good number of recent migrants to Detroit. These men came without their families to make enough money to return to Cleveland.[68] This form of black migration between industrial cities was probably caused by the changing demands for black labor in particular cities at particular times. When black migrants in Detroit failed to find work, they also migrated to other northern industrial areas.[69] Failing to find work there, they often ended up back south.

Lack of housing and jobs were not the only reasons southern migrants returned South. In the fall of 1919, migrants went home for the winter, planning to return to Detroit in early spring. Many black migrants considered "going home" for a while as a natural part of their life. As Gottlieb has pointed out, for migrants returning South from Pittsburgh, "it was not for love of the South that migrants returned, but for love of family, friends and childhood homes."[70]

As soon as spring arrived, southern blacks began their movement north, often to the chagrin of welfare workers, employment managers, state and federal authorities, and private agencies. In March of 1925, many of these agencies went on a kind of red alert as they cooperated with each other "in the hope of diminishing to a minimum all problems which may arise because of this spring's migratory movement, which will probably be of large dimensions." Philadelphia, Detroit, Cleveland, Columbus, Indianapolis, Wheeling, Pittsburgh, and other industrial centers reported an influx of southern black migrants creating problems of housing, employment, and health. Agencies in all these cities knew only too well that such voluntary migration often exceeded the supply of jobs.[71]

There was little anyone could really do to control black migration. There were simply too many uncontrollable factors at work complicating the situation. As production increased in Detroit during the spring of 1922, advertisements appeared in newspapers calling for workers. A year and a half earlier, six to seven thousand blacks had left Detroit since the shutdown of major industries. The Department of Public Welfare was sent about five black families a day who had come back home to the South. In 1922, agencies had to contend with job advertisements which would most certainly stimulate more black migration to Detroit. This problem was compounded by the condemnation and destruction of scores of houses in the main black ghetto on the east side, which was the entry point for arriving migrants and where the majority of black people lived. Knowledgeable observers could only hope and pray that the migration would not be too large.[72]

Thirty-five hundred blacks from virtually all over the country migrated to Detroit during July and August of 1922 in response to the spring advertisement for workers. Gearing up to serve these people, the Detroit Urban League (DUL) had cards printed and delivered to the Traveler's Aid Society at railroad stations to be given out to arriving black migrants so that they could be assisted by the League in finding lodging and employment. Of the entire period between World War I and the beginning of the Great Depression, the year 1923 witnessed the greatest influx of black migrants into Detroit. Close to 14,000 arrived that year. Many of the migrants arrived during the summer months without funds or direction. The DUL had to take care of them.[73]

The migrants who flocked to Detroit between World War I and The Great Depression included more than sharecroppers and other assorted types of common labor. Many were skilled artisans forced to accept unskilled jobs or nothing. Some were business and professional people. As some entire communities migrated to Detroit, doctors, lawyers and ministers had no choice but to follow their patients, clients and parishioners. They left the field they had worked so hard to cultivate, to start all over again in a city bursting with promise. Not all migrants survived without resources, struggling to find any shack to cover their heads. About 20 percent of the migrants interviewed by the League during the spring of 1918 were buying homes. Over one-third commented that they were not used to paying rents and that they had owned their own homes in the South. These migrants also were buying homes in the better sections of Detroit where the newly expanding professional and business class were living.[74] More migrants would join this class as the proletarianization of the black working class improved its economic and social well being. Through it all, black industrial workers adjusted surprisingly well, due to their own initiative to succeed in their new environment against all odds.

The industrial mode of production combined with living in a complex urban center was fraught with social problems that forced black migrants to develop appropriate survival skills on and off the job. They could survive off the job only if they could survive on the job, meaning they had to become efficient industrial workers.

In 1926, a study revealed that the majority of Detroit employers reported that black workers were "as regular and in some cases more regular than white workers on the same job." However, employers who employed the majority of blacks reported that they were less regular than whites. The conclusion drawn from the study was that the black workers were "slightly less regular than a like group of white workers."[75]

Employers also reported on the efficiency of black workers as compared to white workers. Two-thirds of employers that employed 82 percent of all black workers reported that their black workers were as efficient as white workers on the same type of work or more so.[76] By 1929 employers' opinions had not substantially changed. Thirty-one of them who then employed 92.4 percent of the total black work force reaffirmed the 1926 study that blacks were just as efficient as white workers employed on similar jobs, while ten employers who employed 7.6 percent of the total felt blacks were less efficient than white workers.[77]

As the old black saying goes, "Blacks have to be twice as good as whites to make it in this world." During this period when Detroit employers compared black industrial workers to white industrial workers, black industrial workers often had to be far superior to white workers just to survive in industrial work. According to a black electrician working at the Ford Rouge plant, "I have to be better than the average white man to hold this job because they expect more of a colored man. We have to be on our toes all the time." Another black worker echoed the same sentiment: "Of course I'm extra careful. The boss has given me a chance to make good and I'm not going to fall down." These two black workers were the first among the race to obtain jobs in previously all-white industries and they wanted to be the best that they could be so as to pave the way for other blacks. Most wanted to prove to the white industrial world that they were as good as or better than their white counterparts in the same jobs. Some white foremen took advantage of this attitude by pitting black work crews against white work crews to increase productivity. In one case, no doubt representative of others, the black crew turned out a much larger number of castings than the white crew that refused to speed up because they feared rate cuts. As a result, management replaced most of the white crew with blacks who had pushed production tonnage from 226 tons to 650 tons per day. According to the superintendent, notwithstanding some improvement in mechanical technique, he attributed increased tonnage to applying a then favorite method of racial psychology: "These niggers will work their fool heads off if we handle them right." By this he meant "kidding and spurring them on" with a gradual speeding up of the line.[78]

Deliberate pitting of racial groups against one another on the job spilled over into the society at large. The seeds of future racial unrest in Detroit were sown during this period of industrial expansion. Employers obtained their much-valued efficiency and regularity, hence greater productivity, but left a legacy of racial tension and conflict in the larger society.

Black industrial workers became permanent fixtures in Detroit's industrial society by the middle of the "roaring twenties." Captains of Detroit industry no longer considered black workers as temporary relief for labor-starved mills and factories. This acceptance, however, stemmed from the fact that black industrial workers had taken over the most dirty and dangerous jobs in Detroit industries, the "nigger jobs," which white workers, both foreign-born and native, avoided.

But many former southern migrants could not have cared less. Compared to what they had left in the South, the worst industrial jobs in Detroit seemed heaven-sent. In the preceding fifteen years they had experienced more social and economic progress than they could have ever expected in the South. They had leap-frogged from the most backward and underdeveloped sector in the country to the most developed sector of the national economy. No one knew exactly how much economic progress blacks had made in Detroit. In absolute terms they had clearly advanced over their pre-war conditions. But in relative terms, there was a question as to whether they had really made much progress in relation to the rest of society. Since everyone had progressed, how much more or less had blacks progressed? Yet, no one could deny that the process of community building rested squarely on the backs of the merging black industrial working class. But serious problems still hampered this process.

As early as 1920, a mere five years or less after blacks' first significant shift into the industrial sector, a few black leaders felt compelled to engage in premature self-congratulations. Forrester B. Washington rhapsodized that blacks in Detroit had made "greater progress up the industrial scale . . . than in any other city of the United States." To Washington, the black movement up the occupational ladder to semiskilled jobs constituted a great step forward. "The Negro is to be congratulated," he said, "for the advance he has made in the semiskilled occupations." The black community, Washington claimed, "owes at least a small debt of gratitude to the employers of Detroit for the opportunity extended."[79]

Washington apparently forgot or did not think it important that employers hired blacks under wartime duress. Few Detroit employers had opened their arms to blacks before the war-induced labor shortage. But from Washington's perspective, blacks had to understand that there was no other "industrial center in the North where so many Negroes are employed in the semiskilled processes—the most productive section of industry."[80] He shared the belief of many black leaders that northern industry would afford black workers unlimited upward mobility, if only they acquired the necessary skills. According to Washington, in due time the black worker would "graduate from the unskilled to the semiskilled and skilled" jobs. "Other races," he emphasized, "have had to spend a certain length of time in each stage of this industrial revolution and there is no reason to expect that the Negro should find a shortcut."[81] Little did Washington realize that blacks would advance only to a certain point before bumping up against a racial ceiling in Detroit industries. He firmly believed that the black worker had "reasonable assurance of graduating into the skilled processes as soon as he demonstrates his efficiency and as executives and other workers get more used to seeing him about the plants."[82]

This was in 1920. By 1926, black workers had demonstrated their efficiency and regularity. Executives had become accustomed to seeing black workers around their plants, but only in certain jobs allotted by race. In other words, black workers were expected to stay "in their places" and not rock the boat of racial stratification that existed within the occupational structure of most plants. As one employer very frankly pointed out: "We hired them for this hot dirty work and we want them there. If we let a few rise, all the rest will become dissatisfied."[83] As a result, black

Table 2

Percent of Total Black and White Workers in Selected Occupations: 1910–1930

	1910		1920		1930	
	Black	White	Black	White	Black	White
Manufacturing and Mechanical Industries	14.6	40.9	⌐8.5	56.2	48.5	48.4
Transportation	5.5	4.9	5.⌐	8.8	7.9	6.7
Trade	3.5	8.9	3.9	16.8	4.9	14.8
Domestic and Personal Services	46.3	9.2	27.1	8.8	33.0	8.1
Public Service	0.9	1.4	0.6	2.4	1.7	2.4
Other Occupations	29.2	34.7	4.0	6.5	4.0	19.6
Totals	100.0	100.0	100.0	100.0	100.0	100.0

Sources: Computed from *Thirteenth Census of the United States, 1910: Occupations, IV,* 553–55; *Fourteenth Census of the United States, 1920: Occupations, IV,* 1101–04; *Fifteenth Census of the United States, 1930: Occupations, IV,* 803–05.

workers entered new fields only during periods of economic expansion or wars.[84]

Between 1923 and 1929, black workers found new avenues of employment in only eight plants in Detroit. For the most part, the majority of blacks remained confined in plants which had employed them during the war and up to 1923. "We can get all the white workers we need," one employer said, "so why should we take a chance on Negroes?"[85] Black economic progress was largely limited to periods of national crisis and expansion. Black economic stagnation became evident during periods of relative peacefulness. As the nation returned to normalcy, its tradition of racial stratification reasserted itself.

Although the increased percentage of the total black work force in trade and transportation reflected economic progress, it did not reflect the extent and range of industrial expansion nor as high a wage as in manufacturing and mechanical industries. Automobile manufacturing alone in this sector represented the single most important growth industry in the economy, and since the majority of black workers were in automobile and allied industries, the increasing percentage of their total work force within the broader category represented a reliable index of their economic progress (see table 2).

Black workers not only gained a foothold in the manufacturing and mechanical industries between 1910 and 1920 but increased their total work force in that sector from 14.6 percent in 1910 to 58.5 percent in

1920. Whites in the same category increased their percentage from 40.9 to 56.2 percent during the same period. Black workers had started from behind and passed up white workers in the percentage of their total work force in these industries. But this apparent progress was somewhat deceptive. The loss of European immigrants who had been replaced by black workers reduced considerably the percentage of the total white work force in the above industries.[86] This reduction of European immigration—which coincided with the period of increase of black workers—involved largely unskilled jobs and affected only the manufacturing and mechanical industries. This accounted for the increased percentage of the total black work force in those industries.

Because blacks could not overcome racist barriers that restricted their entry into white occupational preserves such as trade, transportation, and public service, their occupational progress slowed down.[87] By 1930, the percentage of the total black work force in the manufacturing and mechanical industries had declined from 58.5 percent in 1920 to 48.6 percent in 1930. White workers' percentage had declined from 49.6 to 42.5 percent of their total work force in the same industries during the same period. From 1920 to 1930, blacks remained concentrated in the domestic and personal services while whites steadily moved out of these low paying jobs (see table 2).

Within the high-wage manufacturing and mechanical industries, black workers were much more concentrated in and thus dependent upon the automobile industry than their American-born and foreign-born white counterparts. For example, by 1930, almost 40 percent of the total black workforce in the above industries were concentrated in automobile production, in contrast to 9.2 percent and 17.3 percent for American-born and foreign-born white workers respectively (see table 3). This concentration of black workers in the automobile industry contributed to the increase of wealth in the black community which, in turn, stimulated and sustained the institutional growth and development within that community; but such concentration in and dependence upon the automobile industry rendered the community vulnerable to the economic swings within the industry itself.

Black industrial workers soon discovered that working in high-wage mills and factories was a mixed blessing. Pouring hot iron and breathing black dust all day wore out body and soul more quickly than picking cotton had ever done. Southern black workers had faced economic crises in the South brought on by crop failure, drought, floods, and the dreaded boll weevil. Their survival skills had been tested in an agricultural society where they could at least read the signs of impending danger in familiar surroundings: cracks in the earth, a touch of dryness in the air, prolonged rain, any number of countless cues programmed into them over the centuries. But business cycles in the Motor City were unpredictable for former rural folk.

Table 3

Number and Percent of Workers in Selected Occupations by Ethnicity and Sex, 1930

Category	Blacks		American Born Whites		Foreign Born Whites	
	Number	Percent	Number	Percent	Number	Percent
Males						
Brick and Stone Masons	248	0.9	1,342	0.9	2,340	1.8
Carpenters	396	1.4	5,961	3.9	6,314	4.9
Electricians and Electrical Engineers	114	0.4	4,861	3.2	1,975	1.5
Foremen and Overseers	102	0.4	7,233	4.7	2,888	2.2
Furnacemen, Smeltermen, Heaters	199	0.7	221	0.1	348	0.3
Grinders (metal)	176	0.6	1,779	1.2	1,298	1.0
Iron Molders, Founders, Casters	304	1.1	376	0.2	773	0.6
Machinists	652	2.3	15,363	10.0	12,367	9.6
Mechanics in Automobile Factories	849	3.0	6,018	3.9	2,852	2.2
Plasters and Cement Finishers	435	1.5	572	0.4	976	0.8
Operatives in Automobile Factories	1,862	6.5	23,941	15.6	17,991	13.9
Laborers in Automobile Factories	11,170	39.2	14,142	9.2	22,349	17.3
Laborers in Building Construction	3,756	13.2	1,666	1.1	2,886	2.2
Total	28,477	100.0	153,295	100.0	129,089	100.0
Females						
Dressmakers and Seamstresses	254	31.9	836	5.9	434	7.4
Tailoresses	40	5.0	117	0.8	151	2.6
Operatives in Automobile Factories	26	3.3	3,975	27.8	1,497	25.5
Operatives in Cigar Factories	27	3.4	1,086	7.6	329	5.6
Laborers in Auto Factories	90	11.3	728	5.1	369	6.3
Total	796	100.0	14,278	100.0	5,870	100.0

Source: Compiled from *Fifteenth Census of the United States, 1930: Occupations,* IV, 803–05.

When the 1920–21 recession hit Detroit, 17,000 black workers found themselves on the streets with no jobs.[88] Many had never experienced urban unemployment.

The foundries where most black industrial workers were employed were the first production units to be shut down in April of 1920. In October local Urban League officials noticed large numbers of blacks, averaging about a hundred a day, leaving the city. In their opinion, this exodus exceeded the usual number going South for the winter.[89] By January 1921, three thousand black families found themselves relying on the Department of Public Welfare. As conditions worsened, some unemployed black workers applied for work at the office of the Detroit Urban League.[90] This short but devastating recession led some blacks to suggest that unemployed black industrial workers should work on the three thousand black-owned farm acres of Michigan.[91]

Two years before the Great Depression, a black writer echoed the above advice in one of the local black newspapers: "More of our people in Michigan should seek agrarian life especially those of us who have dependencies in the form of wife and children; there are far too few of our group enjoying the health and freedom of farm life." Black workers could only hope for work in industry for a few months at a time, the writer warned, because they were "an isolated and insignificant group in the industrial scheme."[92] Others would come to the same conclusions.

The 1927 Ford shutdown, due to a model change, prompted a second warning to black industrial workers to seek more stable employment on Michigan farms. The Ford Motor Company laid off or put on a three-day work week close to 50,000 Ford workers, including 5,000 black workers. In addition, Ford suppliers laid off scores of black and white workers. Black industrial workers bore the brunt of these recessions and auto change-overs because they had such a high percentage of their total work force employed at Ford. In addition black workers' lack of adequate savings put them in a precarious situation during layoffs.[93]

An interesting pattern of black male-female employment began to emerge during these cyclical periods of black industrial unemployment. As black men lost industrial jobs, black women obtained domestic jobs. For example, black women were able to find work during the 1920–21 economic downturn while thousands of black men lost jobs. In November 1920, out of a total of 1,875 black men and women who applied to the Urban League for work, only 363 found work, and the majority of these fortunate souls were black women. A year later in February, all but six of the 179 blacks placed in jobs by the Urban League were women. For the entire year of 1921, out of 11,336 applications for jobs, 2,320 black women found work, compared to 284 black men who found employment.[94]

One possible explanation for this pattern of black women finding more jobs than black men during economic downturns is that, as more black men lost their industrial jobs, their wives were forced to go to work, mainly in domestic and service occupations, to support the family. The reverse occurred during periods of economic upswings. In 1919, the Urban League could not find enough black men for available jobs. On the other hand, black-women job seekers outnumbered available jobs.[95] This interpretation, however, should not be construed as suggesting that black women in Detroit worked only when their husbands were unemployed.

The first generation of black industrial workers in Detroit, especially former southern migrants, carried cultural baggage which impaired their ability to develop necessary survival skills in the North. These workers could not always adjust to northern urban culture with its dazzling consumerism. The northern store practice of allowing all customers, regardless of racial background, to try on hats and shoes without first paying for them overly impressed southern migrants. Blacks were not allowed such social equality in the South. Consequently, many unsuspecting black workers became easy marks for hustling white installment salesmen. Blacks mistakenly perceived that these salesmen were treating them kindly. Black workers, therefore, bought many goods on the installment plan, which kept them perpetually in debt. Such indebtedness forced employers to garnishee black workers' wages more than any other group. This especially hurt them during recessions and depressions.[96]

Considering black workers' lack of bargaining power and the fact that they were the last hired, one would have expected that they would have been the first fired during the economic downs of 1921 and 1927. Yet, this was not always the case. Many plants kept a small black work force in all their departments to insure that black and white workers "be accustomed to each other in case it became necessary later to employ more Negroes."[97] Firms in other industrial cities also adopted this policy. Steel mills in Pittsburgh, for example, kept more black than white workers during the industrial depression of 1924.[98] Some firms that adopted this policy might have had less noble motives: namely, to maintain some blacks in their labor force to draw on in case of strikes by white workers.

Such policies helped many black industrial workers survive the economic downturns of the middle 1920s. Without them, black workers would have been reduced to an urban reserve army of the unemployed before they had the chance to become the economic base for northern black communities and the catalyst for the community building process. The period between the introduction of black industrial workers into Detroit's industries and their arrival at a stage of acceptable regularity and efficiency coincided with the period of dynamic black community building. The black working class, both factory and domestic, male and female, contributed hard-earned dollars to the building and support of churches, fraternal orders, and a wide variety of businesses. The new black professional classes of the 1920s and 1930s were built on the backs of these workers.

It must be remembered that before the Great Migration of black people brought on by the demand for black labor, the process of black community building had come to a virtual standstill because of the lack of a strong economic base and linkages with rapidly growing sections of industrializing Detroit. As we have seen, black industrial workers and, to a lesser extent, black female domestic and personal service workers provided that linkage. As the black working class assumed a more permanent role in the industrial economy of Detroit—albeit an inferior role—it gradually became the catalyst of the community building process. For example, most major black institutions, agencies, and professional classes depended directly or indirectly on the well-being of the black working class. As this class grew and developed it legitimized the role of the Detroit Urban League in the eyes of the white power structure, enabling it to access more resources to facilitate the process of community building through the establishment of community centers, baby clinics, domestic training schools, children's summer camps, and health programs. The same held true for major black churches, such as Second Baptist and St. Matthew Episcopal. Without black Ford auto workers these churches and, by extension, the larger black community they served, would have had no relationship and linkage to industrializing Detroit. It is clear, therefore, that the increasing regularity and efficiency of black industrial workers, along with their ability to overcome countless obstacles, sustained the very tenuous process of black community building in Detroit.[99]

Still, survival in the urban North during industrial depressions proved difficult, at best. Thousands of northern black industrial workers were periodically thrown on the streets, which wreaked havoc upon their families and communities. Black workers and their families would endure much suffering and pain before they developed survival strategies adequate for living through the cyclical economic downturns of northern industrial cities.

And they would need plenty of help from black institutions and organizations. Yet these organizations did not have the necessary resources to address the countless needs of the expanding northern black working class communities. Fortunately, at the time, the arduous task of building black communities meshed rather nicely with the needs of the industrializing North.

Between 1915 and 1930, several key factors set the stage for the black community building process in Detroit: the demand for black labor, black migration from the South, and the emergence of the black industrial working class. While the demand for their labor certainly created the necessary conditions for their introduction into industrializing Detroit, black migrants made a conscious choice to leave home, family, and community to take part in the process. Southern blacks saw jobs in Detroit as a great opportunity to remake their lives.

Not all black migrants who came to Detroit found industrial jobs. Industrial Detroit could not use old men. And only a few young black women found industrial jobs. As much as they tried, the Detroit Urban League could not obtain many industrial jobs for women. Industrial Detroit relegated them to domestic work. Accepting this, the DUL tried to make the best of it by assisting black women to be the best they could be in whatever work they could get. The Domestic Training School was a partial response to this situation.

In order to become the vital link between industrializing Detroit and the black community building process, black migrants had to overcome many obstacles, both personal and social, which they obviously did. By 1930, most had become stable and efficient industrial workers. This stability and efficiency contributed to the meshing of the community building process and the industrialization of Detroit. But arriving at this stage was not easy. Black workers had to endure periods of unemployment, bad housing, and housing shortages, and confinement to the worst jobs. John C. Dancy and the League pulled out all the stops in their efforts to assist black workers in overcoming these problems. But most of the time the workers had to make it on their own. Those who survived the hardships maintained the vital link between a struggling black community and a largely indifferent industrial city.

Three

The Role of the Detroit Urban League in the Community Building Process, 1916–1945

In a program for the adjustment of the Negro, there must be a definite place reserved for the development of industrial efficiency. . . . If the community can be convinced that the Negro is and will always be a business asset, we need not worry much about housing employment and recreation.

Forrester B. Washington, Director, Detroit League on Urban Conditions among Negroes, May, 1917

STABILIZATION OF BLACK LABOR: A NATIONAL CONCERN

As we have already seen, World War I triggered the demand for black industrial workers in northern industrial centers. The emergence and relative stabilization of the black industrial working class provided the crucial link between northern industrial cities and the process of black community building. As black workers became more efficient and regular in the work place, they provided the first essential step in this long and difficult process. Without the Detroit Urban League, this first step would have taken much longer. For all of their initiative, black industrial workers needed black middle-class intermediaries to intervene on their and the larger black community's behalf during critical periods in the history of northern industrial development. These black intermediaries contributed to the stabilization of the industrial working class during periods when the demand for black industrial labor was setting in motion waves of southern black migration to the North, which many northern industrial capitalists feared would be potentially disruptive. Their apprehension was confirmed by the "unpredictable" behavior of southern black migrants who did not always follow the script, as written by industrial capitalists, managers, and black leaders. Even more alarming were the interracial industrial conflicts which flared up in East St. Louis in 1917 and in Chicago in 1919.[1] Industrial capitalists could only succeed by controlling and regulating the flow of southern black migrants to northern industrial cities. But they also had to socialize and program these migrants to be effective and productive industrial workers.

Clearly, white capitalists could not perform all these tasks. They needed assistance from a segment of black society which not only had credibility with the larger black community but could also transmit the values of emerging corporate capitalism to the newly urbanized black communities. Thus, the need for black intermediaries.

Black leaders associated with the National Association of Colored People (NAACP), the National Urban League, and the Tuskegee Institute provided the industrial capitalist class with just the assistance they needed to place black labor in its "proper" relationship to the war-induced industrial demand. In February 1918, Eugene Kinckle Jones, president and secretary of the National Urban League, John R. Shillady, secretary of the NAACP, Robert R. Morton and Emmett J. Scott, principal and secretary, respectively, of Tuskegee Institute, and others asked the Secretary of Labor, William D. Wilson, to appoint a "Negro expert on labor problems." Such an expert, they explained, would help the nation to solve the critical labor problems by effectively deploying black labor. "If the forces at the front are to be munitioned and kept supplied with a continuing stream of labor and food producers and the needs of the home population are adequately to be met," these leaders argued, "every resource of labor and skill must be utilized in the most effective manner."[2] There was too much at stake. The war effort could be harmed if black labor was not used effectively, the argument ran.

This group of black leaders saw themselves as playing a historic role in the war effort via the deployment of black labor. As representatives of organizations "most intimately acquainted with the colored people," they urged the government to see the advantage to the public welfare of including in the proposed labor program "the best possible use and distribution of the tremendous potential labor supply to be found among 12,000,000 Negroes of this country."[3] The extensive migration of black workers to northern cities would cause disturbing maladjustments which would in turn "react unfavorably upon maximum productive efficiency" unless they were wisely directed. According to these leaders, this could only be done by appointing a "Negro expert on labor problems." They pointed out the precedent set by the Secretary of War in appointing a black named Emmett

J. Scott as a special assistant for counseling on matters affecting black people and their relation to the war.[4]

By May of that year, Secretary of Labor Wilson responded to the appeal by appointing Dr. George E. Haynes, professor of sociology and economics at Fisk University, Nashville, Tennessee, as "Director of Negro Economics." Haynes's experiences in promoting industrial betterment among blacks in the North and South made him a solid choice. His two main duties were

> to advise the Secretary and the Directors and Chiefs of the several bureaus and divisions of the Department on matters relating to Negro wage earnings, and to outline and promote plans for greater cooperation between Negro wage earners, white employers and white workers in Agriculture and Industry.[5]

Secretary Wilson decided that the advice of the Director of Negro Economics should be sought before any work affecting black workers be undertaken, and that he be kept aware of the progress of such work "so that the Department might have, at all times, the benefit of his [Haynes's] judgment in all matters affecting Negroes."[6]

Haynes began visiting strategic centers in a number of states where problems related to black workers were of pressing concern. Conferences were held and interracial committees called "Negro Workers' Advisory Committees" were formed to

> study, plan and advise in a cooperative spirit and manner with employees of Negro labor, with Negro workers, and with the United States Department of Labor in securing from Negro laborers greater production in industry and agriculture for winning the war through increasing regularity, application, and efficiency, through increasing the morale of Negro workers, and through improving their general conditions.[7]

It would be too much to go into all of the details associated with these conferences and Negro advisory committees. Basically, they attempted to manage black labor on behalf of the war effort. In some southern states, this translated into "a better understanding of employment matters relating to the Negroes . . . in order that greater production of food and war supplies might be the result."[8] Since northern and southern states were included in this massive effort to stabilize black labor, northern industrial capitalists had to curtail raiding the underdeveloped South for the latter's black labor. But they did not always cooperate.

A whole array of government agencies was involved in the effort to effectively use black labor. In August 1917, representatives from State Councils of Defense, the United States Department of Agriculture, and the United States Department of Labor held a conference in Louisville, Kentucky, for the express purpose of finding ways to stabilize the black labor force. Such efforts also included governors of various states who were seeking ways and means to use black labor more efficiently.[9]

All this concern with black workers and race relations was nothing more than response to war-induced labor shortages and the economic, social, and political disruptions related to the increasing industrial demand for black labor. Both industrial capitalists and government officials were aware of the central role of black labor in the war effort and industrial development, and black leaders were alert enough to see the connection between the war-induced industrial demand for black labor and the building of black communities. However, once the war-induced black labor crisis ended—namely, the need for the mobilization and stabilization of black labor—the government no longer seemed interested in supporting black scholars whose research might be embarrassing. Still, a valuable lesson had been learned during the war: Black industrial labor provided the key to building and maintaining urban black communities.

Even before the war, black and white social reformers had been inspired by the spirit of the Progressive movement to help less fortunate southern blacks to survive in the urban North. But not until the founding of the National Urban League in New York City in 1911—through the merger of three related organizations: the Committee on Urban Conditions Among Negroes in New York, the National League for the Protection of Colored Women, and The Committee for Improving Industrial Conditions Among Negroes—did a really effective national program dedicated to black urban survival emerge.[10]

While the National Urban League (NUL) failed to solve many of the major problems plaguing black urban America, it did provide a safety net without which many black workers and their families would not have survived. It brought together black and white social reformers who, along with well-trained black social workers, greatly facilitated the transition of thousands of southern peasants from the rural South to the industrial urban North. The NUL established a network of invaluable resource people including, among others, powerful capitalist-philanthropists, such as Julius Rosenwald, Jr., John D. Rockefeller, Jr., Ruth Standish Baldwin, and Alfred White, as well as a generation of very bright and professionally trained black social workers.[11]

The training of black professional social workers, along with other NUL programs, was designed to help blacks survive in urban settings. These young black professionals, unquestionably dedicated to the survival and well-being of urban blacks, also eagerly promoted the philosophy of big business. They realized black urban communities could only be built and maintained by forging links with industrial America. So these young people worked diligently to establish ties with industrialists to ensure continual black economic progress. Thus, a symbiotic relationship evolved between local captains of industry and those involved in the black community building process. Two scholars writing in the 1930s understood this relationship when they wrote: "Many of the largest industrial concerns came to regard the local league as a useful agency for procuring labor and as a conservative stabilizing force in the colored community, and contributed substantially to its support."[12]

DETROIT URBAN LEAGUE'S ROLE IN ASSISTING MIGRANTS' ADJUSTMENT TO INDUSTRIALIZING DETROIT

Detroit seemed destined to become one of several midwestern cities where local Urban Leagues and local industrialists would forge alliances based upon mutual needs. The pressing needs of both industry and migrants transformed Detroit into a social laboratory demonstrating the role of the Urban League in aiding southern migrants' adjustment to urban-industrial life.

In October of 1915, Eugene Kinckle Jones of the National Urban League in New York City contacted the Associated Charities of Detroit to ask for financial assistance in establishing a local Urban League chapter. In less than a year, after having worked out a few difficulties, the Detroit branch of the National Urban League opened its doors. Forrester B. Washington, one of the League's newly trained black social workers, became the first director in the summer of 1916.[13]

Washington graduated from Tufts College in 1909 and did graduate work at both Harvard and Columbia, receiving his M.A. from the latter institution in 1917. He spent a year and a half as director of the Detroit Urban League. A year later Washington was appointed supervisor of the Department of Negro Economics in the United States Department of Labor. He returned to Detroit in 1920 and for the next three years worked as Director of the Research Bureau of the Detroit Associated Charities. In 1926, *The Negro in Detroit,* a two-volume study of overall black conditions, was published under his guidance. In the years that followed, Washington continued his social work interests in Philadelphia and Atlanta and was appointed director of the Atlanta School of Social Work at Atlanta University, Atlanta, Georgia in 1927.[14]

As soon as Washington arrived in Detroit in 1916, he began surveying the needs of southern black migrants and the social agencies that served them. He enlisted the assistance of Boyd Fisher, a member of the famous Fisher family and vice president of the Detroit Executive Club and representative of the Detroit Board of Commerce, to help him to secure information on black employment from Detroit employers. Employers were asked to fill out a questionnaire concerning how many black and white workers they employed during past years and their average wages.[15]

The answers to both surveys showed what people had suspected. Few social-service agencies focused on black migrants. And most employers replied that they employed few or no black workers and that the few they did employ worked only in unskilled occupations as porters, furnace tenders, foundry workers, janitors, watchmen, and elevator operators.[16]

The lack of social services for blacks stemmed from a number of factors, including the small number of blacks in Detroit at the time. Various ethnic and religious groups tended to develop and maintain social service agencies for their own use. For example, a pattern of ethnic and religious self-help was well-established in Detroit in 1880. German and Irish Catholics had their own hospitals and orphanages, and Jewish charities sprang up in the late 1880s to address the needs of immigrant East European Jews.[17] No wonder few social service agencies existed exclusively for blacks.

In 1880, Catholic and Protestant leaders recognized the need for greater cooperation and organized the Detroit Association of Charities.[18] It would be close to forty years before the black population in Detroit would be of significant size and strength to command similar attention and support.

Most blacks were forced to live in the most undesirable sections of town, alongside the red light districts. The death rate for blacks was twice as high as that for whites. Probational work among black criminal offenders was practically nonexistent, and it was almost impossible to locate decent boarding homes for black children.[19] Many problems resulted from the social upheavals of the migration.

Undoubtedly shaken by the survey, Washington assessed the situation: "Nothing is being done in the way of adjusting these colored strangers to their new environment and assimilating them healthfully. Hence, a situation is being created which, unless proper preventive measures are soon taken, will present a very difficult problem in the not too distant future.[20]

Washington instinctively knew what it would take some white politicians and scholars decades to see and understand: namely, that unattended urban poverty takes its toll on the larger society. As is still the custom today in many cities, elites in 1916 tended to delegate meager resources to solve the massive and complex problems of the poor. The Detroit Urban League had only three people on its staff to address the problems of finding jobs and homes for thousands of uprooted and disoriented black rural peasants. The responsibility rested on these people's shoulders, especially those of Washington, the director. No black or white social agencies existed that could serve as really effective models. It was to be a new experience with the usual trial-and-error struggles.

For over a year Washington struggled to solve these problems. His efforts exemplified the social work skills that would increasingly come to characterize the work of local Urban League people. Their strategies for black urban survival, notwithstanding their middle-class and at times uncritically pro-employer bias, enabled black migrants to gain a toehold in industrial jobs. In fact, the socialization of the black rural peasant to urban industrial life was partly attributed to people like Washington who ranked among the first advocates and protectors of the black industrial working class. League people constantly reminded black workers to be punctual, zealous, and ambitious in their work. To this end, the League helped organize a group of young black college men, the Young Negro Progressive Association (YNPA). These young men worked during the day and attended college at night. They visited factories during lunch hour to talk to black workers about good work habits. They also worked with the League's prison project, helping former black prison inmates to adjust to the outside.[21]

The League's emphasis upon punctuality, zeal, and ambition, along with the YNPA's lunch hour talks to black workers, contributed to the adjustment and stabilization of the black industrial working class, without which the community building process could not have gone forward. Few local leaders or organizations had the expertise to take charge at this very crucial stage of black community building. The black community could only move beyond its pre–World War I hiatus by implementing effective community building strategies. The demand for black labor provided the initial impetus for this stage of community building, but much more was needed. Labor demand would not build a community. In fact, as we have seen, uncontrolled labor demand during periods of housing shortages created severe problems for the black community, retarding the progress of a healthy community building process. At this stage, according to Washington, job placement was the best strategy for black community building. "As we all know," Washington reported in December 1916, "it is one of the purposes of the League to get Negroes into the more skilled, the better-paid, and the more healthy processes of industry."[22] Once blacks had decent jobs, Washington reasoned, they would be able to "maintain a better standard of living." Furthermore, the more trades and occupations blacks learned, the more valuable they would be to the larger black community.[23]

Washington believed in jobs as the foundation of all black social and economic development. His job placement reflected his belief. He placed more blacks in jobs than most leagues around the country, including New York, which facilitated only several hundred job placements. In his first whirlwind year, Washington placed 6,993 men and 1,279 women! To his credit, 2,000 of these jobs were skilled and semiskilled. Washington enjoyed an advantage few other leaders had. The Employers Association of Detroit paid the salary of his employment secretary. Few urban leagues were as fortunate as Detroit in having "hired help" and financial assistance from their local business associations.[24] The new linkage between the Detroit Urban League and the Detroit business community obviously paid off very well. In all probability, the vast majority of black workers who arrived in Detroit received their first jobs in those industrial firms which had worked with the League. Developing and maintaining such linkages proved to be an effective strategy for community building during the early stages of the black community. Such strategies, however, tended to foster black community dependency upon local white elites, thus retarding the community building process at later stages. (See table 4.)

Table 4

Number of Black Workers Employed on April 27, 1917, by Firms with Which the Detroit Urban League Had Contact

Packard Motor Car Co. (May 18). .	1100	Chalmers Motor Car Co.	62
Buhl Malleable Iron Co.	280	Detroit Pressed Steel	50
Ford Motor Car Co.	200	Hudson Motor Car Co.	50
Continental Motor Car Co.	200	Detroit Stove Works	50
Aluminum Castings Co.	150	Paige Detroit Motor Car Co.	20
Michigan Steel Castings	170	Saxon Motor Car Co.	20
Michigan Copper and Brass	125	Hupp Motor Car Co.	20
Michigan Central Railroad	100	Detroit Seamless Tubes Co.	20
Michigan Malleable Iron Co.	100	Monarch Foundry	15
General Aluminum and Brass	65	Michigan Smelting & Refining . .	100

Estimated Total 2874

Source: Adapted from Table II in George Edmond Haynes's *Negro Newcomers in Detroit, Michigan* (New York: Home Missions Council, 1918).

While the Urban League worked hard on behalf of southern migrants, they could be harsh critics of their peasant charges. A polished and highly cultured person, Washington believed in and fostered middle-class values. He was among the first professionally trained black social workers. He and other young blacks represented the cream of the crop in the emerging black urban professional class whose upward mobility and much-valued social contact with the white upper class depended upon how well they could transform the "crude" black masses into mirror images of themselves. Washington and other League people found jobs and houses for black workers, trained country black women to be good domestics, and "rowdy" men to be efficient, productive workers. In return, the migrants had to become decent citizens, "a credit to the race." They had to stop being so "noisy" and "uncouth," so as not to invite discrimination upon the race. "[A] great deal of discrimination," Washington claimed, "has grown up on account of the loud, noisy type of Negroes unused to city ways that are flocking to Detroit."[25]

Migrant displays of southern folkways greatly disturbed Washington. The sight of southern black women wandering down the business district in "calico mother hubbard" headwear and their male counterparts standing "around the public thoroughfares in overalls and undershirts" worried the Urban League Director. Such behavior would hinder the work of the League in projecting a good image of black community life to the important white folk of the city. Uncouth southern blacks were noticeable. "One hundred of this class are more conspicuous than ten thousand of the better class," reasoned Washington. "There are, of course, untidy and uncouth whites," Washington admitted, "but white people are the judges and colored people are being judged."[26]

Washington's seeming overemphasis on southern migrants' impression on whites was not totally due to his own class and cultural biases. As he conceded, "Whites are the judges," and black migrants were being judged. During these all too precarious years of black industrial breakthroughs, black leaders had to make good impressions on white society if they wanted assistance in opening doors to opportunities and keeping them open. In fact, the impressions made on certain segments of white society determined the extent to which the fledgling black urban community would have access to white-controlled resources which made working and living in Detroit a little less difficult. The Associated Charities and the Employers Association of Detroit, both supporters of the Detroit Urban League, represented such white-controlled resources, and good impressions were very important to them.

So Washington worked on remaking the southern black workers into something more palatable to the taste of sophisticated white urban society. In 1918 the League circulated a small pamphlet designed to help migrants to recognize and abandon their southern ways. Inside the pamphlet, *before* and *after* photographs with captions read, "Generally disorderly appearance" and "Neatly clothed and orderly appearance." The *before* photograph showed a woman sitting on some stairs in a weary posture in the middle of trash lying around. The message was clear: Be like the person in the *after,* not the *before,* photograph. "We want to make Detroit a place free from race prejudice, race friction and discrimination," the pamphlet said. "If you will observe the following suggestions, you can greatly help us in bringing this about. Do not indulge in loud conversations or use vulgar or obscene language in public places. Wear street clothes instead of work clothes in public, but avoid 'flashy clothes.' Do not be late for work and do not sit in front of your house with your shoes off. Do not wear overalls on Sundays or spend all your money on pleasure. Do not braid children's hair in certain ways. Keep the children in school. Do not throw refuse in the back or front yards."[27] There were many other don'ts, but these should suffice to demonstrate how obsessed the League was with socializing the black southern peasants.

The Urban League's almost hysterical concern with black migrants' southern folk ways might have been motivated by the fact that many old resident blacks resented the migrants, blaming them for the white community's growing racist attitudes. Probably many of these "old-guard" blacks blamed the Urban League for the deluge of black migrants. No wonder, then, the old-guard blacks took the 1916 visit of Eugene Kinckle Jones from the National Urban League's New York office to Detroit to set up a Detroit branch, as "less a mission of interracial goodwill than a visitation from an agent of doom." Therefore: "With the frenzy born of fear and of the need to protect themselves and what they had accomplished from the demon, the old guard blacks ran Kinckle Jones out of town."[28]

In order to stay on good terms with the old guard, at least long enough to get established, the fledgling Detroit branch had to prove that they were there to help not to hinder, the black community. This explains some of the League's hysterical concern with migrant "country ways."

The Detroit Urban League's first year challenged both body and soul. Washington might have expected, even hoped, that his primary task would be assisting southern blacks' adjustment to industrial jobs. But the larger black and white community saw his and the League's task much differently. To them, the League would solve all problems related to urban blacks. For example, during November 1916, the League found itself pressed into action to locate a woman who had deserted her child, to investigate the character of a fifteen-year-old girl, to console an aunt whose eighteen-year-old nephew would not work and was expecting her to support him, to reunite an estranged couple, to search for a husband who deserted his family, to ascertain whether a certain woman was a proper guardian for her retarded daughter, to instruct families in the use of the TB clinic, to rescue teenage girls from a house of prostitution, and to locate a young man from a "good family" in the South and then rescue him from the bad section of the city.[29]

No wonder Washington became a first-rate troubleshooter for just about every imaginable urban problem facing black migrants. When a white mob numbering two hundred attacked a house occupied by twenty-five blacks in a previously all-white neighborhood, forcibly evicted the blacks, tore up the house, and threw the furniture in the yard, Washington and the League went to the rescue. They arranged a conference between the blacks and the whites and miraculously brought the parties to a mutual under-standing. The whites agreed to pay damages and the blacks moved back into their home. The League resolved the conflict and succeeded in integrating a neighborhood as well.[30]

Providing a foundation for later stages of community building demanded bold and ingenious strategies. The League persuaded two large foundries to build low-cost homes for their black workers near the plant. The League even figured out a way to buy up the leases from the madams whose houses of prostitution were closed by the Police Department and then persuaded local industrialists to take over the leases and provide housing for families of black workers. To add to this impressive list of accomplishments, the League also established a Housing Bureau that kept lists of vacant houses, many unlisted with commercial realtors. Always concerned with the welfare of incoming immigrants, the League provided employers with lists of respectable rooming houses for their new black employees. Lists of this sort helped steer newcomers away from "the open arms" of "disorderly houses."[31]

Even with all the ingenuity of the League, figuring out newer and more imaginative—and workable—ways to solve the countless problems associated with integrating migrants into industrial Detroit was hard work. Fortunately, several black self-help organizations, some whose roots went back to the pre-migration days and who belonged to the emerging new urban middle class, assisted the League in uplifting struggling migrants. The Detroit Study Club, a group of twenty-five black women, and The Willing Workers, a relief society of black women, invited Washington to address them. These invitations marked a major breakthrough into the established black community, allowing Washington to explain his mission. More substantial aid came from four of the largest black churches which took up a contribution of $25 to give to the League. The Reverend Robert Bradby, pastor of the Second Baptist Church, the largest black church in Detroit at the time, extended an open invitation to the League to use the church auditorium for public meetings.[32] With the cooperation of established black churches, the community building process could advance further.

The small but growing middle class, whose own survival would be increasingly linked to that of the migrants, also supported the League. Washington played a key role in paving the way for segments of this class to work together for the benefit of the larger black community. The League helped to coordinate the activities and functions of several black organizations. In December 1916, Washington suggested to the presidents of the Young Negroes Progressive Association and the Dunbar Lyceum that they consult with other black organizations for the purpose of combining the chief executives of every black church and fraternal, literary, and social organization in the city. Groups of all kinds, shapes, and types of influences began depending upon the League's real and imagined resources. The Colored Mothers' Club asked the League to furnish them with names of expectant mothers. Black businessmen from various parts of the country kept in touch with the Detroit Urban League in order to be on top of whatever developments might benefit them. Black educational institutions depended upon the Detroit Urban League for vital information. For example, Hampton Institute asked the League to supply them with information on blacks in Detroit.[33]

These achievements provided more than feathers in Washington's cap as Urban League director. They bore a broad and strategic significance for the short and long-range process of community building. By establishing linkages with groups in Detroit's black and white power structures, the League enlisted a pool of valuable supporters for the uphill struggle ahead.

The Detroit Urban League became a model of social welfare work in urban areas, which made Washington a national celebrity. Soon after Washington had given an account of his work in Detroit at a New York conference on black migration, Eugene Kinckle Jones, head of the National Urban League, wrote Miss L. Green of the Associated Charities of Detroit, under whose auspices the Detroit Urban League operated: "It will be impossible for me to explain to you the good that Mr. Washington was able to do by his visit to New York and his attendance at the conference on Negro migration. I think that Mr. Washington's account of his work

in Detroit was the most favorably received address of the whole conference."
Jones said Washington had made such a solid contribution to the conference
that "two representatives from Washington who are trying to get an organi-
zation affiliated with the League established in Washington asked that Mr.
Washington's report to be put in pamphlet form for propaganda work in
Washington."[34]

During his tenure as director, Washington became a prominent national
authority on black urban problems. He was in demand as a speaker and
his research and publications on black urban problems won wide respect.
As Washington's views on and approaches to black urban problems became
widely known and accepted, social workers from other cities began looking
at the Detroit Urban League program as a model for their work; still
others used Washington's writings for propaganda work.[35]

In May of 1917, reflecting on what he had learned about black survival
in the urban North, Washington told an audience at St. Mark's Brotherhood
Church that "in a program for the adjustment of the Negro, there must
be a definite place reserved for the development of industry efficiency."
The welfare of the black worker in this new environment, Washington
informed his listeners, depends upon the opinion that the white community
has of him; particularly, Washington stressed, the business community. "If
the [white] community can be convinced that the Negro is and will always
be a business asset, we need not worry much about housing, employment,
and recreation." But Washington warned his audience: "The Negro has
got to convince the captains of industry . . . that he will be just as much
of a necessity to production after the war as he is now."[36]

Had Washington remained a bit longer in his post as director of the
Detroit Urban League, he might have been less convinced that black efficiency on the job provided the panacea for all other urban black problems,
such as housing and unemployment. Of course, he was correct in stressing
the need for black workers to be efficient on the job. No doubt job efficiency
enhanced job security, but Washington's belief that as long as the white
community viewed blacks as a business asset, blacks would not have to
worry much about housing, employment, and recreation, would be proven
wrong. It became evident that the business cycles which ravaged black
workers were not much influenced by a view of blacks as business assets.
Nor would being business assets protect black workers from having their
landlords hike up their rents. Sadly enough, housing and unemployment
would get worse as black workers became more efficient; such problems
were obviously not related to job efficiency but rather to the worsening
conditions of industrial life and to institutional racism.

In all fairness to Washington, from where he stood at the watershed of
the black industrial breakthrough, black workers had to prove themselves,
and quickly, in the industrial sector. If they failed to do so, they would
be relegated back to a rural industrial reserve or forced back into the
domestic and personal-service occupations, while white workers continued

to advance within the expanding industrial sector. On this point, Washington was on target. Building a stable working class community hinged on how quickly and efficiently black rural workers could be absorbed into modern industrial society. Yet, community building also depended on a host of other factors, such as decent housing and adequate recreation.

"The first prerequisite in the task of organizing a local community for the absorption of a large new population of Negro citizens," Washington told a conference of social workers in June of 1917, "is the establishment of a vocational bureau." This had to be the first priority. Without jobs, black migrants would "drift into mischief." Such a situation, Washington explained, "is fraught with danger because in a few days idling about the city in search of a job, the immigrants may come into contact with conditions and people whose influence is demoralizing and may destroy his chance of ever becoming a good citizen." During the first week of his arrival, the migrant needed more "bolstering up" than at any other time. Until his first paycheck, he could not find anyone to trust him. Washington told how the Vocational Bureau of the Detroit Urban League functioned on behalf of the migrants. The Bureau staff gave each new arrival cards with directions on how to get to various places in the city. He explained how the League persuaded the owner of a local theater, known as a hangout for migrants, to publicize the services the League offered.[37]

According to Washington's philosophy, the establishment of a Bureau of Investigation and Information regarding housing was next in importance. "The character of the house into which Negro immigrants go has a direct effect on their health, their morals, and their efficiency." Even recreation played a part in socializing and protecting the new migrants. Organized recreation provided the key in keeping the newcomer away from the "many vicious attractions entirely new to him." Young naive migrants could easily fall into bad social habits so common in the red-light districts. The red-light districts posed the worst and the most dangerous problems because they provided so many allurements to young single black men just off southern plantations. The problem was complicated by the fact that few old resident blacks expressed interest in the welfare of southern black migrants. Nor did they welcome their southern country brethren.

As Washington painfully admitted, the black city slickers of the red-light district did welcome the migrants. "I am sorry to say, but it is true, that he [the southern migrant] gets the warmest welcome from the worst element of the Negro community, the saloon keeper, the poolroom proprietor, the owner of the gambling club and of the disorderly house."[38]

Washington left his audience of social workers with lots of advice and tried-and-tested programs for how best to help newly arriving southern black migrants to adjust to urban industrial life as a first step in building a stable community. He emphasized reshaping the migrant's attitudes and behavior to fit into an industrial mode of production so he would be indispensable to the white business community. Black workers had to be efficient and productive and overcome the obstacle of red-light districts and other "bad" social habits. This strategy of Washington for black urban survival and progress was linked to black social workers' roles in contributing to the difficult process of community building in other industrial cities.

When he left the Detroit Urban League in 1918, Washington was probably pleased with his accomplishments, as indeed he should have been, because he paved the way for his successor. But Washington had never had to face the problems of business slumps, those periodic economic disruptions which would undo a year's work in a week. He had never had to face black unemployment and acute housing shortages, which were destined to ride the back of the fledgling migrant community like twin demons. He produced only a skeletal foundation, at best. His successor would have to flesh out and expand many of his programs. Washington had outlined areas in which migrants needed immediate help, such as job orientation, housing, and recreation, and he had made valuable contacts in the white business and professional communities and initiated cooperative efforts among organizations within the black community. He turned his work over to John C. Dancy, who would be the director of the Urban League for over four decades and would maintain the league's reputation as a major agency of black community building.

A NEW DIRECTOR TAKES OVER:
MAINTAINING THE EMPHASIS ON EMPLOYMENT

John C. Dancy was born on April 13, 1886, in Salisbury, North Carolina. He was educated at Livingstone College and the University of Pennsylvania. After his student days, he became principal of Smallwood Institute, a small black preparatory school in Clairmount, Virginia. In 1914, he left Smallwood to become the Secretary of the black YMCA in Norfolk, Virginia. Dancy developed many practical and important managerial skills in the process of building up that institution. Soon he was eager for more varied experiences in the larger urban centers of the North. A meeting with Eugene Kinckle Jones convinced Dancy to work for the expanding National Urban League. After a stint as Urban league industrial secretary in New York, where he opened up jobs for blacks, and in cities in Connecticut and Massachusetts, Dancy was ready to wrestle with the problems of Detroit's black migrant population.[39]

Dancy joined the Detroit Urban League in June of 1918 and immediately began expanding the League's activities to address the complex problems of black migrants' adjustment to industrial Detroit. Washington had been highly successful in devising community building strategies for the short run, namely, to help blacks get a toehold in industrial jobs. But it was left up to John C. Dancy to devise and perfect long-term community building strategies for the black community. In less than a year Dancy expanded the Urban League's quarters by 300 percent. This growth stemmed directly from new programs initiated by Dancy, who was determined to maintain the Detroit Urban League's reputation which, under Washington, had soared into first place among Urban League chapters around the nation. Dancy succeeded in this goal during his first year. The League handled 11,000 people and became the fastest growing chapter in the country. Dancy's policy of continuing Washington's efforts to unite local black organizations around the needs of black migrants contributed to his successful first year.[40]

The most vital part of Dancy's program of expansion involved the hiring of a vocational secretary. The secretary visited factories, stores, and other places of employment seeking new openings for black workers, especially women, who were having a hard time finding jobs.

By 1919, the DUL had an employment office, which played a key role in the overall community building process. It maintained the vital link between major white employers of black workers and the developing black community by supplying these employers with workers and assisting black workers to find work. Under Dancy's direction, the office also persisted in trying to obtain better employment opportunities for black workers. While other agencies and organizations, such as the state employment service and some black churches, also assisted black workers in finding jobs, none was as intimately connected to the network of employers and black workers as was the DUL. Soon after Dancy arrived and hired his first vocational secretary, the DUL became the most recognized employment agency for black workers. As we will see, even the state employment service deferred to the League on matters relating to black workers. The DUL positioned itself to play a key role in the job-training and placement stage of the community building process and Dancy's unflagging efforts on behalf of black workers kept their interests in the forefront of this process.

The DUL's Employment Office worked unceasingly to get black workers into decent jobs. For decades, the staff processed applications of black men and women seeking work. However, the office had to contend with certain harsh realities of Detroit's job market: Black men and women, however well trained, would be hired only in traditionally "black" jobs. Between the opening of the office and the end of World War II, the greatest demand for black women would be in domestic work, "cleaning white women's kitchens." The office's monthly reports between 1919 and 1945 indicate that many more black women than men were placed on jobs.[41] This could obviously mean many things. But the strongest evidence seems to point to a long-term demand for black domestic labor. Between August and December of 1919, the office placed more black men in jobs than black women. Two years later, a noticeable trend emerged as job placements for black women soared ahead of those for black men. For example, between 1921 and 1930, job placement for black women was from two to three times as high as for black men. Here again, we must be cautious because the office did count each day a domestic worker was placed as a new placement. So one day-worker working seven days could be counted as seven placements.[42]

Monthly job placements provided DUL with a running record of the employment health of the larger black community, which proved useful for mapping out appropriate coping strategies. In May 1920, the Office reported that some black workers were "discriminating in their choice of jobs," warning that "soon most will be eager to take any job offered." Sure enough, five months later, overall employment declined in the city and black unemployed workers were showing up daily at the Office seeking work.[43] The next year, 1921, turned out to be the worst year for both the DUL and black workers. In early January, the Employment Office reported the alarming news that two-thirds of black workers were unemployed. Out of 17,000 black workers, they announced, "it is safe to say that there are not more then 4,000 gainfully employed," and these had been without work for at least two months. A month later, the Office reported that, compared to February of last year (1920), when it had placed 822 black workers, this year it could place only 191. Most of these placements were for general house cleaning. In April, 1,100 people applied for jobs, but, sadly, the Office could place only 192 women and 7 men.[44] As unemployment among blacks worsened, the gap between applicants and job placements widened. During August and September of 1921, the Office could place only 283 workers out of a total of 2,210 applicants. As the year ended, the Mayor appointed Dancy to a committee on "odd jobs" as part of a citywide effort to lessen the effects of the unemployment problem.[45]

The DUL Employment Office cushioned the blows of the 1921 economic downturn somewhat. The few placements it was able to make kept many black families from falling apart. Only through the well-established and well-maintained linkages with key employers was the Office able to place black workers. The DUL Employment Office received a well-earned respite in 1922 as the gap between applicants and job placements began to close. As more blacks returned to work, the relief stations in the black community closed, indicating a decline of black families on welfare. No longer faced with a crisis situation, the Office could resume its normal placement duties—until the next crisis.[46]

In June of 1922, 405 black workers out of a total of 1,325 found jobs through the Office. Expressing relief at the economic upturn, the Office reported: "Just now we are in the position to place all of the physically fit men who apply, not always in positions for which they have been trained but at least a job." The demand for general house work soared during this period. But the Office could not fill the demand. Black women preferred day work for which they received more money and worked fewer hours.

Fewer hours on the job enabled black women more time for their families; this often conflicted with the demands white employers made on black domestic workers.[47]

Increasing demand for black domestics posed some problem for the Employment Office. Dancy saw the role of the Office as an agency that would place black workers in a range of jobs according to their training. If they needed training to get into the more skilled jobs, then the Office would make such training available. For example, the Domestic Training School set up to train "green women" (i.e., rural southern black women) to function in modern kitchens. This practice of training southern migrant black women to become more efficient servants for white households was already well established in southern black industrial schools. Although designed to secure jobs for black women, these training programs as David Katzman has pointed out, prepared these women to "live within the caste system rather than challenging it."[48]

However, institutional racism (which we will discuss in more detail in chapter 5) worked to confine both black men and women, regardless of training and education, to traditional "black jobs," commonly called "nigger work." As much as it wanted to place black women in jobs other than domestic work, the Office found itself fighting an uphill battle. "We are finding it increasingly difficult to find jobs for black women other than domestic work, [particularly] for those with training, graduates of high schools, training schools and colleges," Dancy lamented in September of 1922. Determined to keep trying, Dancy and the Office established a working relationship with the Employment Department of Cass Technical High School, which specialized in placing young people in jobs for which they were qualified.[49]

Reporting on the 1922 year, the Office proclaimed: "There is no unemployment this winter. Those who want work can find it." By April of 1923, the Office must have been elated to be able to report that there were more calls for men than they were able to fill.[50] Over the next few years, the Office continued to place blacks in mostly traditional jobs, as well as placing them in better jobs whenever opportunities arose. Some success occurred in 1924 when the Office was able "to urge the appointment of well prepared Negroes in many fields of endeavors." But, by June of that same year, what little success the Office had achieved was being eroded by another wave of unemployment. Once again black workers flooded the offices of the League looking for work. That fall, increasing black unemployment forced the Office to make the painful decision to place only those black workers who were near the poverty line.[51]

Hard times, however, did not prevent the Office from celebrating its limited progress. In the annual report for 1924, Dancy commented on the work of the Employment Office on behalf of the black community: "In the matter of employment the organization has done more in the placement of men and women than it appears on the surface. Frequently, we have aided persons applying to us who had no home, nor food or a job and of course were necessarily dependent. We have been able on many occasions to provide them with a job where all this was provided." Relating the work of the Office of Employment to blacks on relief, Dancy explained that providing work for blacks "means a tremendous saving in the matter of relief because had this not been provided relief would have been necessary."[52]

As the Great Depression approached, the Employment Office continued its valiant struggle, placing black men and women in whatever jobs it could find and opening up new areas for those blacks who had the training. "We have been able to open," the Office reported for the year 1928, "many jobs of high grade where special training was required of the applicants."[53] Yet, the struggle continued uphill. Although the Office was able to get a few blacks into higher-level skilled jobs, this meant little in the way of major change in the racially stratified labor market. They were less pioneers opening new areas for many others to follow than they were tokens granted by white employers to placate the League. Even these incremental advances moved the community building process forward. The tokens became role models for a generation of black youth, inspiring them to strive for higher goals and contribute to the welfare and pride of the black community.

The Great Depression and the World War II years greatly taxed the DUL's job-placement abilities. The Employment Office had become a life-line for thousands of unemployed black workers. It had provided valuable job information for displaced workers. It had diligently monitored the job market, searching for opportunities in new areas of employment for quali-fied blacks. It had dared to dream that if blacks kept struggling and did not lose faith that things were bound to get better. But then came the Great Depression. Hard enough for whites, it was doubly hard for blacks.

During early 1930, the Office could only place black workers in odd jobs or day work. Having been long considered a key source of expertise on black employment problems, the Office found itself swamped with requests from social workers and economists from around the country who were seeking information on black unemployment in Detroit.[54] As the Depression deepened, blacks in the outlying areas required help from the Office. During November 1931 close to 5,000 blacks in over 400 families in Inkster had the highest rate of unemployment among black communities in the Greater Detroit area. Concerned about this acute condition, the Office began working with local officials in an effort to relieve some of the distress.[55]

As could be expected, the gap between applications for work and job placements grew wider with the passage of time. In 1933, the Office could place only 688 men and women out of a total of 7,000 applicants. "Most of these came over and over again," Dancy reported, "but the best we could do was to take care of the 688." Five years later, the Office confessed that it could not do much more than refer "worthy" people to the W.P.A.

However, between August and October 1938, the Office placed 208 people on jobs out of a total of 1,193 applicants, 584 men and 609 women. At the time the Office reported a shortage of competent domestics, which might explain the much larger number of black women job applicants.[56]

Towards the end of the Great Depression and the beginning of World War II, the Employment Office could see a few flickers of light at the end of a long tunnel. The spring and early fall of 1940 found the Office busy placing black workers in industries throughout the city. In October of that year Dancy served on a Committee of the Michigan Conference on Employment Problems of the Negro set up to address such problems as disproportionate unemployment among black workers, longer duration of black unemployment, vocational preparation for black youth, as well as limited opportunities for them in apprenticeship training, and discrimination in defense-training selection.[57]

The DUL's annual report for 1941 reflected the upswing in not only the resumption of normal job placements but the opening up of new employment opportunities for qualified blacks. "With employment this year we have done fairly well. Not alone have we been content with just getting jobs but we have busied ourselves with the opening of new places for those qualified and have been fairly successful in the attempts made." These "new places" included jobs for stenographers, typists, and electrical and mechanical engineers. Dancy's elation over these particular placements prompted him to elaborate on their unique circumstances. "In the case of an electrical engineer whom we placed, a graduate of the University of Michigan, it is interesting to note that when he took the job his salary was $1,200.00 per year. He has now been raised to $2,400.00 and is the actual head of his department." Another case involved a stenographer the DUL placed with a white company who had "accredited herself so well that frequently she is assigned to work with the General Manager of the concern. This is unusual when it is considered that there are from fifty to sixty women in this office doing stenography. The Manager himself has told the Director that she is a very wonderful young woman. When [she was] first placed in this position one white worker threatened to quit, but since that time she has become the girl's most substantial friend."[58]

As already mentioned, these placements often represented mere token advancements and breakthroughs in the rigid system of employment discrimination in Detroit that confined thousands of blacks to the most menial, dirty, and dangerous jobs. For every "qualified" black The League placed, many others were forced to accept menial work far beneath their qualifications. Notwithstanding, as we noted earlier, these token advancements contributed to the process of community building.

During the 1940s the League began to develop more specialized staff functions such as the Vocational Services Secretary and Group Work and Community Organizations Secretary. Francis A. Kornegay became Vocational Services Secretary in 1944, heading up the Vocational Services

Department. In 1945, this new department serviced 2,339 people of which 911 were seeking work. Out of this group, 246 were placed and 634 were referred. Those remaining received vocational and educational guidance, housing assistance and information, veteran advice and vocational testing. The 246 placements covered a range of occupations from such traditional "Negro" jobs as domestic service and other unskilled occupations to skilled and professional positions such as interviewers for the United States Employment service, recreational leaders, clerks for the Michigan Unemployment Compensation Commission, and Red Cross overseas personnel among others.[59]

Continuing the DUL's practice of opening up employment areas previously closed to black workers, the Vocational Secretary began working with the Retail Merchants Association in Detroit to open up jobs for blacks in various business establishments. Sam's Department Store, a popular downtown establishment was approached by the League for clerical and sales jobs; the Michigan Bell Telephone Company was asked to open up jobs for blacks as linemen and installers. After consenting to hire blacks as linemen and installers, Michigan Bell asked the Vocational Services Department to assist them in recruiting and screening black applicants. The Western Union was asked to give blacks jobs as teletypists. The Vocational Secretary succeeded in obtaining a statement of policy from Cunningham's Drug Stores, a large chain in Detroit, clarifying its practice of nondiscriminatory layoffs. The company also promised to hire more blacks and upgrade those already on the payroll who had the necessary seniority and work performance. Both the Packers Outlet Market and the Reconstruction Finance Corporation promised to hire blacks and asked the League to assist them in recruiting and referring blacks for future job openings. Blacks also found a few job openings in the Police Department, long the bastion of white male power and privilege, as a result of the efforts of the Vocational Secretary.[60]

Late in 1945, the Vocational Secretary became aware of a War Department policy rejecting black applicants for War Department clerical positions in Germany. He contacted the Secretary of War and his civilian aide protesting the policy, which resulted in the policy being rescinded. Soon after, the League began recruiting qualified blacks and referring them to the War Department for possible positions. Realizing the need to prepare the black community for employment during the postwar period, the Vocational Services Department sponsored a Job Workshop Conference soon after V–J Day. The conference focused on marshalling qualified experts and gathering information relating to the job prospects for blacks during reconversion and the post-reconversion periods. The League also participated in the Annual Vocational Opportunity Campaign initiated by the National Urban League by sponsoring a Career Day Program for high school youth.[61] These combined efforts of the League were aimed at preparing the black community for the ongoing struggle of building the community during the rough days ahead.

COMMUNITY CENTERS

In 1918, the growing black community had no YWCA or YMCA, no centers or settlement houses where black migrants fresh from the South could find assistance. Black churches were not yet set up to accommodate the complex needs of uprooted migrants. Recreation was a major need of migrants at the time, but black churches tended to shy away from the recreational activities that migrants favored, such a dancing and games. The League met this need by using a school provided by the Recreation Commission. This way migrants could have supervised parties and dancing, and black churches would not be offended. But the League still needed a community center to address the other needs of the expanding migrant community. At the time, the Jewish Welfare League owned a large building in the area in which the migrant community was expanding. Dancy asked them if they would be willing to allow the League to use the building for just the cost of maintenance. They agreed. Dancy then asked the Recreation Commission to operate the building as a community center. This center, called the Columbia Center, opened in June 1919, representing another step in the black community building process.[62]

The League did not set up the Columbia Community Center a moment too soon. The year 1919 witnessed one of the largest migrations up to that time; and, as already mentioned, Dancy was forced to ask local black ministers to advise their congregations, when writing to relatives and friends, to warn them not to come to Detroit at the present time because of the housing crisis.[63] During its first years of operation, the Columbia Community Center became the hub of community building activities for the surrounding black migrant community. It housed the Domestic Training School, activities for boys and girls, including music and art classes, a reading room for both adults and children, recreation rooms for returning soldiers, debating, literary, and social clubs, a social center where large groups of black men could congregate daily for reading, playing checkers and cards, and listening to music. Unemployed black workers with plenty of idle time visited the Center; it provided a place of "comfort to the unemployed [by] giving him space to pass his leisure in recreation." One of the League's first projects during its very first year of operation was a baby clinic. In a July report, Dancy proudly proclaimed that the baby clinic was "developing more rapidly than any of the other activities. There are always two nurses and a physician present when the babies are brought and they see after every need and care." The baby clinic started with fifty babies and increased to one hundred fifty a month later.[64]

From the very beginning the League operated the Center to benefit all segments of the migrant community, especially the children. Three months after the Center opened, 400 children from Hamtramck, River Rouge, and Detroit gathered at the facility for a picnic on Belle Island, the island park. Several truck companies donated trucks for transporting them to the picnic area. Reporting on the event, the director commented that "the children were provided with ice cream, sandwiches, milk, fruit . . .; they ate until their little tummies bulged out. All the children reported having a very glorious time at the island."[65]

By September, the Center had attracted a wide range of black social clubs and organizations eager to use its facilities: The Tuskegee Club, the women's auxiliary of Dunbar Hospital (one of the first black hospitals in Detroit), the Allied Medical Association, the Board of Trustees of Dunbar Hospital, the Imperial Boys Club, the Young Negroes Progressive Association, and several black college fraternities.[66] All of this community activity pleased Dancy. He seemed particularly proud of the boys clubs which the League had organized into the Wolverine Athletic club. "This club," he reported in October 1919, "promises to do big things in this community. On Saturday night at the Cass High School we had 65 members present who were taking part in various athletic activities. Aside from athletics these boys are doing work in dramatics." Dancy reported, barely concealing his obvious pride, "These boys are doing work in dramatics. So, it is only a matter of time before the organization will be one of the strongest forces for good among the young men in Detroit. We are keenly interested in this group because . . . they were first organized by us."[67]

By October, the Center could not add any more activities. But this was not all bad since, according to reports, the affairs of the Center were "running along smoothly." Both the music school and the baby clinic had expanded and would continue to do so. As the activities in the Center expanded, due to increased use of its facilities by black community organizations and groups and support from the Community Fund and assorted other sources, its role in the community building process became increasingly evident. It not only served the expanding migrant community, providing a central meeting place for all segments of the community, but it galvanized the black community as few organizations and groups could do. Its very existence tended to inspire certain submerged segments of the black community to participate in the community building process. For example, in the spring of 1920, the League assisted in organizing a group of black men and women workers into a club called the Pastoral Club. The men worked as common laborers and the women did day work and laundering. They formed the club because of their interest in the work of the Center. The women then volunteered to launder the curtains in the Center and did such a good job that the director commented that "if their work for their employers is as good as the curtains they did for us then their employers have no reason to complain."[68] An organization of black

The first black baby clinic in Detroit, established by the Detroit Urban League, 1919. (Note John C. Dancy at the top right.) Courtesy of Michigan Historical Collections, Bentley Historical Library, University of Michigan.

The reading room of the Community Center on Columbia Street, 1919. Courtesy of Michigan Historical Collections, Bentley Historical Library, University of Michigan.

taxi drivers, the Taxi Drivers Association, formed in the Center during the same year, adding to the number of black organizations stimulated into being by the Center.[69]

Increased community activities in the Center necessitated a move to a larger building on Chestnut Street located in the heart of the migrant community. Such a location allowed the League to better serve this community because it was also the entry point for arriving migrants. In June of 1920, one year after its establishment, the Center had much of which to be proud. Twenty-one clubs had used the building, 30,925 people had visited the Center, 1,680 babies had been treated in the baby clinic, and the music school had taught 1,920 students. As indicated in its June 1920 report, the Center had evolved into a center of black educational activity. Yet, this was only the beginning. By October, the number of people visiting the Center had reached 30,000.[70]

The Center continued its role as the major black community building institution throughout the 1920s, addressing as best it could the multi-faceted needs of the expanding black migrant community. When large numbers of black workers lost their jobs during the 1921 economic downturn, many would have been forced to hang out on street corners but for the existence of the Center, which provided a place for them to read, relax, and play games. Between January and March of 1921, the Center reported that its rooms were filled "from early morning until late in the evening. Approximately 4,000 persons have visited the Center during the month. This is an increase of about 25% over our usual attendance. Unemployment to a large degree is responsible for this. The men are out of work and as a result come here and spend most of their leisure time." At times as many as 145 unemployed men would use the Center in one day, some arriving in the morning, reading papers and magazines and playing cards and checkers and the piano. Many of these unemployed men probably had families that they brought with them to the Center. In March, the Center reported that its rooms were crowded daily with boys and girls passing leisure time, "great groups of boys and men . . . being taken each night to the school gymnasiums for various sorts of athletics."[71]

Always ready to address new needs of the community, during the fall of 1921 the Center began setting up a course in general house work focusing on modern housekeeping. At the end of the decade, the clinic was still serving black children and had made a special study of rickets among black children. In May of 1929, the clinic was treating eighty-five children for the disease and administering food formula for the children. Functioning many times as a conduit through which city services reached the black community, the Center enabled the educational department of the Board of Health to provide nurses to lecture to black mothers on child care and to expectant mothers on prenatal care. Summing up its year in January 1930, the Center's annual report stated: "Our Community Center has gone along in the even tenor of its way. It has served not only the neighborhood but the city at large . . ."[72]

The league opened another community center on Eight Mile Road where another black migrant community had grown up over the years. Mostly rural, this community did not have access to the social services network available to the League's downtown Community Center. In the Fall of 1928, the League was trying to obtain assistance in building a community center in the area. In May of 1929, the League rented a center from the Episcopal Diocese. However, unlike the steady success story of the first community center, the Eight Mile Road Center had to struggle to get on its feet during the Great Depression. In 1935, the League complained that the Center's quarters were not satisfactory for its purposes. The dental clinic had to be removed for lack of water supply in the building. The Center was also too far away from the black community for people to come on foot in order to avail themselves of the services. The director was forced to report that until the League could find suitable space for the work at this Center, he would advise that it be terminated entirely and the worker shifted to the downtown Center. Fortunately for Blacks residing in the Eight Mile area, the DUL's fortunes changed and it built a new building, which opened in 1937.[73]

Towards the end of World War II, the League operated two community centers serving black neighborhoods, the Chestnut Center in downtown Detroit and the Northwest Center in Northwest Detroit. Both Centers provided a wide range of programs including dramatics, sewing, choral music, piano, scouting, summer day camp, and athletic activities. The Chestnut Center had continued improving its facilities for boys' athletic activities, and the Northwest Center, among its many activities, had organized block clubs. Attendance remained high at both Centers. During 1944 the two Centers averaged a monthly attendance of 2,550. An average of five hundred youth and adults attended the weekly outdoor movies put on by the Chestnut Center. A teenage canteen operated out of this Center two evenings a week, run by a committee of fourteen girls and boys. These youth also ran a snack bar, doing both the buying and selling and cleaning up after dances. About one hundred youth belonged to this committee. Such activities stimulated increased attendance at both Centers. In 1945, attendance totalled 27,075. By the end of the war these community centers had established themselves as major institutions in the community building process.[74]

RECREATION, COMMUNITY HEALTH AND WELFARE

Both Washington and Dancy recognized the vital role that well organized and supervised recreational programs could play in the health and welfare of the migrant community in Detroit. The Young Men's Progressive Association (YMPA), the same group of young black evening college students who spent time talking to black workers concerning good work habits, in 1917 helped establish a weekly community dance at a local school. Organized under the auspices of the DUL and supported by the Detroit Recreation Commission, the community dances provided ghetto youth with a healthy alternative to the other more pathological forms of leisure time activities already mentioned. The first community dances attracted between 30 and 143 youth. Before long, that number had jumped to over 300.[75]

After the Recreation Department ruled that the weekly community dances had to be conducted as a club, membership cards became necessary for participation. Card holders could participate in other recreational activities conducted by the YMPA. Proceeds from the community dance paid for the music, janitor service, printing, and other related expenses. The youth used the remaining proceeds for developing other forms of recreation, such as a black basketball team. Explaining how this recreational program benefited the black community, Washington stated: "Briefly, the proceeds of the YMPA community dance are to be turned back to the community in the form of providing wholesome recreation free or at a nominal fee." Furthermore, the community dances created a spirit of community among the patrons, which Washington felt constituted the nucleus of a "real community centre . . ." From Washington's perspective, the community dances transcended mere recreational activities; they contributed to the needs of the black community. "We now have over three hundred people associated together in an organization interested in promoting healthy dancing. They are conscious that the proceeds are going for the social needs of the community. Probably 90% of these people never gave a thought to the social needs of the neighborhood before."[76]

These community dances, therefore, fostered a spirit of community among patrons, involving them in this early stage of the community building process. Weekly community dances set the tone for other recreational activities designed to improve and maintain the health of the community. Three years after the establishment of the community dances, the DUL was involved in several major recreational projects besides those based in the Community Center. It had a Saturday night recreation center at the Cass High School, where over a hundred boys gathered and sponsored a basketball team that played twice a week and became good enough to play against the Wilberforce University team from Ohio and a baseball team. These recreational activities often depended on resources available from the Recreation Commission, which provided facilities and workers. When such resources were not available, Dancy had to practically go out and "beg and borrow" to keep key programs in operation. His considerable "people skills" served him and the DUL well in negotiating for scarce resources to support his various recreation programs.[77]

Dancy devoted considerable time and effort to the expansion of the

DUL's recreational programs. Like Washington before him, he saw recreational programs as part of the process of building community spirit and pride. In the annual report for 1924, he boasted of the DUL's black basketball team's standing in the newly formed intersettlement basketball league: "Our boys were the only colored group in this organization and they made a very creditable showing, finishing third in a group of six." Two years later, the DUL teams in basketball, baseball, and track won three cups and eight medals, providing Dancy and the League with more reasons to be proud of their recreational programs. With help from the Department of Recreation, which provided them with two recreation workers, the DUL organized a basketball team composed of black boys from around the city to compete in the interracial intersettlement league.[78] Exposing black youth to such interracial competitive sports where they could compete and cooperate with white teams taught them and whites valuable lessons about the real world and generated a greater appreciation for racial harmony.

Among DUL's recreational programs, those devoted to children probably represented the greatest investment in long term community building. By the 1920s Detroit black ghettos had become pockets of poverty, crime, and hopelessness. The lack of adequate housing at reasonable prices, compounded by racial discrimination, eroded black community and family life. Black children had few safe and nurturing recreational activities available to them. So they played in alleys and side streets, many drifting into crime and prison. Over the years the DUL took thousands of these ghetto children and youth on outings, to circuses, baseball games, picnics, fairs, and countless other events to give them opportunities to grow and develop into well-adjusted human beings. But none of these efforts could compare with the DUL's Green Pastures Camp.[79]

GREEN PASTURES CAMP

The opening of Green Pastures Camp by the DUL, in 1931, represented the crowning glory of Dancy's recreational programs. As Forrester B. Washington himself attested: "If John Dancy had not done any more than conceive and bring to actuality Green Pastures Camp he would have justified in a large part his retention for so many years as Director of the Detroit Urban League."[80]

Before the establishment of this camp, most black children in the slums of Detroit had to spend their summers playing on the streets, while white children had access to well-supported summer camps. Summer camps operated by the city and a Detroit daily paper excluded black children, and the YMCA summer camp only allowed black children to attend a few segregated weekly sessions at the beginning or end of each summer. Commenting on the conditions these children had to endure, Washington painted a dreary but accurate picture of the black life in Detroit during the Depression that led to the establishment of Green Pastures Camp:

> Today economic depression and consequent unemployment is affecting the Negro more than any other racial group in Detroit. He was the last brought to the city during the boom days and to a large extent the first discharged now. With the unemployment of the male heads of so many Negro families, the wives and mothers are forced to work away from home and the children are left alone often inadequately fed and improperly clothed and allowed to wander about the streets under-guarded and unsupervised. Or, when mother and father are both unable to find decent employment, they either sit at home and worry or turn to illegal methods of earning a livelihood. In either case the Negro child suffers. He is denied those conditioning factors which lead to wholesome habit formation. "Green Pastures Camp" is a counter-irritant for all these evils so far as the children are concerned.[81]

As he had so many times in the past, Dancy used his network of contacts to address the problem. He approached William J. Norton of the Children's Fund of Michigan to assist in building a summer camp for poor inner city black children. Set up in 1929 by Senator James Couzens, a former business partner of Henry Ford and a former mayor and police commissioner of Detroit, the Children's Fund of Michigan had assets of close to 12 million dollars. The Fund's trustees agreed to support Dancy's proposal and began building what would become the finest summer camp for poor black inner city children in the country. The Children's Fund supported Green Pastures Camp for twenty-three years, with grants totaling 355,000 dollars.[82]

The Fund's first grant of $100,000 purchased the sixty-eight acre lake property located eight miles from the city of Jackson. The grant also paid for the construction of fourteen buildings, including a large dining room used also as a recreation hall with a seating capacity of five hundred, as well as a stage on which plays were held, a director's quarter, a first aid station, and ten cottages for the children. Ten boys or girls lived with a head resident in a cottage, and each had his or her own bunk. The children ate well-prepared meals from a modern kitchen, were watched over by medical personnel, washed in comfortable facilities, and soaked up the rustic beauty of the countryside. By any contemporary standard, this camp for poor black children exceeded expectations. On one of his trips to Green Pastures Camp, Washington was overcome with what he encountered: "Spread out for 1000 feet along the shores of beautiful Little Lake Pleasant and, extending inland to cover 68 acres of woodland, hills, valleys, fields and streams, it includes everything that is beautiful in country life. This variety of scenery is in itself an exception in summer camps."[83]

Poor black parents begged Dancy to allow their children to get into Green Pastures Camp. Year after year he received countless letters from parents who were anxious to expose their children to what was considered a chance of a lifetime. But the camp could accommodate only 600 campers during the five two-week summer sessions. Therefore, many children had to be turned away. Only children between the ages of seven and fourteen who were poor and from Detroit were eligible for the camp. Although the children attending the camp during this period were all black, the camp was always open to all races. Each child had to pass a free physical examination before attending the camp. The examination covered the heart, lungs, and possible parasitic infections. On their arrival at the camp, the children went through a process of being registered, weighed, and examined by a nurse. Once this was over, however, the fun of a lifetime for many of these ghetto youngsters began. Their first experience was a trip to the mess hall for a big meal and being greeted there by the entire staff, including the director, the camp nurse, the cooks, the office assistant, the laundresses, and ten counselors.[84]

The children's first day began at 7:00 at the bugle sound. They raised the flag, ate a good breakfast, and went to their assigned work duties, washing dishes and raking leaves. Children without pocket money could earn some doing these chores. Cottage inspection was next. This activity taught these youngsters the value of cleanliness and engendered in them a sense of group pride by rewarding the winning cottage the honor of displaying the flag for the day. One summer afternoon, probably typical of others, the older boys assisted in the building of log seats for the outdoor amphitheater. The older girls learned weaving and made beaded craft and fern designs. The younger children also had their groups activities. The children swam just before lunch. After lunch, the quiet hour commenced. Campers could nap, go to the camp post office, or spend time at the library. Those campers interested in black history could select books from a collection of over 400 donated to the camp's library in 1934 by the University of Michigan. Other afternoon activities campers could choose from were hiking, boating, and boxing.[85]

On weekends, campers entertained themselves and others with concerts or plays that were often attended by people from nearby towns. Afterwards, campers held "swing dances." Sunday mornings were devoted to "inspirational services" held in the large amphitheater. But the best part of Sunday for the children was that it was visitors' day. Anxious and homesick children could see their parents and share with them the prior week's adventures and excitement. Over 1,000 visitors turned up on visitor's day during the summer of 1932. Visiting parents and other adults had a chance to share in the camp's fun and games by playing baseball and horseshoes and "fishing alongside their children."[86]

While the main purpose of Green Pastures Camp was to provide the children with a fun environment, the League and the summer staff wanted the program also to produce healthier and heavier children. The latter did not always occur. One camp director who ran the summer program between 1931 and 1935 reported that in 1934 each child gained an average of three pounds during a two week session. However, some children gained weight, others remained the same, and still others lost weight. Luckily, the camp staff had other objectives. For example, they worked to stimulate campers' interest in black history.[87]

Realizing that the vast majority of the children had little or no knowledge of black history, since the subject was not taught in the Detroit public schools, Dancy set up the camp in such a way as to promote the history and achievements of black people. Each cottage was named after a famous black person and each camper "was expected to know the history of his and other cottages' namesakes." He invited famous blacks to visit the camp to give inspirational lectures to the campers on how to succeed in life. World Heavyweight Champion Joe Louis visited the camp many times to awe and inspire the youngsters, many of whom were probably from his old neighborhood in Detroit.[88]

Camp counselors had a vital role to play in the success of the summer sessions at The Green Pastures Camp. They were carefully selected because they were expected to be black role models for the children. As one former counselor who worked at the camp as a lifeguard from 1931 to 1937 put it, "John Dancy liked men and women who would stand up strong like the cottages."[89] They were excellent college students with strong leadership ability. In contrast to their charges, they came from the black middle class, considered by some to be the black aristocrats. Dancy remedied this by his policy of selecting at least one of the counselors from a poor background. During the Depression, black college students competed for the chance of working as a counselor at the camp. Only black college students from Detroit could apply. Counselors taught campers valuable lessons about how to succeed, vocational skills, health care, good grooming, proper table manners, and especially proper conduct between the sexes.[90]

Observing these young black counselors at work in the summer of 1931, Washington commented: "Who can measure the inspiring effect of these college student counselors on their impressionable young charges? The children learn to emulate these counselors in small as well as big things, such as deportment, personal cleanliness and the like." Dancy selected a good bunch of young people as counselors because many of them went on to achieve great success in their personal and professional lives. William Patrick, Jr., who was a counselor in 1938 and 1939, went on to become a lawyer and make history by becoming the first black councilman in Detroit. The late Ethelene Crockett, who was one of the first counselors in 1931, achieved success as an obstetrician and gynecologist.[91]

Dancy loved Green Pastures Camp with a passion. He drove to the camp two to three times a week for thirty-one summers even when he had to give up a vacation in the Bahamas to do so. He was proud to boast that during those thirty-one summers he had seen each one of the 15,000 children who attended the camp.[92]

It is easy to understand why Dancy put so much work and effort into Green Pastures Camp. Thousands of poor black children were given a

Children preparing to leave for the Green Pastures Camp. Courtesy of
Michigan Historical Collections, Bentley Historical Library, University of
Michigan.

Staff and children outside a cabin at the Green Pastures Camp. Courtesy
of Michigan Historical Collections, Bentley Historical Library, University
of Michigan.

Staff at the Green Pastures Camp. Courtesy of Michigan Historical Collections, Bentley Historical Library, University of Michigan.

Children playing ball at the camp. Courtesy of Michigan Historical Collections, Bentley Historical Library, University of Michigan.

new lease on life, a fighting chance against poverty, crime, and hopelessness. We probably will never know how many of these poor children became builders of the black community as a result of being exposed to Green Pastures Camp. One thing, however, is clear: They learned that people cared about them and desired very much to see them succeed in life. But above all they learned about the value of serving the black community.

NETWORKING AS A STRATEGY FOR COMMUNITY BUILDING

From the time it set up operation in Detroit in 1916, the DUL networked and cooperated with other institutions, organizations, agencies, and individuals in carrying out its mission of serving the needs of the black urban community. In fact, the DUL could not have contributed as much as it did to the community building process had it not been able to augment its resources via effective networking. From its initial networking with the Employers Association, the Associated Charities, the Detroit Recreation Commission, the Detroit Board of Health, and black churches such as Second Baptist, the DUL, particularly under the leadership of John C. Dancy, steadily built and nurtured a network of resources to assist it in its work. This networking extended from the ranks of the young black college men, the Young Negro Progressive Association, and the black common laborers who contributed their time and energy to fix up the Columbia Community Center to mayors, senators, and corporate and civic leaders in the city, all of whom shared a common belief in the work of the DUL. Furthermore, as a branch of the National Urban League, the DUL was able to tap resources both inside and outside the city of Detroit.

Networking came naturally to many blacks in Detroit, especially members of the new middle class who were anxious to consolidate their base in the rapidly expanding black community. The black elite, as we have already seen, demonstrated less interest in building a strong black community than in securing a niche in white society for themselves and their children. Networking, therefore, as a strategy for community building did not appeal to them. These were the people Washington referred to as the "old Detroiters among the colored people [who] complain that segregation is increasing in the city. There are a great many colored people who call every movement to help the Negro segregation."[93]

Several black churches began networking with the league almost as soon as Washington set up his office. They understood the seriousness of the growing black urban crisis, and they realized that only through networking would they be able to address the problem. In the fall of 1916, the Reverend Mr. Bradby of Second Baptist Church, the largest black Baptist church in Detroit, offered the League a large supply of gym equipment to be used in any recreational center Washington might be planning. The reason behind this offer revealed why the League became the major community building organization in the black community during this period. Bradby had intended to set up the gym equipment in his church to be used by the entire black community. Unfortunately, denominationalism within the black community prevented this intended networking and unification from materializing. Bradby conceded that no individual black church would be able to foster such a community-wide effort. Therefore, he gave the equipment to the League because he felt the League had the best chance of fostering a community center or project.[94] Another black church leader, the Reverend Mr. Bagnall, pastor of the only black Episcopal church in Detroit, asked for the league's cooperation in setting up a parish house to carry on institutional functions connected with his church. The joint project was to be financed by a local pharmaceutical company. The St. Marks Brotherhood of Bethel sent some black women to the League for jobs, and the officers of the organization offered to cooperate in the work of the League. As pointed out earlier, by 1917 the League and major black religious and secular organizations were cooperating on a rather steady basis. But Washington got the process going by such efforts as encouraging the presidents of the Young Negro Progressive Association and the Dunbar Lyceum to assist in unifying the chief executives of every black church and every fraternal, literary, and social organization in the city. Gradually, black organizations began realizing the potential of networking with the League.[95]

As the black community grew in size and complexity, spawning new problems as it struggled to adjust to industrial Detroit, internal and external networking became increasingly vital to its survival and progress. As we will see in the next chapter, dismal living conditions in the ghetto were eroding the health of thousands of blacks. In 1919, smallpox was rampant among black migrants. The League and the Board of Health sent a black social worker to the homes of all recent black migrants to persuade them to be vaccinated. In addition, a nurse instructed migrants how to dress and eat properly in order to maintain their health during the winter months. Notwithstanding these and similar joint efforts of the League and the Board of Health, as well as other health professionals outside the black community, the health of blacks continued to deteriorate. The League and several black doctors began to network with black churches and other community organizations to address this problem. In 1923, two black doctors, Albertus Cleage and Frank P. Raiford, teamed up with the League and conducted a health campaign called the National Negro Health Week. This campaign had been initiated by Booker T. Washington years ago to curtail the heavy death rate among urban blacks. These doctors and the League held health meetings in practically every church in Detroit to explain to blacks how they could improve and maintain their health. This health campaign also extended to isolated black communities on the outskirts of the city.[96]

During the 1930s, the League continued building and consolidating networks within the black community. Dancy served as secretary of the Parkside Hospital Association and as president and treasurer of the Michigan People's Finance Corporation. These two black organizations contributed their share to the community building process during those difficult years. The latter organization provided the League with free rent throughout the Depression, demonstrating the benefits of networking within the black community.[97]

By 1945, the League had become the heart of the black network within the black community and had contributed more to the development of networking than any other black organization or institution in Detroit.[98]

As an affiliate of the National Urban League, the Detroit Urban League had access to a national network of local Leagues concerned with similar problems of community building. These affiliates shared valuable information among themselves, which saved time and energy in the long process of formulating and testing various strategies and programs for black social and economic progress. Since the DUL was one of the fastest growing affiliates in the country—and to many people the most impressive—other Leagues and social welfare organizations looked to the DUL for advice on many aspects of black urban life. In the fall of 1919, the National Urban League showed its recognition of the DUL's status by holding the annual national conference in Detroit. Such conferences stimulated contacts and networking among Urban League affiliates.[99] The DUL, therefore, found itself assuming another vital role in a much larger network that included blacks throughout the country.

Urban League affiliates contacted the DUL about problems of housing, employment, community centers, black businesses, raising community chest funds among blacks, and related concerns. In 1927 and 1928, the Urban League of Pittsburgh asked the DUL for a "digest of [their] experiences with the Employers' Association." "You perhaps know," the Executive Secretary wrote, "that Pittsburgh is a town somewhat on the order of Detroit from an industrial point of view. Because of this fact, I am trying to offer as many parallel reasons for tying in with the Employers' Association here as you have there." Emphasizing the value of networking, he commented: "I am sure you will consider it scientific that we profit by the experiences of others." On at least two other occasions during these two years, the Pittsburgh League requested other kinds of information. One request was for information regarding black thrift and loan companies in Detroit and the other was for support in its efforts to initiate a community fund campaign among blacks in that city. The Boston Urban League also needed advice on fund raising among blacks. "I am having a difficult problem here in the East, that of securing adequate financial aid from the colored people," lamented the Secretary. "I am wondering if you are experiencing this same difficulty in your city, and if so, what means you are employing to meet this situation."[100]

As expected, League affiliates and other social-welfare organizations turned to the DUL for information on black employment. With its enviable relationship with the Employers Association in Detroit as well as its network of contacts within the Detroit black community, including influential black leaders boasting close ties to the Ford family, outsiders rightly perceived the DUL as a good source of reliable information on many aspects of black employment. Leagues in several cities contacted Dancy regarding racial discrimination by the Ford Motor Company in their respective localities. In 1926, the Milwaukee Urban League complained to Dancy that it had been trying to get blacks into jobs in the local Ford plant but with little success. "I do not know whether the Detroit office has any jurisdiction over the policies of the local plant or not," the Secretary wrote. "This you probably know about. If anything can be done from that end, please lend us that assistance through your connections there." The Atlanta league had the same concern about Ford's policy towards black workers in that city. Writing Dancy in 1928, its Secretary complained: "The Branch of the Ford Company in Atlanta not only refuses to employ Negroes, but is not desirous of Negro patronage. This latter phase of our problem is purely local. I hope that you will put these facts strongly before the Detroit Office." Two years earlier, Forrester B. Washington, in one of several positions he held after he left the DUL, was Executive Secretary of the Armstrong Association of Philadelphia, a welfare agency affiliated with the National Urban League. He wanted Dancy to contact a high-ranking black at the Ford Motor Company in Detroit to see if he could influence Henry Ford to visit Philadelphia for a meeting with people working on behalf of black workers.[101] All of these requests reflected how leagues and other social welfare organizations perceived the role of the DUL in the national network.

Networking among agencies and organizations serving black urban communities greatly accelerated the process of community building within these communities nationwide. The pace of community building often depended upon how well a given black community could adapt to particular economic, social, and political problems facing it. In order to adapt effectively, a black community needed critical information from which it could fashion the best possible organizational and institutional strategies for facilitating its growth and development. By sharing its information and strategies for problem solving, an agency in one black community reduced the time and energy spent by agencies, organizations, and institutions in other black communities on solving the same problem. This often resulted in less trial-and-error on the part of the communities receiving problem solving information and strategies, accelerating their community building process.

Throughout the 1920s, these agencies and organizations learned the value of sharing knowledge and experiences. Because of the DUL's reputation in community work among blacks in Detroit, many of these agencies and organizations depended on it for advice on a range of problems they were facing in their cities. Many wanted to know if the DUL's approaches to problems in Detroit were applicable to other settings. For example, they wanted information on blacks working in a major hotel in Detroit, on the nature, activities, and result of its work in industry, housing, health, on homes for the black aged, and on the first black visiting nurses in the city—and these were only a few of the many requests. Scholars also relied on the DUL for relevant data on the conditions of black life in Detroit. These scholars included such names as Charles S. Johnson, Carter G. Woodson, and E. Franklin Frazier, among others.[102]

Networking between the DUL and black educational institutions in the South contributed to the black community building process in both regions. For example, in 1925, representatives from Tuskegee and Hampton chose Dancy to chair a committee based in Detroit as part of their joint campaign fund to raise two million dollars to match a gift from George Eastman, founder of the Eastman Kodak Company and well-known philanthropist.[103]

John C. Dancy and Forrester B. Washington developed one of the best black networks to emerge in the 1920s. Washington became Director of the Atlanta School of Social Work in 1927. The School had been established seven years earlier to focus on the training of professional black social workers for service in southern and northern black communities. As soon as Washington took over the School he contacted Dancy to give a series of lectures on "The Technique of Community Organization among Negroes" in urban communities. The lectures were to be part of a course at the School entitled, "The Technique of Community Work among Negroes," designed to prepare Social-Work students for work in Negro communities. The course exposed students to a case method approach, utilizing "the actual experiences of social agencies in certain Negro communities in different parts of the country." Since Dancy and the DUL represented one of the best case studies around, Washington wanted his students to know about their work. Therefore, he asked Dancy to give some lectures on "the accomplishments of the Detroit Urban League during the last ten years because Detroit is one of the most important industrial centers in the country and has one of the largest Negro populations." According to Washington, the work of the DUL under Dancy's direction was the "ideal example of community organization in urban negro communities."[104]

Dancy gave his lectures and obviously impressed the student body, because several months later Washington contacted him again, this time concerning placements of several graduates of the Atlanta School in Detroit. "I know that you have a great deal to do with creating new positions in social work for colored people in Detroit, and also that you have a great deal to do with recommending colored people for positions in agencies where the policy of using colored workers has been in existence for some time." But Washington explained: "Many of these people have not been especially trained for social work, although frequently they have been college graduates." Washington continued by pointing out the advantages of his graduates over those trained in northern schools: "People in Northern cities have apparently discovered that Negroes trained for social work in the heart of the South among southern Negroes are more successful than Negroes trained in northern schools of social work." He then asked Dancy to help him in placing these graduates with the DUL or some other social work organization in Detroit.[105]

While it is not clear how many graduates of the Atlanta School of Social Work found work in Detroit during the tenure of Washington via the networking between these two architects of community building, it is clear that they complemented each other in addressing the needs of black urban communities. By 1928, the Detroit Friends of the Atlanta School of Social Work was active in Detroit, cementing the ties between two dedicated black men representing the work of a great northern social agency and an equally great southern training institution.[106]

Networking continued to be a major strategy of the DUL. By the 1940s, the DUL was networking with dozens of agencies, organizations, institutions, and individuals, black and white, locally and nationally, to better serve the poor and needy within the black community, as well as to contribute to the social welfare of the larger community. In its 1945 annual report, the DUL listed a number of agencies and organizations that composed its network. These included: the Metropolitan YMCA Counseling and Guidance Committee, Detroit Council for a Permanent FEPC, Red Cross Overseas Personnel Committee, Boy Scouts Advisory Council, Mayor's Youth Advisory Committee and its Area Committee, Popular Education Committee of the City of Detroit Interracial Committee, Area Work Institute Planning Committee, Fair Labor Standards Committee, Reception Committee for European Delegates from the World Youth Council, United Nations Clothing Drive and the Russian War Relief Drive and many others. Concluding the report, the DUL pointed out that "Through such cooperative efforts" it had performed "an important role in community planning in the fields of housing, employment, recreation, health, and education and in *putting* many of the plans into action." It had also continued a tradition of networking which would contribute to the process of black community building for decades to come.[107]

Between 1916 and 1945, the Detroit Urban League played a key role in the community building process in black Detroit. It contributed to the stabilization and adjustment of southern black migrants by providing them with assistance in finding housing, jobs, and wholesome recreation. As thousands of black peasants arrived in Detroit with neither friends nor relatives, the League became their guardian. League staff met them at trains and shepherded them to their destinations. When they needed someone to speak on their behalf or needed to find a relative or a place to sleep, the migrants turned more often to the League than to any other organization or institution in the black community.

The League designed new strategies and programs for building up the internal resources of the black community. It established networks not only among black institutions, classes, and individuals within the black community but it also established and nurtured networks among public and private agencies and influential whites. These networks resulted in financial support for such programs as community dances, community centers, a wide range of educational activities housed and staffed at the centers, and the Green Pastures Camp.

Community building depended upon jobs. Community building among blacks in Detroit would have been greatly retarded without the assistance of the League's Employment Office and, later, the Vocational Service. These programs, although supplemented and superseded by state and other job assistance efforts on behalf of black workers, performed a vital service over the years. While the League failed to place many blacks in jobs for which they were qualified, they did place them in jobs in which they could at least survive until a better day. The Domestic Training School trained black women to work more efficiently in white women's kitchens, but the League did not allow the training to become a barrier to the aspirations of black women. Dancy was always on the lookout for better jobs for black workers.

The Detroit Urban League became a model for other leagues and social welfare agencies around the country. They constantly sought Dancy's advice on problems affecting blacks in urban communities. The exchanges between these organizations and Dancy laid the groundwork for a network which benefited blacks in many urban communities. By 1945, the black community had passed through several key stages in the community building process, and the Detroit Urban League had played a key role in shepherding it through the most critical of those stages.

Four

Weathering the Storm

When Georgia, Tennessee and Mississippi started pouring their thousands of field hands into Detroit . . . [the] black belt became sadly congested. Families doubled up. Sheds unfit for human habitation were pressed into use. Single men and boys coming in from the depots bought sleeping places on pool tables.

Detroit Saturday Night, *December 3, 1927*

PREPARING FOR THE BAD AND THE GOOD

While the DUL cushioned some of the more vulnerable segments of the expanding migrant community from the harsher aspects of urban poverty and despair, it could not extend its net beneath all who so sorely needed its help and encouragement. Many thousands of black men, women, and children simply fell through the cracks, having never caught a single glimpse of the good life they journeyed so far to obtain. For them, the Promised Land of the Motor City turned its back on them, mocking their hopes and dreams. Those who survived had to suffer through cycles of unemployment, dirty and dangerous jobs, substandard housing, crime and violence, poor health, and a clinging social pathology. Such conditions took a steady toll on the black community, retarding an already incremental pace of community building. Yet, these same conditions strengthened the resolve of those who survived and welded them into a community bonded by a common history of struggle. No matter how difficult conditions became in industrial Detroit, blacks pushed on towards some semblance of community.

Weathering the storm of poverty and despair, black Detroit continued the community building process.

Some people doubted that the first waves of southern black migrants would survive the harsh realities of life and work in industrial Detroit. Such doubts, however, soon evaporated thanks to the tremendous efforts put forth by key segments of the black and white communities to ensure that southern blacks had at least a fighting chance. The North was far from being "the promised land" of many southern blacks' dreams and expectations. There were grand and glorious advantages to be sure: the right to vote, opportunities to attend decent schools, much more money, and that "feeling," which few whites could really fathom, of just being "treated like a man." A southern migrant explained it best:

> The first time I went North was in 1924. My pal then was Hines, a young man about eighteen. We were hoping we'd get to see the Mason-Dixon Line. I thought in my mind that it would look like a row of trees with some kind of white mark like the mark in the middle of the highway. We were hoping day would break before we got to the line. The train stopped in Covington, Kentucky just as the sun was rising. Someone said the bridge ahead was the Mason-Dixon Line. We were North. We didn't have to worry about sitting in the back, we felt good. . . .
>
> We agreed that if there was one white man on the train with a seat beside him, we'd sit there to see what he would do. All the things we'd heard before was like reading in the Bible. When I got to heaven I [would] have milk and honey and pearly gates. I wanted to see was I there. We walked through the train feeling shaky. We thought any minute they would tell us to sit in the Negro Coach. I continued to walk until I saw a seat by a white man. I was very uncomfortable for the first hour. . . . I relaxed some. He was reading the paper and when he finished half, he pushed it to me and asked if I wanted to read. He wanted to know where I was going and said, "Detroit is a nice place." This was the most relaxing time I had.[1]

This southern migrant would discover that life in the North, while undeniably better in many ways than life in the South, fell far short of being a land of milk and honey for many blacks. The lack of decent housing and the harshness of industrial work were destined to affect the quality of life in the black community. Northern racism would compound these problems. Without the guidance of such sturdy souls as John R. Dancy, some far-seeing black ministers and professionals, and some dedicated whites, southern black migrants would not have been able to evolve into any kind of community. But they also did "their bit" by suffering through the bad times necessary to bring a community to fruition.

THE HOUSING PROBLEM

No problem retarded the process of community building as much as lack of decent housing. "The housing of the Negro in the North," an observer wrote in 1920, "is the most serious of the Negro's urban problems."[2] Housing problems did not affect just black workers, although racism did determine the availability and allocation of scarce housing for blacks. Before the first waves of black migrants arrived, white workers were already suffering from a lack of housing, which had also caused serious labor shortages. Workers began avoiding Detroit because they could not find housing for themselves and their families. In desperation businessmen offered the highest wages to persuade skilled men to come to Detroit. Housing became so scarce that many observers predicted that thousands of workmen and their families would be forced to live in tents unless something could be done about the housing problem.[3]

During the summer of 1916, 200 carloads of household goods stood idle in the railroad yards because owners had been unable to find housing. The situation became so acute that local officials asked President Woodrow Wilson for the use of army barracks at Fort Wayne to house workers.[4] Rent profiteering compounded the housing shortage problem and indirectly impeded the war effort by burdening war workers with excessive rents. Responding to such practices, the Housing Bureau of the U.S. Housing Corporation, in cooperation with the Council of National Defense, established local committees of the U.S. Home Registration Service to "further the nation's industrial program by assisting war workers in congested districts to find suitable housing accommodation."[5] Detroit's Mayor Couzens was troubled by rent profiteering and the hardships evictions imposed on workers. During the Spring of 1919, he requested assistance from the U.S. Housing Corporation to establish a Detroit committee of the U.S. Home Registration Service to address these problems.[6]

As could be expected, black war workers suffered even more than white workers from housing shortages brought on by rent profiteering and other problems associated with wartime housing shortages. Understanding the acute nature of black housing problems in cities, the U.S. Housing Corporation's Home Registration Service made efforts to place black field agents in heavily populated black areas.[7] Dr. George Haynes, Director of the Division of Negro Economics, contributed to this effort by volunteering his state supervisors of Negro Economics to work with the home-finding section of the U.S. Bureau of Industrial Housing and Transportation to set up room registration offices for addressing the housing needs of urban blacks. These black state supervisors were in place in Chicago and Detroit, but they could do little to address the more complex housing problems of blacks which, because of race, far exceeded those of whites.[8]

As black migrants poured into Detroit during the migration waves of 1916–17 and 1924 they forced the old and only black ghetto—with roots deep in the nineteenth century—to overflow, thus exacerbating the housing problems. Until 1915, this ghetto had been the only distinctly black district in the city, bounded on the west by Brush Street, on the east by Hastings, on the south by Macomb, and on the north by Leland, and bisected by

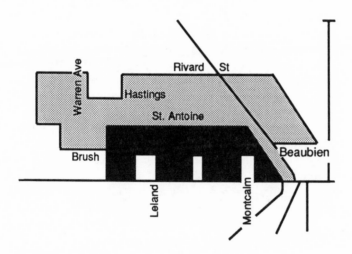

The Hastings Area, 1910–1950. Map prepared by Bradley Davis, Department of Geography and Urban Affairs, Michigan State University.

St. Antoine Street which ran north and south (see map). It was known as the St. Antoine Street District because most of the black hotels, restaurants, barber shops, and other black businesses were located on that street.[9] But five years later the migration caused this east-side ghetto to overflow, creating a number of other black ghettos in other sections of the city.[10] Of all these ghettos, the east-side ghetto would become the main entry point for incoming migrants and the most poverty-ridden, high-rent district in the city. Housing in this ghetto was destined to remain crowded for decades.[11]

In the search for housing, white families had it easy compared to black families. Whites had the advantage of always being considered first whenever new houses were built. Many whites lived two and three families in a house, but when a new house was available and a family moved out, the remaining white families took up the vacant space.[12] As the demand for houses increased and the supply decreased during the first migration wave, black migrants found themselves squeezed into the largest black ghetto, which by then had expanded east to Rivard, west to Beaubien,

south to Lafayette, and north to Brady.[13] In 1918, twelve thousand to
fifteen thousand black residents squeezed into this ghetto; it was constantly
expanding despite the fact that it had previously furnished housing for less
than one-half the current number. One observer said he had "seen rooms
occupied by two people where the most convenient way to dress was to
stand in the middle of the bed."[14] A Board of Health investigator reported
in 1920 that the number of rooms in houses or apartments occupied by
407 families was: 63 families each living in one room, 24 families each
living in two rooms, 34 families each living in three rooms, 71 families
each living in five rooms, 44 families each living in six rooms, 43 families
each living in seven rooms, 13 families each living eight rooms, 14 families
in nine rooms each, and 16 families each living in 10, 11, or 12 rooms.[15]
No available information existed on 50 other families, but his report is
evidence enough of the degree of overcrowding among blacks.

The necessity of having lodgers to help pay excessively high rents worsened the overcrowding. The majority of the above families had no other
choice. Seven families who were living in one room had lodgers; 146
families living in two or more rooms also kept lodgers. Only 100 families
were reported as having no lodgers, and the circumstances of the rest were
doubtful or unknown.[16] Social workers accepted the housing of relatives
as less of a social problem than housing non-relative lodgers, because most
of them were young single males. Many social workers feared that single
male lodgers would disrupt the family structure. One report, referring to
the lodger's problem said: "The . . . lodger is a potential menace to the
family circle. . . . The promiscuous intermixing of children of all ages with
adults and unattached males is highly undesirable."[17]

Many of these lodgers were either detached men without families "or
men who would not venture to bring their families with them into an
unknown country." Yet many were the "floaters and [never] do wells," who
had been easily attracted away from southern towns and cities by the
stories of "easy work at high wages and by free transportation offered
promiscuously by labor agents and railroad companies."[18]

A large number of single black women were also probably lodgers but
were not perceived as contributing to social problems in the same way as
single black males. Lodging of any sort and sex posed problems because
of crowded conditions. As one social worker put it, "seventy-five percent
of the Negro homes have so many lodgers that they are really hotels."
Blacks in New York, Cleveland, and Milwaukee, as well as other urban
centers, faced the same problem of having to take in lodgers in order to
pay the rent.[19]

Lodging became a widely practiced mode of urban survival for blacks
and whites, but in the case of blacks saddled with the additional problem
of racism, lodging persisted much longer as a method of family and community survival. In the late nineteenth century, blacks in Philadelphia took
in lodgers as a means of urban survival. Reports compiled by the Federation

of Churches between 1912 and 1930 pointed out that at least one-third of the black families in the North took in lodgers and/or boarders.[20]

The need for lodgers among northern urban blacks, then, was related to the excessively high rents that white and not a few black landlords imposed upon black workers. Realizing black workers had few options, these landlords squeezed the highest rents possible out of them; but higher rents did not mean better accommodations. In city after city, greedy landlords took advantage of black families' desperate need for housing and charged excessively high rents for bad housing. In the Indianapolis ghetto popularly called "Bucktown," landlords charged $25 a month for "flimsy one-story frame row houses that would have rented to whites for $18." In Chicago between 1909 and 1919, blacks paid 100 percent more for rent than whites.[21]

Following this pattern, Detroit's black east-side ghetto was becoming a sector where landlords could demand and receive excessively high rents for extremely bad housing. Bordering on the main commercial center of the city this ghetto was no longer a favorable location for residential purposes. Factories, garages, and other commercial establishments were increasingly being built in the area, greatly increasing the land value. The majority of houses were so dilapidated that they were beyond the owners' will or resources to make them .suitable for living purposes. But those houses still provided landlords with a golden opportunity to make a profit from desperate black workers and their families who sought any kind of shelter. Such landlords charged what they wanted until they sold their property for commercial purposes.[22]

Desperate black workers would pay anything to get a roof over their families' heads, consequently housing became an increasingly large portion of black workers' budgets. In 1920 the best authorities on family budgets argued that the head of a family "should not, or rather cannot afford to spend over one day's pay per week on rent, if he is going to have enough money left to purchase other necessities."[23] For black workers that would have been a maximum of about 17 percent of their income. Yet they were spending 36 percent of their income, or twice as much as they should, on rent.[24]

Some black workers managed to pay the excessively high rents by working overtime and getting time-and-a-half pay. But when the factories discontinued overtime work these workers could no longer afford to remain in Detroit. Asked how they liked Detroit many black migrants replied: "Except [for] high rent, Detroit is otherwise a good city." "Detroit is all right but for the high rent." "Rent increased from 35 [dollars] to 70 [dollars]. Detroit is good for wages and work but rent is too high—must move and nowhere to go but in the streets now."[25]

Compared to the rent paid by the population in general blacks paid much more. Fifty-five percent of the black population paid more than 40 dollars per month for rent compared to 51.6 percent of the general

Table 5

Average Rents of Unskilled Black Workers for Selected Cities, 1926

Cities	Number of Cases	Rent per Month	Cities	Number of Cases	Rent per Month
Detroit, Mich.	1,000	$47.29	Chicago, Ill.	301	23.61
Buffalo, N.Y.	49	39.09	Louisville, Ky.	203	19.67
Philadelphia, Pa.	1,932	33.45	New Orleans, La.	103	19.58
Gary, Ind.	50	30.60	Richmond, Va.	147	19.33
Columbus Hill	880	19.50	Memphis, Tenn.	110	16.16
(New York, N.Y.)			Lexington, Ky.	110	15.38
Harlem	747	31.09	Knoxville, Tenn.	1,637	14.60
(New York, N.Y.)			Charleston, S.C.	295	13.48
Dayton, Ohio	84	26.00	Charlottesville, Va.	40	13.17
Indianapolis, Ind.	96	24.61	Lynchburg, Va.	33	9.84

Source: Adapted from Glenn E. Carlson, "The Negro in the Industries of Detroit." Ph.D. dissertation, University of Michigan, 1929, p. 83.

population paying that amount in 1920. When we consider that the majority of black workers at the time were in low-wage occupations, one contemporary commented, "it is startling to observe how closely the percentages of the Negro group who pay the higher rents parallel those of the population in general."[26]

Unskilled black workers suffered the most from excessive high rents since they tended to have the least choice of location and had to compete with other workers for the worst housing. In 1926 the average unskilled black workers in Detroit paid rents higher than their counterparts in other major southern and northern cities (see table 5).

As already mentioned, both black and white landlords and real estate agents engaged in rent profiteering. "No less than seven Negro real estate agents have been proceeded against by the County Prosecutor within the last six months for rent profiteering,"[27] a writer reported in 1920. One black businessman with few qualms about exploiting black migrants leased a number of houses in the east-side ghetto which formerly rented for 25 dollars a month and immediately raised the rent to 60 dollars.[28] Of course, black businessmen did not exploit black migrants as much as their white counterparts who had far more property to rent. Compared to the number of black professional men who would help rather than hinder migrants, the above businessmen were, fortunately, few in number.

Throughout the 1920s, 1930s, and well into the World War II period, landlords continued to increase their rents. Many landlords justified such increases on the basis of high taxes. The rent problem in the black ghettoes became so bad that it forced black leaders to make housing a high priority. In October 1941, the Reverend Horace White, pastor of Plymouth Congregational Church, unleashed the full fury of his moral indignation at the perpetrators of high rents in the black community: "The landlords in the Negro neighborhoods are throwing all sense of decency to the winds in their rent profiteering."[29] Illustrating his point, Mr. White told the story of a black family that was paying $35.00 for five rooms in 1940. Two months ago the landlord raised the rent to $40.00; then just a week ago the family received a notice that the rent would be increased to $45.00. "This is ridiculous and unpatriotic", White blasted, "this is happening all over the community. In some places rents are up 50 percent. . . . Families are doubling up to a very dangerous degree in order to keep shelter over their heads." Such overcrowding, White worried, would ultimately result in "tremendous health, fire and police costs."[30]

The indignation of Mr. White and other black leaders, along with black tenants, galvanized people into a small community movement against high rents. Blacks themselves can do something about the problem, White informed his audience. "They can organize and stand together against these outrageous increases." Black preachers should get together, White suggested, and plan a Rent protest day "that will resound from one end of the city to the other." Most of the members of the common council and a few members of the Fair Rent Committee, White argued, are "aware of the extent of the high rent evil among Negroes."[31]

White could see that high rents were forcing blacks to adopt coping strategies that in the long run would endanger the structure of the black family. "Our families," he lamented, "are being drawn to moral decay. [Blacks] cannot rear a family in decency in their present overcrowded conditions. . . . Let us combine to challenge this high rent evil against our people."[32]

Like other black leaders, and certainly the struggling poor tenants who suffered under the added weight of high rents, White had little faith in the Common Council's Fair Rent Committee. Hundreds of tenants were brought before the committee to testify about high rents and the substandard quality of the houses in which they lived. A law was even drafted to keep rents at certain levels and to prevent landlords from "gouging tenants." Yet after hundreds of testimonies and meetings of the committee, rents continued to increase at a faster rate.[33]

In May 1941, the head of the Welfare Rent Division of the city government testified before the rent committee that rents in the poorer neighborhoods of the city had increased during the past few months from 10 to 15 percent. Yet, in black areas, as one black newspaper pointed out, rents increased far above the 10 to 15 percent quoted by the division head. "In many areas," the newspaper stated, "rents have been increased as much as 25 percent."[34]

Occasionally the courts fined landlords for renting substandard houses that violated the building code. But judges faced great difficulty getting tenants to make complaints against their landlords. Tenants were caught in a Catch-22: If the landlord fixed up the house to meet building codes, the already exorbitant rent would be increased to cover the cost of repairs. Consequently many tenants chose not to file a legal complaint against landlords. Some tenants living in squalid conditions not only refused to complain about landlords but said they were satisfied; and in many cases tenants turned hostile when asked for information about the houses.[35]

During the early years of the Great Depression in Detroit, black unemployed workers, at times assisted by local Communists and members of the International Labor Defense, played a leading role in defending the housing rights of black working-class families. Joseph Billups, one of the first black members of the United Auto Workers Ford Local 600, helped organize an unemployment council which, among other tasks, put blacks back into their homes after they were evicted. Interviewed along with his wife in 1967, Billups described how he and other working-class people went to the aid of their fellow workers:

Interviewer: Mr. Billups, I understand that conditions were pretty bad in Detroit in the early 30's with people being evicted from their homes. Was there anything you could do to help out in that situation?

Billups: In that situation I mobilized the Unemployment Council and we set the people back in the house if they were evicted. We left the guard to take care to notify us if the sheriff or deputy sheriff would come back again, but if we put the furniture back, they wouldn't bother them unless the landlord paid them again. So very few landlords would pay it again because the same thing would happen over and over.

Interviewer: You mean they would be evicted; you help them back in—

Billups: Yes.

Interviewer: On it would go, I see.

Billups: And the deputy sheriff said, "just let us set them out and you can set 'em back." Then they are going to pay us to set them back out, so the landlords go to the place they just let them stay there. Because they didn't want to keep paying the deputy sheriff to set them out and then we set them back in, they would have to pay them again to set them out. And it got to the place where after they were in, the deputy sheriff would say, "you have no court eviction, I mean you have to go through court again," and that we may stay in there. I remember one time on Macomb Street they went two blocks just about every house, setting in the street, so we set them back in and we mobilized the people and told them to put the stuff back in. We would have somebody there to take care of the sheriffs if they came around. They wouldn't bother around long as they didn't want to come in contact with them or the Council because they would take us down in front of the judge, and the judge would turn us loose. And then, we used to have demonstrations and go into the Mayor's office and take over, and police didn't care to club the people.[36]

No doubt the tactics of black workers like Billups encouraged other black tenants to resist greedy landlords. Risking eviction, they organized rent strikes against rent increases and substandard conditions. One of several rent strikes occurred in November 1937 when more than 60 black families associated with the Rent and Consumer League refused to pay rents until certain demands were met: They would pay only $15 a month instead of $18 for a basement apartment; $30 a month instead of fifty for a five-room apartment; and $35 instead of $45 to $50 for a six-room apartment. Other demands included: heat in two-room apartments; lights in those apartments; elimination of bedbugs and roaches; and ending the two dollar penalty for three-day late rent payments.[37] While it is not clear if this rent strike achieved all or any of its demands, other tenants in the same general area who belonged to the same tenant organization did win a victory in October when a two-week strike forced the Feldman Realty Company to cancel all rent increases.[38]

In the spring of 1941, a bargaining committee of black striking tenants told the landlord that they would resist any "attempts to increase the rents in the buildings on strike." The landlord, impressed by the determined stand of the tenants, gave in and agreed to reduce the rent increases from $5.00 to $2.50 per month. The tenants accepted this offer.[39]

This strike was the response of the chairperson of the striking tenants to the traditional complaint of landlords that they have to raise rents to cover high taxes. During the meeting the tenant chairperson informed the landlord that his taxes were not being raised at the present time and when they were raised they would not equal or justify an increase of sixty dollars per year per family. "We poor people are having our taxes raised as well as the price of food," the tenant chairman remarked. As a WPA worker getting $54.80 a month with no wage increases in sight, the chairman could not afford a rent increase. Another tenant pointed out to the landlord "that the tenants pay their own as well as the landlord's taxes in addition to the upkeep of the property and his income. It is criminal," she said, "for landlords to increase rents when food costs are rising so fast." Put on the defensive by these striking black tenants the landlord resorted to the timeworn technique of divide and conquer: he retorted that his white tenants were cheerfully paying $40 per month for five rooms, bath and heat. The striking black tenants did not blame the white tenants, but they obviously were not impressed with the landlord's feeble attempt to set one group of tenants against another.[40]

These striking black tenants represented the growing sense of empowerment among the black working class. The more they resisted the exploitation of landlords the more they saw the possibilities of resisting other forms of exploitation. And resistance not only transformed these angry black strikers but added courage and strength to the larger community. Thus, in resisting, they fueled the community building process.

Life was difficult enough for blacks forced to suffer acute housing

Groups of children from the Hastings Street section of Detroit, c. 1930. Courtesy of the Archives of Labor and Urban Affairs, Wayne State University.

shortages and excessive rents. But on top of these problems, they lived in substandard houses. From the very first wave of migrants in 1916–17 to the Depression of the thirties, the majority of blacks in Detroit lived in substandard housing. In 1920 social workers discovered that some migrants lived in a room over a barn with no toilet. Some garages and cellars had been converted into homes for blacks and the "pool-rooms and gambling clubs [were] beginning to charge for the privilege of sleeping on pool-room tables overnight."[41]

Social workers reported that blacks lived in houses where rain poured through the ceiling onto the floor, and that walls and floors were so damp that the tenants had to keep their beds standing well away from the walls to avoid getting wet. In such situations infant death from exposure was common.[42]

Although the majority of black families in the eastside ghettoes had indoor toilets, they were often in kitchens and living rooms with few or no partitions. These conditions, commented one investigator,

> exist mostly in the eastside district and are the result of pressure having been brought on the landlord to move the toilet which was outside, inside the house. . . . The Landlord did the cheapest thing possible. . . . He placed it in one of the existing rooms, usually the kitchen because of the presence of other water pipes.[43]

Twenty percent of those toilets did not work, further compounding the problems of preserving health in such surroundings.[44]

The passage of time did little to solve these problems. As more migrants arrived, they shared the conditions of the majority. During the second migration wave in 1924–25, which doubled the black population, the *Detroit City Directory* observed: "In this east-side district there are three square miles in which people are huddled together as closely as it is possible for human beings to exist."[45]

In 1926 lodgers still lived with families on the east side. Several all-black subdivisions had been built to provide temporary shelter for incoming migrants until they could get settled. These houses had no basements. The structures were flimsy and "subjected to early deterioration." Many of these houses had been built by migrants themselves, who had bought lots but could not afford the high prices asked by white home builders. The majority of houses in these subdivisions did not have bathrooms, although they did have inside toilets. One-tenth had outside toilets.[46]

These all-black subdivisions were built in and near Detroit and varied in size. The Eight-Mile Road subdivision was the largest and contained four thousand families. Inkster had two thousand black families, and Quinn Road had five hundred.[47] These "satellite" ghettos, which were the largest and best known, accommodated some of the overflowing population from the congested east-side ghetto in Detroit. By providing more housing for black workers and their families, these black subdivisions probably helped to reduce the need to have lodgers, as well as to stabilize the rents. Most of these subdivisions had at least a few of the advantages of rural living: clean air and more space. But even these few advantages were often nullified by the poor water supply and inadequate sewage disposal.[48]

Black social workers and businessmen had mixed feelings concerning the advantages and disadvantages of subdivision ghettos. One black real-estate agent claimed subdivisions were moneymaking schemes that attracted many southern blacks who were accustomed to a rural environment. These migrants, he said, tended to remain in "a static condition, raising vegetables and the like"; and they had no chance to develop urban lifestyles. Furthermore, he argued, the municipal government often neglected to require subdivisions to provide new residents with an adequate water supply and sewage disposal which resulted in unhealthy living conditions. One social worker reported that few of the "better-class" blacks invested or lived in these subdivisions and that people tended to slip back into "old Southern ways of doing things." She felt that if they lived in a place where they were exposed to "suggestions of better folk," it would help them to help themselves. A black banker differed with the first two opinions. Few blacks lost money on subdivision property, he countered, whereas many blacks lost money on Detroit downtown property as a result of "careless bargaining." He also pointed out that owners of subdivision property were very considerate of migrants and allowed them the longest terms of credit. The major problem in his mind was the inability of migrants to get houses built.[49]

There was a bit of truth in all the above opinions. Most certainly, building subdivisions made money. In a housing market where the demand was high and the supply was low, any shack would demand almost any price and get it. The east-side ghetto was a good case in point. The subdivisions did tend to perpetuate rural lifestyles, but not just because their inhabitants had little contact with city life. Rather, they had transplanted a viable rural community that worked for them. The subdivisions did not entirely isolate migrants from city life. Most migrants had jobs in the city and were probably being socialized in the factories. Plus, Detroit provided too many attractions for southern migrants to stay isolated in subdivisions.

The realtor's contention that migrants who lived in subdivisions tended to remain in a "static" condition, "raising vegetables and the like," merely demonstrated his class bias against transplanted southern black lifestyles and community life. However, he was correct concerning municipal neglect of subdivisions. The social worker's fear that migrants would slip back into "old Southern ways of doing things" was a common form of class bias. Most black and white social workers, or professionals in general, placed little value on southern black customs and culture, considering them a drag on progress. She was right in arguing that migrants' exposure to "better class" blacks would help them to help themselves—but not because the former was a "better class"; rather, because they had developed urban survival skills as well as urban institutions (such as lodges, churches, hospitals, etc.) that could assist rural blacks in adjusting to an urban industrial culture. In fact, this is what occurred in the programs of the Urban League and the black YMCA and YWCA. The banker was also correct in pointing out that the subdivisions were better for some blacks than the downtown property which we have already shown was subject to high rents and was of bad quality.

The opinions people had of the black subdivisions did not alter the fact that they had emerged in response to the pressing urban needs of migrants. These satellite ghettos expanded black migrants' liveable space, and in those instances where they had to build their own houses, these ghettos provided a sense of community.

It would take some time before the majority of migrants succeeded in gaining the upper hand in solving their housing problems. Housing for the majority of black workers on the east side continued to get worse as more migrants arrived. In 1927 local magazines and newspapers were moved to discuss the problems in increasingly ominous tones. "Detroit is faced with the necessity of finding a satisfactory solution of its Negro problem," a local newspaper stated, and "those who have studied the situation know that the Negro population must be properly housed."[50]

By the mid-1930s, housing conditions had not substantially changed for the majority of blacks; this was of course a living hell for those forced to survive in the east-side ghetto.

In terms of living conditions, the west-side ghetto which had grown up since 1915, contrasted sharply with the east side. Black residents in this ghetto, some with elite family roots predating the first migration wave and who tended to be professionals, had fewer lodgers and represented 60 percent of the black homeowners in Detroit. Their numbers, and undoubtedly their social status, had been augmented by members of the southern black professional class, who, after selling their property in the South, settled in Detroit between 1916 and 1918, and did "own excellent homes."[51] Consequently, this west-side black elite group was spared many of the housing problems burdening their eastside brethren.

By the 1930s, coverage of black housing problems in the east-side ghetto became common in Detroit newspapers. Chances for life in the area between Hastings and Beaubien Streets were half as great as they were for the city as a whole. One local newspaper commented, "The average span of life in the heart of the Detroit slums is 27 years, while for the rest of the city the average resident may expect to live to the age of 54."[52] According to this paper, thousand of blacks in one section of the ghetto lived "in squalid frame shanties and hovels that lie in the ten block area; defective plumbing, darkness, . . . cold, . . . broken windows, vermin, and lack of sanitary food containers contribute to the dangers of human existence."[53]

Another paper reported that "death stalks more frequently through the 40 block east-side area . . . than it does elsewhere in the city;" pneumonia, tuberculosis and, infant mortality rates were 1.5 to 7.4 times as high in that area as for the city as a whole.[54]

The housing conditions in this ghetto in 1930 had not changed since the arrival of the first migrants. City officials made little or no attempt to address the housing problems of this area until the federal government intervened and constructed the 941-unit Brewster Home Project for low-income families in 1937. These new brick structures replaced the substandard houses that formerly occupied the area.[55] Blacks fortunate enough to get in were better off. Except for the surrounding slums, this "island" represented a major improvement in the lives of blacks who lived there. Although limited, it represented the greatest advance in housing for Detroit blacks during this period.

The racial views and policies of the government agencies complicated the housing problems of blacks. For example, the Home Owners Loan Corporation (HOLC) was established by the Home Owners Loan Act of 1933 to provide low-income mortgage loans to financially distressed home owners unable to obtain financing through traditional means. However, in Detroit (and other cities as well) this agency cooperated in conducting economic, real-estate, and mortgage surveys which devalued residential areas in which blacks lived or where they were moving.[56] This had the impact of undermining the economic security of black home owners and of confining blacks to the worst neighborhoods.

Housing problems continued to plague the black community for years. World War II and the postwar period would find Detroit with a rapidly expanding black population and an acute housing problem. The east-side ghetto would become more congested and more federal housing projects would be built because of racist housing policies, including the many white neighborhoods that effectively kept blacks in "their place." As a result, the housing problems of blacks increased and merged with other urban problems to fuel the racial and urban crisis which blew up in the 1942, 1943, and 1968 riots.

HEALTH

Substandard and crowded housing presented major barriers to blacks' uphill struggle to better themselves. At times, migrants must have wondered if overall health conditions in the North were better than those in the South. In 1925, 1,000 black migrant heads of families were asked the question: "Have health conditions of the family improved or worsened since coming to Detroit?" Four hundred thirty-two said health conditions were similar; 312 said they were better; 79 felt they were worse; 173 did not respond; and those remaining did not know.[57]

Whatever regional differences did exist (e.g., poverty, lack of institutionalized health care, clean air, less crowding, etc., in the South versus being a little better off in the North with more access to institutionalized health care but with crowded housing, etc.), they nullified each other. The improved health of the 312 migrants might have resulted from public and private health programs set up in Detroit to monitor and maintain the health of black migrants. As pointed out earlier, the DUL and several black doctors working through the churches conducted yearly health campaigns in poor black neighborhoods. This campaign also included taking children out of congested ghettoes on outings to parks so they could benefit from clean and healthy activities.[58]

The existence of two black owned-and-operated hospitals reinforced these efforts. The Board of Health added to the overall effort by making it possible for an increasing number of black women to give birth in hospitals, greatly reducing the black infant mortality rate. Along with other agencies, such as the Nurses Association which made home visits, the Board of Health monitored the health of black ghetto residents quite effectively.[59]

Despite these efforts, the health of ghetto blacks continued to decline, due to overall poor quality of life in the ghetto itself. For example, in 1926 tuberculosis seemed almost commonplace among poor ghetto blacks. Inadequate sanitation, poor diet, and exposure contributed to the increase of this dreaded disease among the ghetto population. With so many young male migrants attracted both to Detroit's factories and mills and to the "sporting" red light districts, venereal diseases (VD) added to the already acute health problems, especially when these young men were not properly guided in health care or simply in VD detection.[60]

Even with the increased efforts of black and white health professionals, the fight to maintain good health among blacks remained an uphill one. From 1915 to 1920, the peak migration years, the death rate of blacks in Detroit increased from 14.7 per 1,000 to 24.0 per 1,000. During the same period the white death rate of 12.8 remained about the same. Five years later, the black rate decreased to 19.4 as compared to the white rate of 10.4. By 1930 the black death rate was down to 15.6 compared to the white rate of 8.7. And in 1940 the black rate declined to 12.2 compared to the white rate of 8.0 (see table 6).

In 20 years, the death rate for blacks in Detroit had decreased by 12 per thousand, which was a vast improvement in absolute terms. However, in relative terms, compared to the white death rate, the black rate was still about 4 per thousand higher than the white rate. In addition, the declining black death rate was probably very uneven, with most of the decline occurring in areas where blacks enjoyed a better quality of life (see table 6).

Compared to the national death rate for blacks, blacks in Detroit suffered a high death rate in 1920. But by 1930 Detroit's black death rate was even

Table 6

Changes in White and Black Death Rates in Detroit,
1915–1940 (per 1,000)

Year	White Death Rate	Black Death Rate
1915	12.8	14.7
1920	12.8	24.0
1925	10.4	19.4
1930	8.7	15.6
1940	8.0	12.2*

Sources: "Health," *The Negro in Detroit* (Detroit: Bureau of Governmental Research, 1926) pp. 1–9; Ulysses W. Boykin, *A Handbook on the Detroit Negro* (Detroit: Minority Studies Assoc., 1943) p. 49. United States Department of Commerce, *Mortality of Statistics: Thirty-First Annual Report: 1930* (Washington, D.C.: U.S. Government Printing Office, 1934) p. 77; United States Department of Commerce, *Vital Statistics of the United States, 1940, Part I* (Washington, D.C.: U.S. Government Printing Office, 1943) p. 86.
* Rate for non-whites including other races.

with the national black rate. By 1940 the black death rate in Detroit had declined slightly more than the national black death rate (see tables 6 and 7).

Unfortunately, the persistent causes of deaths for blacks slowed the decline in the black death rate in Detroit and the nation. And of all the causes of black deaths in Detroit, tuberculosis (TB) ranked as the highest between 1915 and 1941. In 1915 the rate was 207.7 per 1,000 among blacks compared to 96.5 per 1,000 among whites. In 1920 deaths from TB increased among blacks to 237.0 and decreased among whites to 76.5. Five years later the rate jumped again to 300.2 per 1,000 among blacks while it decreased to 59.5 per 1,000 among whites. In only four years between 1915 and 1941 was tuberculosis not a principal cause of black deaths in Detroit: 1925, 1939, 1940, and 1941. In those years, heart disease and pneumonia competed with each other in claiming black lives.[61] Blacks did not fare much better in other northern cities where tuberculosis often caused half of all deaths.[62]

It was bad enough for black adults to die from the above diseases caused in large part by poverty, but to watch black children die "like flies" in "the promised land" was an unbearable tragedy. Between 1915 and 1919, 149.7 black infants out of every thousand born in the United States died before their first birthdays. White infants were more fortunate; only 92.8 out of every 1,000 died. In 1921 the national black infant mortality rate increased to 161 while the white rate decreased to 84. In 1924 the death rate of black and white infants had declined significantly but black children were still "dying like flies" with a rate of 118 per 1,000 compared to the white rate of 76 per 1,000.[63]

In Detroit between 1926 and 1940, the black infant mortality rate went

Table 7

Changes in National Black and White Death Rates
1910–1940 (per 1,000)

Year	White Death Rate	Black Death Rate
1910	14.5	21.7
1920	12.6	17.7
1930	10.8	15.6
1940	10.4	13.9

Sources: Florete Henri, *Black Migration Movement North, 1900–1920* (New York: Doubleday, 1976) p. 112; United States Department of Commerce, *Mortality Statistics: Thirty-First Annual Report: 1930* (Washington, D.C.: U.S. Government Printing Office, 1934) p.32; *Vital Statistics of the United States, 1940: Part I* (Washington, D.C.: U.S. Government Printing Office, 1943) p. 13.

from 114 per 1,000 to 53.1 per 1,000, while the white rate went from 82 per 1,000 in 1926 to 36.8 per 1,000 in 1940. Interestingly enough, black and white infant mortality increased 7 and 6 deaths per 1,000, respectively, between 1927 and 1928. Throughout this period, the black infant mortality rate was from 17 to 48 per 1,000 higher than the white race. For example, in 1926, 32 more black babies died per 1,000 than white babies. Conditions worsened. Two years later 48 more black infants than white infants died per 1,000. However, by 1940 the gap was closing; only 17 more black than white children were dying out of every thousand, yet the gap was still significant in terms of the human cost to the black community.[64]

Times did get better for the majority of black children in Detroit. They would live longer and get a chance at the life their parents travelled to the North to find. But for many of these children life in the Motor City would be far less than they had hoped for. Ghettoization increased with each passing year and with each arriving southern migrant; and living conditions worsened.

Sometimes the struggle for black survival and progress seemed to be impeded by the black migrants themselves, who tended to rely more upon patent medicines than upon modern medicine and professional health care. Some scholars and lay people have concluded that southern blacks' resistance to modern health care in the North stemmed from their longtime reliance upon "makeshift medicines" necessitated by their lack of access to professional health care in the South.[65]

Considering how little attention and respect was paid to the survival elements in the culture of the transplanted migrant, such interpretations seem reasonable. Few black and white health professionals realized that the southern black folk medicine among recently arrived southern blacks dated back to slavery where, as Genovese points out, it "constituted part of a complex tendency on the part of the slaves to take care of themselves.[66]

The southern black folk-medical-belief system reached across time and place, as many black health professionals would discover. In 1925, two black Detroit druggists with a large southern clientele reported that they had sold large amounts of patent medicines. One druggist discovered to his surprise that even when he did not put patent medicines on display he was unable to curb the demand. Customer demand forced the other druggist to keep a complete stock of these "folk remedies" on hand. Black migrants were not the only users of patent medicines; many whites, probably southerners, also purchased large quantities of folk remedies.[67]

Many years passed before black and white health professionals developed an appreciation of the medical beliefs of blacks socialized in the South and discovered how such beliefs as traditional survival techniques could be reconciled with modern medical practice.[68]

Fortunately, the southern migrant culture adapted to urban life. Migrants soon realized that there were better methods of treating diseases. Southern black folk medicine may have worked in limited circumstances and on limited ailments but in disease-ridden inner cities, blacks needed the best that modern medicine had to offer. Gradually black migrants in Detroit started to respond to the advice and aid of health professionals and social workers. By 1926, the majority were going to private doctors, hospitals and clinics in contrast to a minority who continued to rely upon patent medicines and practices of midwives.[69]

The work environment in industrial Detroit presented yet another major barrier to better health in the black community. Black men had been hired to do the dirty and dangerous work most white men avoided or simply refused to do. White employers, supervisors, and workers shared a common racial belief that black men could "stand heat better than white men."[70] According to some white foremen, blacks liked hot jobs. They also held similar beliefs about Mexican-Americans. "The Mexican," one white foreman commented, "seems to stand the heat better than either Negroes or whites."[71] Since black workers outnumbered Mexican workers, they became the major ethnic workforce in the foundries where the most dangerous and dirtiest industrial work was performed.

Black workers had such jobs as the shakeout, where dust, dirt and sand were cleaned from the molten metal. Coremaking was an even more dangerous and dirty job where many black workers died of gas explosions. If they survived these occupational hazards, they often contracted occupational diseases such as silicosis, bronchitis, pneumonia, heart disease, and various stomach ailments.[72] Notwithstanding Ford's policy of having more black workers on its payroll than any other Detroit manufacturer, its foundry was a deathtrap for many black workers. The lack of safety equipment, poor ventilation, and speed-ups all contributed in one way or another to the deaths of many black workers.[73]

The following account of a black foundry worker in 1924 speaks volumes for the type of work many black workers (and a few whites) had to endure:

As I looked around, all the men were dirty and greasy and smoked up.

They were beyond recognition. There were only three or four whites. These were Polish. Negroes told me later they were the only ones able to stand . . . [the] work. Their faces looked exactly like Negro faces. They were so matted and covered with oil and dirt that no skin showed . . . the job was very rugged. I had to work continuously, as fast as I could move. The heat from cubulos, which were round furnaces for melting the iron, was so hot that in five minutes my clothes would stick with dirt and grease. We'd walk through on our lunch period to talk to a friend. We couldn't recognize him by his clothes or looks. The men working in his section would tell us where he was or we could tell a friend by his voice.[74]

As if the working conditions were not bad enough, white foremen pushed black workers to the limits:

The foreman would curse and holler. They would pay us off right there if we looked back or stopped working. Workers passed out from the heat. The foremen rushed a stretcher over and two workers would take the man out, give him fifteen minutes to revive and then he would have to go back to work. When a man passed out, the foreman would be running out to see if the guy was conscious. He would be cursing all the time. If the worker took too long, he'd shake him.[75]

Since production was more important than the health of black workers, some foremen hesitated to allow black workers to stop work long enough to get medical attention:

The foremen never mentioned a wound serious enough to go to First Aid. Workers would get a layer of iron from the cubulo, bring it to the iron pourers, fifteen to twenty men with long ladles. These would be filled with hot iron running like water. As their ladles filled up, the men had to straighten their arms out level and pour the iron down a little hole the size of a milk bottle. All the time they had to turn slow, like a machine. If they poured too fast, the iron would explode the mold and burn the other men. The iron would drop on a wet spot and hit the men like a bullet and go into the skin. The man getting hit still had to hold the ladling iron level to keep from burning the other men. They would wait their chance and pick out the balls of iron, and sometimes the foremen picked it out as the men went on working. A man would sit a half hour after work too tired to change clothes and go home.[76]

No wonder black industrial workers had such poor health which often shortened their lives. Working in such hazardous environments, where they constantly inhaled smoke and fine particles of dust, contributed to the high rate of respiratory disease among blacks.[77] Even in recent times black workers continue to work in the most dangerous, dirtiest, and lowest-paying jobs. In 1971, a study found that black coke-oven workers "had three times more respiratory cancer, eight times more deaths from lung cancer and a significantly increased death rate from all other causes." At the same time, black males in Pittsburgh, Pennsylvania, the center for the basic steel industry, had the highest rate of lung cancer in the United States.[78]

When we consider how long black workers in these industrial cities have been exposed to these hazardous jobs, we can better understand why the struggle to maintain health was such a difficult one.

Harsh working conditions could be made worse for black workers—as well as some whites in this case—when a foreman or supervisor deliberately encouraged production rivalry between black and white workers. Neither race had any choice but to engage in this vicious rivalry which often occurred at the expense of the workers' health.[79]

As harsh as life in Detroit could be, blacks still preferred the Motor City over the South. For one thing the working day was shorter, which was a sign of progress to some contemporary observers. By about 1926, 81.8 percent of black workers were working nine hours or less per day, 10.6 percent were working ten hours and 7.6 percent were working over ten hours. In the South only 43.2 percent of all black workers worked nine hours or less, 33.2 percent worked ten hours and 23.6 worked over ten hours.[80] In short, black workers in Detroit worked fewer hours than their counterparts in the South. But did shorter working hours in a dirty and dangerous hot Northern foundry really constitute progress? Though some work might have averaged out to be less than nine hours, many black workers in Detroit probably worked irregular hours to perform difficult tasks, as the following black worker did:

> When I had worked for a month, the foreman came and said they were going to change the standard of the job and put it on piece work. We could make more money. I got a nickel for each pan I shaked out. I was glad for the money but I was sorry we were on piece work. We had to work just like a machine. Take a mold, knock it out, set it back. Over and over for nine hours. It was never under nine hours and sometimes ten, eleven and twelve hours a day. We never knew how many hours we were going to work. If they wanted to send us home at ten, ten we went. If a machine broke down, we waited an hour for repairs. The money was taken out of our weekly pay even though it wasn't our fault. We cursed every minute of the day. The main curse was against the foreman. The foreman would say, "God damn it, do it. If you can't do it, there are plenty of men outside who will."[81]

At times the average black factory worker must have wondered whether the trip north was worth the train ticket. They earned more money but high rents ate up most of it. The harsh foremen probably had much in common with southern plantation overseers. Both concerned themselves only with the productivity of black labor and cared little for black workers as human beings.

In the 1920s, contemporary observers pointed out that blacks tended to have better food in Detroit than the southern diet of white bacon, cornmeal, grits, molasses, some greens, "and an occasional chicken." Food was cheaper in Detroit than in the South, and blacks spent more money for food in Detroit than they did in the South, which led some observers to conclude that blacks in Detroit lived better.[82] Whatever the case, one thing is certain: Black workers used their wages to purchase more and better food for their families. They might have worked hard in very unhealthy environments and lived in squalid crowded houses, but they had the money to buy a range of different and better foods.

Yet many southern-born blacks in post–World War II Lansing, Michigan, were probably behaving much like migrants in Detroit during an earlier period when they returned home to replenish their supply of traditional foods and folk remedies. Reporting on this behavior, a scholar commented:

> One informant, who had just returned from her vacation in South Carolina, said she made the trip each year to gather herbs for teas. She brought back pieces for relatives and some southern friends who could not go to get them. She showed me sassafras roots, long leaf pine needles, life everlasting, elderberry roots, catnip, and horehound roots. These roots were used for high blood pressure, flu, common colds, fever, rheumatism, neuritis, and as a tonic during menopause.[83]

Northern blacks tended to ridicule southern blacks when they held on to southern foods and folk medicine. One southern woman whose sister was married to a northern man reported that she had to be very careful about what foods she served. Instead of cooking the traditional southern foods she enjoyed, such as chitterlings, pigs feet, or grits, she cooked buttered beans and roast meat. Whenever she cooked southern foods, she either ate them herself or invited a southern friend to share the meal. Southern women also were reluctant to take southern dishes to church picnics where there would be many northern blacks.[84]

Such practices led to a tendency of southern migrants to limit much of their association to other southern-born blacks in order to protect and maintain their regional culture and values. But the longer they remained in the North, under the transforming influences of both the larger industrializing society and the black community building process, the more they would become like their northern-born brethren.

Perhaps the only legitimate indictment of southern blacks' attachments to southern foods was that such foods seldom formed a balanced diet. Most migrants consumed large quantities of starchy foods and fatty meats and very few raw vegetables or fruits. When put on a diet by a doctor, "they very rarely followed it because they were not used to the type of food."[85] It didn't do migrants much good, therefore, to have high wages to buy the necessary foodstuff for a balanced diet (with which to maintain good health) if they were ignorant of good nutrition. Thus, two steps forward often led to three steps backwards.

Black southern migrants in Lansing and Detroit, therefore, were not very different in cultural background. Both represented the black southern tradition transplanted in the North. Most of all they reflected a process in which traditional modes of survival were being tried, tested and modified for use in an urban environment. The southern migrants brought their cultural baggage north and carefully selected what worked and what did not work. These people were anything but static folk. They had taken the risk to come north. Now that they had arrived, they would adapt for better or for worse.

CRIME AND VICE

Along with poor housing, high rents, and associated health problems such as increasing tuberculosis, the east-side black ghetto in Detroit became a breeding ground for crime and vice. This ghetto, much like other northern ghettoes, was infested with prostitution, gambling, robberies and other assorted forms of vice. In the summer of 1917, the *Detroit News* reported that "there were 12 gambling clubs and countless numbers of disorderly houses in this district prior to the clean up of the city conducted by the police department."[86] Evidently the cleanup, as well as subsequent clean-ups, failed, because the east-side ghetto remained an area of crime and vice for decades to come. And black working class families struggling to rear children in such surroundings could only hope and pray that the crime and vice would not attract their youth into the streets and lead eventually to jail or to an early grave.

Some of the crime and vice in the ghetto came north with the great migration of World War I. With great dismay the Detroit Urban League discovered that crime among blacks increased with every migration wave from the South. The sad result was that southern blacks were generally blamed for these crimes committed by both white and native black citizens.[87]

While the vast majority of southern migrants were hard working folk searching for good jobs with high pay and the freedom to just "be a man," other migrants, mostly from the urban areas of the South such as Bir-mingham, Memphis, and New Orleans, came to Detroit to make the "easy money." As one editor of a local black newspaper put it in 1927: "Word went through the South that Detroit was the town for high wages. The Negro gambler and other vicious characters of the race flocked to the city to get easy money."[88] According to the editor, black crime was caused by these gangs of professional gamblers and "other parasites." Black crime became more vicious during periods of unemployment, the editor added. When these criminals could no longer get money the easy way, they went out and got it by "more drastic methods." They got their guns and went to work, and the race in general has been made to share in their shame."[89]

The Police Commission in Detroit at the time agreed with the editor. "We never had much difficulty with colored folk in the old days," he said, "not until they started coming here by the thousands from the South did the situation become tense. I guess a lot of bad black men came along with the good ones."[90]

Revealing a rare understanding of the underlying social conditions that often breeds criminal behavior, the commission pointed out that when "times became slack, and money scarce . . . some of the good became desperate and went bad." The police commission also recognized that some black leaders were struggling to rid the black ghettoes of "the dangerous elements."[91]

The majority of crimes committed by blacks between 1917 and 1945 were rooted in poverty, despair, and institutional racism. "The colored population as a whole is law-abiding," argued the above editor. "These people have had much to make them otherwise. The frequency with which they are jailed without cause; the ruthlessness that characterizes some of the actions of the police; the struggle they have to keep alive by honest means: all these," the editor stressed, "are elements entering into the problem." Most of the crimes committed by blacks, he said, are "to acquire that which they do not possess, be it money or property. That might indicate that much of the law-breaking can be traced to poverty."[92] Roger Lane's excellent study of black crime and violence in Philadelphia confirms what was also happening in Detroit: namely, that the increase in black crime and violence was a direct result of institutional racism and persistent poverty. "Philadelphia's Afro-American murder rate was higher than its overall murder rate in the late nineteenth century, because, as Lane explains, blacks were involved in criminal activities, such as theft and vice." And most blacks were forced into such activities by "the systematic exclusion of the black population from the opportunities opened up by the urban industrial revolution."[93]

While poverty in some circles provided a plausible explanation for rising crime in the black ghetto, it proved insufficient for those blacks and whites who feared black crime might trigger race riots similar to those that had occurred in East St. Louis in 1917 and in Chicago in 1919.[94] Therefore, black leaders and liberal whites in Detroit stayed on the defensive against racists who argued that increasing crime among blacks was proof of the basic criminality of the race itself.

Whatever explanations proved fashionable for whatever purpose, the disturbing fact remained: crime among blacks in Detroit was becoming a serious social problem. Between 1913 and 1919 the rate of black male arrests per 10,000 population was 4,008 compared to the white male rate of 1,544. The black female rate was 1676.7 compared to the white female rate of 299.4. Between January and June 1926, black male arrests had decreased to 1450.4 but this rate was still much higher than the white male rate of 563, which had also decreased. During the same period, the black-female arrest rate declined to 1008.4 compared to the white female rate of 147.5.[95]

These high rates of black arrests, however, were deceiving. Only about one-fourth of all black males and slightly less than one half of all black females arrested between 1913 and 1919 were convicted; and the same held true for the first six months of 1926. Out of 1,450 black males and 1,008 black females arrested per 10,000 population, only 600 and 506, respectively, were convicted.[96]

John C. Dancy recognized the disparity between black arrests and black convictions and how the former could be used to discredit an entire race. In November 1920 he wrote to Police Commissioner James W. Incher asking for information concerning the extent of crime among blacks in Detroit. Commissioner Incher said he would be happy to provide such information since blacks had been complaining about police brutality. Incher claimed that the police had not been discriminating against blacks and that two police officers had been killed by blacks in the last 30 days. The data showed that blacks committed 31 percent of all the felonies, 18 percent of all robberies, 75 percent of all breaking and entering, 70 percent of all burglaries of dwellings, 25 percent of all grand larcenies, 56 percent of all larcenies from people, 47 percent of all murders, and 37 percent of the carrying-a-concealed-weapon offenses. The commissioner also noted that blacks were only 7 percent of the total population.[97] His meaning was clear: 7 percent of the population committing 31 percent of all serious crimes. Commissioner Incher quickly pointed out, however, that crimes committed by blacks were "the crimes which are attracting most attention and are the cause of general alarm among white people." Whites, the commissioner added, violate the prohibition law more often than blacks, who, as a group, were responsible for only 10 percent of the law violations.[98]

Commissioner Incher told Dancy that he was sure that "the trouble was caused by men who had been induced to come here from the South by the promise of larger wages." He hoped that when unemployment increased during the winter many of the men committing these crimes would return to the South. The commissioner said, "I feel sure that the percentage of crimes committed by the colored population since those men have come from the South has been much higher than it was before."[99]

The high crime figures shocked Dancy. He asked the commissioner if they represented "those compiled before or after the court has acted," adding that maybe it would make a difference.[100] Like most contemporary black leaders, Dancy understood white officers' tendency to arrest blacks on any number of "trivial infractions." He agreed with the commissioner that unemployment could help reduce crimes among blacks by forcing some of the "undesirable elements" to return South. But Dancy made it clear that other solutions should be employed, such as using black officers in the east-side ghetto.[101]

As early as 1917 the Urban League had sought help from the Police

Department in controlling crime among blacks. The League, reflecting the contemporary social work philosophy, urged the police department to control black crime by preventive rather than punitive measures. As a result, the police commissioner appointed a special officer selected by the League to work entirely with recently arrived black migrants. This officer watched the streets where migrants hung out and kept the black underworld under surveillance. The League also had its own special agents who were used to inform the police of "questionable organizations and clubs."[102]

Little did the Urban League realize that the problem of crime among blacks would become increasingly serious. Industrialization and urbanization not only transformed southern peasants into industrial workers but also reduced many of them to surplus workers, who were forced at times to "steal or starve." The hope that cyclical unemployment would siphon off the so-called bad elements and send them back to the South, thus reducing crime among blacks, was simplistic and futile. More than likely, the bad elements (blacks who committed the crimes) stayed in Detroit during the unemployment periods and survived by hook or by crook through their ties to the black underground economy. Unemployed workers, left with no legal means of survival and little knowledge or inclination to survive by illegal means, were forced to return to the South.[103]

Throughout the 1920s and 1930s, crime among blacks, particularly black-on-black crime, remained an intractable problem woven into the fabric of black urban life. As long as poverty persisted, black crime would flourish. Violence constantly erupted in the crowded east-side ghetto. Overcrowding, with a lack of privacy that forced members of both sexes to occupy the same quarters, was aggravated further by a large population of young males, and was undoubtedly responsible for the frequency of several types of crimes.[104]

Though it is difficult to determine the extent of black-on-black crime during this period, the local black press commonly reported such crimes. Most black-on-black crimes tended to be violent, erupting between friends, relatives and lovers, caught up in the social pathology of poverty, frustration, and conflict. "Many such crimes," one observer noted in 1926, "are hasty explosions due to quarrels which may even have had their origin in good-natured joking."[105]

However, most crimes of violence between blacks had their origin in the tensions and conflicts of everyday ghetto life. The prevalence of single males and females living together in "common law" (i.e., "shacking up") did not always make for a stable relationship. With no legal restraints, either partner could eventually leave and take a lover if he or she chose to do so. In such relationships men could easily take advantage of women.

Yet in both legal and common-law marriage, black men and women often found themselves in heated battles ending in serious injuries and/or death. For example, in 1925, out of 19 murders of black people by black women, 10 killed their husbands and 4 killed men other than their husbands as a result of quarrels. Five killed other black women, also as a result of heated arguments. In the majority of cases in which black women killed their husbands and men other than their husbands, the violent acts had been provoked by the men's brutal treatment of the women.[106]

Black-on-black crime gave rise to news items about such violent acts as: Man stabbed in fight over women. Woman fatally shot when she attempted to break off a two-year common-law marriage; common-law husband turns himself over to the police. Husband cuts wife's lover. Man shoots wife and kills son who was trying to stop him from beating mother. Two men stabbed to death in brawl. Tavern owner shot to death by irate partner. Spouse's ear shot away by blast of gun. Teenager kills black business-man for insulting mother. Jealous woman shoots at lover, kills innocent bystander. Man killed in argument between women over who spilled "voo-doo" powder in the basement of a four-family apartment.[107]

The transplantation of southern cultural elements to the North, of which the medical beliefs already mentioned are an example, accounted for some of this violence. For example, southern authorities tended to be less con-cerned with black crime as long as it affected only blacks; therefore, many southern blacks in Detroit could not understand why white authorities interfered in black-on-black violence.[108]

Carrying concealed weapons was also a part of southern culture, being more common among blacks and whites in the South than in the North. But carrying a weapon in the tense and conflict-oriented street culture of the black ghetto was courting trouble, both with other urban dwellers as well as the white police who commonly arrested blacks as a form of social control. Between 1930 and 1945 police arrested more black males for carrying concealed and/or possessing concealed weapons than any other ethnic group.[109] Some of these men arrested probably carried weapons only for protecting themselves and their families. But more often than not this practice contributed to the increase of black-on-black crime.

Because the black population was younger, poorer, and less educated than the white majority population, black crime tended to reflect the social and economic profile of the larger black community. In 1925 black crim-inals tended to be younger than white criminals, with a greater proportion of offenders in the 20 to 40 year age group. Black criminals committed far fewer white-collar crimes, such as embezzlement and forgery, which required more formal education. Instead, the common black criminals concentrated on such crimes as gambling, robbery, and larceny. The lack of education explained the choice of crimes among black males, but this explanation did not always apply to black female offenders, who generally were better educated than their black male counterparts. According to a contemporary source, black women generally had even fewer economic opportunities than black men and engaged primarily in prostitution, lar-ceny, and gambling.[110] These crimes were directly related to the plight of black females struggling to survive in an urban society dominated and controlled by white and black men.

By the mid-1930s, crime among blacks had become a local disgrace for both black and white leaders. Blaming black crime on the inability of southern black migrants to adjust to northern life and culture and on the "bad elements" among the good folk of the ghetto was no longer acceptable in certain circles. Black crime had become so prevalent in the public mind that some white criminals committed crimes disguised as blacks, knowing that most white policemen and the public in general would never question whether the crime had been committed by a nonblack person.[111]

Concerned black leaders placed part of the blame for crime among blacks on the black press. In an article published in the *Detroit Tribune* in December 1940, two club women, Geraldine Bledsoe and Nellie Watts, took the black press to task for its sensationalistic coverage of black crime. "There is a serious struggle going on in the world today to evolve a new and better social order where the average man may enjoy the better things of life," the women reminded the paper and its readers. "Surely the Negro is part of this struggle. The press can ill afford to miss the opportunity to be in the vanguard of this movement to help integrate the masses." Therefore, the women argued, to "that end, they should mold public opinion along constructive lines by headlining constructive, worthwhile efforts that the Negro is making, rather than devote so much space to murder, brawls, and other destructive experiences." Since the *Detroit Tribune* was owned and edited in Detroit, Bledsoe and Watts commented that "it must assume leadership in such a movement if it is to keep pace with the progressive leaders within its own group who are working to bring about the complete integration of the Negro into this new order." Ending their letter, the two women assured the paper and its readers that other people in the community shared their opinions and also deplored "this negative situation." They asked for other readers to express their views through the column.[112]

In the next issue of the paper a veteran newspaper man challenged the women head on. "I have been in the newspaper business since 1928 . . . I am in sympathy with Miss Watts and Mrs. Bledsoe's complaints," the writer said warming up to his topic, "but I must admit that their requests are unreasonable." Agreeing that black newspapers had a responsibility to help their communities, the newsman argued that newspapers are also primarily businesses, "and the first consideration of any business is to satisfy as many of their customers as is humanly possible." Publishing crime among blacks in the local black press was simply good business practice—and profitable. "Crime news and the information dealing with the intimate side of human lives sell more papers," the newspaper man explained, "than any other single feature except the comics, which few colored papers carry." Then hammering home a truth which few contemporary editors and publishers of black newspapers could deny, the newspaper man laid it out: "I have found those most guilty of community crimes and living in blighted areas contribute more to the sale of newspapers than any other group." Ending his response to the women, he said, "Don't tell papers how to run their business."[113]

No one questioned the fact that "number playing" was illegal and contributed to crime among blacks.[114] However, blacks of all social classes in Detroit participated in this "crime"; and during the worst years of the depression black college graduates found well-paid employment in this line of work. In fact, some of these college-educated young people did so well in the numbers racket that they decided to remain in it even after the depression ended and legitimate jobs were available.[115]

Legitimate black businessmen not only assisted in the development and expansion of the numbers racket in Detroit—where, unlike other cities, blacks dominated this particular criminal activity—but they legitimized the practice within the black community itself. For example, in 1916, two black businessmen, John Roxborough (who later became Joe Louis's manager) and Everett Watson, set up a club called the Waiters and Bellmans Club, a gambling establishment specializing in dice and cards. Club members played popular card games such as stud poker and "Georgia skin." The latter game was played mostly by blacks. The next year, these two "legitimate" businessmen further expanded their illegitimate operations by establishing the first major numbers gambling house in Detroit called the "Big Four." In 1920, Watson sold his interests in the business to Roxborough who in turn set up three more numbers houses which as late as 1935 were still going strong.[116]

Between 1921 and 1935, the numbers gambling racket began engulfing the storefront spiritualist churches that catered to the black urban poor. Soon storefront preachers were helping to fleece the black poor of what little money they had by giving out "lucky numbers" to their eager congregations. People started attending certain churches for the sake of "hitting the number" (i.e., winning a bet).[117] One of those churchgoers said it best:

> I joined this church because it is the only church I have attended in Detroit that had anything to offer me. Most of them want you to give them something but don't want to give you anything. Before I joined this church I used to play as big as fifty cents almost every day in policy [number gambling] and never hit. I went to visit the church, got a private reading. She told me to fast. I did three days; and one day I played fifty cents and won. I then thought I ought to have played more so I put fifty cents in the next day and won.[118]

These black spiritualistic churches became so integrated into the numbers racket that the police department started treating them like other gambling establishments. As one contemporary scholar of the numbers racket said: "It is not uncommon for a congregation to be interrupted in the midst of 'Onward, Christian Soldiers' or 'Nearer My God to Thee' by some burly police sergeant." The same scholar added that the "modern world has witnessed few things more paradoxical than a pastor and his congregation being loaded into a patrol wagon and whisked away to the police station."[119]

Numbers playing became so pervasive in black urban communities during the depression that it affected their language and folklore. People bought "dream books" to interpret and decode dreams, and, of course, the publishers raked in money through sales of these books.[120]

As a boy growing up in the Detroit of the 1940s and 1950s, the writer remembers the tremendous faith placed in dream books by his close relatives and their adult friends. These people really believed that there was a connection between their dreams and numbers playing. The social pathology of poverty generated and maintained this belief system, interwoven into the cultural fabric of northern black urban life, that one day "the big hit" would come. The writer's father repeatedly told him that one day his "ship would come in," meaning that he would hit the number for a lot of money. He never did. Waiting for the ship to come in fueled many abortive hopes.

In all fairness to the moral guardians of the black community, before 1929 most leaders attacked the numbers racket for what it really was: plain gambling. In 1928 the Colored Ministers Association organized an uncompromising crusade against the practice of numbers gambling in the press and on the pulpit. Determined to uproot this vice from the community, they called it "an insidious practice which feeds upon the poverty and ignorance of the masses. We must unite," the preachers cried out, "to do away with this cancer that pauperizes our people."[121]

But as cruel fate would have it, the harsh depression years of 1930–32 forced the bravest of these black moral leaders to surrender high principles for basic survival. Numbers gambling produced jobs for some blacks and offered the black masses at least some hope—however small—of hitting the big number and "bringing home the bacon." Numbers gamblers provided financial aid to hard pressed churches during these years.[122]

These ministers knew the score: They could not win against the powerful influence of the numbers racket which, by then, had evolved into a solid institution in the black community, supported by people from all levels of black social life and unquestionably a key factor in the community building process.

So instead of condemning the numbers racket as before, as an "insidious practice" and a "vice" that "pauperizes" black people, the moral leaders switched to apologizing for the practice. "Numbers gambling is no worse than going out to "Lefty' Ryan's and losing $3 at a shot; 'the numbers' are not an evil because the money is spent right in our community and the bankers are our best charity givers."[123] Thus, the moral guardians of the community, in many cases the cream of black leadership, legitimized what was essentially another form of black crime.

Numbers gambling rapidly became respectable, and the men associated with it, who in an earlier day were considered gamblers, were now "men of unquestioned integrity, fairness, and honesty." Even John C. Dancy, who as a young idealistic social worker more than a decade earlier had sought assistance from the police department in protecting migrants from such vices as gambling, now had only praise for numbers gamblers: "Whenever I need financial help for any of my work I can count on these men."[124] Time and circumstances had mellowed Dancy's earlier moral indignation over gambling. He had learned to be moral in a practical way, to be flexible concerning certain community "customs." Numbers gambling was simply too popular among blacks and it involved too many blacks with money and influence. In fact, numbers gambling constituted the heart of the "underground" ghetto economy. So Dancy learned to accept and even praise "big shot" numbers bosses, such as Bill Mosley.

Any embarrassment suffered by these moral guardians as a result of reversing their moral stand on gambling in the black community was rendered less painful by the fact that many of the most successful men in the numbers rackets were also equally successful men in the legitimate business world. Bill Mosley, one of the biggest and most powerful numbers bankers, did quite well before engaging in the numbers racket. During the Depression he owned the *Detroit Tribune Independent,* Detroit's largest black newspaper; he had controlling interest in the McFall Brothers Undertaking business, the largest of its kind in black Detroit; and he had a half interest in the City Cab Company, the largest in the black community. If these were not sufficient to establish his preeminence in the legitimate black business community, Mosley also owned three store buildings, two poolrooms, and seven houses. And to top it all off, he and John Roxborough owned the controlling shares in Great Lakes Insurance Company, one of the largest and fastest growing black businesses in Detroit.[125]

These men enjoyed such status and influence in the black community that few legitimate business people who valued their black clientele dared to criticize numbers gambling. Black professional and business people, who normally might have looked down their noses at numbers gambling as a poor man's vice, discovered soon enough that their success in the black economy depended on how favorably they viewed the practice. One such professional, a prominent dentist, put it well: "This numbers playing is a terrible business, and to think that I have to help it along. But what can I do when one of my patients asks me to buy a number? If I don't play with him, he'll go somewhere else for his dental work. I can't afford to lose any business in these times."[126]

The legitimization of numbers gambling in the black community blurred the line between criminal and noncriminal behavior and eroded the credibility of those black leaders who tried to curb crime and juvenile delinquency among blacks. But, whatever contradictory feelings they might have had endorsing numbers gambling while campaigning against crime among blacks, such feelings did not deter them from vigorously attacking other forms of crime within the community.

For decades, black leaders had been obsessed with controlling the anti-social behavior of the mostly lower-class blacks within the community. Such control was crucial to the credibility of black leaders who had the nonissuable and awesome responsibility of assimilating the black masses into Detroit's urban and industrial culture. Dancy and Bradby had been performing this task since before the end of World War I, at least. But by the 1940s, black crime—and particularly juvenile delinquency—became unbearable to black leaders and community groups. Black youth gangs were crashing and breaking up private parties and roaming the streets beating up people. A gang of boys beat up a police officer who made the mistake of trying to break up a dice game. A near riot almost occurred during the summer of 1941 in the east-side ghetto when police arrested some youths who had had a little too much to drink. That same summer, a group of young boys boarded a bus, refused to pay, snatched a $20.00 roll of coins from the driver, and fled.[127]

These and similar incidents led the Reverend Mr. Bradby in the fall of 1941 to declare that "young upstarts and jitterbugs have wrecked everything that Negro leaders have fought for in Detroit." He called on black parents to clamp down on their children.[128]

Focusing on the more criminal and frivolous aspects of black youth behavior, Bradby said the "switch blades and unlawful acts, fights and clowning are not part of a responsible society."[129] He blamed just about everybody and everything for the problems of black youth crime and delinquency. "Cults and profit-making religions," as well as "fine homes and big automobiles," were corrupting black youth. He was much more on target, however, when he advised black youth to "stop fighting battles for criminals and let the police arrest law violators, and fight for those who are right."[130]

Other black leaders and community groups joined in this campaign to combat black crime and delinquency. The Civic Action Committee of the Omega Detroit Chapter of the Omega Psi Phi Fraternity had been studying the problem for several months and organized a network of black organizations to work on solutions. "It is our considered judgment," the committee reported, "that our spiritual and intellectual leaders must furnish the vision that will point to a solution of this vexing problem."[131]

Several months earlier, Senator Charles C. Diggs, the first black Democrat to be elected to the Michigan legislature, urged that an anti-reefer (marijuana cigarette) drive be organized to prevent the corruption of black youth. Diggs's concern was prompted by the increase of delinquency and crime in his district, which he attributed to drug dealers. In a letter to the police commissioner he urged that "steps be taken to curb this growing evil" and made suggestions to accomplish that end: A special group of police officers, both men and women, should be assigned to the task. A conference of blacks should be called, under the supervision of the police department, for the dual purpose of acquainting them with the methods used by drug dealers and involving blacks in fighting the drug problem.[132] Little else is known about the results of these suggestions but Diggs's efforts demonstrated how some black leaders attempted to tackle a problem destined to increase in the black community.

An organization of west-side ministers, called the Northwest Pastors Union, representing all the black churches on the west side of Detroit, held a mass meeting in November of 1941 "to help improve conditions caused by some of the "reckless youth of the community."[133] Much like other black leaders around the city, the sponsors were troubled by the increasing crime among blacks and what it meant for the larger black struggle. Addressing the meeting, one sponsor declared:

> In view of the precarious position of our race today, after its long climb upwards, and since our course ought to be forward, in spite of the stony road we're travelling, we deplore the upward surge of juvenile delinquency, murdering, knifing, all kinds of debasing actions with tendency to defame us.[134]

Concern over crime and delinquency was compounded by the ministers' abhorrence of an emerging "fad" among many black urban youth called the "jitterbug," consisting of certain nontraditional forms of dress, speech, and dance.[135] "Our hearts are made sad because of the funny suits and large hats, clownish in appearance, worn by so many of our own young people."[136]

Black leaders' concern over the jitterbug fad stemmed partially from their fear that such behavior would undermine important social values held dear by the black upper and middle classes. Too much was at stake, according to these leaders, to lose it all because of the irresponsible jitterbugs. Similar concerns led a group of both young and old black citizens of the north end black community, area of mostly middle class blacks, to launch a drive in May of 1941 to counter what they called the "disorderly jitterbugs." One of their handbills dramatically stated: "Down with the disorderly jitterbugs."[137] Blaming the jitterbugs for undermining the values of the youth of their community, the organizers of the drive claimed that "a few disorderly, indecent jitterbugs of our fine community are having a demoralizing influence on future citizens and young ladies." The citizens of the north end, therefore, have the duty and obligation for "breaking up the demoralizing conduct of our youth on the streets, in theaters, and in business establishments."[138]

Jitterbugging was only a fad and would pass away as do most fads, but black crime and delinquency, rooted in the pervasive poverty of the ghetto, remained serious problems. In October 1942, one of Detroit's major white newspapers, the *Detroit News,* ran a series of five articles, again focusing on the "Negro problem in Detroit." Emphasizing the seriousness of the problem, the first article opened up with a candid statement: "The Negro factor in Detroit is a keg of powder with a short fuse, and one of many possible incidents, fairly insignificant in themselves, may be the match put to the fuse."[139] One such "insignificant incident" had already occurred and was reported in the article. Recently, a group of black boys confronted the police after one of their friends was arrested for allegedly disturbing the peace. The paper raised the question: Why was a gang of boys on the street at night ready for trouble? The reason, the paper argued, was that "the boys had nothing better to do or think about. They were squeezed by economic and social conditions, . . . restless to the point of breaking down some fences." These black boys, the paper continued, "were old enough to take many kind of jobs that would bring in real wages. They wanted work—had wanted it for a long time."[140]

Four years later in 1946, and three years after the first and worst race riot in modern American history, the *Detroit News* ran another series on blacks in Detroit, entitled "Negro life in Detroit." As expected, black crime and delinquency remained serious problems, although some progress had occurred. The robbery record for blacks had decreased from previous years, a remarkable sign given the decline in jobs. According to the paper, the decreased black crime rate resulted from blacks saving money and investing in war bonds, "surviving without resort to crime or welfare relief." The other reason was a "greatly improved attitude toward law and the police."[141] The paper seemed hopeful that black conditions would improve with time, but unfortunately blacks and white Detroit had a long way to go.

These harsh conditions of the promised land did not murder or maim the spirit of black Detroit—though they came awfully close to doing so. Health, housing, jobs, crime and delinquency were all problems—and many still are—that blacks had to bear in order to build a community in Detroit.

Weathering the storm for blacks in industrializing Detroit involved surviving substandard housing, high rents, dirty and dangerous jobs, and crime and violence. Not all blacks lived and worked in such miserable conditions, but most did. Many blacks not only had to live in substandard housing, they also had to pay exorbitant rents for the privilege. High rents eroded already low wages earned in dirty and dangerous jobs. These conditions combined to undermine the health of thousands of blacks.

For decades blacks had to endure high rates of adult and infant mortality. Unable to break the cycle of poverty, many succumbed to the pervasive social pathology of crime and violence. Unable to strike out against the forces which robbed them of fruitful lives, they turned in on themselves.

But some were able to escape, to move out of poverty into stable black middle class neighborhoods on the west side. So the struggle continued on behalf of those still mired in poverty. Black leaders joined by poor tenants fought against high rents and crime in the black community, and numbers bosses and social workers joined hands to support a community in which they all had a stake.

"Weathering the storm" also involved surviving and transcending the manifest forms of racism rampant in industrial Detroit. Ironically, racial discrimination in housing, employment, education, and public accommodations contributed to certain aspects of the community building process. For example, had white charitable organizations and settlement houses been integrated before the establishment of the Detroit Urban League, a separate black social welfare agency would not have been necessary. Black migrants would have been integrated into existing white organizations. As happened, racial policies at the time dictated separate organizations for social work among racial groups. Yet, without the DUL, as well as the Green Pastures Camp, itself a benign by-product of racial segregation, the black community building process would have been quite different. Negative aspects themselves—racial discrimination in housing, employment, and public accommodations—stimulated the social consciousness of the black community and led to a variety of movements which, in turn, nurtured and sustained the community building process.

Five

Racial Discrimination in Industrial Detroit: Preparing the Ground for Community Social Consciousness

The herding of Southern Negroes into a city that was unprepared for them pushed our race problem to the front, and has given city officials, police officers, and others something to think about. What to do with the 81,800 Negroes now estimated to be living in greater Detroit is a subject that has engaged the thoughts of many able minds.

Detroit Saturday Night,
December 31, 1927

The Detroit Housing Commission will in no way change the racial characteristics of any neighborhood in Detroit through occupancy standards of housing projects under their jurisdiction.

Minutes of the Detroit
Housing Commission,
April 29, 1943

CHANGING RACE RELATIONS IN INDUSTRIAL DETROIT

After arriving in the North, many southern blacks mistakenly believed they had finally outrun white racism. Little did they know that their mere presence would cause it to rise up to haunt them once again from cradle to grave. Though not nearly as pervasive in custom and particularly non-existent in law, northern racism differed from southern racism only in degrees. Northern and southern whites shared a common cultural heritage of white supremacy and paternalism. Before World War I, the North tended to be less racist than the South, partially due to its small black population. Between 1915 and 1945, northern racism and racial conflicts began exploding in the face of the nation that for too long had believed racism to be exclusively a southern problem.[1]

Northern racism, which evolved between 1915 and 1945, stemmed largely from the economic, social, and demographic changes disrupting northern industrial cities. Black migration led to increased conflicts in northern urban centers as blacks settled in to live and work in a region unaccustomed to interacting with blacks in such large numbers.[2]

Spared the early bloody race riots that bludgeoned northern cities, including East St. Louis and Chicago in 1917 and 1919, respectively,[3] Detroit considered itself lucky. Such good fortune did not go unnoticed or unappreciated by alert local social observers. As one newspaper writer explained it:

> Gradually, for more than a year and with little or no warning until the East St. Louis outbreak of a few weeks ago gave it presentation in a terrifying form, a race problem fraught with peril for both whites and blacks and the continuance of law, order and decency, has been developing in the North.[4]

The "race problem" the writer referred to stemmed from "the influx of Negroes in large numbers to the North without proper guidance," which, the writer feared, left these blacks to be manipulated "by various unscrupulous persons with ends of their own to achieve."[5] But Detroit was most fortunate, according to this writer, because it already had an active Urban League and a director, Forrester B. Washington, "who was well on his way toward solving the problems of his race in Detroit."[6]

This writer probably lived long enough to regret his premature optimism. Washington and the fledgling local Urban League were not even close to adequately understanding the complexity of the problems of race in industrial Detroit. But whites, such as the above writer, perceived Washington and other black leaders and agencies as being responsible for solving the race problem in Detroit. They assumed that all or most racial problems were essentially "black problems." Blacks had to adjust to white society, certainly not the converse. Years of urban race riots and needless death and destruction would occur before socially responsible and sensitive whites would admit that white racism was the root cause of most social problems affecting blacks in urban America.[7]

As we have already seen, the industrial demand for cheap and abundant southern black labor during World War I greatly increased the black population in Detroit and other northern industrial centers. Such a rapid increase in a largely rural population created countless and unprecedented problems of social adjustment. Had the thousands of southern blacks been white, it would have been serious enough; but they were black at a time when white Americans held the worst racial stereotypes concerning blacks.[8] Only the wisest of the wise could have fathomed the social and historical consequences of viewing this problem as just a black problem. At the bare minimum the problem was one of racial adjustment, facing both blacks and whites in a new industrial society. However, capitalists wanted profits and the city fathers wanted social peace, so the task of bringing about racial adjustment fell to social workers and preachers, whose unquestioned good intentions often lagged far behind their ability to meet this new challenge.

While some whites viewed the racial problem in Detroit as a black problem of social adjustment to white industrial society, other whites frantically and often ingeniously designed ways to contain blacks, to maintain the racial status quo. This meant "keeping the niggers in their place," based upon the logic that even though blacks enjoyed considerably more freedom in Detroit than in the South, they still should be racially restricted. If allowed to move out of their "place," blacks would disrupt the social order, these whites believed. This is what one employer meant when he explained why blacks were not moving up in the occupational structure of most plants: "We hired them for this hot dirty work and we want them there. If we let a few rise, all the rest will become dissatisfied."[9]

In the 1920s, the black population increased and overflowed the boundaries of the pre-war ghettos (see map). Blacks appeared in increasing numbers in public places, such as parks, schools, street cars, theaters, and eating places. Had this population increase been more gradual, perhaps whites might have adjusted better than they did. Perhaps if whites in Detroit had been better prepared for such radical changes in the racial status quo, the entire history of race relations in Detroit would have taken a different course—that we can never know. What we do know is that between 1915 and 1943, race relations in Detroit sped steadily and disastrously downhill, characterized by more and more volatile skirmishes, which accumulated and exploded in the hate filled bloody race riot of 1943. As a result, blacks became increasingly race conscious, realizing that their progress depended upon their functioning as a community.

Throughout this period, white racism was expressed and practiced almost by common consent. Many whites who believed racism to be crude and morally wrong failed to mount a serious challenge to stop it. Since most whites of the period frowned on social equality with blacks, they accepted racism as the lesser evil. Blacks rarely received equal treatment in public places. A black could expect to be turned down or charged a higher price at theaters in downtown Detroit. Most white hotels and restaurants flatly refused to serve blacks. In the 1930s, owners of the Hoffman building attempted to ban blacks from working on the premises. Some whites fumed when they saw blacks occupying box seats at the local race track, and blacks were ejected once for being so daring. Racism in Detroit followed blacks to the grave. Until 1935 the white-owned Roseland Park Cemetery directed blacks to use its side entrance.[10]

At times, white racism in Detroit could be downright pathetic as when the Salvation Army refused to give Christmas baskets to blacks because of their race. Then, too, white racism could be comically cruel as in stereotype advertisements in white newspapers featuring blacks gambling and eating watermelon. In the 1940s, A&P stores in Detroit never thought

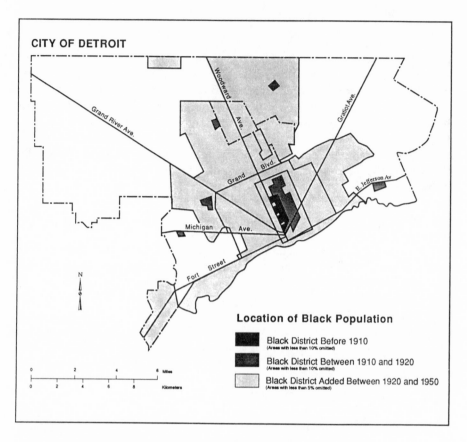

Location of black population, 1910– 1950. Map prepared by Bradley Davis, Department of Geography and Urban Affairs, Michigan State University.

twice—until blacks protested—about advertising a shoe polish called "Nigger-head."[11] Such racial attitudes revealed the pervasive nature of white feelings toward blacks and the negative images of blacks most whites carried around in their heads.

Some of these racial attitudes predated the large-scale migration of southern blacks. Blacks in nineteenth-century Detroit faced racial discrimination in public schools, hotels, restaurants, and other public places. The passage of the 1875 Civil Rights Act discouraged some of these practices, but it had little effect on the more determined whites who found ways to circumvent the law. Some white hotel proprietors, for example, charged blacks double what whites had to pay for the same accommodations.[12]

Racist whites continued to employ this subterfuge in the early 1930s to avoid compliance with the public accommodation section of the 1885 Michigan Civil Rights Act.[13]

RACIAL DISCRIMINATION IN PUBLIC ACCOMMODATION

Some of the worst discrimination occurred in white restaurants in Detroit, and they proved to be the most resistant to equal accommodation laws and social pressure. Even with the full weight and authority of the federal Civil Rights Act of 1875 and the Michigan Civil Rights Act of 1885 (both of which "dealt directly with the elimination of segregation in public accommodations") behind blacks in the 1880s, many white restaurants continued to bar blacks or to serve them only in back rooms.[14]

Black leaders fought this racism in court, lost several cases in the lower courts, but were finally vindicated by the Michigan Supreme Court in 1890 when it unanimously ruled that "the white man can have no rights or privileges under the law that are denied to the black man."[15] But racial discrimination against blacks in white restaurants continued.[16]

What was it about restaurants that made whites so resistant to complying with the law? Why was eating with blacks so threatening to whites in the late nineteenth and the greater part of the twentieth centuries? Several scholars who have studied American race relations have concluded that "Segregated restaurants were designed to prevent whites and blacks from partaking in the social ritual of eating together," since in most societies in the world the act of breaking bread is "a ritual symbol of brotherhood and at least of potential equality."[17] The continuance of restaurant discrimination against blacks in Detroit well into the twentieth century gives credence to this point.

Restaurant discrimination against blacks continued during and after periods of black population expansion. As black ghettos began swallowing up white establishments, some whites, unable to adjust to a racially changing community, held firm in their racist practices.

In 1920, in a case representative of others, the Greek owners of a restaurant, which was located in a black ghetto and which catered to blacks, threatened two black police officers when they refused to pay more than the standard price for a glass of milk. According to the *Detroit Contender*, a local black newspaper, racial discrimination against blacks by Greeks was common practice.[18] Blacks were further annoyed by the fact that such discrimination occurred in the heart of the black community. Angry and insulted, the *Detroit Contender* publicized these racist practices, which frightened one Greek owner into trying to bribe the newspaper into shelving the issue.[19] But the editor and the newspaper could not be bought off. In a blast of indignation the editor informed its readers of the bribe and threw down the gauntlet to the Greeks: "We propose—God being our helper—to show these Greeks who are getting rich off of our people and at the same time giving vent to their dirty prejudices, that this kind of a thing don't go with us anymore. They will either have to play the game like men or get out of our territory."[20]

Racist whites neither "played the game like men" nor got out of black territory; the practice of charging blacks more than whites for a service or a product had not ceased by the early 1930s. In June of 1930, the white owner of a tavern and grocery store charged two black men in his tavern 75 cents for two bottles of beer, which he sold to white customers for 15 cents. The practice seemed paradoxical; the white proprietor welcomed black customers in his grocery store but discriminated against them in his tavern. "If Negroes are not considered good enough to be served in his beer garden, they should feel themselves too good to patronize a grocery store operated by the same proprietor."[21]

When blacks began setting up their own eating establishments and catering to their own people they did not have to expose themselves to such indignities. But many blacks, motivated more by pride and principle than by anything else, refused to allow racism to go unchallenged. They wanted the right to be served anyplace and not just in black restaurants that were located in black communities. It was rather awkward and inconvenient for blacks working or shopping outside black communities to have to return home just to get a meal. But in the 1920s and 1930s, white restaurant owners were unrelenting in barring blacks, just when the black community was expanding and a new generation of radical young people were coming of age. One black who remembered this period commented on the restaurant issue:

> It was just about out of the question to talk about going in restaurants to eat, to get a meal, etc. No matter . . . any place in the city of Detroit, as far as the so-called white restaurants. You just couldn't do it. . . . I tell you very frankly, Detroit was just as bad as Mississippi or Georgia in a way of speaking.[22]

Conflicts over racial discrimination in white restaurants increased in the 1930s and 1940s, largely because of middle class blacks who worked downtown and refused to accept the racial status quo. In 1934, when the United States decided not to reopen a cafeteria in the new federal building in downtown Detroit, 400 black federal employees were put in a bind. Previously they had been served in the cooperative cafeteria. Now that it was closed these black federal workers had no place to eat. Most white restaurants in the surrounding area either refused to serve blacks or did so reluctantly. One white restaurant refused to serve a black federal worker at the counter but told him he could get a sandwich at the back door.[23]

Similar cases followed, so the black federal employees took the case to court, accusing white restaurant owners of violating the civil rights laws. In one case in June of 1934, a white who discriminated against blacks admitted that he had violated the law, so the judge ordered a suspended sentence. In explaining his reason for granting such a light sentence, the judge said the law was not meant to inflict vengeance but to establish justice. When questioned by the lawyer for the black worker, the judge claimed that the suspended sentence would deter the defendant from any future acts of discrimination against the black federal workers.[24]

When white restaurant employees did serve blacks, they often treated them disrespectfully. In August of 1934, a black was first refused service, and then when he was finally served his food, it was covered with salt. He took the case to court, where the judge excluded the only black from the jury, and the remaining all-white jury found no cause for action.[25] Realizing that blacks could get little relief with existing civil-rights laws, Charles C. Diggs (who in 1936 became the first black Democrat elected to the Michigan Senate), with the help of others, succeeded in 1937 in putting a stronger civil rights law on the books.[26]

Although this new law had more teeth in it than previous laws, racial discrimination against blacks in white restaurants persisted. In March 1938, a black woman invited to lunch in a downtown white restaurant by her white friend was refused service. The waitress informed the white woman that she could be served but that the management did not allow blacks to be served on the premises. The white friend then invited her black companion to another restaurant across the street where they met with similar treatment. The black woman then filed suit under the new civil-rights law.[27]

As indignant blacks began taking whites to court over restaurant discrimination under the new law, judges in turn began handing down appropriate sentences. In another case in March 1938, police arrested a waitress and restaurant owner for violating the new law; this was the first time that criminal proceedings were instituted against violators.[28] The white owner of a beer tavern, who in 1937 had instructed his waitress not to serve a black, was charged with violation of the new civil rights law and ordered to pay the plaintiff $75.00, in addition to paying $3.00 court costs and $5.00 in attorney fees.

Either some white restaurant owners were ignorant of the new civil rights law or knew about it and chose to ignore it, because discrimination against blacks continued. In October 1938, two friends, one white and the other black, stopped in a restaurant for a glass of beer. The waitress declined to serve them, claiming she was under orders not to serve blacks. The two men left the restaurant and returned with Senator Charles Diggs. The waitress decided to serve them but told them that the white would be charged 10 cents for his glass of beer but the two black men would be charged 25 cents each for their drinks. The three men left and reported the incident to the assistant prosecutor.[29]

In another case, when a black man entered a restaurant and ordered something to eat, the owner promptly asked him, "Don't you know it is against the rules of the Board of Health to serve a 'nigger' in here?" When the black refused to leave, the white owner tried to remove him by force. A policeman passing by the restaurant hurried in and parted the two men. The black man then rushed to the prosecutor's office where he lodged a complaint against the white proprietor. After hearing the complaint, the prosecutor suggested a warrant be taken out against the white owner.[30]

White restaurant owners who resisted the new civil-rights law often showed deference to their customers who did not want their racist sensibilities disturbed. In such cases these owners, caught between complying with the new law or honoring the racism of their customers, often deferred to the latter, even if that choice meant paying a fine. That is exactly what one white part-time owner and waitress chose to do. In September 1941, after the law had been in effect for four years, a white woman was found guilty of violating the Diggs civil-rights law. When given the choice of paying $25 or spending 15 days in jail, she decided to pay the fine. She explained in her testimony that many of her white customers objected to blacks eating in her restaurant. As a result, she adopted the policy of serving blacks their food only on paper plates, which they had to take outside. When questioned by the judge as to whether she knew that she was violating the law, she replied, "I cannot help that."[31]

Not all whites objected to sharing eating accommodations with blacks. Some whites strongly believed in racial equality and were angered and embarrassed by the crude and relentless racist practices of white restaurant owners, especially since such practice represented a blatant disregard of the law.

By the early 1940s, many white restaurants still discriminated against blacks. These indignities got under the skin of younger, more militant blacks in the city. In 1937 during the Annual Convention of the National Association for the Advancement of Colored People (NAACP) Youth Councils, a group of these militant youths descended on one of the most infamous racist eating establishments in Detroit, Greenfield Restaurant, and forced the proprietor to serve them. But four years later, Greenfield's racist practices remained firmly in place. Therefore, in December 1941, after a Sunday meeting of the NAACP Youth Council, the young militant band decided to test the civil-rights law at Greenfield. Led by their two leaders, Stanley Evans and Gloster Current, the youths entered the restaurant. The manager attempted to persuade them not to force service but the youths moved on towards the steam table, unobstructed. When the waitress at the steam tables refused to serve them, the youths went to the counter, where they selected salads, pie, and other dishes. After eating their meals, they paid their bills, but the waitresses refused to clean off any of the tables. The youths had to clean off their own tables. Several white customers, observing the events, became angry over such racist treatment. Two white women decided to act out their moral convictions, left their own tables, and joined the black youths at their tables. One of the white women protested the manager's treatment of blacks, calling it ridiculous. Obviously moved by the protests of these white customers, the manager backed down and ordered the waitresses to clean the tables. The police had been sent for, but they informed the manager that they could do nothing since the youths were not causing any problems.[32]

Racial discrimination in restaurants would have persisted had other developments not intervened. Black employment in downtown Detroit grew steadily after World War II, due to the government's hiring of young blacks for clerk and office work. Major utility companies such as Michigan Bell Telephone Company contributed greatly to this trend by expanding the pool of black professionals working downtown. Finally by 1952, major restaurants and hotels had relaxed some racial barriers. However, blacks shopping downtown had to pick their places carefully if they wanted to have a pleasant lunch free of embarrassment and hassles.[33]

Throughout the 1920s and 1930s, blacks established their own recreational facilities within the black ghettos, but these rarely met the growing demands of the expanding black population. As a result, many blacks ventured out to test the water and exercise their rights under the law. Had blacks stayed within the crowded ghetto, satisfying themselves with meager recreation, most whites would have been more than happy to let them do so. But blacks could see the flashing new lights downtown and the grand hotels and dance halls, and they craved them.

This craving for better things was particularly strong among the restless middle class. They refused to be hemmed in by ghetto walls built and maintained by whites who profited by keeping blacks out of the larger society. For example, whites owned all of the nine theaters in the black community, most of which were located on Hastings Street within the heart of the ghetto. These theaters featured stage performances by black theatrical troupes of the musical comedy variety, with much dancing and singing. Second rate films completed the repertoire.[34] Such entertainment more than met the needs of the working class blacks, who had little time or inclination to search for other forms of entertainment outside the ghetto.

When blacks sought entertainment outside the ghetto, they often had to conform to white racist policies and practices, particularly in large white-owned dance halls. In the 1920s, there was only one hall in the entire city owned-and-operated by blacks that was large enough to be suitable for dancing—the Masonic Hall. This hall could only hold 100 couples. Larger black dances had to be held on a segregated basis in white dance halls such as the Arcadian and the Graystone. One white dance hall, the Palois de Dance, had a policy that barred blacks from using its facilities except on holidays between midnight and five or six o'clock in the morning. The other two, the Arcadian and the Graystone, allowed blacks to use their halls only when they had an open night, usually on Mondays.[35]

Blacks also found themselves unwelcome at other amusement centers. In the 1920s Tashmon Flats and Bob-Lo barred blacks entirely, while

Put-in-Bay and Sugar Island accepted blacks only on special days. Boat companies flatly refused to take black passengers on general excursions. One boat company even refused to transport a staff picnic to an amusement center because black members of the staff were included.[36]

By the 1920s, blacks could attend all of the best theaters in downtown Detroit, but often had to sit in the balconies and galleries. Some theaters would sell blacks tickets only for certain rows and sections. Evidently this policy was not written in stone since, in those instances when blacks protested the segregated seating policy, management generally relented.[37]

Theater managers had had plenty of experiences with blacks who would not accept segregation. Back in 1914, the Detroit branch of the NAACP took fourteen cases of racial discrimination in theaters to court.[38] Although they won only four, the message was clear: Blacks would not passively accept segregation in theaters or in other places of public accommodation.

Much like the trend in restaurant discrimination, white theater owners and managers chose to resist Michigan's civil rights laws. In May 1933, a theater overcharged a black doctor and his wife for tickets. The doctor complained to the manager, who informed him that the management reserved the right to charge black patrons any price they pleased. The doctor called the police, who told him they could do nothing about the incident and that he should see the prosecutor. The case went to trial. Luckily for the black couple, a white person who witnessed the incident testified on their behalf. The couple won the case and the jury awarded the black doctor $50 in his suit against the theater.[39]

In 1935, one theater manager attracted considerable attention in his efforts to segregate black patrons. When one black couple refused to sit in the black section, the management called in an officer, who forced the couple to give up their seats. The couple filed a suit, but before the trial the manager promised that he would stop discriminating against blacks if the couple dropped their suit against the theater.[40]

Later that same year, another theater refused to sell tickets to a black couple to see Show Boat. The ticket seller claimed the theater ran special shows for blacks and that they could not attend any other shows at the theater. Asked when the theater ran these special shows, the ticket seller replied they were advertised in the paper. The couple then wanted to know if the ticket seller realized that such discriminatory action violated the Michigan Civil Rights Act. His reply was simple and to the point: "I do not care to argue."[41]

Laws or no laws, many whites in Detroit felt justified in defending the racial status quo. Even passenger elevators were considered too good for blacks, as a black woman discovered as late as 1938. On a visit to the Belcrest Hotel, a black woman accompanied by a white friend was told by the black elevator operator that she would have to use the freight elevator by order of the management. She refused and rode upstairs. After she returned to the lobby, the manager grabbed her and told her she would have to leave by the servants' entrance. Objecting to such humiliation, the woman declared she was not a servant and refused to use the entrance. The manager physically forced her out through the servants' entrance.[42]

In the 1930s, the more perceptive racist whites in Detroit knew they were fighting a losing battle against black social equality, but that did not stop them from employing all the tricks of the trade to slow down black advancement. If anything grated on their racial sensibilities, it was seeing blacks in positions of high social status. Little wonder, therefore, that in the summer of 1934 the officials at the Michigan fairgrounds barred the black guest of a white patron from occupying a box seat at the race track. The usher claimed black people were not allowed to occupy box seats at the race track. The usher's statement received backing from the secretary of the Detroit Racing Association who, in turn, stated that there was a clause in the contract between the association and the state of Michigan and signed by the governor that prohibited blacks from occupying box seats at race tracks. As it turned out, the officials were lying. The editor of the local black newspaper received a copy of the contract and, after a careful reading of the document, wrote that he was "gratified to find . . . no clause or implication discriminating against colored people nor prohibiting them from purchasing and occupying box seats at the race track."[43]

The governor's office also examined the contract and reported that no such clause discriminating against blacks existed. Replying to a letter on the matter sent by the Reverend Mr. Bradby to the governor, the governor's executive secretary wrote, on behalf of the governor who was absent at the time:

> I am sure from the Governor's attitude both past and present that he would never tolerate a contract which contained a clause providing for racial discrimination. Should you come to the Governor's office I am sure that I could convince you that the Governor is not inclined to discriminate between . . . races, religions or nationalities. In this office under the employ of the state and directly responsible to the Governor are persons of your race . . . along with other groups occupying places and positions on the basis of equality.

The Executive Secretary assured the black leader that if the Governor had been there he would have joined "in an expression of regret that the incident . . . occurred." He then informed Reverend Bradby that he would send him a copy of his complaint as well as a copy of his reply to the Racing Commission.[44]

The governor's office found itself in the unhappy position of opposing a social norm approved by the vast majority of whites at the time. To many whites, blacks were moving too fast, threatening the comfortable racial status quo, challenging the rights of whites to determine the racial characteristics of their environments. Many white-dominated institutions, however, remained on the side of the racial status quo.

In 1926, the Detroit public schools maintained a general policy of segregated swimming for black and white students. Wayne University found it necessary in the late 1930s to rent a hotel swimming pool a block away to accommodate its black students, a policy which it had probably been following for some time. The university worked hard at discouraging blacks from taking courses in physical education, but when black students insisted, they had to swim at the Brewster Street Community Center pool in a black neighborhood located over a mile from the university.[45]

Interracial swimming was most common in the public swimming pools provided by the Department of Recreation. On occasion, racial conflicts did occur, such as in February 1926, when blacks entered the Kronk Community Center pool against the wishes of whites. But such conflicts, according to one observer, rarely occurred when blacks "were decidedly in the majority,"[46] suggesting perhaps that such conflicts occurred more often when whites felt they had the numbers to reinforce the racial status quo. Even more to the point, blacks seemed much more willing than whites to accept interracial settings.

The sanctified domain of medical practice played its part in Detroit's history of institutional racism. Between 1915 and 1945, many white hospitals in Detroit discriminated against both black patients and black doctors, forcing the latter to develop their own independent black hospitals as early as 1917. In 1926, no white hospital in Detroit employed black physicians on its in-patient or out-patient staff. Some, however, did allow black physicians to treat their patients in their facilities, while others flatly refused to do so. At this time few if any black nurses could be found on the staffs of white hospitals, and only one black intern was reported working in a white hospital. At least five white hospitals maintained some degree of racial segregation of black and white patients.[47]

This policy persisted throughout the 1930s, 1940s, and 1950s. By the early 1950s a local black newspaper reported that it "is hard to say just how many beds are available to Negro patients in Detroit. There are almost as many policies for handling Negro patients as there are hospitals." Only black hospitals, the newspaper reported, "will admit Negroes at any time under any circumstances."[48]

A black physician reported in the 1920s that on many occasions when he had called municipal hospitals to have patients admitted, hospital officials had enquired as to the patient's race. If the patient was black, the hospital officials either claimed they had no vacant beds or had only a limited number of beds set aside for blacks. Considerable controversy surrounded such allegations. One of the few black physicians employed in the city hospitals explained that, since there were few hospitals besides Receiving Hospital for black charity patients, black patients' physicians were often informed that a particular hospital at a particular time had no vacant beds for any more black charity patients. In such cases, the black physician further explained, the physician often jumped to the conclusion that the hospital was discriminating against his patient because of his race.[49]

According to the superintendent of Receiving Hospital in 1926, the institution did not have a policy for segregating black and white patients. But he admitted to shifting patients around whenever he received a great number of complaints from white patients, most of which came from northern whites.[50]

With few exceptions, white hospitals in Detroit, both public and private, practiced various degrees of institutional racism. Both Herman Kiefer Hospital and Receiving Hospital discriminated against blacks in employment. In 1926, Herman Kiefer Hospital had an all white staff, and little had changed by 1937. Receiving Hospital was no different. Over ten years after a black physician reported that white hospital officials routinely requested information on the race of prospective patients, the practice had not stopped. As the number of black hospitals grew in the 1930s, white hospital officials offered the dubious courtesy of arranging for beds in a private black hospital for black patients they could not or would not accommodate.[51]

Some white hospitals' racial practices defied the most basic principles of human conduct. During the spring of 1938, Women's Hospital refused to accept a seriously injured man when they discovered he was black. The man had been brutally beaten by white police officers and suffered a broken spine, fractured legs, and other internal injuries. Not knowing his race, the hospital had agreed to accept him, but upon his arrival, rejected him. The police had to be called to remove him from the hospital room where he had been placed. The injured man did not receive medical care until an hour and forty-five minutes later. This case of shameless racism infuriated the local NAACP, which demanded an investigation of conditions at Women's Hospital and pointed out that it received money from the county to treat all patients regardless of race.[52] NAACP protests notwithstanding, the majority of white hospitals in Detroit took their time changing their racial practices.

KEEPING BLACKS OUT OF WHITE NEIGHBORHOODS

Racial discrimination in housing and employment plagued the black community at every turn. Blacks could survive quite easily without eating in white restaurants or sitting where they pleased in white theaters. Racism in white hospitals created difficulties but at least black hospitals lessened the impact. But racial discrimination in housing and employment struck at the roots of the struggling black community.

As already mentioned, black southern immigrants faced horrendous housing and employment conditions, which greatly affected their health. These conditions worsened over the years as racist whites developed and perfected various institutional and legal arrangements to contain the expanding black population within "acceptable" racial boundaries. Nowhere were these racial boundaries more important to racists than in the area of housing and employment. And of the two areas, housing was the most sacred to those whites bent on maintaining the racial status quo.

The black population increase during World War I placed tremendous pressure upon an already inadequate supply of housing, which eventually generated an impetus for racial segregation in housing. As one scholar explained: "It is presumably no accident, therefore, that we find segregation practices with their concomitants becoming more entrenched with the passage of time, and with the continued growth of Negro population."[53]

Housing restrictions against blacks in Detroit were not apparent until 1910; they quickly increased during the boom years of subdivision building in the 1920s. These racial practices gained wide support. After the 1923 Michigan Supreme Court ruling that supported restrictive covenants,[54] racist whites had the full weight of the law behind them to support their racial attitudes and practices.

Conflict was inevitable. Blacks in the rising middle and upper classes who wanted to rent and buy houses outside poverty stricken ghettos had to face the full fury of white resistance.

In June of 1925, Dr. Alex L. Turner bought a nice expensive brick house on the northwest side of Detroit in the all-white Grand River Avenue district. Like many other black professionals, Turner and his family saw this move as a long awaited opportunity to escape the congested living conditions of the black ghettos. The Turner family had been in their new house only a few hours when they were forced to leave by a crowd of whites 5,000 strong, hooting and throwing stones at the house. White men, women, and children participated in this shameless demonstration until the Turners left under police guard. Even as the family were leaving, the white crowd heaped further abuse upon them by stoning their car, breaking the glass and slightly injuring Dr. Turner. He later agreed to sell the house to a group of whites.[55]

In less than a month, a similar incident occurred on Stoepel Avenue in the same general area, resulting in the wounding of a white youth. Once again, a large crowd of whites numbering close to 4,000 gathered in the vicinity of a house recently purchased by a black family. The crowd choked the streets for seven blocks shouting, jeering, and throwing rocks, bricks, or anything they could find at the house. A white woman living next door to the house went so far as to purchase five tons of coke to supply the crowd with ammunition. By the time the crowd had thrown all the coke at the house, they had shattered almost every window in the house. Finally, the blacks opened fire on the mob, hitting a white youth twice in the thigh. All available police in the area rushed to the scene and arrested the five blacks in the house, including a husband and wife, their two teenaged boys and another adult male. Fifty policemen were stationed to guard the house. After the arrest, large placards were placed on telephone posts in the area announcing a mass meeting of members and friends of the Ku Klux Klan. Large crowds of whites gathered around the placards discussing the meeting.[56]

Although few in number and fully aware of white resistance, professional blacks continued to exercise their right to purchase homes in whatever area they could afford. Vollington A. Bristol, a black undertaker, purchased a home on American and Tireman Avenues, a location considered by police and newspaper reporters as one of the "storm centers." He paid for his boldness by having to suffer through several successive nights of demonstrations by whites. White resistance to blacks moving into the area became so intense that the police prepared an armored car for service in the "storm centers."[57]

Several days after the shooting on Stoepel Avenue, Mayor John W. Smith pleaded with citizens to stop rioting. In an open letter to the police commissioner, Smith blamed the violence on the KKK and asked the commissioner to enforce laws against rioters. "The police department can have but one duty in connection with all such incidents—that is to use endeavors to prevent the destruction of life and property. I trust that every police officer will be unremitting in his efforts. The law recognizes no distinction in color or race." Smith understood how racial problems over housing effected other cities as well. "The condition which faces Detroit is one which faced Washington, East St. Louis, Chicago, and other large cities. The result in those cities was one that Detroit must avoid if possible. A single fatal riot would injure this city beyond remedy." While he argued that "the avoidance of further disorder belongs to the good sense of the leaders of thought in both white and colored races," one of his recommendations for solving the racial conflict over housing asked blacks to help preserve the peace of the community by forgoing some of their liberties. This could be done if blacks avoided moving into white neighborhoods where such action would cause conflict. As if he had not heaped enough of a burden of responsibility upon blacks, he then proceeded to denigrate and misrepresent the motives of those blacks who might choose not to forgo their liberty to purchase homes in whatever area they desired: "I believe that any colored person who endangers life and property to gratify his personal pride possesses a murderous pride and is an enemy of his own race."[58]

Dr. Henry O. Sweet, a young black dentist, and his wife were not about to give up their hard-earned liberties to placate either the mayor or hostile whites. Sweet was born in Orlando, Florida, and graduated from two of the best black schools in America, Wilberforce and Howard Universities. He received his M.D. from the latter institution. In 1921, he joined the wave of young black professionals setting up business in the expanding black community. A year later he married Gladys Mitchell, a daughter of a small black elite family living in a white neighborhood. In 1924 they

traveled to Europe, where Dr. Sweet studied radiology in Paris and pedi-
atrics and gynecology in Vienna. In Paris the young couple was blessed
with a baby girl but cursed by the long shadow of American racism: The
American Hospital in the city would not admit Mrs. Sweet for delivery
of her baby because of her race. But the Sweets were still on top of the
world when they returned to America and the Motor City.[59]

What happened next in the lives of this young black couple had tremendous consequences for black communities all over America. In early
September, the Sweets decided to follow the path of other upwardly mobile
black professionals and move into a nice house, which just happened to
be in a white neighborhood. Well aware of the white violence against
blacks in other white neighborhoods, Dr. Sweet prepared himself for what
he and his wife undoubtedly hoped would not occur but which unfortunately did occur. He provided a gun to each of the ten persons who
accompanied him to his new home. In short, he prepared himself to protect
his home.[60]

As soon as the word got out that a black family had moved into the
neighborhood, crowds of whites gathered around. Soon rocks and stones
were hitting the house and breaking windows. Shots rang out from the
house, and one white man was dead and another wounded. The police
arrived and arrested all ten blacks in the house. At the police station, a
white officer asked Dr. Sweet and Mrs. Sweet separately why they had
moved into a white neighborhood where they were not wanted. Mrs. Sweet
replied, "I think it is my perfect right to move where I please". The Sweets
and the other occupants of the house were charged with murder.[61]

The Sweet trial put black Detroit on the map and raised the social
consciousness of blacks all over America. Nothing up to this time had so
galvanized the black community in Detroit as did this tragic event. The
NAACP asked Clarence Darrow, then the best criminal lawyer in America,
to take the case. He accepted the case because, as he put it: "There is a
principle involved. These colored people are entitled to a fair shake. . . .
I have a deep-felt interest in the colored race and hope for an improvement
in their condition." Darrow firmly believed that white racism was a force
that had to be dealt with in arguing the case: "Dr. Sweet and the other
defendants are in jail, not because they have committed a crime, but because
they are Negroes and dared to defend their homes and their lives against
a mob." He also understood the historical significance of the trial for black
civil rights. The Sweets, he continued, "are in the forefront of the battle
being waged for all Negroes in America and, in the larger sense they are
fighting for justice and fair play for all Americans".[62]

At the same time that James Weldon Johnson, secretary of the NAACP,
announced that Clarence Darrow would assume the role of chief counsel
in the Sweet case, he also explained the significance of the case for all
blacks in America. "The Detroit case involves the . . . most dangerous phase
of segregation. The NAACP has fought and won segregation by ordinance

or law. We shall very soon argue in the Supreme Court the question of segregation by private agreement among white property owners. We are now facing in Detroit, segregation by mob violence." The NAACP saw the Sweet case in Detroit as key to their overall strategy to combat racial segregation, because, as Johnson argued: "If in the Detroit case the Negro is not upheld in the right to defend his home against eviction by a riotous mob, no decent Negro home anywhere in the United States will be secured."[63]

Almost overnight, the ten black defendants in the Sweet murder trial became a cause célèbre in black communities throughout the country. Major black newspapers carried detailed accounts of the proceedings. After the first trial, which ended in a mistrial, the Sweets, freed on bail, visited various cities, including New York and Baltimore, where they discussed their experiences. The NAACP started a Defense Fund for the Sweets, imploring blacks throughout the country to rally around the Sweets because of its importance to the larger struggle against racial segregation. The Messenger magazine reinforced the NAACP's plea for funds to defend the Sweets: "The NAACP has gone to bat for the defense and preservation of a great principle, the right of a man, regardless of his race, creed, color, or nationality, to be secure in his own home." Speaking specifically to blacks, the magazine stated: "Every Negro in America should rally to Dr. Sweet, because by so doing, he is rallying to himself. But the only effective kind of rallying now is the dollar. There is no use giving lip support. We can only win with power and money is a big factor in the struggle to secure power."[64]

As a result of the efforts of the NAACP, the brilliant defense of Clarence Darrow, thousands of supporters of all classes and colors, and the moral courage and guidance of the presiding Judge, Frank Murphy, the next Sweet trial ended in acquittal on May 13, 1926. Throughout the long months, the black community in Detroit never wavered in its support for the Sweets. Walter White of the NAACP national office, moved by the devotion of Detroit blacks for one of their own, wrote: "One of the most impressive sights I have ever seen was the way in which colored people in Detroit flocked to the trial." He recounted how local blacks stuck it out even at odd hours: "At half after midnight on Thanksgiving morning, when the jury was still arguing and sent out for instructions, the court was packed. At 2:10 in the morning, when the jury was sent to bed, bailiffs had to make way through the crowd for the jurymen. All Thanksgiving day, many of them going without Thanksgiving dinner in order to be on hand."[65]

After the trial, Clarence Darrow commented that he believed that the outcome would benefit both blacks and whites. The NAACP felt that the acquittal was "one of the most important steps ever taken in the struggle for justice to the Negro in the United States." Judge Frank Murphy became one of the greatest white heroes in the black community.[66]

Some saw the Sweet acquittal as a vindication of the rights of blacks to protect their property, but the vast majority of whites in Detroit continued to resist what they perceived to be a black invasion of their neighborhoods. Throughout the 1930s and 1940s, whites used every tactic at their disposal to keep blacks out of their neighborhoods. They stoned black houses, burned crosses, petitioned for injunctions to enforce racially exclusive covenants, and organized neighborhood associations, all calculated and designed to effectively keep blacks from moving into white neighborhoods.[67]

By the 1940s, white resistance to blacks moving into white neighborhoods had intensified and assumed several forms, reinforced by the courts, the Federal Housing Administration (FHA), and the Detroit Housing Commission. Some whites, working through neighborhood improvement associations, signed petitions, took blacks to court, and when all else failed, resorted to violence. In situations in which black families purchased property in white neighborhoods where restrictive covenants did not run with the land, white petitioners had no legal recourse.[68]

In March 1940, a circuit-court judge ruled against whites who had signed a restrictive covenant to bar blacks from occupying a house they had purchased. These legal setbacks, however, rarely discouraged whites determined to keep blacks out of their neighborhoods. Soon after the judge's decision, white residents began signing more petitions to prohibit the renting or selling of houses in the neighborhoods to blacks.[69]

Later that same year, white residents on the northeast side of Detroit signed petitions asking the court to oust a black family from a house because black occupancy violated certain building restrictions based upon agreements that the owners would sell to "pure caucasians only." The lawyer for the association added that black occupancy was "injurious to the value of the property."[70]

White lawyers who shared prevailing notions that blacks should be restricted to black areas could be extremely helpful in devising effective strategies to keep them out of white neighborhoods. In August of 1940, one such lawyer, Phillip H. Cale, gave a talk at the luncheon meeting of the Eastern Detroit Realty Association entitled "Benefits of an Improvement Association." Cale's main theme centered on how to "effect legal restrictions against the influx of colored residents into white communities."[71]

Using the widespread allegation that black influx into white communities lowered property values, Cale laid out a strategy for his white listeners. He urged them to form improvement associations, obtain competent legal advice regarding restrictions, and then determine the first area to be covered. "Every owner in that area," he advised, "must then be approached with a restrictive conveyance prepared by the group's legal counsel binding the owners not to sell to Negroes."[72]

Cale informed his audience that real-estate dealers "have been known to cover a district of two miles square in which the owners were not able to sell to anyone but members of the white race." But he cautioned them that such a task was too much for one man. "Organizations are essential for such work and such results," Cale pointed out. The first step is to pick a community, then "block it out by streets or subdivisions or square miles. Select the community most liable to have trouble, or better yet one in which a Negro family is already a resident. The people of that section will be in a most receptive mood."[73] He then pointed out that under the present law, racially restrictive covenants were not legal unless everyone in a subdivision signed a restrictive contract.[74] Here was white legalized racism at its worst. No wonder housing discrimination against blacks in Detroit proved so intransigent.

Keeping blacks out of white neighborhoods proved especially difficult when white sellers violated restrictive covenants by selling to blacks. In one such case in 1941, a white neighbor not only got an injunction to stop blacks from occupying a house sold to them by a white neighbor but also named the white seller's lawyer as one of the defendants.[75] Restrictive covenants in Michigan, therefore, began losing their legal weight when one white owner's right to sell or rent property was challenged by other whites desiring to keep neighborhoods all white.

In June 1941, the Michigan State Supreme Court upheld a decision of a circuit-court judge that refused to grant a temporary restraining injunction to prohibit a white man from renting his apartment to black families.[76] The walls of legalized racism began to crumble, but only because some whites' legal right to sell conflicted with other whites' legal right to exclude blacks from their neighborhoods.

Some whites did not mind if a black owned property in their neighborhoods as long as neither they nor any other black occupied the premises. For example, in August 1941 a black owner of a house in a white neighborhood rented his house to a black coworker after his white tenants moved out. A committee of white residents protested to the black owner, who informed them that he had lived in the same house and had raised his family there, moving only because the house was too small. He refused their demand to evict his black tenant. The whites then paid the black tenant a visit and told him they did not want blacks in their neighborhood. They ordered him to move or suffer the consequences. He refused and called the police.[77]

Unfortunately, in most cases the police offered little assistance in protecting the rights of blacks buying or renting houses in white neighborhoods. Blacks moving into white neighborhoods were seen as "invaders," a perception reinforced by major institutions in the city and the nation, such as the Detroit Housing Commission and the Federal Housing Administration. White policemen shared this common racist perception of the black invader and often supported or acquiesced to white violence against blacks who dared to move into white neighborhoods.

It is difficult to determine at what stage of resistance to blacks moving into their neighborhoods whites resorted to violence and at what stage the local authorities chose to intervene to restore order. In some cases restrictive covenants did not run with the land, which provided a legal loophole for blacks to purchase homes in white neighborhoods. As a result whites resorted to violence as their only alternative to keeping blacks out of their neighborhoods.

In March 1940, in a case representative of others, a black family succeeded in purchasing a home in Ferndale, a white suburb in northwest Detroit, but the family left after a Ku Klux Klan (KKK) group burned a ten-foot cross by their house. After the black family had gone, leaders of the mob gathered in front of the house broke windows.[78]

During the 1940s, Ferndale employed a range of methods to keep blacks out, including violence and a brick wall eight feet high and a half-mile long, built in 1941 to separate black and white residents in the area. The wall represented a blatant affront to blacks as well as a glaring symbol of white racism in a northern city. One of Detroit's black leaders, the Reverend Horace A. White, who was both a state representative and a member of the Detroit Housing Commission, commented: "This is the only place in the world, except under Hitlerism, where groups are being segregated in a . . . ghetto." The building of the wall "is sociologically disgraceful in these times of strain to unify the people."[79]

But whites opposed to equal treatment for blacks cared little about the disgrace of racism during war or peace. In the late summer of 1941, two hundred whites met in a Ferndale neighborhood bakery to discuss methods of keeping blacks out of their subdivision and getting rid of those already residing there. No blacks were admitted to the meeting. The methods discussed included buying out black families who had not yet moved into their houses; applying pressure on black families already living in the area; and, if they did not move, burning them out.[80]

Some blacks could have lived in white neighborhoods for years with no trouble, and then suddenly whites insisted that they move. Hostile whites warned one black woman who had lived in Ferndale for fourteen years to move to the black section of the subdivision. During the same period in the suburb of Hazel Park on the eastern border of Ferndale, the house of a black family who had resided in the area for eighteen years and whose sons had played on the Hazel Park high school football team for eleven of those years, was stoned several nights in a row by whites. Finally, after whites threw bricks through the windows, a family member fired a warning shot. The police arrived and arrested two of the ring leaders of the crowd, who were later released. One was from Ferndale. Whites had demonstrated in front of the house for four successive nights because the black family had plans to enlarge the house. The family refused to be intimidated and informed officials of the Detroit NAACP that they had no intention of moving out of the area.[81]

The NAACP accused the Hazel Park Police Department and the county sheriff's office of allowing the racial disturbance to get out of hand by lack of adequate protection for the family. The governor responded by sending Michigan State Police to Hazel Park to support the Hazel Park Police. Deputies from the county sheriff's office were also ordered into Hazel Park to protect the family.[82]

Racial conflicts over housing reached fever pitch during World War II, aggravated by the rapid increase in population growth brought on by the labor demands of Detroit's war industries. Almost overnight Detroit metamorphosed into a bustling war production center attracting tens of thousands of black and white workers to the city. Providing housing for these war workers soon became a problem of mammoth proportions. For black war workers, the housing problem seemed insoluble simply because they could live only in racially designated areas of the city. But some believed relief was in sight.

In September 1941, a temporary housing project, named Sojourner Truth after the famous black fugitive slave woman and financed by the federal government under contract to the Detroit Housing Commission, was built for black war workers and their families.[83] The project was segregated, in keeping with declared public policy of both the Federal Housing Administration (FHA) and the Detroit Housing Commission. In fact, the minutes of one of the meetings of the Housing Commission were explicit concerning this policy:

> The Detroit Housing Commission will in no way change the racial characteristics of any neighborhood in Detroit through occupancy standards of housing projects under its jurisdiction. The importance of housing war workers is recognized by [us] and every effort will be made to accomplish this task. It is [our] opinion . . . that any attempt to change the racial pattern of any area in Detroit will result in violent opposition to the housing program. This could very easily reach a point where war production efforts of this entire community could be endangered.[84]

In the 1930s, this policy of segregated public housing had been pushed down the throats of liberal blacks and whites associated with the NAACP and the Urban League who wanted to see public housing used to destroy racial segregation. One of the white fathers of the city called local black leaders together and informed them: "Either we have a segregated project, or we won't have any. So make up your minds." And they did.[85] Segregated public housing became the rule.

THE SOJOURNER TRUTH HOUSING PROJECT

The Sojourner Truth Housing Project was racially segregated. But this policy did little to allay the racial hysteria of whites who lived nearby. Before long, whites in the neighborhood in which the project was built began objecting not to the housing project but to the blacks who would be living in them. These blacks were too close for white comfort. The Reverend C. Dzink wrote the federal coordinator of Defense Housing and asked him not to allow blacks to occupy the housing project because it would mean utter ruin for many people who had mortgaged their homes to the FHA. Dzink also told the federal coordinator that black occupancy would "jeopardize the safety of many of our white girls, as no colored people live close by [and] it would [also] ruin the neighborhood."[86]

Racial demagogues rushed to fan the flames of white racial hysteria. A newly organized Fenelon–Seven Mile Road Development Association led by Joseph Buffa, a local real-estate man, protested to the Housing Commission that the housing project would destroy property values in the neighborhood. The Housing Commission refused to change its policy. Buffa and the Improvement Association then appealed to Michigan Congressman Rudolph G. Tenerowicz, who after some political dealings succeeded in getting Washington to turn the housing project over to whites.[87]

Working class ethnic whites were not the only people opposed to black war workers occupying the project. Middle-class blacks in nearby Conant Gardens also opposed the housing project and for some of the same reasons, namely, the fear of an influx of lower class black migrants. These middle-class blacks, however, changed their minds when they understood the racial purposes of the white opposition. The white opposition, according to two scholars, reflected the racial attitudes of "a generation of upwardly mobile American-born Poles . . . coming of age, [and] resentful of competing with increasing numbers of blacks in the job market and bitterly opposed to them as neighbors."[88] In 1942, a government investigator's report for the Office of War Information attempted to explain this white opposition:

> The conflict over the Sojourner Truth Housing Project illustrates the changing attitudes of the Poles toward the Negroes. Until the time when the project was to be occupied by Negroes, the Poles and Negroes lived amicably in Hamtramck on the same street and in the same house. The Poles expressed no anxiety over depreciated property values in a united neighborhood until real estate agents and the subversive groups involved in the Sojourner Truth fight gave it to them when the projects were to be opened. The second generation Poles were the first to take up the battle cry for segregation and discrimination. Like others of foreign descent in Detroit, they were beginning to fear the competition of young and status-conscious Negroes in jobs. The younger Poles are now inducing anti-Negro attitudes among the older generation and the Negroes are being forced out of Hamtramck.[89]

After the project was handed over to whites, blacks and their white allies began mobilizing to have it returned to black workers. Joined by the national offices of the NAACP and the Urban League, the local black community dug in for an aggressive campaign. Because similar situations were occurring in Buffalo, Baltimore, Indianapolis, and other places where black war workers needed housing, Lester Granger, head of the national office of the Urban League, wrote John C. Dancy, director of the Detroit Urban League, informing him they must get "as much pressure organized around the Detroit situation as possible so as to use it in correcting alarming tendencies observed on the national picture."[90]

In their efforts to have the Detroit housing project returned to black war workers, the national office of the Urban League sent telegrams to President Roosevelt, Mrs. Eleanor Roosevelt, and key governmental figures such as Charles F. Palmer, coordinator of Defense Housing, and Baird Snyder, third acting administrator of the Federal Works Agency and one of the Washington bureaucrats responsible for the change from black to white occupancy.[91]

The telegram to Snyder accused his office of "yielding under the pressure of selfish Detroit groups and reactionary congressmen that seek to bar Negro families from these homes." "We cannot believe," the telegram continued, "that a governmental agency would be guilty of so unworthy an act." The telegram to Mrs. Roosevelt, who headed an office responsible for boosting civilian morale, pointed out that the federal government's action was "impairing the morale of Negroes who [were] being called on for all-out support of a war for democracy." Granger reminded Palmer that "facts already produced by [him] show the need for more, not less, provisions for Negro defense workers." He was asked to bring the full influence of his office into the situation and warned that Detroit was then "a symbol of what may happen on a wider scale if federal officials retreat under the pressure of local prejudice and reactionary opinions." President Roosevelt was urged to use his office to correct the situation.[92]

Local black leaders began sending telegrams to President Roosevelt and Governor Van Wagoner as soon as the news of the change in occupancy hit the papers. The telegrams in part said that there was no time to raise "the color issue in the arsenal of democracy and rob Negro defense workers of homes." Later that week there was a mass meeting at the Calvary Baptist Church to rally support for a reversal of the decision.[93]

Under the leadership of a local black leader, the Reverend Charles A. Hill of Calvary Baptist Church, blacks prepared to picket the meeting of the Detroit Housing Commission. The meeting was postponed, so the pickets returned the following day. When the Commission finally met, a delegation of black leaders asked them to intervene in the situation. The Commission refused, shifting the blame to Washington. But strength was slowly building on the side of black war workers. A coalition of groups called the Sojourner Truth Citizens Committee, headed by Hill, emerged to challenge those supporting white occupancy of the project. Originally all-black, this committee soon became interracial in membership, including Jewish organizations, Protestant liberals in the Detroit Council of Churches, and trade unionists. Perhaps because most of the whites resisting black occupancy were Polish Catholics, few other Catholics became involved at this stage. However, after a riot a month later at the housing project, some white Catholics did become involved on the side of the black war worker, such as the League of Catholic Women, some faculty members at the University of Detroit and several priests. The Socialist Party also joined in and gave their support.[94]

The Sojourner Truth Citizens Committee started applying pressure by nighttime picketing of the offices of City Hall and the Detroit Housing Commission. Finally, the mayor and the common council gave in and asked the housing authorities in Washington to reverse themselves and give the housing project back to the black war workers. Realizing that they had to act fast, the Sojourner Truth Citizens Committee held an emergency mass meeting to raise money to send an interracial delegation to Washington to help convince the Federal Housing Authority. Overwhelmed by the militant blacks in the group as well as by the fact that the city fathers endorsed black occupancy, the federal housing officials rescinded their last decision and returned the housing project to blacks.[95]

Predictably outraged over this new decision of the federal authorities, whites opposing black occupancy protested at the Detroit city hall against the mayor and the common council but failed to budge them. Hearings broke up in an uproar, with the protesting group threatening to return to demand another audience. Mayor Jeffries told one angry group: "If you can work out a proposition where people can live peacefully and harmoniously, I will send taxicabs for you." The whites shouted him down.[96]

This latest demonstration by whites opposing black occupancy convinced the Sojourner Truth Citizens Committee that they should return to Washington, in case the federal authorities had second thoughts about giving the project back to blacks. Once again an interracial delegation visited the federal housing officials, who assured them that the decision would stand and that the first tenants could move in on February 28, 1942.[97]

At this stage, the racial conflict moved to a more volatile level. The night before the move-in, the KKK became involved, and 150 cheering whites burned a cross near the project. Before dawn the mob had swelled to 1,200, many of them openly armed. That morning, as the first black tenants arrived in trucks, lines of white pickets blocked their way. Tempers flared, and before long a riot broke out, with blacks and whites on opposite sides of the street throwing bricks at each other. Whites turned over the blacks' furniture vans. Police armed with tear gas and a riot car made frequent runs into the melee. Scores of people, mainly blacks, were injured by the police, who tended to side with the whites by arresting blacks. When news of the riot reached nearby black ghettos, hundreds of black youth rushed to the aid of the black tenants and fought the white mobs and the police. Finally, authorities decided to postpone the move.[98]

Later, the whites around the housing project, under the leadership of Buffa, president of the Seven Mile Improvement Association, began reorganizing their forces. On March 10, 1942, Buffa led a march of five

HELP THE **WHITE PEOPLE**

To Keep This District WHITE

MEN NEEDED

TO KEEP OUR LINES SOLID

COME TO NEVADA and FENLON

Sunday and Monday

WE NEED HELP

Don't BE YELLOW   COME OUT

We Need Every WHITE MAN

WE WANT OUR GIRLS TO WALK ON THE STREET NOT RAPED

A handbill distributed during white resistance to blacks' moving into the Sojourner Truth Housing Project in Detroit, 1942. Courtesy of the Archives of Labor and Urban Affairs, Wayne State University.

hundred whites on the project. The police broke it up with tear gas. Buffa was jailed, but later returned because of insufficient evidence, and his organization went back to picketing. Circulars passed around in the vicinity of the project said, "Help the white people to keep this district white. Men wanted to keep our line solid."[99]

Racism, however, failed to win the day. The Congress of Industrial Organizations (CIO) unions, particularly the United Auto Workers (UAW), increased their support for black occupancy of the project. White trade unionists picketed city hall alongside the blacks. The UAW president, R. J. Thomas, backed by the International Executive Board, took a public stand on behalf of the blacks. Polish union members in the vicinity of the housing project denounced his stand, but he and the UAW held firm. Even the Catholics among the UAW leadership "openly supported blacks in the housing controversy."[100] Not all Poles shared the racist sentiments of the mostly Polish group that opposed black occupancy. At a mass meeting on March 28, 1942, the Polish Women's Division of the International Workers Order made a twenty-five dollar donation toward success of the fight for black occupancy of the project. Two Polish women gave short talks assuring the audience that progressive groups throughout the country were backing the black war workers' occupancy of the Sojourner Truth Housing Project.[101]

Finally, on April 29, 1942, as a result of the efforts of a coalition of black organizations, prominent white Catholic and Protestant clergymen, the UAW-CIO leadership, and the black press, and due to the pressing demands of the war, black families began moving into the housing project. Twelve hundred state homeguard troops, three hundred state police, and eight hundred Detroit police escorted them to the housing project. The troops remained on guard in the neighborhood for several weeks, and there was no further violence in the area.[102]

Four years later, a picture of black and white children playing together in a field in Sojourner Truth Housing Project appeared in *Collier's,* a national magazine. Sadly, the photo was in an article entitled "Housing, Detroit's Time Bomb."[103]

RACISM IN THE JOB MARKET

Employment was the other battlefield in which racist whites waged a relentless struggle to maintain the racial status quo. In America, as elsewhere, work has always determined social status, and this is the case even more in interracial relations. The industrial demand for black labor during World War I altered somewhat the traditional relations between blacks and whites in the Detroit work force by incorporating southern blacks into the industrial work force. By any measure, this represented significant occupational upward mobility.

Throughout the 1920s, however, black industrial workers could advance only within a predetermined racial occupational structure. Most white employers were determined to keep black workers confined to the worst jobs.[104] The message was clear. Race, not merit, would determine the allocation of jobs in the industrial work force. To some extent, Henry Ford proved an exception to this rule, since black workers in his plants tended to be more widely distributed throughout various occupations. But then, too, Ford had his own hidden agenda, which will be explained later.

Both white bosses and white workers had something to gain from practicing employment discrimination against blacks. For example, as discussed earlier, productivity could be greatly increased by pitting one racial group against another.[105] Generating racial conflicts between two racial groups already competing over housing, schools, and recreational facilities proved profitable for shortsighted bosses who cared little for interracial harmony. To them, racism and racial conflicts were destined by the natural order of things. Most white workers, on the other hand, desired to be protected from competing with black workers for the choice jobs. Racism kept black workers out of jobs traditionally preserved for white workers without obligating white workers to compete on the basis of merit. White workers, therefore, needed racism to protect and maintain their edge over black workers. Several cases demonstrate how such employment discrimination affected black workers.

During the 1930s and 1940s, whites bent on maintaining the racial status quo in the labor market used every means at their disposal to achieve their malevolent ends. Although blacks suffered much higher rates of unemployment than white workers during the Depression, some white businesses fired their black workers and replaced them with white workers rather than pay blacks higher wages as dictated by the industrial codes initiated by the New Deal planners.[106]

As long as black workers received low wages for certain jobs that white employers and employees considered "nigger work," their jobs remained secure. But as soon as jobs became scarce and some employers increased the wages in the "nigger jobs," to conform to the industrial codes, black labor lost its value as a cheap commodity. And white employers fired black workers in Detroit and other cities around the country.[107]

In December 1933, seventeen black workers of the Webster Hall Hotel in Detroit got "the boot" in just this fashion, as soon as the hotel began operating under the new code. Under the new code the black women's wages of fifty dollars a month were raised to sixty-five dollars. Other black workers received comparable raises, as well as a reduction of hours. These changes altered traditional racial work patterns where blacks were expected to work long hours for low wages. So the white manager of the hotel fired the black workers and hired white workers.[108]

The summer before this, the manager of a Sears & Roebuck store had fired three black workers from the tire and battery department; all three workers had worked for the company for many years and had a record of efficiency. The manager gave their jobs to white workers, because white customers demanded that they be fired. Two black janitors were retained.[109] The lesson in this case is key. The store's white customers evidently felt that black workers should be confined to janitorial work and that any job above such work should be reserved for whites only. An editorial in the local black press expressed concern for this racist tendency and suggested what blacks should do about it:

> There are many citizens . . . who are so blinded by race prejudice and the clan (KKK) spirit, that they seem to feel that Negroes need no consideration

or sympathy in the present crisis, although we as a group are at the base of [the] economic pyramid where the pinch of the depression is felt first with the keenest severity. There are certain individuals and agencies who for some time have been active in their efforts to influence employers in Detroit and elsewhere to fire Negro workers and hire white employees, often alien, in their places. We grant that white firms have a legal right to dismiss colored workers in this way, if they so desire, but we question their moral right to take such an unjust course. . . . Public sentiment is indeed a mighty force, but it can be made to work for us, as well as against us. When public sentiment among our people is strengthened to the point that we refuse to spend our money with business concerns that discriminate against us unjustly, then we shall receive a much greater measure of justice and consideration than we receive at the present time.[110]

The editorial also reminded its black readers that "colored citizens spend large sums of money with the Sears & Roebuck stores in Detroit."[111]

Discriminatory firings of blacks and their replacement by whites represented just the tip of the iceberg of employment discrimination. Black workers were practically nonexistent in city and county jobs. In 1937, blacks made up 7.6 percent of the total population of Detroit yet held less than one-half of one percent of the jobs supported by public taxes. Of a total number of 3,734 policemen, only 35 were black. The Detroit Fire Department employed 1,748 firemen, but no blacks. The Water Board employed more than 1,000 people, but no blacks. The Detroit Board of Education (DBE) employed 10,183 people, but only 72 of them were black. The Detroit Street Railway's labor force numbered 4,579, but only 59 were black. The two major public hospitals, Receiving and Herman Kiefer, had a combined work force of 1,427, yet they employed a total of only five blacks. The city employed only four black nurses out of a total nursing staff of 362. The public libraries had a staff of 551, of which only three were black.[112]

According to figures calculated by Snow Grigsby in 1937, if blacks had received 7 percent of the employment in the police and fire departments, Receiving and Herman Kiefer hospitals, the board of education, and the public libraries, they would have earned a grand total of $20,175,793.50 between 1923 and 1933 (see table 8).

In short, employment discrimination in just six areas of public employment in four years cost the black community in Detroit over twenty million dollars. One can only imagine how much more the black community lost as a result of the combined racial discrimination of the public and private sectors. Extending the period to cover the years of this study, 1915–1945, the amount of the loss would climb much higher.

The Detroit Board of Education (DBE) was one of the city departments that discriminated against blacks in a major way, followed by the fire and police departments. In 1937, the DBE allowed black teachers to teach in or be transferred to only 13 of 252 public schools. White teachers, however,

Table 8

Total Wages Blacks Would Have Received Had They Received a
Seven Percent Share of Employment in City Departments, 1923–1933

Police Department		$6,516,969.80
Board of Education		9,862,041.60
Receiving Hospital		475,358.90
Herman Kiefer Hospital		425,605.00
Library Department		439,886.60
Fire Department		2,455,931.60
	Total	$20,175,793.50

Source: Snow Grigsby, *White Hypocrisy and Black Lethargy* (Detroit, Michigan: Snow F. Grigsby, 1937) p. 17.

had the option of being placed or transferred into any of the 252 schools. In some sections of the city where blacks comprised from 50 to 98 percent of the total school enrollment, the teachers were all white.[113]

Black teachers not only were limited in their choice of where they could teach, they also had to jump through hoops for promotion. In response to some black teachers who requested promotions, the superintendent of schools informed them that once they received their Master's Degrees they would then be promoted to the high school and other divisions. But in 1936 the school superintendent was presented with a list of 36 blacks holding the Master's and Ph.D. degrees. He then introduced other criteria for promotion, such as individual merit and the order of their names on the employee roster.[114] These tactics were not new and would be employed constantly by the whites who were intent on confining blacks to traditional jobs.

Of all the city departments, the fire department appeared to be the most resistant to changing its policy of racial exclusion. In 1934, the local black newspaper lamented the fact that the Detroit Fire Department had no black firemen, while other cities, "notably New York, . . . Chicago, Kansas City, and Philadelphia," employed a fair proportion of Negro firemen who were making a success of the job of firefighting. "Colored firemen," the paper exclaimed, "when given a fair chance, soon become firefighters of the most efficient and loyal type, for as a race, we are forced every day of our lives to fight the hellish fires of race prejudice and injustice."[115]

Four years later, after a long and bitter struggle by black citizens led by a local black protest group, the Detroit Civic Rights Committee and its aggressive chairman, Snow Grigsby (See chapter 7), Mayor Richard W. Reading issued an order to the Civil Service Commission to appoint the top ten applicants, of whom three were black, to the fire department.[116]

But what to many contemporary observers appeared to be a happy ending to a tragic story of senseless and shameful discrimination only opened another chapter of white racist resistance to black occupational advancement.

This chapter opened in August 1938 as two of the newly appointed black firemen reported for work at a fire station located on the southwest side of Detroit. These two black firemen, Marvin White and Marcellus Taylor, had passed rigid civil-service examinations with high honors and had successfully completed the equally rigorous firemen's training school. Despite their qualifications, however, 1,800 racist whites in the mostly-Polish area of the fire station signed and presented a petition to the fire commission asking them not to assign the black firemen to the stations in their neighborhood. The petitioners claimed that the presence of black firemen in white neighborhoods was a violation of particular restrictive residential clauses in their land contracts.[117]

The fire commission rejected their request, so the petitioners went to the common council, who passed the buck to the mayor, who in turn stood firm on his decision and informed the white petitioners that the two black firemen had passed the required rigid civil-service tests and that if they (the white petitioners) felt that the assignment of black firemen to a station in their neighborhood violated their civil rights, then they should take the issue to court.[118]

Frustrated by the failure of their petition to have the black firemen reassigned, some whites decided to block the entrance to the fire station to prevent the black firemen from reporting for duty. When one of the black firemen arrived for his first day at work, he found a barricade of white women, with close to a hundred white men on their flanks, barring his way. The white men warned him not to touch the white women. The black fireman remained cool while police officers attempted to control the menacing crowd. The police soon restored order, and the black fireman went to work. The other black fireman entered the fire house later. Several days after the incident, the captain of the fire station reported that the black firemen were performing satisfactory service and getting along well with their white coworkers.[119]

These congratulatory comments proved premature. The black and white firemen might have been "getting along," but it was happening within a social setting still resistant to racial change. A fire station was a home away from home, where firemen worked, ate, played, and slept together. The introduction of black firemen into this type of intimate living environment created difficult problems for interracial adjustment. The first problem that had to be faced by the new black firemen was the refusal of the local firemen's union to admit them into the union, solely because of their race. This sent an obvious signal to white firemen and the white public that the union supported racial segregation. Next, the fire station established a separate washroom for the two black firemen. Three years later in 1941, black firemen at this fire station had separate living quarters and toilet facilities. The fire department explained that racial discrimination was a social problem which would "work itself out." The mayor agreed. But it would be many decades before the problem worked itself out.[120]

The spirit of patriotism during World War II had little effect upon white racism within the labor market. In fact, many white employers and employees saw no contradiction in fighting a war against Nazism abroad and maintaining racial segregation at home. When the government launched the defense program in 1939, black workers had known high unemployment for some time. An expert in black labor concluded that black workers were losing ground. Between 1910 and 1930 the proportion of blacks in manufacturing nationally had increased from 6.2 percent to 7.3 percent. By 1940 it had declined to a new low, 5.1 percent.[121]

Even before America entered World War II, black workers appeared to be expendable in war production because of their traditional restriction to unskilled and semiskilled occupations. Defense training appeared to be the answer for blacks; it was an opportunity to pick up the necessary skills to obtain a good-paying defense job. But blacks were either discouraged or barred from this training.[122]

In Detroit, defense training got off to an early and successful start. Many instances of discrimination existed during the earlier stages of the program. But the militant leadership of the black community turned the tide (See chapter 7). As a result, a black employee of the board of education was soon appointed as coordinator of defense training for blacks; with the support of the black community, he opened many types of defense training to black workers. By the summer of 1941, blacks made up close to a quarter of the total enrollment in the pre-employment training.[123]

Much of the success of this program in the early stages of enrollment and training was due to the concern of people like John C. Dancy, who, along with other concerned citizens, held a statewide conference in October 1940 on the employment problems of blacks. This conference reported disproportionate unemployment among blacks, longer duration of unemployment for blacks than for whites, more limited vocational preparation for black youth than for white youth, apprenticeships being closed to black youth, except at the Henry Ford Trade School, and discrimination in defense-training selection on the theory that employers would not hire blacks even after they had been trained.[124]

The conference recommended that industry, public utilities, department stores, chain stores and "other employing units be stimulated and encouraged to develop further employment opportunities for qualified Negroes." Other recommendations included: that all community groups and community workers be encouraged to remold public opinion "as it affects employment, health, education, and other factors concerning Negro workers"; that all unions should give thorough consideration to admitting qualified black workers to full membership; that increased and equitable participation be granted to all qualified blacks in the administration of municipal, county, state, and federal services; and that local National

Defense Councils and related cooperating agencies provide more adequate and realistic vocational preparation and guidance for all workers, with particular study and attention to the vocational problems of black youth. Of obvious importance was a recommendation that private enterprise and public agencies direct their attention to more adequate low-cost housing developments for blacks, as well as for other groups. Lastly, they recommended that efforts be made to provide more adequate medical and dental care for low-income groups, including blacks.[125]

These recommendations and the availability of defense training for blacks were mere straws in the wind. If anything, the forces of racism were beginning to entrench themselves. Many white employers and workers alike were not the least bit interested in the plight of black workers or, for that matter, in meeting war production needs if it meant employing blacks in traditionally white jobs. Patriotism, to many white workers, certainly did not mean abandoning their white skin privileges. As one white worker said during a walkout at the Packard plant in Detroit, protesting the upgrading of three black workers, "I'd rather see Hitler and Hirohito win than work next to a nigger."[126]

Most employers held similar thoughts. Federal agencies, such as the War Manpower Commission (WMC),[127] had their hands full trying to meet war production, because many employers simply refused to use black workers. More than once this agency reported confidential findings such as the following:

> Discrimination against Negroes continues to restrict the available unskilled labor supply. . . . Few firms expect to increase their employment of nonwhites significantly unless forced to by greatly increased labor stringencies or by compulsory labor market controls. All available information shows that employer discrimination is the major cause of low utilization of Negro workers.[128]

Since defense training undermined many employers' major excuse that blacks were unqualified, some employers permitted black workers to take dexterity tests but then refused to hire those who passed. This led to both the hiring of substandard white workers and labor shortages.[129]

In 1942 in Detroit, the WMC reported a rapidly shrinking supply of labor and predicted a shortage of almost 100,000 workers by the spring of the next year. Because of the continuing need for skilled workers in all the war industries and the complete absence of any such supply, it became necessary to break down jobs into smaller components in the metal working machinery industry.[130]

The industry had several alternatives: pooling labor and/or relaxing the racial barriers against black workers. Industry officials considered the latter alternative to be an "important method of increasing the effective utilization of local labor." As a result, the WMC reported that "to the extent that Negro labor is not fully utilized, [white] in-migration will have to be increased, with consequent aggravation of housing shortages and over-crowding of other facilities."[131] White employers had a choice. They could hire trained black workers already in Detroit or bring in more white workers and risk other kinds of social problems. Clearly, the cost of maintaining racism, particularly in a time of national crisis, was going up.

Blacks had no trouble finding defense jobs where the work was too hot, dirty, and dangerous for white workers. For example, in the cotton textile industry, the WMC reported that black workers were hired in those plants where the manufacturing of rubberized fabrics was detrimental to white workers' health.[132] The undesirability of certain jobs, then, could ironically work in the black workers' favor.

In 1944, the shortage of common labor created a bottleneck in the forge and foundry industries, having far-reaching effects on the production of major war items such as tanks, trucks, and ducks. Although the jobs represented only one percent of the country's production, they affected 50 percent of the total war production. The reasons for the shortage were simple: "The work [was] hot, much of it [was] of a heavy nature, and conditions [were] none too attractive at best."[133]

Men would stay a few days and quit. At a war production board meeting in Detroit in 1944, the official in charge seriously discussed the employment of Italian prisoners-of-war and Mexicans as possible solutions to the problem. Only anticipated problems with the Mexican government and the U.S. Secretary of State forced them to consider black workers. Reluctantly, the officials decided that "in view of all the difficulties, the only way still open [was] to bring up more Negroes from the South." This would, the report pointed out, increase the already large black population in Detroit and Muskegon, causing local repercussions, including the resistance of local white communities, probably postwar unemployment problems, and the need for additional housing, etc. They concluded that "any results from a move in this direction would be dubious."[134]

As much as they wanted to dismiss it, the demands of the war forced government and private officials to come to grips with racism and its effects. Only the exigencies of war forced them to admit that the price of racism could be high indeed. Notwithstanding, many of them persisted in their stand.

Thus, while the nation prepared for war production and while defense contractors clamored for more skilled men, skilled black workers were rejected at the gates of many plants. "They were turned away almost to a man," one observer noted. When employers chose not to be subtle they simply said, "We can't use skilled Negroes." Skilled black workers in Hartford, Chicago, Cleveland, Camden, Pittsburgh, Newport News, Houston, Los Angeles, and Detroit were "walking the streets while the communities talked of extreme shortages of skilled workers."[135] Plants continued to train white recruits with backgrounds similar to black applicants while consistently barring local black workers.[136]

In 1943, this problem prompted a writer to say: "That a nation at war would delay the use of its total manpower resources for three years is the most striking instance of the tenacity with which America has clung to its established color caste system in occupations."[137]

Black workers and their supporters responded to this entrenchment of racism against black workers by staging massive protests all over the country that were geared toward all levels of government. In January 1941, an administrator of the Federal Work Administration issued a ruling banning racial discrimination in the employment of workers on defense housing projects. A couple of weeks later, the NAACP sponsored mass meetings in 24 states to protest discrimination against black workers in defense jobs. In March, the National Urban League presented a one-hour radio program over CBS featuring prominent persons in various fields of activity who spoke against discrimination. The next month, a six-point program for the greater employment of black labor in industrial phases of national defense was submitted to the United States Office of Production Management (OPM) by the Committee on Participation of Negroes in the National Defense Program. Sidney Hillman, the associate director and veteran labor leader, who was devoted to the integration of blacks into the national defense program, created a new section in the OPM. This new section was headed up by a black economist named Robert C. Weaver. In June, President Roosevelt, responding to the earlier threats of A. Phillip Randolph to lead a mass march on Washington, directed the OPM to act immediately toward ending nationwide discrimination against blacks in defense industries. And after a meeting with leaders of the March-on-Washington Committee, he issued an executive order prohibiting discrimination in government and defense industries.[138] Black workers and their allies had won the first battle, but the war was far from over, and one of the major battlefields was to be Detroit.

The plight of black workers in Detroit was certainly alleviated by the issuing of the executive order, but they still could not rest assured that everything would now fall into place. Racial occupational patterns had been well established in policy, practice, and the public mind since the 1920s. Although many automobile plants had hired black skilled and semiskilled production workers during the 1920s, the majority of black workers at the outbreak of World War II were still concentrated in foundries, general labor, and janitorial assignments. The Ford Motor Company, for all its resistance to unionism, was the one outstanding exception.[139]

In 1941, the Ford Motor Company employed 11,000 black workers, who made up over 12 percent of the total number of Ford workers. Yet even with their use of blacks in production and highly skilled jobs, the majority of black workers remained concentrated in the foundry, which reflected the general racial pattern in the auto industry. The Chrysler Motor Corporation hired about 1,850 black workers in the spring of 1941; this number was 2.5 percent of its total work force. Close to 1,400 of these black workers were employed as foundry workers and janitors. The Packard Corporation was second to Ford, employing 10,000 black workers, who constituted 11 percent of their total labor supply. Most of these were also in the foundry. At the Hudson Motor Car Company in 1941, only about 225 unskilled black workers were employed among the estimated 12,200. The companies which supplied parts and accessories to the major automobile manufacturers followed the above occupational pattern.[140]

In 1941, the Murray Corporation of America had 350 black workers, making up 5 percent of the total labor supply. They were used as production assemblers, welders, press operators, janitors, and laborers. Kelsey Hayes Wheel Company employed close to 350 black workers, most of whom were in the foundry. Black workers at the Briggs Manufacturing Company in 1941 constituted 7 percent of the 22,000 workers employed; they were material handlers and laborers. Vicker, Inc., employed 80 to 90 black janitors and stock handlers out of a work force of 3,000. And Aeronautical Products, Inc., boasted one black machine cleaner in a labor force of 450 workers.[141]

The occupational pattern of black industrial workers in the above industries exposed them to mass layoffs during the conversion of civilian production to war production. Many of these black workers had barely gained a foothold in peacetime industry before war production threatened to undo much of the progress over the preceding few years. Converted wartime industry by its very nature posed serious problems for black workers, which were complicated by racism. Its highly mechanized production required new skills and a larger proportion of trained workers than peacetime industry.

Wartime industry also required more manpower in the traditionally white jobs. Since more than 50 percent of the black workers in the peacetime industry worked in automobile foundries, which were scheduled to be closed down or used on a limited basis, black, as well as white foundry workers, would have to be absorbed into general war production jobs or else be unemployed. Black workers stood in danger not only of losing their jobs but, if they kept them or obtained others, of being paid lower wages. Wartime labor shortages developed mainly in occupations in which black workers had been excluded, such as the assembly line, and where the opposition to black infiltration was the most violent and uncompromising. The handwriting was certainly on the wall: Black workers could survive conversion and remain employed only if they could obtain skilled and semiskilled jobs.[142] This meant upgrading black workers into traditionally white occupations, which was obviously threatening to white workers.

Black workers were understandably upset. A writer in the local press voiced their sentiments when he said:

Negroes are facing an extremely dangerous situation in the automobile industry. . . . The change from civilian production . . . to production of tanks and airplanes . . . involves laying off 45,000 civilian[s] . . . within the next ninety days and there are only 7,500 new jobs open in defense production. Of course, you can imagine that there is going to be some scramble to see who gets them.[143]

The union would have to get into the act, and fast. "If the union would adopt a policy of insisting that men be transferred on the basis of seniority," the writer commented, "it would keep Negroes from being squeezed entirely out of the industry."[144] As we shall see, the seniority question opened the proverbial can of worms.

A group of black workers were well aware of the problems associated with conversion and knew what had to be done. They prepared to fight for jobs. They formed a committee and later broadened it to include all black automobile workers in Detroit. This committee established another committee on September 15, 1941, to meet with the local union officials to discuss conversion and seniority. Feeling they had met with little or no success, they went to Chicago, where the International Executive Board of the UAW was meeting. After a two-hour conference, they made two demands: that a system of transferring eligible black workers, based on seniority, be immediately put into effect; and that a well-planned educational program to bring about unity of all groups in the union be established to forestall the repercussions which might follow within the union when blacks were transferred to airplane production machine shops, where they had not been previously employed. After three hours or more of "buckpassing" and evasion of issues, the international officers came out with a rather strong resolution condemning discrimination and establishing a committee composed of six black workers: Walter Hardin, John Conyers, Al Johnson, William Bowman, Oscar Noble, and Leon Bates, along with four members of the international board.[145]

The resolution and the new committee notwithstanding, the international board did not fully adopt the methods needed to resolve the problem. When U.S. Office of Production Management (OPM) officials asked the president of the UAW how far he wanted to go on black workers' transferals to defense production, he answered he did not know.[146]

The union president and the board found themselves in a tough situation, generated by the confusion and conflicts associated with conversion, seniority rights, and the demands of militant black unionists. At this point, conversion had forced many submerged issues relating to traditional occupational racial practices of the UAW-CIO and management to surface.

In the past most black workers in the automobile industry had paid little attention to upgrading. Their main concern was job security. Management offered little general in-plant training, and the majority of black workers did not protest for admittance into apprenticeship schools. Although the official position of the UAW-CIO was equal seniority rights and promotion opportunities for all workers, regardless of race, color, or creed, black workers were seldom employed on jobs traditionally considered "white," such as on assembly lines; and the union did not bother to challenge these occupational patterns. Many black union members not only accepted this situation but encouraged its development because it provided them with security. This security was based on departmental seniority as contrasted to plantwide seniority. It meant that black workers had seniority in a department only, and that white workers in other departments could not, during layoffs, take the jobs of black workers in the blacks' department on the basis of seniority. Yet the drawback was that it limited old and new black workers to traditionally black jobs. In many ways it was a perfect device for maintaining the racial-occupational status quo, because seniority for black workers applied only to those few departments and occupations where they were concentrated. This arrangement proved equally nonthreatening to white workers, who by this time had come to think of black workers as static occupational types.[147]

While some black workers before conversion were satisfied with the questionable security of "black" jobs, and the seniority related to them, others were not satisfied. They saw the situation as "a thinly disguised ruse to keep them concentrated in the poorer and less desirable departments and occupations." This feeling was confirmed by their failure to profit when plantwide seniority had been in effect. In many such situations, black workers had been discriminated against when their seniority plantwide entitled them to promotion to occupations or departments which traditionally hired only white workers. In order to get around the seniority question, management and union officials told black workers that they were not qualified to perform the job. The real reason, however, was white workers' opposition to working with blacks on the better jobs and the reluctance of both union and management to confront this issue.[148]

Wartime conversion (from civilian production to war production) forced all this out into the open for a full airing. Conversion soon became the catalyst that triggered many other problems. In 1941 in Detroit, black workers, UAW-CIO officials, management, white workers, and the various governmental agencies charged with war production and equal employment opportunities were caught in an unprecedented racial maelstrom with nothing to guide them. Black workers had already met with the unions' international governing board and, for all intents and purposes, had the green light to advance their position. Unions and management both attempted to place the full responsibility upon the government. White workers let it be known that they would not work with blacks. These problems would have to be resolved if war production was to be successful; and black workers would have to find a place in that production.

By the fall of 1941, the upgrading of black workers in Detroit's converted plants, which was the only way for black workers to obtain war jobs, was ready to be put to the test. An executive order had been passed that summer, and soon the Fair Employment Practices Committee (FEPC) machinery for monitoring discrimination in war industries would be fully operative. At this stage of war production certain influential officials considered the opening of new types of jobs (white jobs) for black workers a "prime necessity" for any realistic program for the mobilization of manpower.[149]

Management was still dragging its feet on upgrading black workers, because they feared white workers would walk out. Black workers, on the other hand, refused to stand around and watch only white workers being transferred to war production jobs. In August 1941, a group of black workers in the Dodge foundry stopped work twice to protest the refusal of management to transfer black workers to production jobs at the Chrysler Tank Arsenal, although whites with less seniority were being transferred there. A group of black workers attempted to discuss the matter with management and were told that management alone determined who should be transferred. The local union established an official committee to talk with management, but still the management refused to budge. The matter was then referred to the OPM for settlement and the black workers returned to work.[150]

Later, Dodge management transferred some white janitors to war production at the Arsenal while black workers with more seniority and wider occupational experience were refused such jobs. Black workers again met and discussed striking. Some white workers were ready to join them. But they could not get enough support from other workers for strike action. Once again the local and international officers invited federal OPM officials to intervene, which they did in early October. Management admitted to discrimination in transfers but placed most of the blame on the local union. Top UAW-CIO officials then assumed responsibility and, at the request of its black staff members, the union established an International Interracial Committee to aid in finding solutions. Soon similar committees were organized on a local basis.[151]

Meanwhile, Packard management had taken action in accordance with its earlier commitments to OPM. They transferred two black metal polishers from civilian to defense production. When the black workers began their new work, close to 250 white polishers staged a sit-down strike, which halted production in the unit. The two black workers were asked to return to civilian production until the local union could decide on the matter. After the local union voted on the matter, its officers declined to take action. Black union members had no luck in obtaining intervention from the international representative; the local interracial committee made excuses and refused to refer the matter to the UAW-CIO International Interracial Committee that had been established by the executive board.[152]

Due to the insistence of OPM, the case was referred to the committee a month after the transfer. After some hesitation, the UAW-CIO International president sent a letter to the Packard local re-emphasizing their position and purpose for setting up the Interracial Committee and stating that he would stand by that committee and the executive board in seeing that there would be no discrimination in the transfer of workers.[153]

Despite this letter, the local again refused to act, and the Executive Board called for a conference with the local's officers. The international UAW-CIO leaders stood firm on the union's policy of equal treatment. After the meeting, the shop committee of the Packard local told management that the local and international unions wanted the black workers transferred to defense production.[154]

The personnel department then warned the black workers that if they accepted the transfer there would be bloodshed. The shop stewards told them to accept, and they did. Management then refused to transfer the workers, claiming that it would cause racial conflict and stop production. This prompted the international president of the UAW-CIO to send a letter to management stating that he believed that there would be no problem and that the UAW-CIO would take the responsibility for anything that occurred as a result of the transfers. Finally in April of the following year, the two black polishers were successfully transferred.[155]

Similar problems of upgrading black workers occurred at other plants and continued for several years, complicated by the Sojourner Truth war-housing riot in February of 1942, and, finally, by the eruption of the June 1943 race riot. Other major strikes included: four at Chrysler during February and June of 1942; two at Timken-Detroit Axle in July 1942; and one at Hudson Naval Ordinance in June 1942. Other major strikes occurred in 1943.[156]

Although several of the strikes against the upgrading of black workers prevented some from gaining defense work, a considerable number were successfully transferred, thanks to the leadership of the UAW-CIO International Board. Time and time again they stood firm on their racial policy, even against the balking of locals. During the walkout of white workers at the Chrysler Highland Park plant in February 1942 in reaction to the upgrading of black workers, the international and local union representatives advised the company to fire all workers who did not return to work. The following day, black and white workers were working together without trouble. A day later management reported that all was well at the Highland Park plant, and that one black worker had been promoted to a crane operator.[157]

Earlier that month, the local at the Chrysler Tank Arsenal received word from their union officials that the UAW-CIO International Union and the Chrysler Corporation "now insisted that Negroes be employed on defense work for any job to which they were entitled and for which they could qualify." As the word spread throughout the plant, many white workers were reported to have told black workers they would help them in every way they could.[158]

On June 11, 1943, just nine days before the race riot, union leaders told an overflowing crowd at the Olympia Stadium that discrimination must be banished. A representative of Phillip Murray, the CIO president, read a message which said: "There is no room in the CIO for racial discrimination." R. J. Thomas, president of the UAW-CIO, vehemently denounced "those who have been stirring up racial disputes in war plants with strikes." He went on to pledge to use every available means of legal and union procedure to stamp out the influence of the KKK and other promoters of race hatred within the UAW. He was applauded repeatedly. The union leaders blamed the racial turmoil on the KKK and the Black Legion which flourished among those whites who had just arrived from the South, but who "lacked the education and the understanding to cope with some of the economic problems of modern industrial society." They also reaffirmed their support for the FEPC. Due largely to the efforts of the UAW-CIO, by the summer of 1942 Detroit had begun to alter "the color-caste occupational pattern in its industries."[159]

Hardly had the issue of upgrading black workers been tackled when another problem, which had been an issue all along, came into focus: What would be the role of black women workers during the war production period? As already mentioned, in the past, black women had been the mainstay of domestic and personal services occupations. During World War II they were the very last resource to be tapped by the war industries. In one industrial city in Connecticut the manager of the local U.S. Employment Service said he feared that encouraging black women to seek work in manufacturing would greatly upset the wives of influential white employers in the area. Yet at the same time local industries accepted white women and lamented the lack of female workers, saying that they "could not be recruited fast enough." One observer noted that "vital war production was being delayed because a segment of available labor in the community was ignored in the program for recruiting much-needed workers." In all industrial communities with black populations, "racism led to a serious waste of available black manpower and womanpower."[160]

Black women were concentrated in nonessential service jobs while white women were being trained for high-paying defense jobs. When black women attempted to abandon their low-paying jobs, some cities interpreted their actions as being subversive and "designed for a general exodus from their servants' jobs."[161]

Black women in Detroit could find almost no work in the automobile industry when it first began to recruit women workers. Not even the Ford Motor company was eager to hire them. The personnel office at Willow Run began hiring white women in the spring of 1942. Black women had to wait until December, and then only a few received jobs. The same situation prevailed at most of the other plants. Kelsey-Haynes, Murray, and Briggs employed a few black women during the winter of 1942 but, as a group, black women had far more obstacles placed in their path than white women and black men.[162]

Only 74 of 280 establishments in the industry using female labor employed black women, who made up 3 percent of their total female labor force. General Motors employed 407 black women, which was 1.1 percent of its total female work force, but they were employed in only 13 of the 27 plants using women workers. Out of the 15 Chrysler plants using women, only 7 used black women, but they comprised 10.4 percent of its total female work force. Ford had eight plants that used women workers, five of which used blacks. These women comprised 3.6 percent of the total female work force in all eight plants; and of these about two-thirds worked at the Rouge plant.[163]

By 1943, a growing number of black women in Detroit found work in production jobs, yet a union survey revealed that the majority of black women workers still worked in such jobs as janitresses and matrons. Although the total of black women in the work force had been increasing, hiring restrictions continued to hamper the full use of the available supply of black women workers.

A release from the U.S. Employment Service in April 1943 pointed out that although the majority of employers did not discriminate against non-whites in job orders, it was still difficult to place them in other than unskilled work, and that this was particularly true of black women.[164]

In June 1943, the employment service in the Detroit area estimated that there were 28,000 black women available for war work, comprising the largest neglected source of labor living in the area. Yet Detroit had an acute labor shortage!

When black women did get a foothold in defense work, they had to suffer much of the same abuse as black men. Soon after Packard management placed four black women in a new department in February 1943, white workers walked out. Members of the UAW-CIO Interracial Committee attempted to intervene, but the white workers refused to return to work. Management took the black women off their jobs. A report circulated that a large segment of the KKK in the plant had instigated the work stoppage.[165]

An interesting irony of this period involved the struggle to get black women workers into the Ford Willow Run plant. Alone among all of the companies, Ford had not had any work stoppages by whites because of upgrading blacks. Since 1920, Rouge management had followed a definite policy of using blacks in semiskilled and skilled jobs. Ford management had made it clear that demonstrations by white workers over black employment and upgrading would result in the former losing their jobs. As a result, the rigid racial-occupational patterns which existed at other plants were much less prevalent at Ford. And upgrading blacks did not disturb the racial status quo.[166]

Nevertheless, Ford management put up more of a fight than most other companies over the issue of employing black women in defense work. In fact, the struggle to get black women into the Willow Run Bomber Plant in 1942 became one of the most pressing issues of the war years. The Ford Motor Company trotted out any excuse it could marshal to justify its policy of excluding black women from the Willow Run Plant; but finally, under pressure from a wide range of community groups, the company conceded and a few black women moved a notch up the occupation ladder.[167] The hiring of black women at the Willow Run bomber plant contributed to the overall stability of black families and, by extension, the larger black community. The movement to pressure Ford into using black women at Willow Run was led by working class blacks in the plants grounded in both the black protest tradition and in the trade union movement, demonstrating once again how the black community creatively utilized both internal and external resources in the community building process.

POLICE BRUTALITY

Job discrimination exacted more than its pound of flesh from the black community, but the struggle against police brutality took its toll both physically and emotionally on the black community.

If blacks in Detroit had been polled anytime between 1925 and 1945 concerning the worst racial abuses they had to encounter, they would have said white police brutality. White police officers in the black ghettoes in Detroit and elsewhere symbolized a form of unbridled racism. In some ways, the white police in the black ghetto functioned as the first line of white defense against what many whites considered to be an expanding black horde which, if not checked, would overwhelm surrounding white neighborhoods. White police brutality, therefore, often functioned, whether deliberately or not, as an effective method of racial-social control at times when the forces of industrialization were undermining traditional relations among social groups and classes. White police brutality could and often did maintain the racial status quo when all other efforts failed or were weakening in the face of black protest and white liberalism.

Although Detroit's black population increased between 1915 and 1920, only 15 black officers were numbered among the 3,000 member police force by 1920. As the black population expanded during the 1920s, the Detroit Police Department (DPD) hired only 32 additional black officers. The black population increased by 25 percent, compared to a white increase of 1.7 percent during the 1930s, but the Detroit police department hired only 16 more blacks during that period.[168]

As crime increased in the black ghetto due to the horrid living conditions generated and maintained by racial discrimination in housing and employment, the police department expected these black policemen to keep "their people" in line. But the major responsibility of "keeping the niggers in line" fell to the predominantly white DPD, which tended to go overboard in combating crimes in black neighborhoods. Such overzealousness in the 1920s contributed to increased racial conflicts between the black and white communities. A report of the mayor's Committee on Race Relations published in 1926 placed much of the blame for poor race relations on the police department:

> There is evidence that in many cases Negroes are treated with undue severity, not to say brutality, by the police. The assumption among many police officers that Negro criminals offer a special peril to the life of the officer and that consideration of self-defense, therefore, justifies unusually precipitate action in firing upon Negro criminals is not borne out by the facts. This unjustified assumption has resulted in needless loss of life on occasion of Negro arrests. This condition will probably not be remedied without much greater vigilance on the part of the department in disciplining officers guilty of unwarranted brutality.[169]

While questioning the impression in the black community that many white police working in black districts were southerners venting their racist feelings against blacks, the Mayor's Interracial Committee recommended that "the police department formulate a policy of excluding from precincts in which colored people predominate, officers whose social backgrounds or previous history prompt them to an undue measure of race prejudice." Furthermore, the committee suggested that "it might be a wise policy for the department to investigate the personal bias of officers it intends to use in colored districts."[170] Sadly enough, no significant change occurred in the practices of the Detroit Police Department.

White police brutality against blacks increased during the 1930s. Blacks were indiscriminately beaten, repeatedly harassed, and often killed at the hands of racist policemen for doing little more than saying the wrong thing or making the wrong move at the wrong time. And more often than not, white policemen were not punished for such racist actions.

In 1933, white policemen killed several blacks in rapid succession, prompting the black community along with concerned civic organizations to lodge complaints against "the promiscuous shooting of Negroes by police." Two years later, white policemen were still shooting blacks on the slightest pretense. In one case in 1935, a white policeman fatally shot a young black man in the abdomen while he was sitting in the rear seat of a car that the officer had stopped for exceeding the speed limit. The officer claimed he thought the victim was armed. At his trial, the jury could not reach a verdict, despite the testimony of eyewitnesses that the shooting was unjustified. Several months later, another white officer seriously wounded a sixteen-year-old black youth. The officer explained that he really shot at the rear of a garage the youth was attempting to open and the kid "ducked into the line of fire."[171] This trend continued. (See Chapter 7).

According to the paper, "the orgy of brutality" began in January when a white policeman shot a black citizen to death while he was sitting at the wheel of a car he had just purchased. Seven months later the officer had not even been given a reprimand. In June, a white policeman shot and killed a sixteen-year-old boy "for allegedly taking a sweater" from a store.[172]

Even in cases which warranted some use of force in protecting lives, many white officers greatly abused such force. In February 1939, a white officer allegedly threatened by a sixty-three-year-old black man, who had just slashed a white tailor over an argument about repairing a coat, found it necessary to shoot his alleged attacker three times.[173]

When obviously racist white policemen were not engaged in unjustified killings of black citizens—which is not to say that all killing of black criminals or black criminal suspects were unjustified, since black policemen also killed blacks—they commonly engaged in a social ritual of beating up blacks. This treatment was consistent with the dominant racial attitudes of white Detroit—the desire to keep blacks "in their place," legally or otherwise. It explains why so few whites expressed concern about white police brutality against black citizens. The vast majority of whites believed that blacks deserved such treatment because they were either criminals or criminally inclined. If they were neither, then they were "uppity" or "radical" niggers trying to push themselves into white neighborhoods and white jobs.

Beating blacks in precinct stations was a common practice of many white policemen, and this was the main reason why black policemen were kept outside of some stations. A former black policeman commented on this practice, which was still quite common in the 1950s: "They [white police officers] did it for kicks just for fun."[174] Beating black citizens just for fun indicated the degree to which racism had infected the mentality of many white policemen.

The war years of the 1940s provided even more opportunities for white policemen to vent their racist feelings against the black citizens of Detroit. During the racial disorder of the 1942 Sojourner Truth housing controversy and the 1943 race riots, white policemen unabashedly took the side of whites; and in the racial confrontation, they not only sided with white mobs but refused to respect and protect the lives and property of black citizens. Blacks and their white allies continued to protest against white police brutality, to little avail. White police brutality continued well into the 1970s.[175]

THE 1943 RACE RIOT

The long history of white racism and black resistance was destined to explode. While reasonable people hoped and prayed that Detroit might be spared a serious race riot, they knew in their souls that the fuse of racial tension was burning shorter each day. Fifteen months before the riot of June 1943, the Office of Facts and Figures in Washington, D.C., submitted a confidential report on Detroit. It warned that unless some "socially constructive steps" were taken shortly, the "tension that [was] developing was likely to burst into active conflict." Officials suppressed the report until a day after the riot when the *Detroit Free Press* obtained a copy.[176]

Another paper, the *Wage Earner,* warned in its June issue that there was a growing "subterranean race war going on in the city of Detroit, which can have no other ultimate result than an explosion of violence, unless something is done to stop it."[177] Walter White, national director of the NAACP, bluntly told a Detroit audience on June 3: "Let us drag out into the open what has been whispered throughout Detroit for months—that a race riot may break out here at any time."[178]

City officials also feared and expected racial violence. But they refused to give any serious thought to solving the causes of the unrest. Instead they waited as the police officials and the military met to discuss "procedures to follow in the event of a serious outbreak requiring federal forces."[179]

Who knows just what will spark a race riot? The fighting between blacks and whites was becoming increasingly common in both the plants and on the streets. The June 20, 1943, racial conflict on the Island Park, Belle Isle, on a typical hot Sunday evening, was as good a cause as any. Before long, two hundred white sailors from the nearby armory joined a white mob attacking isolated blacks, and the riot started.[180] Rumors spread throughout the city. One such rumor said that whites had killed a black woman and thrown her baby over the bridge.

Blacks who heard the rumor started stoning unsuspecting white motorists driving through the ghetto.[181] The police commissioner would later place all the blame on the blacks, ignoring the white sailors, much like the white policemen who sided with the white mob during the Sojourner Truth riot. During this 1943 outbreak, the police killed 17 blacks (some were shot in the back) but not one white, despite the fact that white rioters numbered in the thousands compared to blacks, who numbered in the hundreds. Many blacks were beaten up by police for little or no reason. On Woodward Avenue, a major thoroughfare on the edge of the ghetto, white mobs beat blacks under the very eyes of the police. The next morning, downtown Detroit was in turmoil as "thousands of whites roamed the streets searching for black victims."[182]

The country found this hard to believe until newspapers printed a photograph of a black World War I veteran being held by white police while a white man hit him. The mayor tried to ignore the seriousness of the situation. He refused the request of black leaders to bring in federal troops. But when the numbers of whites increased, the mayor reversed himself. By Wednesday, the intervention of the army had calmed things down. Only a few gangs still slugged it out. Within a week, the city was back to wartime normalcy, but emotional wounds were open and raw; worse, 31 people had died, and over two hundred were injured.[183]

Only the UAW and a few black leaders offered any program to halt the bloodshed and create some social stability in the city. That next Monday at a meeting of the Detroit Citizens Committee, headed by Mayor Jeffries, the UAW president attacked the city and police officials for failing to stop the riot. The union called a citywide meeting of union leaders in all the plants to coordinate efforts to calm the situation and maintain peace in the factories. Because over half of the whites and between 50 and 80 percent of the black workers were absent, no fights occurred in any auto plant during the riots. Two days after the meeting with the city officials, the UAW president, on behalf of the union, presented an eight-point program "to forestall future riots." The program called for: "(1) a special grand jury to investigate facilities; (2) adequate park and recreational facilities; (3) new housing plans for Negro slums; (4) effective curbs on racial intolerance and discrimination in industry; (5) investigation as to why drastic action to subdue mobs had not been taken earlier; (6) impartial justice to the rioters, regardless of color; (7) restitution of losses to innocent sufferers from the reign of terror; and (8) creation by the Mayor of a special biracial committee of ten to make further recommendations towards elimination of racial differences and friction."[184]

The union president selected the high schools for a "concentrated campaign," since the schools had allowed racial hatred "to grow and thrive," during recent years.[185]

The Detroit Free Press endorsed the proposals, but they died an early death, particularly the one asking for a grand-jury investigation. Had such an investigation been held, city, state, and police officials would have been exposed by some very influential people, such as William E. Guthner, who headed the federal troops in Detroit during the riot and complained of the vicious and harsh treatment the police meted out to blacks.[186]

The union proposals contradicted the majority of reports, which basically blamed the riot on blacks. A member of a fact-finding committee set up by the governor also blamed blacks. Wayne County Prosecutor William E. Dowling blamed the black press and the NAACP "as the principal instigators of the race riot." The police commissioner supported him.[187]

During a speech in June of the following year (1944), Dowling revealed much of the racist thinking commonly harbored by whites in Detroit: "The white man in the South has met the problem. Although we may not agree with what he has done, we must go along with the thought that he has met the problem." Dowling could have meant only one thing by his statement "The white man in the South has met the problem"—namely, that the southern system of racial segregation of blacks was the only way to meet "the problem." According to Dowling, Detroit blacks already had political and economic equality, but they had been influenced by the communists to want "social equality" as well. So these "communists" preached social equality. Negro churches took up the cry for social equality. Then Negro newspapers became vocal for social equality. The papers kept demanding it until every incident involving a Negro person came to be seen as a problem of discrimination.[188]

The official report of the committee blamed the racial tension and riot on black leaders' "positive exhortations . . . to be militant in the struggle for racial equality." According to this report, black leaders caused the outbreak by comparing "victory over the axis . . . [with] a corresponding overthrow in the country of those forces which . . . prevent true racial equality." As expected, the report pleased Mayor Jeffries, who said it was good. The *Detroit Free Press* called the governor's committee report a whitewash and pointed out that it "was largely drawn up by Police Commissioner Witherspoon . . . with [him] furnishing much of the evidence." "The tragedy for Detroit," one writer stated, "was that most whites were more than willing to believe the report."[189]

The national organization of the CIO in Washington blamed "Nazi-minded hoodlums" and the "influence of the KKK, the Christian Front, the Black Dragon Society, the National Workers League, the Knights of the White Camelia, the Southern Voters League, and similar organizations based on a policy of terror and . . . white supremacy."[190]

A delegation of white and black trade unionists—with representatives from Ford Local 600, including Shelton Tappes, recording secretary, and from the UAW, the CIO, the AFL, and black and Jewish organizations—called on President Roosevelt to put down "with a firm hand the organized campaign of violence" that was being carried out against blacks, Mexicans, Jews, and other minority groups, as well as against organized labor in the industrial centers.[191] In his letter to President Roosevelt requesting help, CIO President Phillip Murray mentioned that "the Detroit violence followed a pattern written in blood in other war production centers." He asked Roosevelt to issue orders to the Departments of Justice, War, and Navy and to the Office of War Information "to offset the plotting of disruptive agencies that have fermented this hysteria and with a view to severe punishment of those found guilty."[192]

UAW President R. J. Thomas declared that there was a "substantial nucleus of KKK and Black Legion elements here [in Detroit] and nobody in political life has the intestinal fortitude to move in and prosecute." He added that it was no secret that "the KKK whooped it up here during the last couple of days and [that he was] willing to give names before a grand jury."[193]

During the week of July 12, the CIO executive board passed a resolution at a special board meeting that riots and mob violence against blacks and other minorities were seriously endangering the war effort. The resolution had been introduced by Willard S. Townsend, president of the Transport Service Employees and secretary of the CIO Committee to Abolish Racial Discrimination. "Labor must recognize," the resolution said, "that the forces which fermented racial strife are identical with those which would destroy the . . . labor movement." It further pointed out that as a means of "strengthening democracy and for its very self preservation," the labor movement must "wage an all-out attack on [those] disintegrating forces," and it must deal "resolutely with the basic causes in its day-to-day operations." Tying the fight against domestic racism with the fight against Hitler, as the Detroit NAACP has been accused of doing, the board declared:

> We express our solidarity again with our Negro fellow citizens and fellow workers, and renew our fight against discrimination and persecution . . . as a necessary part of our common fight against the enemies of our country and of the United Nations.[194]

The CIO's brave pronouncements masked what many labor leaders knew to be the case—that a rabid homegrown racism was shared by a broad cross section of white workers, not all of them southern, but foreign and northern as well. The CIO was stretching the truth when it attributed "the absence of racial conflict in the shops" to the "CIO leadership in Michigan." As we have already pointed out, half of the white work force was gone, while from 50 to 80 percent of the blacks were also absent. However, the CIO did work hard to calm things down; and CIO leaders understandably were grabbing for any ray of hope that their union had some semblance of racial unity. To the CIO's credit, as early as 1943 they had pointed out that "curative measures [were] not sufficient," and that "a nationwide program of prevention [was] imperative" and most importantly, "it must include every segment of our community life."[195]

Detroit black pressure groups blamed for the riot by several blue-ribbon committees were defended by CIO leaders like Thomas. He accused Detroit public officials of making irresponsible statements, which he considered "the most serious incitement to race riots . . . since the riots themselves." He challenged Detroit Prosecutor William E. Dowling to present his evidence pointing to blacks as "instigators of riots." If "Dowling believes that the NAACP is responsible for the riots, it is his sworn duty to present evidence before a grand jury," Thomas said, "and not run off at the mouth in public. I think," he continued, "that the NAACP [would] welcome an investigation of all factors in the situation including its own role." He then said that the NAACP was an organization of which all Americans, regardless of race or color, may be proud. "It includes among its warm supporters and members," Thomas added, "Wendell L. Willkie, Judge Ira W. Jayne, Justice Frank Murphy, General Theodore Roosevelt, and Herbert H. Lehman."[196]

A report of a survey of race relations in Detroit authored by a field consultant of the Office of Civilian Defense, which included "the underlying causes of the Detroit Riot," explained the tragic event as the outcome of the black struggle for human rights as American citizens: "The basic underlying cause of the Detroit Riot is, of course, the struggle of colored Americans for full, unrestricted, and non-discriminatory enjoyment of the rights, privileges, and immunities of American citizenship under the Constitution and for non-discriminatory participation in the political, economic, and social life of the American community." Continuing, the report stated that this struggle has historic roots that "ante-date the formation of the Republic . . . [and] may well be characterized as the most important feature of our economic and political development." While it was not the purpose of the report to discuss the national and international ramifications of this struggle on the war effort, this "equalitarian struggle, however, points up the areas of racial conflict in Detroit, and due to the penetration of the struggle, touches all the community problems. . . . The most pressing, however, in colored-white relationships, are employment and housing."[197]

The police were also targeted for a much-needed expose in the *CIO News*.[198] But, as supportive as their allies were, the masses of blacks in Detroit had become increasingly antiwhite. It was not an easy task, nor a popular one, for black leaders to continue struggling for that elusive dream called democracy.

The national and local black leadership responded to the race riot in various ways. The national office of the NAACP stayed on top of the race riots from the very beginning. Walter White, as national secretary of the NAACP, wrote a detailed analysis of conditions leading to the riots.[199] Thurgood Marshall, the special counsel for the NAACP, using the services of two private investigators from New York, one black and the other white, collected affidavits related to the role of the police during the riot. According to Marshall's final report in July, which was to be used as evidence for a Grand Jury investigation, the police "ran true to form":

> In the June riots of this year, the Detroit police ran true to form. The trouble reached riot proportion because the police of Detroit once again enforced the law under an unequal hand. They used 'persuasion' rather than firm action with white rioters while against Negroes they used the ultimate in force: nightsticks, revolvers, riot guns, sub-machine guns, and deer guns. As a result, 25 of the 34 persons killed were Negroes. Of the 25 Negroes killed, 17 were killed by police. The excuses of the Police Department for the disproportionate number of Negroes killed is that the majority of them [were] killed while committing felonies; . . . It is true that some Negroes were looting stores on Hastings Street and were shot while committing these crimes. It is equally true that white persons were turning over and burning automobiles on Woodward Avenue. This is arson. Others were beating Negroes with iron pipes, clubs and rocks. This is felonious assault. Several Negroes were stabbed. This is assault with intent to murder.

All of these crimes are matters of record. Many were committed in the presence of police officers, several on the pavement around the city hall. Yet, the record remains: Negroes killed by police—17; white persons killed by police—none. Eighty-five percent of persons arrested were Negroes.[200]

Several months after the riot, the editor of the *Michigan Chronicle* said, "The race riot and all that has gone before have made my people more nationalistic and more chauvinistic and antiwhite than ever before. Even some of us who were half-liberal and were willing to believe in the possibilities of improving race relations have begun to have doubts—and . . . worse, have given up hope."[201]

Fortunately, most of these leaders went back to struggling for a sane and more humane society. A citizens committee headed by the Reverend Charles A. Hill met daily at the YWCA to discuss racial problems. When the mayor appointed an Interracial Committee of 12 members, several black leaders accepted appointments: Hill, pastor of the Hartford Avenue Baptist Church; Louis E. Martin, editor of the *Michigan Chronicle;* Mrs. Beulah Whitby, executive secretary of the Emergency Welfare Evacuation Service, Detroit Office of Civilian Defense; Walter Hardin, director of the Interracial Division of the UAW-CIO; Charles H. Mahoney, of the State of Michigan Department of Labor; and the Reverend George W. Baber.[202]

These leaders and others worked throughout the war and postwar period to promote better race relations in Detroit. But those years were not much better than the ones that preceded the riot. Housing for blacks during this period remained poor. Discrimination in employment continued. Blacks had to fight inch by inch for every bit of progress they made. The Urban League and the NAACP, aided by the FEPC and other governmental agencies, pushed steadily forward, gaining ground and losing ground. By the mid 1940s, blacks had learned a lot about northern racism and how to struggle against it. Detroit was their promised land and no amount of white racism would turn them around. What they had to do was survive— in order to continue to build a community strong and secure enough to transcend racism.

As blacks sought to grow and develop as a community in industrial Detroit, they came up against countless barriers of racial discrimination. At every turn, they were reminded of their color and "their place" in society. Racist whites attempted to restrict blacks to the ghetto and dictate their place in the larger society. Blacks had to challenge the racial status quo in public accommodations, and the housing and job markets and confront relentless police brutality. Had blacks decided not to challenge the racial status quo, the entire history of black Detroit would have been different. Had they decided to sit passively in the place allotted to them by whites, they would have been partners in their own disempowerment. That they chose to challenge a racist system determined the future course of the community building process.

Racial discrimination gave rise to black pioneers who dared to venture out from the ghetto to exercise their right to live wherever they pleased. In the process, they expanded the horizons of the more passive members of the community who would have taken the path of least resistance by staying in "their place." In this sense, the Sweets provided a rallying point for blacks in Detroit and elsewhere. The Sweet trial galvanized the entire black community. However little or much blacks in Detroit thought of themselves as a community before the trial, wherever they lived—in the worst black ghettoes or in the elite black sections on the fringes of white neighborhoods—the Sweet trial made them one community. As they continued to confront racial barriers in housing and employment and to confront white police brutality, they increasingly did so as a community. Although racial discrimination did retard the process of community building, it also prepared the ground of black social consciousness, which gave rise to self-help, protest, and political development.

Six

Social Consciousness
and Self-Help:
The Heart and Soul of
Community Building

*There is no survival for the
Negro except it be
guaranteed by his own
concentrated efforts.*

The Detroit Tribune,
August 20, 1938

PLANTING THE SEEDS OF SELF-HELP IN INDUSTRIAL DETROIT

As blacks faced seemingly endless hardships in industrial Detroit pushing back the barriers of racial discrimination, their social consciousness expanded and developed. From the very beginning they knew that building a community meant relying ultimately upon their own meager resources. Even Forrester B. Washington and John C. Dancy, who depended upon the wealth and influence of white captains of industry to keep the fledgling Detroit Urban League afloat, never allowed the black community to become too dependent upon whites. When and where they could, they sought to raise the social consciousness of blacks to lift themselves up by their own bootstraps. Each successive trial in industrial Detroit impressed upon black Detroiters that their destinies and their children's destinies were in their own hands. Now and then they could count on a few white friends and supporters, such as Henry Ford and Clarence Darrow, but these white men had their own agendas.

If blacks in Detroit were to survive and progress beyond the narrow margin of life grudgingly allotted to them by whites, they would have to expand their horizons far beyond even their own limited expectations. They would have to be makers of their own visions and shapers of their own futures. In short, they would have to become firm believers in their own abilities to raise themselves above poverty, racism, and, especially, hopelessness.

To some blacks, hopelessness posed the biggest problem, especially as expressed in its most popular cultural form, singing the blues. As one black editor put it:

> Colored people are the greatest singers of the "blues" the world over. . . .
> There are times when the blues can be appreciated even by the most discreet
> of music lovers and then there are times when no music is as thoroughly out
> of place as the blues, and such are the present times.[1]

He said singing the blues defeated the spirit of the present time because "brave men [were] trying to improve conditions and not to immortalize hard times with a funeral dirge." According to this editor, blacks should not spend their leisure time applauding blues singers, whom he called "apostles of tough luck," because "such rot . . . poisons the soul and dwarfs the intellect." Instead of singing the blues, blacks, he said, needed "the song of hope, which 'would start the wheels of fortune rolling.'" The editor went on to say that blacks must change their attitudes, "and one of the natural consequences of this will be a change in racial music." He ended his editorial with a call for a new spirit, and put in a note of encouragement: "There is too much sunshine on the hilltop for us to be forever groping in the valley."[2]

Written in the spring of 1921, when a recession yet lingered over the black community, the editor may have been too harsh. Most blacks in Detroit had been in the city for less than half a decade. Perhaps their faith in the promised land was wavering, but the writer was correct in saying that brave men and women were trying to improve conditions.

THE CHURCH

Many of these brave men and women worked through the black church, the core institution of the black community. Black churches in Detroit and elsewhere planted and nurtured the seeds of black social consciousness and self-help. Although there would be times when some of these institutions would fall prey to the blandishments and bribes of powerful white leaders, most of them remained true to their historic mission of raising the social consciousness of the black community and leading the way in self-help activities. Three major churches paved the way for black self-help in Detroit: Second Baptist, Bethel African Methodist Episcopal and St. Matthew's Episcopal. All three date back to before the Civil War.

Beginning in 1914, when large numbers of blacks started to settle in Detroit, the Reverend Robert L. Bradby from Second Baptist Church, began setting up self-help programs. A committee in this church carried on an extensive social service program to assist migrants in adjusting to urban life.[3] Other churches, finding themselves confronted with thousands of migrants from the South, began shifting increasingly to social service work. Some developed social welfare departments to provide sewing, cooking, millinery, and employment information and recreation.[4]

During the peak migration period, committees from Second Baptist Church met every train arriving in Detroit from the South to greet and offer assistance to bewildered migrants. Unlike some established blacks who tended to shun southern blacks, members of Second Baptist Church embraced their southern brethren. Between 1917 and 1918, Second Baptist Church served as the major social service center for blacks in the city. Much of this work was later turned over to the Detroit Urban League. But Second Baptist continued to assist southern black migrants. In 1924 the church established a Big Sister's Auxiliary to build a home for homeless black girls. Two years later Second Baptist opened a social service educational institution staffed with eighteen teachers and classes. The classes lasted from 1926 to 1929. By 1933 Second Baptist, still under the leadership of Mr. Bradby, had raised and spent more than half a million dollars in serving the black community in Detroit;[5] the vast majority of these people had come from the South since the war. Second Baptist continues to serve the black community to the present day.

Bethel African Methodist Episcopal Church (AME) embodied the same self-help philosophy as Second Baptist. Both churches shared similar histories of community building and have continued as institutional symbols of black struggle. In 1898 the Association of Colored Women's Clubs of Michigan held its first meeting at Bethel. Educators of the Colored Youths of America met at the church in the summer of 1899. The Association of Colored Women met in the church again in 1913; and in 1919 black Detroiters celebrated the signing of the Armistice at Bethel AME.[6]

Between 1930 and 1945, Bethel AME developed the most effective model of black self-help. The two people essentially responsible for the church's success in this area were the Reverend William H. Peck and his wife Mrs. Fannie B. Peck. The Pecks arrived in Detroit in 1930 when the church was suffering both spiritually and materially.[7] Later Mr. Peck helped establish the Booker T. Washington Trade Association, and Mrs. Peck organized the Housewives League of Detroit. These two organizations soon became models of black self-help throughout the city, as well as the state and

Church gathering outside the Bethel AME Church. Courtesy of the Burton Historical Collection of the Detroit Public Library.

nation (see the section on "Developing a Philosophy of Black Economic Self-Help" in this chapter).

Like other black churches, Bethel AME opened her doors to the black poor and hungry during the Great Depression of the 1930s. Church members devoted time and effort providing meals for the poor. But the church went farther than traditional church responses to the needy. Bethel AME also developed a mutual benefit association, The Bethel Benefit Association. This association paid three dollars per week in any calendar year to members unable to work because of sickness and paid the family of deceased members a $75 death benefit. The Bethel Benefit Association charged a 25 cents per month fee, in addition to 50 cents for joining.[8]

Most black churches had nurses who provided emergency first aid for members during church services. However, Bethel AME organized the Bethel Nurses Guild in 1926, which provided for members during church services and provided free services in the community. The Guild also conducted practical nursing classes for the larger black community.[9] The Fannie B. Peck Credit Union was organized at the church in 1936 (more on this in a later section). In 1940, church members established the William H. Peck History Club to study and disseminate black history and culture.[10] The study of black history would provide members with an appreciation of the long standing traditions of black self-help and the role played by the church in that tradition.

St. Matthew's Episcopal Church was not among the ten largest black churches in Detroit, but it was the third oldest in the black community, having been founded in 1846. While the church did contribute to black self-help during the period, its efforts did not seem as impressive or widespread as those of Second Baptist and Bethel AME. The reason was probably the class structure of the church membership. St. Matthew's had always been a church for upper-class blacks, and it enjoyed considerable prestige in both the black and white communities in Detroit.[11] While St. Matthew's did extend the hand of assistance to poor struggling blacks, it was more to help them on their way rather than to welcome them into the fold of the church, as was the case with Second Baptist and Bethel AME.

Under the direction of Father Everand W. Daniel, St. Matthew's Episcopal church established The Dorcas Society in April, 1923, which converted members' discarded clothing into usable garments for poor children. In 1924 the church began planning a parish house to house an adequate program for community services. The church completed the parish house in 1927. St. Matthew's also developed educational programs for members and nonmembers, which included lecture series featuring prominent speakers.[12]

Unfortunately, these efforts fell short because the professional skills necessary for addressing migrant problems were lacking.[13] Had the Urban League with its trained professional staff not been established during the first migration wave, the churches as institutions would have been overwhelmed.

Institutional self-help as represented by the black church simply was not sufficient to address the need to prepare thousands of southern peasants for life in a modern industrial city. The black church, however, continued to develop black self-help programs, which came to embody the very essence of community building.

While the migration generated a need for additional self-help institutions, it also stimulated the growth and expansion of churches. "There has been such a rapid development of Negro churches in Detroit within the last ten years," an observer in 1926 said, "that it is impossible to give the exact number." Continuing, he said: "As one walks through the several Negro

Table 9

Membership in 10 Largest Churches,* 1915–1926

Church	Year Established	Membership 1915	Membership 1926
Second Baptist	1836	1,400	4,000
Bethel AME	1841	2,737 (1919)	3,500
Calvary	—	—	2,000
St. Johns CME	1918	—	2,000
Shiloh Baptist	1913	104	1,600
Ebenezer AME	1887	500	1,500
Mt. Olivet	—	500 (1919)	1,200
Hartford Ave. Baptist	1915	—	1,200
Scott ME	1900	—	1,100
St. Paul AMEZ	1893	—	1,100

Source: "Religion," in *The Negro in Detroit* (Detroit: Bureau of Governmental Research, 1926) pp. 2–3.
*Other recognized black churches ranged in membership from 100 to 200; smaller churches, from 50 to 150.

neighborhoods, he finds numerous storefronts, basements, front rooms, . . . platforms in vacant lots, and other small and insignificant places being used as church buildings."[14]

These storefront churches did not contribute much to institutional self-help. They were far too small and scattered, and unstable. Instead, the more stable self-help occurred primarily through the established denominational churches, such as Second Baptist Church and Bethel AME. These institutions grew and consolidated their power and influence as a direct result of money flowing into their coffers from migrants' wages.[15]

In 1926, aggregate black church membership reached 44,907, about seven times more than the total black population in Detroit in 1910 and half of the total black population in Detroit in 1926. The distribution of black membership by denominations was an indication of the preference of the migrant population. Thus, the migration had a differential effect on the growth of black churches (see table 9). The Baptists experienced the greatest growth between 1915 and 1926 because 66 percent of the aggregate church membership in Detroit was Baptist.[16] This helped the Second Baptist Church, the largest of the Baptist churches, to maintain its premigration institutional status in the black community. Half of the churches were founded before the migration, while the other half were established as a direct result of the arrival of the migrants. Premigration churches included the Second Baptist, Bethel AME, St. Paul AMEZ, Ebenezer AME, and Scott ME. The churches founded as a result of the migration were St. John's CME, Shiloh Baptist, Hartford Avenue Baptist, Calvary, and Mt. Olivet. Long before the migration, African Methodist boasted the largest denomination (with its several churches), while Bethel AME had the largest congregation. The Baptists had the second largest denomination and Second Baptist was the second largest congregation.[17]

St. Matthew's had no more than 10 percent of the black community membership.[18] In terms of social status within the black community, St. Matthew's, was on top, followed by Bethel AME, with Second Baptist Church on the bottom rung.[19] As the migration brought in more Baptists, other churches sprang up, such as Shiloh Baptist (1913), Hartford Avenue Baptist (1915), and Calvary Baptist (1926). Eventually the Baptist churches grew into the largest denomination among all black churches in Detroit (see table 9).

Between 1919 and 1926 the property of the established churches increased phenomenally. The total value of property owned by these institutions was $2,297,000, of which more than half had been obtained during the above mentioned seven-year period.[20] This rapid increase of institutional wealth obviously resulted from the increased membership of church-going black workers, who made generous contributions to Baptist churches. This is also confirmed by the fact that over one-half of this accumulated wealth was in the hands of the Baptist churches[21] that had experienced the greatest increase of membership from southern migrants, by then seasoned industrial workers whose earnings provided the economic foundation of these churches.

But what did this mean for black self-help? Some established churches carried out large building programs that included expansion of social services and supervised recreation for migrants. With the possible exception of the movies, church entertainment provided the major forms of recreation for churchgoers.[22] Before long, there evolved a symbiotic relationship between the new black working class and those churches whose membership and wealth they had increased. Churches that failed to respond to the needs of the black workers did not grow, and many "old fashioned" churches were forced to "acquire a broader vision" in order to survive. Churches that experienced the most rapid growth embodied a social consciousness stressing self-help in servicing the expanding migrant population, thus they made vital contributions to community building.

BLACK HOSPITALS

Between World War I and the Great Depression, black hospitals in Detroit emerged as major self-help institutions. They developed in response to the rising medical needs of the expanding black community and also provided an institutional base for black medical professionals.

Because black doctors were having a difficult time obtaining internships in white hospitals, they were forced to organize themselves and establish their own. Mercy Hospital, founded in 1917 by David Northcross, became

Staff, Board of Trustees, and Corps of Nurses of Dunbar Memorial Hospital, c. 1925. Courtesy of the *Detroit News* Historic Film Library.

the first black hospital in Detroit.[23] A year later a group of black doctors incorporated the Dunbar Hospital Association, which later changed its name to Parkside Hospital. This association studied sanitation, hygiene, and related sciences, treated advanced diseases, and performed surgical operations.[24] In 1918, Mercy Hospital had 37 beds and space for an operating room. By the early 1940s, the hospital had acquired an operating room, had been approved by both the American Hospital Association and the American College of Surgeons, and had increased its bed capacity to 52. Blacks funded two other hospitals during the Depression: the Trinity Hospital in 1933, which grew from a 35-bed to a 110-bed capacity in ten years; and the Edyth K. Thomas Memorial Hospital in 1935, with a 100-bed capacity. Two years later, Thomas Memorial had expanded to become the Thomas Medical Center, making it the largest privately-owned black hospital in the United States.[25] Other black hospitals established between the Depression and the early 1940s included Fairview Sanitarium, Bethesda Hospital, Good Samaritan, Mercy Hospital, Wayne Sanitarium, St. Aubin General, and Kirwood Hospital.[26]

Of all of the black self-help institutions that emerged between World Wars I and II, the black hospitals were among some of the more stable and permanent ones. They furnished striking evidence of the ability of the black community to develop self-help institutions even in the midst of a depression. Considering that black doctors did not significantly increase their numbers per 1,000 black people in the total population from 1910 to 1940 (1.0, 1910; 0.7, 1920; 0.6, 1930; 0.6, 1940).[27] These hospitals were a monument to their efforts. Few other black professional groups contributed as much to institutional self-help. Preachers built their churches, undertakers flourished and enlarged their facilities, and insurance brokers founded the Great Lakes Mutual Insurance Company; but the black hospitals provided the working class folk with medical care without which they could not work to pay for the churches, the burials, or the insurance policies.

Black hospitals also provided jobs for the black community as few other black institutions were able to do. In 1943, black hospitals furnished employment for more than 500 blacks.[28] Although this contribution seems very small compared to the number of jobs outside the black community, these job opportunities loomed large in comparison to the offerings of other job-generating institutions within the black community.

Black self-help institutions and organizations also generated black pride and raised the social consciousness of the struggling community. The black community became proud that it possessed the knowledge and tools by which it could lift itself up. This social consciousness often generated tremendous community support. Beginning in 1919, the Parkside Auxiliary, formerly the Dunbar Auxiliary, contributed linens, rugs, radios, dishes, and a washing machine to the Parkside Hospital.[29] Mrs. Fannie Peck, the founder of the Housewives League, the sister organization of the Booker T. Washington Trade Association, both of which were founded in 1930, once lent her valuable time and organizing skills to organize an open house for this institution.[30]

Fund-raising and donations were common methods of community support. Social clubs, such as the Century of Progress Club, donated money outright, while other groups held dances at the popular Graystone Ballroom to generate funds to support black hospitals.[31] Without these black self-help efforts, black hospitals in Detroit would not have survived.

Black community support of black institutions also reflected growing cooperation between black self-help institutions and various professional classes. As already mentioned, in 1923, the Urban League, under John Dancy and several black doctors, organized a National Negro Health Week campaign, which met in black churches. Such cooperation helped the black professional classes to perform their jobs more effectively and strengthened the previously loosely-knit institutional self-help networks that character- ized the early stages of the black community. Nonmedical professionals like Dancy sat on the boards of trustees of black hospitals and contributed their expertise to this developing self-help network.[32]

Though black hospitals were originally created in reaction to racial discrimination, many blacks deserted black hospitals once white institu- tions ceased discriminating because white hospitals offered a greater range of medical services and employment. As one observer pointed out, a "point against Negro-owned hospitals is that the majority of Negroes desire to work in and receive care in large tax-supported or white-owned private hospitals because of the better pay and more adequate facilities. Loyalty, however, has caused many blacks to help support Negro institutions that employ Negroes."[33]

Torn between the desire to benefit from the greater resources of white hospitals and loyalty to less endowed black hospitals, many blacks chose the former. Whether or not this choice stemmed from a lack of race pride or from the wish to exercise long-desired and sought after freedoms, such as the right to integrate or not to integrate into white society, would remain ambiguous for some time.

One thing seemed abundantly clear: black social consciousness repre- sented a mosaic of contradictory agendas for blacks' survival and progress. If black hospitals existed mainly because black doctors could not practice in white hospitals, should the black community support black doctors in their struggle to integrate these facilities or support black hospitals staffed by black doctors? Could the struggles for black self-help and racial inte- gration proceed simultaneously or were they contradictory social forces? What approach was best for building a strong, secure black community?

According to Snow Grigsby, a black radical of the 1930s and a founder of the Civic Rights Committee (CRC), black hospitals stood in the way of racial integration. "The Negro race and Negro doctors can never advance under the 'Jim Crow' set up," Grigsby argued in the 1930s. Whenever blacks have established black hospitals, white hospitals that had been admitting blacks either stopped doing so or admitted only a certain quota; the rest, Grigsby claimed, were referred to black hospitals. As a result, black patients with urgent needs who ended up in poorly equipped black hospitals suffered the consequences of the segregated setup. "In this way the mortality and morbidity rate of colored people in the North will be immensely increased, Grigsby said."[34]

Finally, Grigsby believed black hospitals produced "a sense of servility, suppressed inspiration and created artificial and dishonest standards." Black doctors and nurses "should be accepted in universities and hospitals and trained as all-American students. . . . To do otherwise," he continued "is to create a menace to the training of the Negro in medicine." Concluding, Grigsby pointed to the fact that the two racial hospital systems in Detroit set blacks "apart from all other citizens as being a different kind of citizen and a different kind of medical student or physician."[35]

Grigsby's criticism of black hospitals did not stop black doctors and their associates from establishing hospitals. But his criticism did add to the ongoing debate over where institutional black self-help ends and self-imposed segregation begins.

INSURANCE COMPANIES, LOAN COMPANIES, AND CREDIT UNIONS

Black insurance companies in Detroit and elsewhere did not depart from this general historical and occasionally contradictory pattern of institutional development. Much like black hospitals, black insurance companies also emerged partially from racist practices. White insurance companies simply refused to provide blacks with the same quality of policy they provided to their white policyholders. They regarded blacks as poor risks by virtue of the conditions in which they lived and worked. Blacks were limited to certain types of policies, rates of premiums, and benefits. However, these white companies did contribute to educating blacks to the importance of carrying some kind of insurance.[36] But they also exploited blacks. A section of the Michigan state law passed in 1893 stated in part "that no life insurance company doing business in this state shall make any distinction or discriminations between white persons and colored persons . . . or to the premium or rates charged for policies upon the lives of such persons." Yet in 1937 white insurance companies in Michigan were reported charging black customers no less than a million and a half dollars extra a year for being black. For example, in 1937, thirty-year old whites paid about $42 per thousand for an endorsement policy. Blacks paid $47 per thousand.[37]

White insurance companies exploited the black community taking millions of dollars out of the community and giving back little in return.

Beginning in 1922 black insurance companies started setting up operations in Detroit black communities to offer blacks more and better insurance premiums for their money. Four years later when the amount of insurance in force among blacks in Detroit was about $17,351,468, three black insurance companies held close to $5,000,000. Blacks benefited more from these companies because they offered them more beneficial policies (e.g., ordinary and casualty) in contrast to the less beneficial policies (e.g., industrial) offered by white corporations.[38]

Black insurance companies also generated jobs for blacks, something that white insurance companies rarely did. As a rule, white insurance companies did not employ blacks even as agents to represent them in black communities.[39] Such gross racism added considerable insult to the injury of exploitation. Black insurance companies, like black hospitals, retained black dollars within the community, creating jobs and providing a capital base for further economic development. Between 1915 and 1925, black workers were making more money and demanding more services, yet most of their money was being siphoned off by white professionals and businessmen. Gradually, as blacks became more conscious of whites' taking money out of their communities, they began seeing the wisdom of supporting their own insurance companies.

Great Lakes Mutual Insurance Company came along just at the right time. This company was one of the most successful black companies in the history of black business in Detroit. Incorporated in 1927, it started operating in 1928. Services provided to policyholders without cost included a visiting nurse service, provided through the Visiting Nurses Association. During 1939, visiting nurses made a total of 3,367 visits to black communities in Detroit, Flint, and River Rouge at a cost of $3,452 to the company. Between 1935 and 1943, 9,537 visits were made, which cost the company $9,629.[40]

The enterprising business people associated with Great Lakes Mutual soon expanded into other ventures. They formed the Great Lakes Agency Company and in 1936 purchased the Great Lakes Manor, one of the most elegant apartment buildings in Detroit. Two years later these same business people acquired a fabulous 250-acre country club located in the Oakland Lakes north of Pontiac with clubhouses, tennis courts, and an enclosed private lake; the facilities included a lounge, a dining room, and a spacious ballroom. The Great Lakes Country Club, according to its buyers, would provide a place for "rest and recreation" for blacks in Detroit and nearby cities.[41]

In 1941, the Great Lakes Insurance Company employed 112 blacks and had over $11 million worth of insurance in force on 33,273 policyholders, from whom the company received $1,342,252.74 in premiums. Furthermore, the company had paid a total of $239,587.80 to beneficiaries of policyholders. By 1943, Great Lakes Mutual had accumulated unassigned surplus funds amounting to $131,397 in cash on hand and $97,235 in banks, which were neither stocks nor speculative securities; and their first mortgage loan on real estate totaled $50,000.[42]

Black insurance companies rarely obtained white policyholders, yet they were forced to compete with large white companies for black customers. In spite of these handicaps, they succeeded in becoming some of the largest businesses in Detroit operated by blacks. They provided jobs and loans to protect black homes and businesses, which contributed to the stability of the institutional structure of the black community.

Small black loan companies complemented the self-help thrust of black hospitals and insurance companies. Throughout the 1920s, the Michigan People's Finance Company, the Watson Enterprises, and the St. Antoine Branch of the Michigan Mutual Savings Association aided many black workers in financing the purchasing of homes. In 1925, Michigan Mutual, with a mixed-race directorate and several thousand members, financed the purchasing of 240 homes for black workers.[43]

The Michigan People's Finance Company proved its worth to the black community by granting the Urban League, which had offices in the company's building, free rent for the duration of the Depression.[44] This networking of black self-help enabled the Urban League to continue providing essential services to the black community.

In the late 1930s and early 1940s, blacks began setting up their own credit unions to eliminate the cut-throat activities of black and white loan sharks who exploited black workers.[45] The largest and best known of these credit unions included the Westside Improvement Association Credit Union, the Fannie B. Peck Credit Union, the National Alliance of Postal Employees Credit Union, and the Second Baptist Church Credit Union. The Fannie B. Peck Credit Union best exemplified local black self-help. Fannie B. Peck and a group of young men from her church's Sunday school class organized the credit union in 1936. By 1941 the Fannie B. Peck Credit Union had 220 members. Between 1936 and 1941, the credit union made loans of more than $14,000.00 to black members to pay school bills and hospital and doctor bills, to buy with cash instead of installment payments, and to take advantage of sales. Dividends were declared annually. A five percent dividend was declared in 1940. The Fannie B. Peck Credit Union was the first black credit union in America to receive a state charter.[46] These financial institutions demonstrated the black community's ability to marshal and use its own limited resources. The growth and development of such institutions also reflected an evolving social consciousness among blacks in Detroit.

Black self-help efforts were not limited to black-controlled institutions. Blacks in Detroit and other cities often developed or operated projects and organizations controlled by predominantly white regional or national boards of directors. In such cases, blacks still promoted the self-help philosophy. In the case of the black Ys (segregated YMCA and YWCA) in Detroit, blacks played a key role in supporting the organization's work in poor black communities. In 1923, the black community pledged $40,000 in a financial campaign, to which was added $375,000 by the Metropolitan Board of the YMCA, to build a local black branch. By 1926, it had developed programs for both sexes. In 1927, several black women's organizations started a $4,000,000 building campaign to accommodate the rapidly expanding black women's membership, which had been on the rise since the establishment of the black YWCA in 1920. The new building was completed in 1932. As soon as it opened for business, this new branch was pressed into service within the black community to provide food and shelter for unemployed black women. At the outbreak of World War II, the branch helped to house black women and girls who had come to Detroit to work in the tank section in the war industries. Both the black

YMCA and YWCA became strong internal institutions, encouraging black self-help and community building. Along with the Urban League these black branches also provided excellent training grounds for young black professionals.[47]

BLACK NEWSPAPERS AND SOCIAL CONSCIOUSNESS

Black newspapers in Detroit tended to be the most influential institutions in shaping black social consciousness and inculcating in the collective black mind the spirit of black self-help. They represented the only means of communication beyond the information-gathering social centers such as barbershops, poolrooms, and churches. Black newspapers expanded the sense of community among diverse groups of blacks. At times they tended to favor those social classes that bought advertising, but they at least addressed major problems facing the black community as a whole.

The black press in Detroit had nineteenth-century roots, as did the older black churches and lodges. The *Western Excelsior,* the first black newspaper in Detroit, began operation on March 28, 1848. The *Plain Dealer* was established on May 19, 1883, and for a while was the major black newspaper in Detroit. Frederick Douglass once wrote for the paper. This paper ran for eleven years and was one of the first newspapers in the midwest to realize the great significance of typesetting machines; it became the second newspaper in Michigan to purchase such machinery.[48]

Most of the Detroit black newspapers were weeklies and rarely lasted longer than fifteen years. These included: The *Detroit Owl* (1926–30), the *Guardian* (1932–34), the *Detroit People's News* (1930–36), the *Michigan World* and the *Detroit World* (1931–32), the *Detroit Independent* (1921–32), and the *Paradise Valley News* (1937). Unlike most black newspapers, which collapsed during the Great Depression, the *Detroit Tribune* was established during this period and served the black community until January 1966.[49]

In 1936, John H. Sengstacke, a black Chicago publisher, realized that Detroit was becoming a labor town and that the United Auto Workers (UAW) were on the move. He sent Lucius Harper, a veteran *Chicago Defender* editor, to Detroit to change the former Detroit edition of the *Chicago Defender* into a full-scale local paper; it was called the *Michigan Chronicle.*[50] Along with the *Detroit Tribune,* the *Michigan Chronicle* joined the long struggle to stimulate the development of black social consciousness. The *Detroit Tribune* tended, on occasion, to be more conservative. Both, however, embraced the philosophy of black self-help.

The *Detroit Tribune* stated at the outset it would be a progressive newspaper for "the humble wage-earners and the unemployed workers," but the economic realities were such that the paper was forced to be almost "a mouthpiece for the business and professional people." The first five issues carried a complete directory of local black professionals and business people, to encourage blacks to patronize their own race.[51]

As expected, most of the news items and editorials focused upon church-related and professional functions, conventions and activities, the NAACP, and the Booker T. Washington Trade Association. Both newspapers clearly favored segments of the black bourgeoisie such as doctors, lawyers, dentists, druggists, undertakers, and beauticians. The *Detroit Tribune* also covered membership drives for the NAACP and the Urban League, which proved essential for the survival of those organizations. Black people's consciousness had to be raised before they would join or support self-help organizations.

In simple economic terms, black newspapers had to depend on the black bourgeoisie. White businesses had not made it a practice to advertise much in the black press. Moreover black newspapers had to compete amongst themselves for a share of the ghetto market. The only hope black newspapers had for survival during the 1930s was to cater to those social and economic groups that could buy space—for whatever political or social reasons. And since fraternal orders and merchants needed and bought large advertisements, the paper's general approach and outlook tended to reflect these class biases and values.

White department stores purchased some space, but the majority of advertisements were bought by small local stores, auto repair garages, and restaurants and clubs in the black community. The paper was also influenced in this direction by its business manager, Robert C. Peak, an advocate of black economic self-help and a supporter of the Booker T. Washington Trade Association. After a merger with the *Detroit Independent* in the mid 1930s, designed to reduce competition and build a strong black newspaper, the paper focused on the migration and southern injustices. But evidently this approach brought too little payoff because the paper soon returned to the same content and remained consistent up until the 1940s.[52]

In contrast to the explicit prolabor focus of the *Michigan Chronicle,* the *Tribune* was proindustry and pro–black capitalism. The differences in the philosophy and orientation of these two major black newspapers are attributed to their very different institutional histories. The *Michigan Chronicle* was set up by a well-established outside black newspaper publisher whose fortunes were not directly tied to the proindustry orientation of the Detroit black leadership. The *Michigan Chronicle,* therefore, had the advantage of riding into town on the crest of the wave of industrial unionism. They had few long or delicate community ties to break. In addition, the *Chronicle* was established during a time when the Detroit black community and its leadership were undergoing a radical ideological transformation, deciding whether to side with labor or Mr. "tried and true" Ford (see Chapter 7).

On the other hand, the *Tribune* had evolved within the unique institutional history of a black community heavily indebted to and dependent upon industrialists such as Henry Ford. Despite this, in the late 1920s and 1940s, the *Tribune* began drifting away from its proindustry position toward a more open position on labor.[53]

Though it was initially conservative on issues related to industry and labor, the *Tribune* contributed its share to raising black consciousness in Detroit on several key social issues. The paper reported racial discrimination of all types in its pages, as well as the heroic black struggles to counter such discrimination. The *Tribune* encouraged blacks to vote and stressed black economic development. In additon, the paper aired ongoing controversy. It even encouraged black readers to support *all* black newspapers in Detroit. In 1935, the *Tribune* reminded blacks that they had been freed from slavery seventy years; at the same time, it also mentioned Italy's oppression of Ethiopia.[54]

Between 1933 and 1945, hardly an issue of any relevance to the political, economic, and social development of the black community escaped the attention of the *Detroit Tribune*. As could be expected, certain subjects received more attention than others—for example, the Booker T. Washington Trade Association and its sister organization, the Housewives League. This emphasis reflected the ideological orientation of those who believed that black economic self-help represented the best means of black community building in industrial Detroit.[55]

Throughout this period, the *Tribune* never wavered in its promotion of black business. The paper carried on a constant campaign to educate the black public about the necessity of "cooperation and team work among the members of our race." "We cannot build Negro business unless we support it," the paper scolded its readers in the mid 1930s. When we spend 95 percent of our money with business people of other racial groups, we should not expect the 5 percent we spend with Negro firms to provide our children and ourselves with all the jobs we think they should provide." The *Tribune* pointed to the fact that many blacks were spending hundreds of thousands of dollars weekly with nonblack businesses "from which Negroes receive little, if any, economic returns, in the form of jobs or reciprocal patronage." The paper criticized black professional and business people, churches, clubs, and fraternal organizations that depended on the black press to defend them and publish news about their organizations and activities, while they in turn subscribed to the white press, which seldom published such news items.[56]

Some blacks even bragged, reported the *Detroit Tribine* in early 1942, that they did not read black newspapers. No doubt these blacks felt the black press too restrictive and "race conscious," too preoccupied with issues of black survival and progress. Obviously, they did not understand the relationship between supporting black institutions and providing jobs for blacks. "The time has come," the *Tribune* appealed to its readers, "when we must spend the bulk of our money where it will help make jobs for Negro workers. Otherwise, the number of our jobless men and women increases, and they will not have the purchasing power with which to support Negro organizations and institutions."[57]

As the Great Depression gave way to the prosperity of the war years, the *Detroit Tribune* drew attention to the fact that many defense orders were being filled by local factories which, in turn, were hiring more and more workers—including blacks. These workers were spending their high wages on a wide range of consumer goods supplied by local merchants. But the *Tribune* asked: "What share of this prosperity and patronage is being received by local Negro businesses?" "Only a small percentage," the *Tribune* commented, notwithstanding the fact that "thousands of the workers who are reaping a harvest of good wages in local industrial plants are members of our own race."[58]

The paper warned black business people that the war-related prosperity would not last forever; and while money was being abundantly spent in the black community, local black business leaders "must put forth vigorous efforts to secure a larger share of the trade." Business will not just come to black businesses unsolicited, warned the *Tribune*. Black business people will have to "go after it in a systematic and concerned manner." There are new dollars out there "for aggressive, progressive Negro business men and women to claim them." And once these new dollars are in the hands of these aggressive black entrepreneurs, then, the *Tribune* advised, the black business community will be able to expand, modernize, provide employment for young blacks, and set up other businesses. "This goal," the *Tribune* added, "is worth striving for."[59]

By the time the *Michigan Chronicle* was established in 1936 and Louis Martin, a recent young graduate of the University of Michigan, had taken over as editor,[60] the *Tribune* had almost single-handedly developed the social consciousness of the black community. Martin was undeniably more radical and prolabor than his counterpart at the *Detroit Tribune,* but his newspaper probably drew its more radical readership from segments of the black community whose social consciousness had been raised already by the *Detroit Tribune.*

Martin and the *Michigan Chronicle* stimulated and energized key segments of the black community that were breaking away from the Republican Party and antiunionism (see Chapters 7 and 8). In 1939, Martin attacked Henry Ford and "his Angels of Darkness"[61] (i.e., his black supporters for antiunion positions) saying what many black leaders felt but were too frightened to say in public or private. According to two scholars of the period, "Martin with his New Deal and union sympathies consciously developed for the *Chronicle* a new constituency."[62]

This "new constituency" emerged as a result of the radical transformation of the social consciousness of black Detroit between 1936 and 1941. In fact, without Martin and the *Michigan Chronicle,* black social consciousness would not have been able to take the iedological leap from what many blacks considered the old tried and tested political orthodoxy, with its heavy dependency upon the Republican party, the industrial elites, and black capitalism, to the Democratic party and industrial unionism. Therefore, the *Michigan Chronicle's* first major contributions to black consciousness and self-help were in providing a channel for the expression of the new political and economic ideas coursing through and transforming the black community.

In contrast to the *Detroit Tribune,* which leaned toward the Republicans, the *Michigan Chronicle* was unapologetically Democratic at a time when some blacks still considered it economic suicide to be a Democrat (see Chapter 7). But by the time Louis Martin joined the staff of the Democratic National Committee in 1944,[63] the majority of black voters in Detroit were Democratic and Martin and the *Michigan Chronicle* had contributed their share in making the difference.

However much the *Detroit Tribune* and the *Michigan Chronicle* might have differed from each other, both maintained a consistent focus on similar overriding issues that plagued the black community. Both fought against racial discrimination in all of its ugly forms and both encouraged the black community to fight back and to strive for unity of purpose and the betterment of the overall black community. "[O]ur plight demands the very best efforts of all of us for mutual help and betterment," the *Chronicle* informed its readers in the spring of 1939 on the occasion of an ideological conflict among black leaders. "Our public men who are doing their utmost for the common good do not have the time to seek personal applause nor indulge in petty jealousies. Our position is too precarious to afford an individual leadership or a divided people."[64]

Any community newspaper could have reported bad news, but the black press in Detroit, particularly the *Michigan Chronicle,* had a knack for using bad news to raise the consciousness of the black community and inspire it to struggle on. "However discouraging the studies of Negro progress in America may prove to be," the *Michigan Chronicle* warned its readers in January of 1939, "we cannot permit ourselves any pessimism in considering either our present or our future, we inhabit no vale of tears despite the fact that we represent the most oppressed minority in America. . . . To some extent, at least, life for us is what we make it."[65]

Here was the black self-help philosophy expressed in its purist form. As hard as times were, blacks had to carve their destiny out of stone and not permit themselves to inherit "a vale of tears."

Occasionally in the midst of circumstances which belied all hope and encouragement, the black press in Detroit revived hope in order to inspire the community, worn and tired from constant struggle and more than enough setbacks. Much like other years, 1940 was a tough year for blacks in Detroit, but the *Michigan Chronicle* called it a "banner year" and informed its readers that the community of which they were a part was "materially and spiritually richer. In our community today, there is no lack of confidence."[66]

Lack of confidence resulting from the groundswell of white racist resistance to legitimate black rights during the war years would have certainly overwhelmed the black community had not the black press been present to encourage blacks to counter and transcend such resistance. Here again, the *Michigan Chronicle* played a leading role in directing black moral indignation and protest against racist forces bent on keeping blacks from benefiting from the prosperity of the war years.

When blacks and their white allies in Detroit and elsewhere began protesting against racial discrimination, which evoked unsolicited advice from high officials to "cool off," the *Chronicle* retorted, "if we fall victims to this cooling off technique, we can kiss all of our gains against industry good-bye. Instead of cooling off, we need to get hot and stay hot until effective machinery is established to guarantee equal job opportunities to all Americans regardless of color, creed, or national origin. Let the stooges of Hitler and the Negro-haters do the cooling."[67]

This was tough black talk for the time and probably led to the accusations by members of the 1943 race-riot fact-finding committee that the black press (and the NAACP) were the principal instigators in the riot because they had encouraged blacks to be militant in the struggle for racial equality (see chapter 5). Of course, such one-sided racist views ignored the long train of racial abuse heaped upon the black community for decades.

No one denied that the black press, particularly the *Chronicle,* did in fact encourage blacks to be militant in the struggle for equality. This had been the purpose and glory of the black press dating back for over a century. And the black press in Detroit never deviated far from this historic and honorable tradition and mandate. As long as white racism persisted, the black press was bound by its legacy of struggle to alert and lead the community to resist and overcome it; and few black papers fulfilled this honorable mandate as well as the *Michigan Chronicle.*

The black press in Detroit could and did cherish dreams and visions of a better day beyond racism and war. As the end of World War II approached, the *Michigan Chronicle,* rising above its own pressing historic mission of leading the race in struggle, gallantly encouraged its readers to participate in the larger struggle for world unity and peace:

> No period in modern history has been more challenging than the present. And this challenge, like this war, demands something of every one of us.
>
> In the winning of the war and the peace as well, there is one factor without which we cannot hope to succeed. Unless we have unity among men of good will in our own country and in the world, we shall fail again, as generations before us, to achieve a warless world. This unity does not mean a mere general agreement on common ends by those who are in positions of leadership, but rather a unity which stems from the hearts and minds of the great masses of the people.
>
> Racial, religious, and cultural prejudices which can be exploited by men

of ill-will must not be permitted to check our progress toward the unity that we shall need to make life livable again. In destroying the divisive influences in our midst, everyone of us can participate in the building of unity. All colors and minds of men have a contribution to make and the future of civilization demands that we make it.

Too often in the past the so-called "common man" has left the business of shaping the future to those aggressive egotists who lust for power and the glory it brings. Even in our own community, some of us shirk our social and civic responsibilities and leave our own interests in the hands of the other fellow. This "other fellow" has made a mess of things here at home and the more we lean upon him the bigger mess we can expect.

For the coming year, we of the rank and file must resolve to take a new view and a new responsibility for the building of a warless world. We can start in our own backyard. It is the "common man" who has fought all the wars of history and it is time for the common man to speak and be heard regarding the shape of the future.[68]

While both the *Detroit Tribune* and the *Michigan Chronicle* emphasized black pride and self-help, they often projected an obvious color preference which hampered the full development of black social consciousness. Earlier we mentioned the *Tribune's* negative attitudes towards the singing of the blues, which suggested at least a tendency towards class and cultural bias. In some ways both the black press also had a tendency toward color bias. Both tendencies revealed a persistent historical contradiction in the developing black social consciousness, which advocated black pride and self-help on one hand while shying away from anything too "black" in looks and culture on the other hand. In short, the black press in Detroit went only so far in the development of black social consciousness.

Neither the *Chronicle* nor the *Tribune* fully encouraged a black consciousness based upon a deep appreciation of dark-complexioned blacks. On the contrary, both newspapers published advertisements which denigrated dark complexion. At the same time that they protested against white newspaper advertisements depicting blacks in a negative light, such as a little boy eating a watermelon, both newspapers published advertisements which strongly suggested that lighter complexioned blacks, especially women, were better off than those with darker complexions. While such advertisements reflected the history of racial preferences within the black community, we have to wonder why the black press did not consider such advertisements as racist as those that appeared in white newspapers. The answer is clear: The social consciousness of black newspapers themselves lagged far behind.[69]

Bleaching cream dominated most of the anti–dark complexion advertisements in the black press. According to these advertisements, by using these bleaching creams and "skin whiteners," black women could "know the joy of lovely, *fairer, brighter,* smoother skin." By using Doctor Palmer's skin whitener black women would not suffer, their romance would not "hit the rocks because of rough, harsh, uneven, and too dark skin." The "dark skin" was always emphasized in these advertisements. Lighter skin would even help a person obtain employment (which unfortunately, in many cases was true). "Lighter, brighter skin helps win big money jobs." The message of the advertisements could not be mistaken. As one put it, "brighter, lighter skin is prettier."[70]

The advertisements in the black press also emphasized "long, smooth hair" as a standard of beauty for black women. In 1941 a similar advertisement with a picture of a light complected woman with hair flowing down over her shoulders promised black women that they too could "have beautiful hair." Four years later, an advertisement for a scalp ointment appealed to black women by asking: "Do you want the long smooth hair that attracts love and adoration?"[71]

Much like the advertisements for skin whiteners, bleaching cream, and long hair, the social pages of both the *Detroit Tribune* and the *Michigan Chronicle* focused upon the "lighter side" of the black community. If there were ever any doubts in the minds of the readers of these newspapers as to the value placed upon light complexions, they had only to scan the society sections of both papers. The Alpha Kappa Alpha and the "charming sweethearts at the Sigma Gamma Rho ball" sororities tended to be predominantly light complected, as was the black elite.[72] Black social consciousness, therefore, as reflected in these two major black newspapers of the late 1930s and early 1940s, rarely addressed the problems of color prejudice within the black community itself. Yet in all fairness to the black press in Detroit, it both influenced black social consciousness and self-help and was itself influenced by unresolved contradictions inherent within that same consciousness.

THE UNIVERSAL NEGRO IMPROVEMENT ASSOCIATION:
MARCUS GARVEY'S FOLLOWERS IN DETROIT

Of all of the black self-help organizations in Detroit, the Detroit area division of the United Negro Improvement Association was one of the most colorful. Notwithstanding a relatively short period of activity compared to other black self-help movements, organizations, and institutions in Detroit, the movement made a major contribution to the black self-help philosophy. Its mass appeal uplifted the hearts and souls of thousands of black working people who had left the repressive conditions of the South. The colorful parades and heady talk of race pride provided a much needed balm to those souls who had suffered for so long at the hands of arrogant, racist whites, in both the North and the South. But the appeal was not just to working-class blacks. In fact, the Garvey movement in Detroit and in other cities tended to be headed by members of the black petite bourgeoisie. As historian Judith Stein has pointed out: "The language of Garveyism was racial; its ideology was bourgeois." According to Stein, "Garveyism was stamped by the leadership and immediate purpose of more middling strata, people who were the cause of its passionate hopes and social instability."[73]

It was to some members of this class in Detroit that Garvey attempted to make his appeals for funds for The Black Star Line in the spring of 1919. However, he was blocked for a time by a member of the black upper class, Charles S. Smith, the African Methodist Episcopal bishop of Michigan, who reported Garvey to the Justice Department as a "Red" who was pushing a project which was "a fake pure and simple . . . [who] should either be required to discontinue his present vicious propaganda and fake practices or be deported as an undesirable."[74]

Garvey was not discouraged by the bishop. By then, he had probably become accustomed to such reactions from the members of the black upper classes. He must have been somewhat encouraged, however, as he wrote to his "Fellow men of the Negro Race" from the black owned-and-operated Biltmore Hotel, an establishment then reflecting the economic growth and development of the expanding black petite bourgeoisie:

> Greetings:—Through pressure of work I was rendered unable for several weeks to send you the accustomed message of cheer and good will. Today I write to you from the city of Detroit, bidding you be steadfast in your hope of the glorious future that awaits us.
> The Universal Negro Improvement Association is now starting in earnest to cover the entire world in its campaign to inaugurate the "The Black Star Line."[75]

A year later, a division of the UNIA was established in Detroit. John Charles Zampty was one of the first blacks in Detroit to join the UNIA. Zampty was born on July 12, 1889, in Belmont Port of Spain, Trinidad, then the British West Indies. After a series of jobs that took him from Trinidad to Nigeria, West Africa, he met Marcus Garvey in 1912 in Colon, Panama. Garvey was "moving from place to place advocating unity among the Black race because of the conditions he experienced when he first saw them in every place he had traveled. When I met him he was circulating a paper known as *Liberty*. He was financially able to move from one area to the next, and by selling these magazines or papers periodically he was able to maintain a cashflow."[76]

According to Zampty, the Detroit UNIA division was organized in Detroit in 1920 under the following circumstances:

> The UNIA's Detroit Division was organized in Detroit in 1920. A. D. Williams, who was a preacher then, went to the UNIA Convention in New York, and came back to Detroit with a red, black, and green flag, and he walked the streets of Detroit accompanied by others, played the tambourine and so on, and that began the organization of the Detroit Division. Through

that method we got our charter, Detroit Division No. 407. The first officers were President W. Meyers, First Vice President L. K. Nerks, Secretary Reynold Smith, and Treasurer Douglas [no other name given]. Soon we had a membership of over three hundred whose ages ranged from eighteen to seventy-five years old.[77]

The UNIA had a mass appeal which would suggest that many working class blacks belonged to it. It would seem reasonable to surmise that the methods used by A. D. Williams, walking the streets playing the tambourine, were geared to appeal to certain segments of the black working and lower classes. One could not imagine John C. Dancy using such a method to build support for the Detroit Urban League, which was unabashedly middle class in its programmatic orientation.

Garvey visited Detroit again in 1922 speaking several times to huge crowds of blacks who turned out in the thousands to hear him. Such huge turnouts must have alarmed the likes of Bishop C. S. Smith, who reported Garvey to the Justice Department. Garvey probably felt himself properly vindicated as he spoke to thousands of blacks, mostly newly arrived southern migrants, of his vision of uplifting the race:

> I appeared in Detroit three nights. I spoke two nights at . . . Turner Hall, wherein there was jammed 2,000 people to hear me each night, and there was turned away twice as many on both occasions. On the third night I spoke in the arcadia, to 4,000 Negroes, each of whom paid 50 cents admission, and they stayed . . . until 12 o'clock, as they did [at] the two previous meetings, to give their moral and financial support to the work of the Universal Negro improvement Association.[78]

No doubt there were also members of the black petite bourgeoisie among those throngs that hailed Garvey. As Stein has argued, the urban black professional and business classes were also drawn to the UNIA in Detroit and dominated the leadership. F. Levi Lord, one of the major leaders of the Local and a former school teacher from Barbados and skilled shoe maker, "recruited an able leadership of businessmen and professionals," including such personages as Alonzo Pettiford, a lawyer with ties to the black elite. Pettiford presided over the Detroit Local during the early 1920s. In the fall of 1923, both Lord and Pettiford were honored by the UNIA international office with the award of the order of Knight Commander of the Cross of African Redemption.

J. A. Craigen took over the presidency after Pettiford. Craigen was born in British Guiana and came to the United States to work for the Navy Department at Muscle Shoals, Alabama. Craigen then migrated to Detroit and worked at Ford. Years later he would become a lawyer. Charles Diggs arrived in Detroit in 1913 and established a business in 1922. He was the leader of the Board of Trustees that managed the division's property.

J. Milton Van Lowe was another member of the black professional class who played a leading role in the Detroit UNIA. Born in the British West Indies, Van Lowe attended the University of California and the University of Pennsylvania before coming to Detroit, where he received a law degree from the Detroit College of Law. He was a member of the Bethel AME church in Detroit. In 1924, he had achieved sufficient prominence in the UNIA as to be accorded the privilege of addressing the UNIA Convention. Robert Lincoln Poston, another member of Detroit's black petite bourgeoisie, attended Princeton University and protested Woodrow Wilson's (then president of the university) policy of racial segregation on campus which led to his forced departure. In 1920, he and his brother Ulysses published the short-lived *Detroit Contender* (1920–21), which the UNIA newspaper, the *Negro World,* highly commended for its role in rendering a "signal service to the UNIA in winning Detroit against the strongest opposition that has been encountered in any northern city." Poston was a close associate of Garvey, "a Garvey favorite," who became "Sir" Robert Poston. He moved up in the UNIA and became a member of the *Negro World* editorial staff. In February 1924, he led a UNIA mission to Liberia to discuss terms for Afro-American immigration. On the way back to New York, he contracted pneumonia and died.[79]

It seems clear from the above that the members of the black professional and business classes played a leading role in running the affairs of the Detroit UNIA. The black working class most probably played little or no major role in the leadership positions. Owing in large part to the well-paid black industrial working class that made up the bulk of its membership of about four thousand, the Detroit UNIA was able to contribute more than its share to the parent body. Its economic activities were limited to purchasing a building for its meetings and buying stock in the Black Star Line. While individual UNIA members, such as Charles Diggs, would develop major businesses in Detroit, the division did not initiate any economic activities of any great import. It did establish a restaurant in its Liberty Hall to serve its members. However, its leaders did not use it to teach entrepreneurial skills but rather hired trained blacks to run it.[80]

The bulk of the members probably worked in the industrial plants, as Zampty did. But few had Zampty's educational background. Zampty had initially come to Detroit to work for the Ford Motor Company. He had been educated at the Roman Catholic Academical College and worked in Nigeria as a sanitary inspector for the Trinidad Sanitary Corporation. Just after the start of World War I, Zampty wrote the Ford Motor Company in Detroit and sent them his qualifications. The company invited him to come to Detroit and work for it. When he arrived at the Ford office, Zampty discovered that being qualified was not sufficient:

> I took my communications to the office of employment of the Ford Motor Company, where they were hiring men in large numbers. But I was told it was a mistake. When I learned what the mistake was, I realized that they

thought I was a white man and they had an official job for him, but when they saw me, they would not hire me in that capacity.

There was a great deal of work, my type of work, in the City of Detroit but to my disadvantage because, wherever I went, I was not allowed to receive the same pay as white workers. I had to keep that in mind as I went through life. I retired from Ford Motor Company in 1957.[81]

In 1922, Zampty traveled with Garvey throughout the United States as the UNIA's auditor and remained active in the Detroit UNIA all his life.[82] Zampty's life as a member of the Detroit UNIA paralleled the life and work of John C. Dancy. Both men were equally concerned with uplifting the black community but used different approaches. As in many other similar situations, blacks working on behalf of the same cause more often than not disagreed over the best method to address the cause. As one of the major leaders in the Detroit UNIA, Zampty did not think highly of the Detroit Urban League and the local NAACP:

> There are other political organizations, such as National Association for the Advancement of Colored People (NAACP). Their program has been in existence since 1909, and I have watched its activities among its officers and members in every area and I do not think they have accomplished what we have accomplished. I am not in sympathy with the program of the NAACP. Their program is advocating integration, and no one—no power on earth or in heaven—can force integration unless they themselves are willing to open their hearts and their minds to accept others. As a result of that from 1909 to the present, I do not see any good that the NAACP has done or is doing as far as their program is concerned. I must also say the same thing for the Urban League, which is asking for open doors and handouts.[83]

Zampty's indictment of the work of the Detroit Urban League and the NAACP was based more on ideological differences than on any objective analysis of the comparable contributions of these organizations to the black community building process. As we have seen, the Detroit Urban League contributed to the stability of the black working class during its critical formative period. Without this stability the Detroit UNIA would not have the economic base on which to support themselves and the parent body. No doubt, the vast majority of the Detroit UNIA members probably worked in jobs obtained for them by the persistent efforts of Dancy and his always hard-pressed staff. Therefore, it is inconceivable that the Detroit UNIA did not benefit in some way, directly or indirectly, from the work of the League.

Similarly with the local NAACP, UNIA members faced the same racial oppression visited upon all blacks in housing and public accommodations. No doubt, they also were probably occasionally brutalized by white police officers. Their lives could not have been totally unaffected by the work of the NAACP in these areas. According to Zampty, the economic work of the UNIA suffered after the "expatriation of our leader."[84] This would suggest that local UNIA was no longer able to contribute, at least not economically, to the community building process. Yet that process did not come to a halt. It continued, as it had before the establishment of the local UNIA, through the work of the Local Urban League, the NAACP, and other community organizations.

Notwithstanding its unfortunate decline in the economic area, resulting from the expatriation of Garvey in 1925, the UNIA left its mark on the self-consciousness of thousands of blacks in Detroit. Following the trends in other black urban communities, thousands of blacks attended UNIA gatherings in Detroit. And the Detroit UNIA did influence Elijah Muhammad, the founder of the Nation of Islam. Zampty explained the historical connection between the Detroit UNIA and the Nation of Islam (called the Black Muslims by some nonmembers):

> I have to give credit to Elijah Poole of the Nation of Islam. He was a good member of the UNIA and worked with us for many years, and when he came in contact with Fared, Poole left Detroit. After leaving The Detroit Division, [UNIA] he went to Chicago and was captain of the legion there. He saw the opportunity of organizing under the name of Black Muslim. . . . Elijah Poole was wise enough in arousing the Black people here in certain areas . . . to recognize that they must do something . . . economic . . . for their race, and that since they are Black Muslims, then they must work as Black people. If he had left that word "Muslim" out, I think he would have gotten more cooperation from even those who were at one time former members of the UNIA.[85]

Elijah Poole, later Elijah Muhammad, was not the only UNIA member in Detroit who, in the wake of the decline of the UNIA, sought other means of community building. Two other former leaders, Charles Diggs and J. A. Craigen, abandoned the UNIA for more effective approaches of community building (see the discussion in this chapter and later chapters). Garvey's incarceration and subsequent deportation led to factional conflicts within the parent organization that sapped the energy of the Detroit UNIA.

An attempt to revitalize the UNIA was made in 1926, when four of Garvey's major division leaders from Cincinnati, Detroit, Pittsburgh, and Philadelphia held an emergency meeting in Detroit. The gathering rededicated itself to Garvey and "mapped out a UNIA holding action until the return of the movement's dynamic founder"; but, to little avail. As one scholar of the movement put it: "[W]ithout Garvey's inspirational leadership the delegates were unable to generate the enthusiasm which had been so notable a characteristic of the earlier UNIA conventions."[86]

Local blacks continued to support Garvey and the UNIA with their donations and other forms of support.[87] On May 6, 1927, the Detroit *Independent*, a black newspaper, published a moving article on Garvey, reminding the black community that regardless of Garvey's "mistakes" and beliefs, he had still contributed to the development of black social consciousness:

> News comes from the Federal Prison at Atlanta that Marcus Garvey, the world-famous U.N.I.A. founder and president who has been incarcerated there for some two years, is confined in the prison hospital. He is suffering from bronchitis and asthma, developed from a recent attack of lagrippe, and it is reported he has lost fifteen pounds in weight.
>
> Why is Garvey in prison, anyway? Hasn't the end of justice already been served, during the years he has been imprisoned in Atlanta? These are questions that thoughtful Negroes should consider. Marcus Garvey is a member of our racial group and is just as human as we are. He may have made mistakes, just as others make them. We may not all agree in our views concerning the Garvey Movement, but this is not the issue. The same lamentable fate and imprisonment that befell Marcus Garvey, regardless of innocence or guilt, might probably befall any other Negro leader with the universal Pan-African ideas and ideals and the wonderful organizing power that Garvey possesses. Garvey has the ability to make millions of Negroes think and act together on the "Africa for Africans" idea. He has the power to purchase steamships, to man them, and to send them on the high seas to develop international trade and commerce among Negroes and to transport members of the race to the African fatherland. The white world does not like that. Such power might endanger white colonial rule in Africa. It might also stimulate millions of colored Americans and natives of the islands and countries to the South to follow the Garvey movement to Africa, thereby depleting the colored labor supply in the Western Hemisphere, and at the same time awakening a keener sense of race consciousness and unity among the African natives. If Marcus Garvey did not possess this potential ability, he would not now be in prison.
>
> On Sunday, May 8, sympathizers of Marcus Garvey in Detroit and elsewhere are planning to hold great mass meetings and silent parades of protest against his continued incarceration. . . . Marcus Garvey is sick, he has already suffered in prison sufficiently to serve the ends of justice. We believe he should be set free.[88]

On the appointed day, May 8, the Detroit UNIA held a silent parade and a mass meeting, which attracted thousands of people who stood on crowded sidewalks to watch the event.[89] Even as the Detroit UNIA rallied behind Garvey to secure his release from prison, it was on the decline. Two years later, both the local and the parent organization suffered a tremendous blow when one of Detroit's leading UNIA members, Craigen, along with some other major leaders from other cities, resigned at the 1929 UNIA convention held by Garvey in Jamaica after his release. They accused Garvey of using the UNIA limited resources to foster his own personal and political aims. Craigen and William Ware of Cincinnati joined forces to try and create a new organization without Garvey. Predictably, the plan failed and the UNIAs in Detroit and other cities broke into factions.[90]

While the Detroit UNIA did not last long as a viable organization—wasting away because of internal strife within the parent organization and the resignation, desertion, and dissaffection of major leaders—it left its imprint on the collective self-consciousness of black Detroit. Like UNIA divisions in other cities and indeed around the Black World, the Detroit UNIA contributed to the building and consolidating of an international network of black communities, all engaged in various forms of community building. The Detroit UNIA division spawned some major black leaders: Elijah Poole, Charles Diggs, J. A. Craigen, and others who would use their apprenticeship in the UNIA to develop new strategies of community building during the 1930s, 1940s, 1950s, and 1960s. As Stein has pointed out so well, several former members of the Detroit UNIA successfully made such a transition.[91]

BLACK BUSINESS AND PROFESSIONAL CLASSES

So far we have discussed black institutions and their relationship to black social consciousness and self-help and the UNIA Division of Detroit. Now we will take a broader look at the black business and professional classes which formed the base of these developments, focusing exclusively upon how these classes grew and developed within the internal market of the black community. We will then examine how black social consciousness and self-help contributed to this process.

Black institutions grew and developed in response to the expressed needs of the black community. The economic aspects of these needs viewed collectively were called "the Negro market," a segregated economic sector of the black ghetto over which both black and white business and professional people fought. Survival and progress for black business and professional people demanded that they control as much of "the Negro market" as possible.

But this was not always easy because, as we have seen, black social consciousness as related to black self-help often lagged far behind the required needs of the black community. Blacks had to be educated to support black institutions and the business and professional classes in Detroit could not wait for the black conscience to realize "its duty." Instead, between 1915 and 1945 it moved aggressively to take advantage of the black community's expanding internal market. The results of these efforts constitute impressive examples of black social consciousness and self-help during this period.

Black business and professional classes had existed in the late nineteenth century but not to the extent of their twentieth-century counterparts, who obviously shared economic advantages totally lacking in the earlier period. The World War I migration created an industrial working class consumer base that enabled twentieth century black business and professional classes to thrive much better than those of the late nineteenth century. The latter depended upon a small, low-wage black clientele and steadily declining service occupations based almost entirely upon serving whites. Barbering was the single most lucrative black service-occupation in the white work force of late nineteenth-century Detroit and the only service-occupation providing blacks with assurance of upward mobility to the middle class. But all this would soon come to an end as white racism and foreign competition combined to destroy black barbering in the white community.[92]

In 1870, blacks made up 55 percent of Detroit's 138 male barbers. By 1910 only 7.3 percent were black. In 1884, blacks owned 25 percent of the barber shops in the city; by 1908, black ownership had declined to .06 percent. By 1910, as a result of "white only" advertisements for barbers dating from the 1880s, black barbers were restricted to cutting only black men's hair.[93]

The decline of black barbering was catastrophic for the premigration black community because it was the single most important black business during that period. But more importantly its decline revealed how dependent the majority of black businessmen and professionals were on the white community. Because of the lack of a large black working class demand for their goods and services, the black business and professional classes had to rely upon a white clientele.

The handwriting was on the wall: black business and professional classes that traditionally depended upon a white clientele began turning toward "the Negro market." Interestingly enough, the descendants of these late nineteenth-century black business and professional classes failed to capitalize on the expanding, higher-wage black industrial workforce. In fact, they tended to shun the business world for work in the government. Into their places stepped "newcomers" from the South who soon made up the majority of black business and professional people. Increasingly the black doctor, lawyer, and grocer was a recent arrival from the South, serving an expanding black migrant community.[94] The World War I migration, therefore, saved the black business and professional classes in Detroit from further decline.

Unlike their nineteenth-century counterparts, forced by grim necessity to depend upon a white clientele, the new black business and professional classes had access to a rapidly expanding internal market. The problem would be how to acquire and maintain black control of it.

Less than a decade after the first migration wave, these classes pointed with pride to a number of business and professional accomplishments that resulted from catering to a mostly black clientele. H. S. Ferguson, the first black to establish a chain of restaurants in Detroit, in 1920 had made $222,000. In 1920, a black also owned and operated one of the largest modern garages in Detroit and the modern-equipped Biltmore Hotel. In the spring of 1923, Cynthia Thompson opened an apron shop "with only a few yards of cloth and a sewing machine." As her business picked up she hired other workers to meet the demand. Soon she diversified into mens' and womens' clothing and made quilts from castoff pieces. A year later, she had a greater demand for quilts than she could supply.[95]

Charles C. Diggs, Jr., started an undertaking business in 1922. Two years later he owned the largest black funeral home in Michigan. Since hairdressing for black women was one of the major businesses in the black community, several black business women capitalized upon it. Eleanora A. DeVere opened a hairdressing parlor in 1920. She had studied with Madame C. J. Walker, the famous black woman who popularized the straightening of hair and who became a millionaire from the manufacture of hair and skin preparations. DeVere was a wholesaler and retailer for Walker hair products and toilet articles and supplied Walker merchandise to agents throughout Michigan.[96] A black owned-and-operated film company, The Apex Film Manufacturing Company, was founded in 1923 and produced films of black life, *Events in Negrodom,* and of stories produced by black writers. The company started specializing in short newsreels and comedies focusing on miscellaneous aspects of black life. These films were sold directly to producing firms. The largest demand for these films came from Germany, France, and Mexico because, at the time, the local black market had not developed sufficiently. Yet the black demand was fairly good. The lack of good local black screen actors and actresses however limited the company's success.[97]

In 1922, several black brothers established the Superior Bottling Works. Unlike some black business people at the time, the Dixon brothers were well informed in the art of running a business. Their success in the manufacturing and sale of carbonated beverages created much demand. During the summer the demand for their carbonated drinks increased beyond their capacity to meet it. Although limited in equipment, they succeeded in gaining a foothold in the industry and became a member of the city, state and national associations of Manufacturers of Carbonated Beverages.[98]

On several occasions the expanding southern black community in Detroit provided markets for very specialized needs. For example, the Home Milling Company, owned and operated by blacks, was set up in 1922 to manufacture corn meal, hominy grits, and wheat flour to meet the demand of thousands of transplanted southern black folk who longed for "soul food." The great secret behind the success of this black milling company was simple: They made corn meal from white corn like southern blacks liked it, instead of from yellow corn.[99]

In 1911, a black doctor, Robert Greenridge, established one of the first black chains of drug stores in Detroit to provide employment for black professionals. The project proved so successful that by 1924 a cluster of black owned-and-operated stores emerged in the black community. Considering the fact that in 1926 about one-third of the stores in the black community were controlled by outsiders, this early move by Greenridge helped to lay the foundations for the growth and development of similar stores. Greenridge contributed further to black economic growth and development in 1919 by establishing an x-ray laboratory to provide service to the increasing numbers of black doctors and dentists who, in turn, supported the laboratory by referring their patients to him. Greenridge provided a good model for young black business people. A decade later, Sidney Barthwell, a young black pharmacist, started another black drug store chain with $500. He set up his own ice cream plant to eliminate the middleman and soon became the owner and operator of the largest black drug store chain in America.[100]

Despite the impact of the Depression, the more enterprising black business and professional people continued to push forward, growing, developing, and consolidating their economic ventures. One such venture involved moving out of the old blighted areas of the black ghetto into a new business area located around East Warren Avenue, Canfield, and Hancock between Beaubien and Russell (see map 1 in chapter 4). By 1935, several major black business and professional groups had moved into this area. Once again Dr. Robert Greenridge provided the impetus and the direction for black economic growth and development by opening a modern office building in the area. The "Walgreen" building, located on the corner of E. Warren and Beaubien streets was "thoroughly modernized" and was soon occupied by up-and-coming black business and professional people.[101]

Commending Dr. Greenridge for his contribution to this new direction, as well as the business and professional groups that took up the challenge, the *Detroit Tribune* commented:

> By investing in this modern office building and making it available to members of the race, Dr. Greenridge has rendered a real service to the community which is worthy of our unstinted gratitude and support.
>
> Despite the business depression, which has been more keenly felt in Detroit than in most other large cities, the colored business men and women of this community are not only holding their own, but are courageously pushing forward to greater achievement. We congratulate them, one and all. We also commend the masses of our people here who are so loyally giving their financial support to Negro business.[102]

In 1943, a group of black businessmen led by then state Senator Charles C. Diggs formed Wayne County Better Homes, Inc., a $100,000 construction corporation set up to build 500 Federal Housing Authority (FHA) houses. The day that the actual construction began was called by one of the local black press "a red-letter day for the Negroes of Detroit."[103]

All the black businessmen involved in this impressive project had proven records of success in their fields. Among them were: Richard H. Austin, auditor and controller, the only black certified public accountant in Michigan as well as one of the few in the United States; Everette I. Watson, the first vice president of the corporation, president of the Watson Insurance Agency, and vice president of Great Lakes Mutual Insurance Company;

Fred Allen, treasurer, who owned and operated the Supreme Linen and Laundry Company, and who was also a member of the board of trustees of Parkside Hospital and vice president of the National Negro Business League; Louis C. Blount, director, was secretary and general manager of the Great Lakes Mutual Insurance Company of Detroit, president of the Booker T. Washington Trade Association, regional vice president of the National Negro Business League, and former president of the National Negro Insurance Association; and William L. Maynard, a builder and owner of his own construction company, Maynard Construction, that represented three generations of black builders (he was a man who had personally supervised the construction of some of the most elegant houses in the city of Detroit).[104]

That same year (1943), several black businessmen purchased the fabulous nine-story, 300-room Gotham Hotel. This purchase contributed to the already impressive history of black business in Detroit by giving black Detroit "the finest hotel in the country owned and operated by Negroes." The Gotham was originally built in 1925 by Architect Albert Kahn for the opulent taste of Albert D. Hartz, the rich owner of a medical supply house, at a cost of $590,000. When the black businessmen purchased it, it became the only black-owned building on the block, and this, according to some contemporary observers, "was a milestone" in the long, slow, but relentless struggle to break out of the black ghetto.[105]

The Gotham's impressiveness was enhanced by its contrast to the long tradition of third-rate black hotels with their poor service and high prices. Soon after its purchase, the name "Gotham" became "a coast-to-coast byword" among black travellers, and black entertainers looked upon the hotel as an oasis. Prominent whites remained patrons of the hotel for a while after its purchase by blacks. Millionaire contractor Charles R. Lenmane, famous for his construction of some of Detroit's biggest viaducts, and Stanislaw Szmulewicz, famous violinist in the Detroit Symphony orchestra, among others, were still residing at the Gotham in 1947.[106] Other black business and professional men and women also made substantial contributions to the black community.

Some black businesses and professional people were able to increase their numbers more than others, because they had almost total access to particular segments of the segregated ghetto market. For example, in 1910 black barbers, hairdressers, and manicurists comprised seven percent of all such occupations in Detroit. By 1930, they had increased to thirteen percent of the total. Racial preference and segregation protected these black professions from white competition. Between 1910 and 1940, similar racial factors contributed to the greater growth of boarding and lodging establishments, restaurants, cafes, lunchrooms, barbershops, hairdressing and manicuring salons (see table 10).

In 1910, black doctors, teachers, and lawyers made up less than one percent of people in their professions in Detroit. Thirty years later, black

Table 10

Blacks as Percent of Selected Professionals and Business People* in Detroit

Occupation	1910	1920	1930	1940
Physicians and surgeons	0.7	2.1	3.8	4.1
Dentists	—	4.2	4.3	3.4
Lawyers, justices and judges	1.3	2.6	2.3	2.0
Teachers	0.4	0.8	1.1	1.6
Clergymen	—	14.1	19.4	10.7
Real estate agents and officials	0.1	0.7	2.1	3.8
Retail dealers*	0.0	1.1	3.0	2.2
Wholesale dealers*	—	0.1	—	3.5
Barbers, hairdressers and manicurists	6.6	13.0	10.8	10.2
Boarding and lodging housekeepers	2.9	9.8	15.8	27.2
Restaurants, cafe and lunchroom keepers	—	2.5	6.6	3.2

Sources: Compiled from *Thirteenth Census of the United States, 1910: Occupations, IV,* 535–55; *Fourteenth Census of the United States, 1920: Occupations, IV,* 1101–04; *Fifteenth Census of the United States, 1930: Occupations, IV,* 803–05; *Sixteenth Census of the United States, 1940: The Labor Force, III,* 612–13.
*Note: Change to wholesale and retail "trade" in 1940.

doctors comprised four percent of all doctors in the city. Black teachers and lawyers trailed behind at two percent of all teachers and lawyers. Unlike black doctors, who steadily increased their percentage of the total number of doctors in Detroit between 1910 and 1940, black dentists comprised four percent of all dentists in both 1920 and 1930, declining to three percent in 1940 (see table 10).

The expansion of the black population tended to nullify whatever increases occurred among black professional and business groups. In 1910, there were six black doctors, eleven black lawyers, and eight black teachers in a total black population of 5,741. By 1930, the black population had increased the 120,066 souls. But the number of black doctors had increased only to 78; black lawyers had increased to 51; and black teachers had increased to 145. This was not very impressive, given the large increase of the black population (see tables 11, 12, 13, 14, and 15).

As pointed out above, certain black business and professional groups grew faster than others, due to racial factors inherent in the ghetto economy. In some cases, racial factors (such as racial segregation) combined with other equally significant factors (such as particular group needs at certain stages of community growth and development) to generate different rates of growth among segments of the ghetto economy. Between 1910 and 1930, the rate of growth among black real estate agents and officials was greater than that among black lawyers, physicians, and teachers (see tables 10 and 11). No doubt the growing need and demand for housing among middle-class blacks during this period accounted for this greater rate of growth.

Table 11

Changes in Aggregate Black and White Business and Professional Classes per 1,000 Population: 1910–1940

Category	1910	1920	1930	1940
Black professionals	4.3	5.0	3.9	2.8
Black businessmen	25.3	20.2	18.5	14.0
White professionals	8.0	8.8	9.4	10.4
White businessmen	27.3	28.4	31.0	22.6

Source: Computed from Table 5.

Some segments of the black community that grew faster than others did not represent qualitative growth. For example, while the growth among black retail dealers was greater than that among black doctors between 1910 and 1930, the increase in retail dealers did not represent qualitative growth to the extent that the increase in doctors did. According to a survey, many blacks in retail lacked sufficient training for the business they were conducting. Only 14 percent had been in business more than ten years, while the average was about six years. The majority were in businesses "in no way similar to or connected with their present occupation."[107]

Compared to some black professional and business groups, black insurance agents' rate of growth during this period was greater both in number and quality. They met an obvious need in protecting black families from financial loss due to the death of the head of a household. Growth of restaurants, cafes, and lunchrooms was related to the needs of the single men who made up the industrial working class. The growth of black lawyers probably reflected the rise of black protest over violations of their civil rights.

Most black professionals and businessmen in aggregate (i.e.: doctors, lawyers, dentists, teachers, clergymen, insurance agents, and officials, etc., as "professionals"; and retail dealers, barbers, hairdressers, manicurists, keepers of boarding and lodging establishments, and restaurant, cafe and lunchroom owners, etc., as "businessmen") did not appear to increase much when viewed as a percentage of the population during this period, due to the rapid increase in population (see table 11).

Black professionals as a class increased by about one professional per 1,000 between 1910 and 1920 but declined steadily to a total of less than 3 per 1,000 in 1940. Compared to white professionals, who increased steadily, blacks did poorly. There were many more black businessmen as a class. Black businesses declined per 1,000 population from 1910 to 1920, but this decline was more a function of a rapid population increase of blacks far outpacing the rise of black businessmen. By 1940, the percentages of both black and white businessmen steadily declined. During this entire period, 1910–40, whites had a larger aggregate of business and professional classes per 1,000 population than blacks (see table 15).

Again we must emphasize the fact that the decline of some occupational groups probably affected the process of community building more than the decline of others. For example, because of the health problems in black ghettoes in Detroit, the decline of black doctors and dentists between 1930 and 1940 probably retarded the process more than the decline of clergymen, barbers, hairdressers, and manicurists during the same period.

Perhaps the most we can say about the growth and development of selected business and professional classes in the black community between 1910 and 1940 is that much of it was uneven, absorbed, and nullified by population increases and the devastation of the Depression. Yet enough growth and development did occur to keep the larger black community moving forward. The spirit animating this forward movement was rooted in a philosophy of black economic self-help.

DEVELOPING A PHILOSOPHY OF BLACK ECONOMIC SELF-HELP FOR
COMMUNITY BUILDING

In order for black business and professional people to take advantage of the expanding ghetto market so vital to this stage of community building, to which they were confined by institutional racism, they needed to develop a philosophy of black economic self-help that appealed to the larger black community. They had to educate both themselves and black consumers about the need to support black businesses and professions.

Black business and professional classes encountered countless obstacles as they struggled to survive and progress in the only market to which they had access. Realizing that they were dependent upon the internal market of the black ghetto, they set out to protect and expand their share of it; and this was no easy task. White competitors were well aware of the potential for profit within the black ghetto, where racial segregation fostered a captive consumer market. But black business and professional people were also captives, in a sense, because while white business and professional people could penetrate and exploit the ghetto market, their black counterparts could barely get within reach of the white consumer market. Therefore, both systematic white racism and the problems of a yet-undeveloped black social consciousness had to be overcome before black business and professional classes would be able to tap the full potential of the black consumer market within the ghetto.

As the black business and professional classes struggled through various problems of growth and development, they developed an economic philosophy. Realizing that they were mainly dependent upon workers in the community, they set out to protect and expand their share of internal

Table 12

Number and Percent of Black and White Selected Professionals and Business People, 1910

Category	Blacks		Whites		Total	
	Number	Percent	Number	Percent	Number	Percent
Physicians and Surgeons	6	0.7	865	99.3	871	100.0
Dentists	0	0.0	0	0.0	0	0.0
Lawyers, Justices, & Judges	11	1.3	823	98.7	834	100.0
Teachers	8	0.4	2,025	99.6	2,033	100.0
Clergymen	0	0.0	0	0.0	0	0.0
Real Estate Agents & Officials	1	0.1	669	99.9	670	100.0
Insurance Agents	0	0.0	746	100.0	746	100.0
Retail Dealers	26	0.3	7,878	99.7	7,904	100.0
Wholesale Dealers	0	0.0	0	0.0	0	0.0
Barbers, Hairdressers & Manicurists	78	6.6	1,097	93.4	1,175	100.0
Boarding & Lodging Housekeepers	40	2.9	1,345	97.1	1,385	100.0
Restaurant, Cafe, & Lunchroom Keepers	0	0.0	0	0.0	0	0.0

Sources: Compiled from *Thirteenth Census of the United States, 1910: Occupations*, IV, 554–55; *Fourteenth Census of the United States, 1920: Occupations*, IV, 1101–04; *Fifteenth Census of the United States, 1930: Occupations*, IV, 803–05; *Sixteenth Census of the United States, 1940: The Labor Force*, III, 612–13.

Table 13

Number and Percent of Black and White Selected Professionals and Business People, 1920

Category	Blacks		Whites		Total	
	Number	Percent	Number	Percent	Number	Percent
Physicians and Surgeons	28	2.1	1,291	97.9	1,319	100.0
Dentists	24	4.2	552	95.8	576	100.0
Lawyers, Justices, & Judges	32	2.6	1,180	97.4	1,212	100.0
Teachers	40	0.8	4,825	99.2	4,865	100.0
Clergymen	82	14.1	500	85.9	582	100.0
Real Estate Agents & Officials	41	0.7	5,148	99.3	5,189	100.0
Insurance Agents	6	0.5	1,213	99.5	1,219	100.0
Retail Dealers	165	1.1	14,314	98.9	14,479	100.0
Wholesale Dealers	1	0.1	830	99.9	831	100.0
Barbers, Hairdressers & Manicurists	355	13.0	2,379	87.0	2,734	100.0
Boarding & Lodging Housekeepers	226	9.8	2,072	90.2	2,298	100.0
Restaurant, Cafe, & Lunchroom Keepers	29	2.5	1,131	97.5	1,160	100.0

Sources: Compiled from *Thirteenth Census of the United States, 1910: Occupations, IV, 554–55; Fourteenth Census of the United States, 1920: Occupations, IV, 1101–04; Fifteenth Census of the United States, 1930: Occupations, IV, 803–05; Sixteenth Census of the United States, 1940: The Labor Force, III, 612–13.*

Table 14

Number and Percent of Black and White Selected Professionals and Business People, 1930

Category	Blacks		Whites		Total	
	Number	Percent	Number	Percent	Number	Percent
Physicians and Surgeons	78	3.8	1,951	96.2	2,029	100.0
Dentists	42	4.3	927	96.7	969	100.0
Lawyers, Justices, & Judges	51	2.3	2,141	97.7	2,192	100.0
Teachers	104	1.1	9,437	98.9	9,541	100.0
Clergymen	193	19.4	802	80.6	995	100.0
Real Estate Agents & Officials	133	2.1	6,113	97.9	6,246	100.0
Insurance Agents	61	1.4	4,137	98.6	4,198	100.0
Retail Dealers	675	3.0	21,952	97.0	22,627	100.0
Wholesale Dealers	0	0.0	1,219	100.0	1,219	100.0
Barbers, Hairdressers & Manicurists	669	10.8	5,522	89.2	6,191	100.0
Boarding & Lodging Housekeepers	520	15.8	2,778	84.2	3,298	100.0
Restaurant, Cafe, & Lunchroom Keepers	167	6.6	2,382	93.4	2,549	100.0

Sources: Compiled from *Thirteenth Census of the United States, 1910: Occupations,* IV, 554–55; *Fourteenth Census of the United States, 1920: Occupations,* IV, 1101–04; *Fifteenth Census of the United States, 1930: Occupations,* IV, 803–05; *Sixteenth Census of the United States, 1940: The Labor Force,* III, 612–13.

Table 15

Number and Percent of Black and White Selected Professionals and Business People, 1940

Category	Blacks		Whites		Total	
	Number	Percent	Number	Percent	Number	Percent
Physicians and Surgeons	95	4.1	2,221	95.9	2,316	100.0
Dentists	30	3.4	841	96.6	871	100.0
Lawyers, Justices, & Judges	49	2.0	2,404	98.0	2,453	100.0
Teachers	145	1.6	8,994	98.4	9,139	100.0
Clergymen	111	10.7	924	89.3	1,035	100.0
Real Estate Agents & Officials	89	3.8	2,260	96.2	2,349	100.0
Insurance Agents	98	2.9	3,218	97.1	3,316	100.0
Retail Dealers	311	2.2	13,642	97.8	13,953	100.0
Wholesale Dealers	183	3.5	5,079	96.5	5,262	100.0
Barbers, Hairdressers & Manicurists	652	10.2	5,738	89.8	6,390	100.0
Boarding & Lodging Housekeepers	666	27.2	1,781	72.8	2,447	100.0
Restaurant, Cafe, & Lunchroom Keepers	111	3.2	3,328	96.8	3,439	100.0

Sources: Compiled from *Thirteenth Census of the United States, 1910: Occupations,* IV, 554–55; *Fourteenth Census of the United States, 1920: Occupations,* IV, 1101–04; *Fifteenth Census of the United States, 1930: Occupations,* IV, 803–05; *Sixteenth Census of the United States, 1940: The Labor Force,* III, 612–13.

markets. This proved quite difficult because of white competition within the ghetto market.

In addition to these problems, black businessmen and professionals were often denied locations in downtown areas where other racial and ethnic groups were allowed to set up businesses. In some cases these other groups could afford to pay the higher rents. During the 1930s and 1940s, black merchants had a difficult time obtaining liquor licenses. The police department and the liquor commission created barriers that restricted black merchants from participating in one of the most lucrative businesses in the black community. These barriers against black merchants reduced black competition against white merchants, who were able to make fortunes selling liquor to blacks. Of course the irony of this issue was that blacks found themselves fighting for the right to make money by supplying other blacks with liquor, which contributed to alcoholism in the larger community.[108]

The most painful problem faced by black businessmen and professionals centered on the distrust of them by their own people. Understandably, black consumers in many ways were not unlike other consumers: they were out to save a buck and get a good deal on commodities; if white stores gave better deals and provided more savings than black stores, it was too bad for the latter.

Another problem already discussed is that of black businesses being poorly run by persons with little prior experience. This might explain why black consumers sometimes patronized white stores instead of black stores. But this was not the whole of it. More than likely a good number of black consumers lacked confidence in those blacks in untraditional economic ventures. Black doctors and other black professionals were novelties to many former migrants, so they doubted their abilities.[109] In many cases, "whiteness was rightness." If Detroit black businessmen and professionals were to succeed, they were going to have to raise the social consciousness of black consumers by cultivating their racial pride.

The use of organized racial pride as a means to strengthen black businesses and professions received its greatest impetus from Booker T. Washington, who founded the National Negro Business League in 1900. An earlier attempt, the Fourth Atlanta University Conference in 1898, adopted a resolution that declared: "Negroes ought to enter into business life in increasing numbers. . . . The mass of Negroes must learn to patronize business enterprises conducted by their own race, even at some slight disadvantage."[110] Two years later, Washington called a group of black businessmen together in Boston and organized the National Negro Business League. This stimulated the formation of many local groups, and by 1907 the national organization had 320 branches.[111] This group laid the ideological foundation for black economic nationalism in the twentieth century.[112]

Detroit black business and professional classes also shared in this national movement. The Detroit Negro Business League (DNBL) was founded on July 14, 1926, with sixty members. Their objectives were: to work for the development of a sense of unity of interests among black businesses; to educate black businessmen in the best business practices and to point out the necessity of considering their various problems, handicaps, opportunities, and responsibilities; to educate the black public about the special advantages the Business League could offer them; and to "disabuse the black public's mind of the many misapprehensions it entertains towards Negro concerns."[113]

Other efforts aimed at spreading the economic philosophy among the black public included those of the *Detroit Independent,* a local black newspaper, which started a financial review section edited by the managers of a black company, the Michigan People's Finance Corporation; it devoted space to discussions of good business practices. This section generated a large readership by discussing technical aspects of financial and general business matters in a popular readable style. The St. Antoine branch (black) of the YMCA contributed its share in early 1926 by putting on an industrial exhibit featuring products of black businesses. The Underwriters Cooperative Association, composed of the three black insurance companies operating in Detroit, performed the task of educating the black public in "thrift and pride in their own enterprises and confidence in their own business leaders."[114]

These efforts represented the first stumbling steps toward the development of a racially and economically conscious community. But by 1930, the black community still lacked an effective and organized strategy for marshalling the consumer power of the black community. Before the year ended, however, two black self-help organizations emerged, marking a historical watershed in black consciousness and economic self-help in Detroit.

THE BOOKER T. WASHINGTON TRADE ASSOCIATION AND THE
HOUSEWIVES LEAGUE OF DETROIT

When the Reverend William H. Peck and his wife, Fannie B. Peck, came to Detroit in 1930, where he assumed the pastorate of Bethel AME Church, they found not only the black masses struggling to survive, but also black business and professionals trying to fight off white competition. In April of that year Mr. Peck called a meeting of black businessmen and professionals and organized the Booker T. Washington Trade Association (BTWTA). But not until A. L. Holsey, secretary of the National Negro Business League, spoke at Bethel AME, did things really start happening. Holsey focused on the economic power of black housewives. If black housewives would "wisely" direct their economic power, Holsey advised, it would lead to the development of black businesses. He told how black housewives in Harlem used their economic power to help the black community. Holsey's speech struck a responsive chord in Mrs. Fannie Peck and other women in the congregation. Black housewives had to become more conscious of their potential economic power. Acting on this impulse, Fannie Peck discussed the idea with her husband. Black housewives in Detroit, they concluded, could be organized to support black businesses and professionals. On June 10, 1930, about 50 black women held a meeting in the gymnasium of Bethel AME church. They had been invited by Mrs. Peck to make history. She told them of her plan, stressing that it would be a pioneering effort. The assembled black women unanimously agreed to set up a permanent organization, and they elected Mrs. Peck president. The organization was named the "Housewives League of Detroit" (HWLD).[115]

In a joint statement of their declaration of principles the BTWTA and HWLD explained their purposes, as well as their relationship to other black organizations: "We emphasize and declare it to be the most desirable to own our own business and manage it ourselves. While we recognize as an act of fairness the employment of Negroes in businesses owned and operated by other racial groups, yet we feel that the solution of our economic problem is the ownership [of] business, and to this end we shall confine our efforts."[116] They said they were not "an organization which seeks to right the many injustices we have forced upon us or as a result of discrimination within the field of civil and property rights." Neither were they a religious, political, or charity organization, but they recognized the great necessity of such organizations.

They would not protest against any nonblack business with a large black patronage but would just support their own. Nor would they take action against those blacks

> who, in the face of the struggles of the Negro businessmen and professionals, saw fit to support those of other racial groups. We see the great need of our social, educational, religious, and economic improvement, and we have selected the economic as our field of endeavor.[117]

The economic welfare of blacks was uppermost in the minds of both organizations; and this concern, often seen as merely a reflection of the class interests of the black bourgeoisie, was in most cases sincere:

> The great loss of employment upon the part of our people has reduced us to the place where we have not sustenance of our bodies, clothes to wear, homes to live in, books to read, and none of the many things which are not any longer luxuries but are prime necessities to the home life of modern standards. Our children graduating from school are left helpless in our world because of our lack of vision and non-loyalty in support of such business effort among us which promises for them a future. In our great cities of America where we are in large numbers we are regarded as the great charity

load. Our organizations recognize all these great discouragements and resolutely sets its face against them and dedicates itself toward their correction.[118]

As could be expected, the Booker T. Washington Trade Association
represented a cross section of the classes in whose interest it was founded.
Doctors, pharmacists, dentists, salesmen, lawyers, newspaper editors,
social workers, ministers and others; but few, if any, blue collar workers
were members. Since the Housewives League was the sister organization,
its composition was somewhat similar.

In the following years, both groups engaged in activities and programs
designed to develop a strong black business and professional class. In 1932
the Booker T. Washington Trade Association organized the Noonday
Luncheon Club (NLC), whose membership was restricted to members of
the association. This club met every Wednesday at the YWCA and often
hosted some of the major black figures in the country, such as C. C.
Spaulding, president of North Carolina Mutual Life Insurance Company,
the largest black insurance company in America. The club organized its
programs around certain businesses and professions such as "Doctors' Day,
Lawyers' Day," "Insurance Day"; it also sponsored annual essay contests
for high school graduates, with $500 cash prizes for writing on "Why We
Should Support the Booker T. Washington Trade Association and the
Detroit Housewives League." The BTWTA and the HWLD often jointly
sponsored programs featuring prominent black and white speakers such
as Mayor Frank Couzens and the Reverend R. L. Bradby of Second Baptist
church. These programs included concerts and shows for children.[119]

The Noonday Luncheon Club's speaker-program provided valuable information for struggling black business and professional groups in Detroit
and functioned as a black "think tank" for sorting out the best strategies
for black economic development. It also formed part of the first large-
scale black network in America, where successful black professionals and
business people shared economic ideas with their counterparts in other
cities. In the spring of 1934, twenty members of the BTWTA organization
traveled to Cleveland, Ohio, to help launch the Noonday Luncheon Club
set up by the Progressive Business Alliance of Cleveland. Carlton W. Gaines,
president of the BTWTA, was the main speaker. He told the Cleveland
audience how the Detroit organization had been founded and talked about
the effectiveness of its work. At his historic meeting, the black Detroiter
pointed out that "Booker T. Washington's greatest achievement was the
forming of the National Negro Business League." According to Gaines,
"this achievement . . . was greater even than the founding of Tuskegee Institute, because it stimulated the formation of many local Negro business
organizations throughout the country, created business ambition in the
minds of many of our people, fostered cooperation among [black] business
men and women, and led the way for greater development and stabilization
of Negro business." Gaines then reminded his listeners "that only through

the development of business and industry will the race gain its economic freedom."[120]

The president of the BTWTA could afford to give advice because the Detroit black business and professional association had come a long way in a short time. In 1933, three years after founding the BTWTA, it had not only raised the consciousness of blacks in Detroit but had also stimulated blacks' consciousness of economic self-help around the country. The BTWTA had organized two black merchant clubs that met weekly to discuss the state of black business in the city. The organization established a trade school and held several trade exhibits. As a result, membership in BTWTA increased tremendously. The BTWTA members were so proud of their success that they held a big first anniversary celebration to mark their progress.[121]

The BTWTA had even more to be proud of in 1938. In February, Gaines attended the sessions of the small businessmen held in Washington, D.C. He was invited only after members of the Noonday Luncheon Club (NLC) pressured two Michigan senators and congressmen to use their influence to persuade President Roosevelt to invite him. The following summer, the BTWTA held an annual trade exhibit that attracted more than 10,000 people. That fall, the BTWTA sent the second largest delegation (Atlanta had the largest) to the 38th annual convention of the National Negro Business League held in Houston, Texas. They superseded black Atlanta as the delegation from a city and an organization contributing more to black business development than any black organization in any city in the United States. Talk at the convention often centered on Detroit as the city where blacks were really doing things; the BTWTA, the HWLD, and the Noonday Luncheon Club had become well known.[122]

The Detroit black business and professional community won the honor of hosting the 40th annual convention of the National Negro Business League in 1940. The theme of the convention was "Trends and Opportunities for the Negro in Business." Panel discussions covered such topics as "How do present Negro consumers' attitudes affect Negro businesses"; "Should united efforts be made to integrate Negroes into general business"; "What are some effective methods for building strong local Negro trade associations"; "How may cooperative efforts strengthen Negro business;" and "What improved business techniques are needed in Negro business today."[123]

Not all whites who supported the idea of black self-help understood its deeper meaning of racial solidarity. In fact, some aspects of black racial consciousness disturbed some prominent whites in Detroit, such as Mayor Couzens. During a speech at the Noonday Luncheon Club in December of 1935, Mayor Couzens warned the assembled black business and professional people to be aware of overpatronizing black businesses and professionals, because such efforts might result in segregation. Real progress, the mayor suggested, could only occur through cooperative efforts between

First group of the Housewives League of Detroit Boosters. Courtesy of the Burton
Historical Collection of the Detroit Public Library.

blacks and whites.[124] The mayor's heart was certainly in the right place,
but economic survival for blacks dictated that they cooperate with whites
as well as support racial solidarity.

While the predominantly male BTWTA and Noonday Luncheon Club
tended to attract most of the local and national attention, the HWLD
performed the more pedestrian tasks of working in "the field." In fact, the
HWLD consciousness-raising work in black neighborhoods laid the foundation for the success of the BTWTA and black business and professional
classes. The HWLD disseminated the message of black economic self-help
through their *Housewives League Bulletin,* a bimonthly report on black
business in Detroit, and a *Trade Week Guide.*

In May 1934, the HWLD announced in its bulletin that its membership
had increased from 50 to 10,000 members. Commenting on this spectac-

ular growth, the bulletin attributed it to "the realization on the part of the Negro woman that she has been traveling through a blind alley, making sacrifices to educate her children, with no thought as to their obtaining employment after leaving school." Now the black woman is aware that while educating her children she can also "prepare employment for them after they leave school; but that this can only be done by spending the money that comes into her hands with her own people and with those who employ them."[125]

The HWLD worked mainly through its booster committees, which conducted house-to-house canvasses in black neighborhoods on behalf of local black merchants and black-made products. The committees also circulated booklets to the general public that contained information on the locations of black professions and businesses.

Boosters often took militant positions in pushing black economic self-help. They argued that black professional and business classes deserved a fair share of the black consumer's dollar because they lived in the black community and supported black churches and social agencies. Those black institutions, the boosters argued, "cannot grow and serve their communities as they should until the people have the opportunities for the [black] boys and girls of tomorrow."[126]

The booster committees urged black housewives to "Think! Think! Think! before you give your business to any place, before you purchase what you're going to eat today, or before you purchase anything you need today. Can't you see the need of keeping as much as possible [of] your little money in the hands of your own race?" To black housewives who might have interpreted such militant self-help propaganda as a form of segregation, as did Mayor Couzens, the boosters' response was: "It is not a case of advocating segregation, or of encouraging race prejudice, it is a case of advocating self-respect and thinking as much of ourselves as other races think of themselves." The time has come when blacks should "have sense enough" to service themselves. "Why do we have to have other races of men to serve us as physicians, dentists and lawyers, sell us life insurance, drugs, foods, wash and make our clothes, and do all the thousand and more things for us, that other races are doing for themselves?"[127]

This militant black consciousness raising often went beyond certain express purposes of the HWLD, one of which stated that it was not a protest organization. However, the HWLD did send committees to urge white stores located in black neighborhoods that did not hire blacks to do so. If they changed their policy and hired blacks they were not bothered; if they refused, the HWLD picketed the stores until they hired blacks or went out of business.[128]

The boosters' militant campaign worked wonders for black businesses and black professionals. As early as 1933 the majority of black merchants in the city had benefited from their efforts. Toward the end of the Depression many black business and professional people claimed that the HWLD and the boosters were responsible not only for their tremendous growth but also for helping them to remain in business during the Depression.[129]

The black women of the HWLD were largely responsible for the survival and progress of black businesses and professionals. In May 1934, HWLD reported on its housewives' page, that its greatest accomplishments "have been the vision of self-help it has given the Negro women; the confidence it has inspired in Negro business and professional men and women; [and] the courage it has imparted to your young people to continue their education."[130]

By this time, HWLD had already become nationally known for its work in Detroit and had become a model for the national Housewives' League established in Durham, North Carolina, in 1933. The League elected Mrs. Peck as its first president. During World War II, the HWLD added to its accomplishments by assisting the U.S. Bond drive and the USO and being selected as the first black organization to participate in training people in the use of rationing stamps as well as teaching them about rationing regulations.[131]

Not all blacks accepted the philosophy of black economic self-help as promulgated by the BTWTA and the HWLD. One of the earliest challenges to this form of black social consciousness and self-help surfaced during the fall of 1935. The Reverend H. H. Williams of the Metropolitan Baptist Church started a movement to cooperate with Jews, Syrians, and other non-blacks in black neighborhoods. In November of 1934, Williams gave a speech at the Bethel AME church before 300 members of the BTWTA and the HWLD. He argued that Jews, Syrians, and other outsiders dominate the economy of the black community because they control the channel of domestic trade. But blacks and Jews are "brothers in distress"; the Jews in black communities should work to bridge the gap and promote good relations between the two peoples. According to Williams, the Jewish capitalists in black communities should feel duty-bound to promote the economic welfare of the black community; in turn, blacks should stop trying to dislodge them.[132]

Predictably, the BTWTA disagreed. Williams's philosophy was unfair to struggling black business people. How could Williams, they argued, as head of a black institution dedicated to the welfare of blacks, urge blacks to support the interests of outsiders as opposed to blacks? Williams should be opposed, one BTWTA member said, because his speech would destroy the spirit of any black trade protectionist movement like the BTWTA. Members of the BTWTA and HWLD might not have been so upset over Williams's speech had there not been large numbers of the National Negro Youth Congress in the audience who, some felt, might be influenced by the speech. One observer who disagreed with Williams felt the speech could inculcate in the young people's minds "the admitted failure and the vain efforts of the struggle of the Negroes for the trade emancipation from the neighborhood retailers." Someone asked Williams who was paying him to represent them. After a short time Williams's movement died.[133]

The BTWTA and the HWLD revolutionized black social consciousness and self-help in Detroit. Few black organizations or social movements contributed so much to racial solidarity and economic self-help between 1915 and 1945. In some ways, the spirit of the BTWTA and the HWLD galvanized other black self-help institutions such as the churches, hospitals, and newspapers. Although geared to the interests of the fledgling business and professional classes, these two organizations understood the connection between the welfare of the business and professional classes and the masses of black people. While class interest was present, it was not the major driving force behind these two organizations. Instead, they were driven by the desire to develop a strong black economic base upon which to build a secure community.

BLACK WOMEN'S SELF-HELP CLUBS AND RELATED EFFORTS

Mrs. Peck and her Housewives League of Detroit became part of a long tradition of black women's involvement in black community building. The black housewives had been primed and prepared long ago for the role that they eventually played as militant members of the HWLD. During the middle 1890s, black women throughout the state began organizing self-help clubs to find solutions to such black community problems as the homeless, deprived young mothers, unfortunate youth, and other needy segments of the black community. The "In as Much Circle of King's Daughters and Sons Clubs," founded in Detroit in 1895, was one of the earliest of these black women's self-help clubs. Mary McCoy, often called the "Mother of Clubs," who was the wife of the famous black inventor, Elijah McCoy, played a major role in the founding of this first club. Mrs. McCoy also assisted in establishing other black women's self-help clubs, which pioneered in addressing particular problems in the black community. For example, she contributed to the establishment of the Phyllis Wheatley Home for the aged, the McCoy Home for Colored Children, The Lydian Association of Detroit, the Guilding Star Chapter Order of the Eastern Star, and the Willing Workers. Mrs. McCoy's club activities also extended outside the black community. She became the only black charter member of the famous Twentieth Century Club established in 1894.[134]

In 1898, black club women in Detroit hosted the first meeting to organize black club women into a statewide organization. Stimulated by a group of Michigan women who had attended the annual meeting of the National Association of Colored Women in Chicago, these women founded the Michigan State Association of Colored Women. The women elected Lucy Thurman, an "internationally renowned lecturer for the Women's Christian

Temperance Union," as their first state president. Several decades later, Detroit club women had organized eight women's clubs making it "the hub of black women's club work in Michigan." On April 8, 1921, under the leadership of Veronica Lucas, these clubs joined together to form the Detroit Association of Colored Women's Clubs (DACWC). The Association was federated that same year, and twenty years later, in 1941, it was incorporated.[135]

Several of the member clubs of the DACWC contributed impressively to the black self-help tradition in Detroit. The Entre Nous Club organized in 1924 to assist black girls associated with the YWCA to go to camp and to establish a branch on the West Side of the city. In 1925, black women formed the Progressive Women's Civic Association. One contemporary writer described the approach of this association in the following manner: "These ladies are always on the alert to any problems pertaining to our race, and they aid in remedying them if possible." The women made their mark by successfully campaigning for black clerk positions in Kroger's stores in black neighborhoods on the West Side.[136]

When the DACWC incorporated in 1941, its president, Rosa Gragg, began working on getting a clubhouse for the organization. After every attempt to obtain money failed, she and her husband decided to mortgage their home, their furnishings, their car and Mr. Gragg's business to make the down payment. Mrs. Gragg persisted in obtaining a clubhouse for the DACWC, because she firmly believed that it would demonstrate the spirit of black self-help. As she explained, blacks cannot "advance dependent on other people." By 1945, the membership had paid off the mortgage by such fund raising activities as candy and bake sales, baby and beauty contests, teas and bridge parties; in addition, the DACWC boasted 73 clubs.[137]

Self-help efforts by black women were not limited to women's clubs. Several black women founded major institutions that contributed to the economic and social development of the black community, particularly when they were established at crucial junctures of the black community building process. Such a juncture existed in 1938, when the Detroit Chamber of Commerce wrote Dr. Violet T. Lewis, a black woman who had founded the Lewis College of Business in 1929 in Indianapolis, Indiana. The Chamber asked Dr. Lewis to open a branch of her school in Detroit. During this time, blacks in Detroit were not welcomed in vocational schools—with the exception of the Henry Ford Trade School. Dr. Lewis visited Detroit and accepted the challenge. The Detroit branch of the Lewis College of Business opened in September 1939.[138]

As soon as the Detroit Branch opened, the school was overwhelmed with eager black students. They were finally getting an opportunity to be trained in the business skills necessary to break into Detroit's segregated business world. Within a year, Dr. Lewis had to move to Detroit to oversee her rapidly growing Detroit branch. Soon the school needed more space to expand, so Dr. Lewis purchased a permanent site at John R and Ferry in 1941. Because of its location in an all-white area—The Cultural Center—the zoning commission found reasons to prevent the opening of the school for violation of zoning laws. The school was ordered to move within twenty-four hours. Local black leaders rushed to the school's defense. Louis C. Blount, Horace A. White, Carlton Gaines, and attorney Herbert Dudley devised a strategy of incorporating the school as a nonprofit corporation to conform with the "alleged zoning laws." The strategy worked and the Lewis Business College incorporated in 1941 under the name of Lewis Association for the Study and Practical Application of Business and Commercial Science. These efforts, led by a black woman pioneer, paved the way for a generation of blacks to enter the offices and board rooms of Detroit's business world. As one current official of the school points out: "The first minorities hired by private industry, government agencies, and utility companies, in the area of office occupations, usually had either attended or graduated from the Lewis Business College."[139]

THE SEVENTY-FIVE YEARS OF NEGRO PROGRESS EXPOSITION

In May 1940, Black Detroit was host to the Seventy-Five Years of Negro Progress Exposition. Notwithstanding the many barriers that still stood in its way, the black community in Detroit still symbolized the progress of blacks in industrial America. According to the sponsors of this historic event, the Seventy-Five Years of Negro Progress Exposition was "the first of its kind to give Negros an opportunity to show their progress to the world." A month prior to the event, the general chairman of the exposition pointed out that "This event has been keenly anticipated by the Negro people of America."[140] One black newspaper boasted: "The exposition will give Negros one of the few opportunities they have had to show the facts of their progress to the world."[141] According to one organizer of the event, "we are attempting an exposition which will be an interpretation of Negro life and a focal point for the past seventy-five years of culture and progress."[142]

The focus on black progress as reflected in art, science, technology, industry, literature, and religion was designed to create "interracial goodwill and understanding." Two days were reserved "for a concrete demonstration of this theme . . . Race Relations Day . . . and Patriotic Day."[143] The theme of interracial goodwill and understanding found its most dramatic expression in the Negro Hall of Fame erected for the Exposition. Black and white Americans who had made important contributions "to the progress of the Negro race" were honored through pictures, statues, and busts. Among those honored were: Abraham Lincoln, Frederick Douglass, John Brown, Sojourner Truth, Col. Robert Gould Shaw, and Booker T. Washington.[144] White political, civic, and religious leaders were involved in various aspects of the event, as well as representatives and agencies from the local, state, and federal governments. Local black and white industry and business rented exhibit space to show the contributions blacks had made as producers and consumers.[145] The event generated a lot of interest among some large local white businesses. A few took out large advertisements in local black newspapers congratulating blacks on "Seventy-Five Years of Negro Progress." The Stroh Brewery Company placed the following very large advertisement:

> OUR CONGRATULATIONS ON SEVENTY-FIVE YEARS OF NEGRO PROGRESS
>
> In the seventy-five years of its emancipation, the [sic] negro race has made tremendous strides in all cultural, education, and economic phases of life.
>
> It has produced great leaders such as Booker T. Washington and George Washington-Carver—men gigantic in stature by any means of measurement.
>
> Great artists have come from their ranks—Paul Robeson and Marion Anderson and that grand composer of [sic] Negro music, Samuel Coleridge Taylor.
>
> But it is not even in these great leaders that the [sic] Negro race should find deepest satisfaction.
>
> Rather should they take greatest pride in the raising of the standard of living of their entire people—in the thousands of doctors, lawyers, dentists and businessmen located in towns and cities all over the country—who are contributing to the upbuilding of America and their race by fine citizenship.
>
> Progress in the past seventy-five years has been phenomenal, but even greater things lie ahead!
>
> THE STROH BREWERY COMPANY, DETROIT, MICHIGAN[146]

Beginning in February, as part of the preparation, the Seventy-Five Years of Negro Progress Exposition began a weekly evening radio program entitled, "Song of Progress." The program featured a choir of sixteen singers from the General Conference Chorus, which was directed by Dolly Brown. Both spiritual and secular songs were featured. Robert E. Hayden, a local black young poet destined to become world-famous for his poems, was the commentator and explained the stories contained in the songs. Hayden also wrote the scripts for the program.[147] As the day of the great event grew nearer, the Exposition attracted more and more attention among not only the local population but major white political leaders. A week before the opening of the Exposition, one such leader, Michigan Congressman Rudolph Tenerowicz, explained to the representatives that "an event which seems destined to prove both unique and symbolic is to take place this month in Detroit. . . . the city is to be the scene of an exposition of a type never before presented to the public. It is to be an exposition conceived, planned, and executed by members of the colored race, and promises to be broad enough in scope to constitute a Negro's World's Fair."[148]

When the Exposition finally opened on May 10, black Detroit had much

Poster and advertisement of the Negro Progress
Exposition, Detroit, 1940. Courtesy of the *Detroit
Tribune.*

of which to be proud. The Negro Hall of Fame housed busts, pictures, relics, and personal belongings of those famous blacks and whites who had contributed so much to the long struggle of black peoples. Directly in front of the Hall stood an 18-foot plinth with a gilded hand at its top holding a torch. On the four sides of the plinth stood imposing statues of Booker T. Washington, John Brown, Frederick Douglass, and Sojourner Truth. Hundreds of exhibits from Africa, Latin America, and other places were presented. Several dozen musical organizations, including instrumental ensembles, choral groups, and a thirty piece orchestra took part in the event. Several nationally known groups, such as the Hampton Institute Quartet and the Karamu Dancers of Cleveland, were part of the program. Each day of this "Negro World's Fair" was dedicated to a specific activity or field of interest such as Education Day, Woman's Day, Race Relations Day, Science Day, and the like. The most prized exhibit of the exposition was, of course, the George Washington Carver exhibit, which was a reproduction of the great black scientist's laboratory with specimens of his work. Unfortunately, Dr. Carver was unable to attend the exposition because of illness. But he was represented by his assistant, Dr. Austin Curtis, who received a medal from the Exposition Executive Director to present to Dr. Carver. The largest crowd of the Exposition assembled to see the hometown hero and one of the most famous black Americans at that time, boxing champion, Joe Louis, receive a medal.[149]

At the close of this "largest Negro affair of its kind ever staged in Michigan,"[150] more than 85,000 persons had seen the various expressions and production of seventy-five years of black progress.[151] Both blacks and whites had participated in the event and its chief aim of creating a better interracial climate was at least achieved in part. The Exposition educated both whites and blacks; but since whites needed to know more about how blacks had struggled and progressed than did blacks, the exposition performed a vital function of creating "racial goodwill." A white newspaper editor understood this need to educate whites about the black struggle for survival and progress when he made the following comments about the exposition:

> Such an exposition is in itself an indication that the Negroes have made great progress in "working up from slavery." They have had to do this in the face of many handicaps. The obstacles which had to be overcome by men like Booker T. Washington and George Washington Carver before they obtained recognition would have daunted men of smaller caliber. A good many younger Negro men and women are today working in the same way to improve the condition of their race within the framework of our political, economic, and social system. They can point already to many inspiring examples of Negros who have attained recognition in education, science, art and literature, the theater and the concert stage, as well as in sports. All things considered, we doubt if the history of the human race contains a more

interesting chapter than that which tells of the rise of the Negros in this country in the first three quarters of a century of their freedom from slavery.[152]

Several years after this great event, Detroit would become the scene of the worst race riot in American history. Whatever bonds of interracial goodwill and understanding emerged during the 1940 Seventy-Five Years of Negro Progress Exposition were strained to the breaking point. But many of these bonds held firm, and many blacks and whites continued to join hands in working for black social progress—inspired by the spirit of the oldest tradition in black American history: black pride and black self-help.

Black social consciousness and self-help comprised the heart and soul of community building in Detroit. As blacks struggled to overcome their common problems of racial discrimination and poverty, they gradually evolved into a vibrant urban community. Black institutions played a leading role in generating a sense of community. Black churches, hospitals, insurance and loan companies, along with credit unions and black newspapers, represented tangible examples of how self-help contributed to the process of community building.

But community building was complex and needed more than just institutions and people; it required a vision of what a people is and what it is capable of becoming. For this a philosophy was needed to energize people to flesh out the vision in their own lives. Black newspapers played a key role in this process. In addition, blacks needed to understand the relationship between black support for black business and professions and building a strong black community. The Booker T. Washington Trade Association and the Housewives League of Detroit led the way in educating the black community about the need to support black professional and business people, not just to make them more profitable, but because they supported black institutions, provided jobs for blacks, and contributed to the overall well-being of the larger black community. As blacks in Detroit became more socially aware of their responsibility for each other, they increasingly thought of themselves as one community, regardless of class and political differences.

Seven

Protest and Politics: Emerging Forms of Community Empowerment

Colored citizens of Detroit have been protesting for some time to those in local authority, and appealing to them to put a stop to this police brutality, but our protests thus far seem to have fallen on deaf ears.

Editorial, The Detroit Tribune, *July 15, 1939.*

My independent actions as a lawmaker have not been to the liking of certain interests, especially in the City of Detroit, who would like to control the Negro vote through me.

State Senator Charles C. Diggs, The Michigan Chronicle, *July 29, 1944.*

GEARING UP FOR STRUGGLE

While blacks in Detroit set up and promoted black businesses and institutions within the black community, they also engaged in protests and politics to dismantle the network of white institutional racism and challenge the hegemony of white political power. Although the BTWTA and the HWLD claimed that they were not protest or political organizations, their members and major supporters often wore several hats at different times. For example, businessmen L. C. Blout and Moses Walters, president and treasurer, respectively, of the Great Lakes Mutual Insurance Company, belonged to both the BTWTA and the NAACP.[1] These emerging forms of community empowerment complemented the development of black businesses. Clearly, the needs of the times required that blacks' talents be used wherever needed.

Furthermore, the generation of blacks born and reared in Detroit between 1915 and 1945 expected and demanded more from life than their parents and grandparents, most of whom could do little more than inspire their children to want and demand more from life. This same spirit motivated many blacks who came to Detroit to seek their fortune. Racist whites in Detroit systemically locked blacks out of the best jobs and neighborhoods, demeaning them in print, intimidating them with unjustifiable police violence; but try as they might, the powers of white racism could not crush the spirit of this new black generation or those who came to Detroit looking for opportunities and were determined to fight for them.

White racism pervaded every corner of black community life, yet seldom did it go unchallenged by blacks. From 1911, when the Detroit branch of the NAACP was established, to the 1940s, when blacks led interracial protests against housing and employment discriminations, this generation of blacks knew they could overcome any and all obstacles placed in their paths.

These blacks also witnessed the first stirrings of real black political power in Detroit. As blacks became aware of their increasing numbers in certain electoral districts, they began the long process of challenging white political hegemony in those areas. Black political control of Detroit was yet a long way off but the migrants, the generation of blacks born and reared between the world wars, sowed the first seeds of future black political control in Detroit. Black self-help, protest, and politics, therefore, emerged and reinforced one another within the same developing black social consciousness. Black protest and politics, however, were aimed solely at challenging white institutional racism and political power as they affected the black community.

THE DETROIT NAACP

Between 1915 and 1945, black protest took as many forms as there were incidents of racial discrimination. Not all of these forms of protest proved successful or evolved into effective long-term strategies against racism. A big difference existed between an individual black protesting against a particular racist practice and a well-organized protest or mass movement against that same practice. Some racist practices such as housing and employment discrimination and police brutality called for mass black community protest—even biracial protest. Lesser forms of racial discrimination, such as racial stereotypes in white newspapers, discrimination against blacks in cemeteries, restriction on black acquisitions of liquor licenses, refusal to serve blacks in public places, among others, were not quite as threatening to the overall well-being of the black community, but they still represented racial barriers which the new black generation, coming of age, did not allow to go unchallenged. Members of this generation—many of them southern-born—had been influenced by the radicalism of W. E. B.

DuBois, editor of the *Crisis,* Marcus Garvey's United-Negro Improvement Association (UNIA), and the hope and promises of World War I.

Several years before the first large-scale black migrations from the South, the Detroit branch of the NAACP, founded in 1911, laid the groundwork for systematic black protest in Detroit. The growth and development of the Detroit NAACP paralleled the rising tide of racial discrimination in industrial Detroit. Between 1911 and 1918, the NAACP focused primarily upon national issues and local cases of racial discrimination. In 1914, for example, the NAACP took fourteen cases of discrimination in theaters to court. They won four. Several years later, they protested against discrimination in the U.S. Civil Service and succeeded in placing a black woman postal clerk in a job she had earned by examination, but which had been denied.[2]

As important as these protests and court cases were to the early stages of the NAACP's struggle against racism in Detroit, they did not stimulate any great increase in membership.[3] Some blacks might have felt racial discrimination only affected a few unlucky souls, that it was not a prevalent practice or mood among whites of sufficient gravity to warrant joining a radical protest movement such as the NAACP.

The great migration of 1917–18 changed this attitude. As thousands of southern blacks arrived in Detroit, racial patterns in housing and some occupations changed dramatically, generating fear and anxiety among whites who reacted by instituting racist measures to control the movement of the expanding black population. Serious racial problems began arising in housing, recreation, and the courts. Membership in the Detroit branch gradually increased, which enabled it in 1926 to fight one of the toughest battles in its history. That year it marshaled national support to protest the rights of the Sweet family, charged with murder resulting from their efforts to protect their home.

The mobilization of both the city and the nation behind the Sweet family, as well as the role played by Judge Frank Murphy who presided over the case, enhanced the Detroit branch's reputation among liberal whites.[4] The black community could not help but be proud of its local branch. Yet the victory in the Sweet case did not mean that the local NAACP had overcome racism in housing or in any other area in which blacks were affected. (See chapter 5)

The victory of the Sweet case marked a high point for black protest and struggle of the 1920s, but many more struggles remained to be fought in the 1930s and 1940s. Throughout this period, the Detroit NAACP branch spent much of its resources protesting against police brutality.

In 1933, the branch and the International Labor Defense lodged protests against what some people considered the promiscuous shooting of blacks by white police. These shootings continued, prompting more protests from the NAACP. In July of 1938, Dr. James J. McClendon, president of the branch, protested the beating of a black man by white policemen while in custody in the Canfield station, which was known for its brutality against blacks. At a conference consisting of Mayor Richard Reading, the superintendent of police, and officials of the branch called to discuss the matter, McClendon told the mayor that "this sort of thing must stop. Officers of the Canfield station are noted for their brutality toward colored citizens and we are assembled here [to] protest against their attitudes and we are asking you, the Chief Executive of our city, to put a stop to it." The mayor responded by ordering an investigation of charges of police brutality against black citizens. One such charge filed by the branch was found to be invalid by the police report.[5]

Incidents of police brutality stepped up in 1939. Early in the year, the president of the North Detroit Youth Council of the NAACP addressed a mass meeting at a local church organized to protest a recent killing of a black autoworker by a white policeman. He declared: "Negroes are being shot down like rats and unless we put up a bigger fight such conditions will continue to exist."[6] Speaking at the same mass meeting, the NAACP president informed the audience that "the case will not be over until the policeman is punished for the slaying of Jesse James [the black worker]." The Reverend Horace White, then pastor of the Plymouth Congregational Church and chairman of the Legal Redress Committee of the NAACP, informed the crowd that they "should get mad about it, and then you'll get something done." Referring to those white elected officials who many blacks believed were dragging their feet on the issue of police brutality, White told the people to "vote for the one who promises to abolish police brutality." Another speaker urged interested organizations to concentrate their efforts in a coordinated drive to achieve justice for the victim.[7]

White public officials appeared insensitive to both black victims of police brutality and black protest. Few, if any, white policemen were punished for killing a black. Alarmed over this situation, the NAACP, in April 1939, called for a conference to plan a mass protest against "the alaming increase in beatings, killings, and illegal arrests of colored citizens by police." Later that month concerned organizations began planning a "Brutality Week" to protest the killings by police.[8]

A week before the mass meeting, one of the local black newspapers ran this editorial:

> The Detroit Police Department is apparently trying to establish a national record for brutality to Negro citizens. In spite of the many protests made to those in authority, the brutality continues. . . . Since January 1, this year, the number of Negroes slain in cold blood and savagely beaten and clubbed by local police officers has steadily mounted. . . . In addition to these and other murders by Detroit policemen in recent months, many other members of our race have been brutally clubbed and beaten by officers of the law, without just cause. . . . Policemen are paid by the taxpayers to preserve law and order and to protect human lives and public and private property, but they have no right to take the law into their own hands, as so many of them do. It is

not their duty to act as judges, juries and executioners, in their dealings with Negroes. Policemen have no legal or moral right to let their racial or religious prejudices lead them to persecute members of our race or any other racial group, and when policemen . . . forget their duty as to indulge in such lawless acts of violence, they should be curbed, reprimanded, and in flagrant cases they should be dismissed from the Police Department and punished by the courts of justice.

Colored citizens of Detroit have been protesting for some time to those in local authority, and appealing to them to put a stop to this police brutality, but our protests thus far seem to have fallen on deaf ears.[9]

Close to 1,500 people attended the mass meeting on police brutality held in Bethel AME Church. The dominant theme was removal of city officials who tolerate police brutality against citizens. The speakers included Charles H. Houston, the famous black lawyer from Washington, D.C. and special counsel for the national headquarters of the NAACP; John P. Davis, executive secretary of the National Negro Congress; attorney Henry Fried, Civil Rights Federation; attorney Harold E. Bledsoe, and Dr. James McClendon, president of the local NAACP and chairman of the Committee to End Police Brutality.[10]

Houston told the audience that they should not attribute police brutalities just to the policeman on the street when such brutalities continue months and months. "Instead," he explained, "Go after the City Hall gang." When a policeman "cracks the head of a Negro," Houston continued, "he is saying, 'I don't agree with you about poor housing conditions and intolerable slum environment.' To the laborer and Jew, he is saying, 'Shut up or you'll get what the Nigger got.'" Davis's talk had a special relevance because he had led the fight against police brutality in Washington, D.C. After discussing the protest campaign in D.C., Davis pointed out that "the nightstick that cracks the Negro's head is held not alone in the policeman's hands, but in the hands of the Mayor." McClendon discussed the recent wave of police brutality and the problems the committee had encountered attempting to obtain warrants for the arrest of police responsible for killing and beating black men. "We intend to do something about that," McClendon warned, "if we have to vote out every person in the City Hall." The mass meeting did not end with participants denouncing officials they claimed tolerated police brutalities, but petitions were circulated advocating the removal of the police commissioner.[11]

In late August, the Committee to End Police Brutality, still under the leadership of the NAACP president, Dr. James J. McClendon, staged mass protest meetings against police brutality on nine playgrounds throughout the city. Speakers discussed the objectives of the meetings and listed incidents of police brutality. People were then encouraged to sign petitions for the removal of the police commissioner from office. The next month, the committee submitted a petition to the Detroit Common Council requesting the council to investigate the policies and practices of the police department, which, the committee was convinced, would lead to firing the police commissioner. The attorney for the Committee informed the Council that they had filed countless protests with the commissioner and the mayor but to no avail.[12]

On the surface the protests of the NAACP and the Committee to End Police Brutality seemed little more than periodic aggravation of public officials. Other than a 1942 judgement of $890.26 awarded to a 22-year-old black male in a suit against a white officer for breaking his jaw, no major concessions were ever granted to either organization. Below the surface of the seemingly glacial and ineffective black struggle against police brutality, a steady and constant transformation of black self-consciousness was taking place. Each bold verbal blast and rally against white policy brutality chipped away at what far too many blacks had thought to be the invincibility of the pervasive system of white power and control over the black community. Blacks no longer had to feel helpless in the face of white policy brutality. It did not matter that they lost many battles in bringing white police officers to justice. They were at least waging a struggle; they were fighting back; and such actions on their part transformed them from passive creatures kowtowing to oppression to proud black people fighting for dignity as human beings. Therefore, the protest against quasi-legal white policy brutality and intimidation—bordering at times on a form of "terrorism"—however limited, stimulated and sustained the process of community building. Police brutality continued throughout the 1940s, followed by continual black protest in which the NAACP played a leading role. Occasionally, blacks were able to get back at white public officials for tolerating police brutality. Because Mayor Reading refused to remove the police commissioner, in the fall of 1939, blacks voted against the mayor in his bid for reelection. A year later, the local NAACP led the fight to defeat a local judge. And in case anyone had any doubts about the political power of black protest organizations, a writer for one of the local black newspapers commented: "The margin of his defeat was just enough to let the judge know that Negro voters defeated him."[13]

The local NAACP also protested against other forms of racial discrimination. In the summer of 1935, the Detroit NAACP protested against the Detroit Department of Public Welfare for alleged racial segregation of black and white social workers. Three years later, the Branch assailed a CIO Union, the United Dairy Workers Local 83, for refusing to support a black milkman who lost his job when his company sold his route to another company. By 1941, the focus of the NAACP's attention had expanded to include white owned-and-operated businesses in predominately black areas. The Branch asked these businesses to hire blacks since they were located in mostly all-black areas.[14]

The NAACP's greatest challenges of the war years involved the protracted struggle over the Sojourner Truth housing projects in 1942 and harsh treatment of black citizens during the 1943 race riot (See Chapter 8).

Another protest launched by the local NAACP in 1943 was against a
newscaster employed by radio station WWJ who overemphasized the fact
that a man who robbed a downtown store was black. The branch lodged
a protest with the station and sponsor, pointing out the man's color was
irrelevant and such usage on the air contributed to racist attitudes. The
radio station responded to the protest by issuing a memorandum to all its
announcers instructing them to be more careful in their use of terms in
the future.

In another case, the branch protested the insulting questioning of black
female employees of the Post Office by an assistant superintendent of mail.
The protest resulted in the postmaster reprimanding the assistant superintendent and expressing regrets to the women. Employment discrimination
in war industries kept the NAACP busy. In January 1943, they protested
the discriminatory furloughing of black women by the Briggs Naval Ordinance. The company decided to let the women go rather than place them
in inspection jobs for which they were trained. That same year, the Michigan Bell Telephone Company abandoned some of its discriminatory practices after meeting with the local NAACP. Firms that placed discriminatory
advertisements in newspapers found themselves in trouble with the branch
which protested to the District Director of the War Manpower Commission. The commission then wrote the firm asking them to "delete from
future advertisements all references to race and color." The same message
also was conveyed to the three major white newspapers.[15]

Realizing the role of movies in perpetuating racist attitudes and practices,
the National Office of the NAACP began urging Hollywood to select better
movie roles for blacks. In the spring of 1943, the Detroit Branch followed
their lead by protesting to Mayor Jefferies against the showing of *Tennessee
Johnson,* arguing that it lacked historical accuracy. "This picture is inac-
curate in its presentation and the selection of statements out of context
seem deliberately designed to assuage the prejudices of anti-Negro people,"
the branch protested.[16] The film portrayed President Andrew Johnson, who
opposed black freedom, as a victim of the 40th Congressional Congress
which sought to impeach him. According to the NAACP, such Hollywood
films encouraged a dangerous antiabolitionist trend in movie making which
perverted "the truth of the struggle for emancipation, paint abolitionists
as either fanatics or selfish and insincere people." The NAACP asked Mayor
Jeffries to take such films off Detroit's screens because they contributed to
racial stereotypes and racial conflicts. The mayor referred the matter to
the police commissioner who reported that the police department could
not censor films except when they contained immoral or obscene material.[17]
In other words, racism was neither immoral nor obscene.

These setbacks did not dampen the ardor or halt the forward movement
of the local NAACP. Led by its able president, Dr. James J. McClendon,
and its young radical executive secretary, Gloster B. Current, the branch
played a leading role in black protest against racial discrimination in the

late 1930s and early 1940s. It should be pointed out, however, that contemporary observers differed over the relative contributions of the branch to the black protest movement during this period of great upheaval. One such observer, a member of the local branch, acknowledged the contributions of the local NAACP, but felt it depended too much on "legal avenues." When asked how effective the local branch was between 1935 and 1945, another observer noted that this period was one of its most effective: "It had, I believe . . . the highest membership in its history." If in this observer's mind, "effectiveness" was measured by the number of members, then we can understand why some other observers felt the local branch was overly concerned with membership drives and tended to ignore mass action on the part of the masses of black people. Still another contemporary pointed out that many people felt that from the time of the Sweet trial in 1925 to the rise of the union movement in the mid 1930s, the local branch was dominated by the black professional class.[18] Although many of these contemporaries differed on the relative influence of the NAACP, the historical record clearly shows that the branch shouldered its part in the protracted struggle against racial discrimination, which greatly facilitated the process of community building.

SNOW F. GRIGSBY AND THE DETROIT CIVIC RIGHTS COMMITTEE

In December 1933, more than two decades after the establishment of the Detroit NAACP, a group of blacks headed by an aggressive, intellectual postal employee named Snow F. Grigsby founded the Detroit Civic Rights Commitee (CRC). Inspired by a talk given by Grigsby at a church forum where he presented impressive statistics showing the lack of blacks in city jobs, a group of concerned black citizens decided that a new organization was needed to address the problem.[19]

The CRC's first mission would be to locate the proper officials and demand that qualified blacks be given jobs in city departments. In case some people worried about the CRC taking over other black protest organizations' functions in the black community, the CRC organization assured them that it would not usurp any other organization's power or authority. Rather, its aim would be to seek support from everybody and to prod "those who have hitherto been dilatory in their activity." It would, however, assume the lead when necessary in all struggles for the betterment of the black community.[20]

Although not mentioned by name, the Detroit NAACP was probably the organization the CRC considered "dilatory in their activity." Snow Grigsby, the chairman of the CRC, was also a member of the NAACP. He would not have helped form another rival civil-rights organization if he had been satisfied with the branch's work. Instead, Grigsby decided to work through the CRC rather than the NAACP because in his words, he "had a freer hand . . . I wasn't tied down . . . you have to go through so many different channels and you have to observe national policy. We made our own policy here. It was local."[21] The CRC started out then with the mark of Snow Grigsby on its forehead and his fire in its soul.

Between 1933 and 1945, the CRC developed into an effective black protest organization far surpassing the local NAACP in raising the social consciousness of the black community and achieving results in the area of employment discrimination. Most of CRC's success can be attributed to the energizing personality of its chairman, Snow Grigsby, who at times almost single-handedly masterminded its strategies for challenging racial discrimination. Unlike other black protest leaders in Detroit, Grigsby expended as much energy educating blacks as he did leading them into battle. He also wrote pamphlets and books in which he outlined his philosophy of struggle.

In one of his publications, *White Hypocrisy and Black Lethargy,* which he published in 1937, he covered such topics as Christianity and Race Relations, Justice Negroes Receive in the Courts, Board of Education and the Negroes, Religious Institutions and Their Policies from an Inside View, Exploitation of Negroes by Certain White Insurance Companies, Discrimination Against Negroes in Public Places, the Negroes in Business, Wayne County and State Employment, and the Road to Recognition.[22]

Several of the topics in *White Hypocrisy and Black Lethargy* originated as talks such as "Christianity and Race Relations," which was given at People's Church in East Lansing, Michigan, in the spring of 1935. Other topics include Letters and Responses, sort of a running record of the man and his involvement in the black struggle.[23]

Snow F. Grigsby came to Detroit from Chatsville, South Carolina, in 1920. He studied pharmacology at the Detroit Institute of Technology (DIT) where he encountered the racist practices which would lead him into a career of protest. All students at the school had to take physical education. White students had access to the YMCA gym which was operated by the school. Black students, however, had to go to the segregated black YMCA. Grigsby balked at this practice, hired a lawyer, and forced the YMCA to change its policy. Evidently Grigsby won his case based on sound research and facts regarding the illegality of the racist policy. About forty years later he recalled that that experience taught him that "you have to have facts and figures to present your cause, and I thought one of the best ways, especially in these public institutions maintained by public funds, was to see what the budget was, how many employees they had, and how many of them were from minority groups."[24] After graduating from the DIT, Grigsby could not find work in his field. So following the worn path of other well-educated blacks of his time, who had risked money and time to obtain training in fields considered nontraditional by both blacks and whites, Grigsby went to the Post Office. He also found racism there, although in a slightly different, but no less repugnant form.

Throughout the 1920s, black postal workers in Detroit were not allowed to work at windows selling stamps. Grigsby challenged this practice. The postmaster responded that white people would not tolerate buying stamps from blacks. Grigsby's response was that "the Post Office has a monopoly on selling stamps, and . . . if they [whites] don't buy them at the Post Office, where are they going to buy them?" Before long, blacks were selling stamps at the windows.[25] And Grigsby was on his way to becoming the most effective spokesman for black civil rights in Detroit.

From the time he helped organize the CRC in 1933 to his forced retirement from the organization in 1939, Grigsby maintained a relentless struggle against racial discrimination in city government. He emphasized the importance of placing research at the core of the struggle for racial justice. Unlike many black leaders, Grigsby took on the behemoths of racism in Detroit—the Detroit Board of Education (DBE) and the Detroit Edison Company—and forced them to grant reluctant concessions. He kept the heat on an incorrigibly racist fire department for their treatment of newly hired black firemen and engaged in numerous other battles against racial discrimination in Detroit. Grigsby also took on blacks whom he suspected of compromising with racism.

Before accusing city departments of discriminating against blacks, Grigsby and the CRC gathered facts and figures of the numbers of blacks in the various departments. In 1933 he published the results of his research in a pamphlet entitled *X-Ray Survey of Detroit* and presented it to the public. At that time, the Detroit Board of Education had only 72 black employees out of a total workforce of 10,183. Fifty of the black employees were teachers and 22 were janitors. By figuring the percentage of blacks of the total population in the city, the CRC took the position that blacks were entitled to 820 jobs from the Board of Education. Armed with this information, the CRC confidently went forth to do battle.[26]

They held public programs at various churches and brought in speakers who focused attention on the employment situation.[27] This move obviously heightened black social consciousness of the role of the DBE in contributing to and maintaining a racially segregated job structure in Detroit—what future scholars would define as a dual labor market.[28] For example, although a number of black women graduated as stenographers and office clerks each year from the Detroit public schools, not one black held a position in these jobs in the school system. Nor could there be found in the system a single black counselor or truant officer.[29]

Next, the CRC sent a letter to Frank Cody, then school superintendent. He failed to respond. Thirty days later, the CRC sent another letter, this time registered, with a return receipt, to ensure that Cody received it. Finally, the CRC got its opportunity to go before the DBE. A war of wits and strategies followed. On one side stood Grigsby and the CRC employing some of the most sophisticated tactics ever used in the history of the black protracted struggle against institutional racism in Detroit, and on the other side stood the DBE, one of the bulwarks of that very institutional racism. The CRC won the first scrimmage by anticipating how the white DBE official would respond to their requests for jobs for blacks.[30]

Before approaching the DBE, the CRC had developed a brief-like document containing all the relevant research supporting their position. The brief contained data which showed that in the 91 years of the DBE's history, they had hired only 72 blacks. Under questioning, the DBE focused on the depression and claimed that they had not hired anyone recently, not even a substitute teacher. Anticipating this resort to falsehood, the CRC had already sent letters to the presidents of all colleges in Michigan asking how many of their students had been hired by the DBE in the last year and what schools presently employed them. They compiled their list and waited to spring the trap. The CRC had also anticipated another response from the DBE: They would argue that they could not find any qualified blacks. So the CRC wrote to fifteen colleges and universities around the country requesting job credentials of black men and women qualified to teach in various areas. Included among these were the black presidents of Howard University in Washington, D.C., and Fisk University in Nashville, Tennessee. The CRC informed them of their efforts to break down racial barriers in the DBE. Both presidents promised to give the CRC any faculty members needed to support their efforts.[31] When the DBE's anticipated response occurred, CRC bombarded them with facts relating to their recent hires and a list of qualified blacks. After embarrassing moments and hot interchanges, the DBE relented and to the surprise of the CRC hired 19 blacks that day. A year later, one hundred blacks had obtained employment in the school system.[32] But by 1936 only 57 blacks worked as regular teachers, up from 50 three years earlier, out of a total number of 7,408.[33] Clearly, the struggle against racial discrimination was not over. In fact, it would continue for several decades.

Between the struggle over increasing black jobs in the school system in 1933 and the 1939 confrontation with Detroit Edison, one of the city's biggest and most powerful utility companies, the CRC continued to pressure city officials to hire blacks in jobs supported by public funds. In September 1934, the CRC consulted with two judges regarding jobs for blacks in the Friends of the Court Department and the Elections Commission. The organization had already published figures on the racial distribution of jobs by the commission and other departments supported by public funds. In early 1935, the CRC sent letters to various judges on the Recorders Court bench informing them that it would be periodically issuing bulletins to reach every black club, congregation, fraternity and black home containing figures on the status of black employment in city jobs supported by public funds. Furthermore, the letter continued:

> We have noted that there is no Negro clerk stenographer in the Recorder's Court office. We are also aware of the fact that the judges tell us often of

their fairness to the Negro and their respect for him in our public meetings, along with promises to see that everyone gets a square deal. Seeing no Negro employed in this particular office speaks for itself. We are not only requesting that a Negro clerk or stenographer be given a position, but also that a social worker be given the part made vacant by death.[34]

Continuing, the letter alerted judges that the CRC had already compiled a list of competent black social workers, stenographers, and clerks who should "fill these positions immediately." Interested judges, the letter hinted, will convene a meeting to make arrangements as to what day jobs could be assigned. To those judges who claimed their willingness to support the CRC's position but blamed other judges for opposing it, the letter merely stated: "We are now requesting that some agreement be reached among you regarding this matter." Black citizens are no "longer being fooled by public officials and it is the duty of this committee to point out to Negro citizens as well as public office holders the unfairness of this matter." Concluding, the letter stated that the CRC would be "very pleased to announce in our bulletins the names of the persons who are to fill these vacancies and the day they are to go to work." If the judges preferred, the CRC could send people to them for job interviews. "We assure you that we will send you personnel that will not only be a credit to the race but to the department as well." The letter was signed by Grigsby.[35]

The CRC's letter contained obvious veiled threats and subtle pressure tactics designed to force judges to take a position against employment discrimination in their workplaces. If the judges did not respond favorably to the requests in the letter, blacks would know who not to support for reelection.

In 1937, the Recorder's Court employed 101 people; only four were black. Two years later, little had changed. The CRC reported that only four blacks had been appointed among nine judges each of whom had nine appointments available to him. Such glacial progress in Recorder's Court disillusioned Grigsby to the point that that same year, 1939, he went so far as to accuse a well-known white judge, who was also a member of the local NAACP as well as an associate of Dr. McClendon, of double-crossing blacks and attempting to take away their constitutional rights by pushing a bill through the state senate which gave common pleas judges the power to appoint judges. Grigsby viewed the bill as a way of restricting the power of the people, especially minorities, in the selection of judges. "It is hard to understand," Grigsby commented in a newspaper interview several days before election day, "that you, from a minority group, would ever assist in taking away another minority group's rights. We urge you to have your friends . . . withdraw this bill immediately, or it will be necessary for our Civic Rights Committee to inform the public."[36]

Since the letter was published two days before an election (in which the judge lost) and, according to the judge, it had failed to acknowledge the fact that he had refuted Grigsby's charges in sufficient time to clarify the issue, he accused both Grigsby and the newspaper of being unfair: "Publication of your story just two days before election was the most unfair type of journalism, as it gave me no opportunity to reply," the former judge commented. Concerning Grigsby and the CRC, he said that "it becomes apparent to me why the Civic Rights Committee accomplishes so little for your group if its Chairman goes about making unfounded and unfair accusations against public officials."[37]

Grigsby and the CRC might well have blundered in this situation. In their eagerness to achieve results in the court system, they probably made some tactical errors—perhaps bordering on the unethical. Grigsby and the CRC probably came close to colliding with the local NAACP over their attacks on this judge who as already mentioned was also a member of the local NAACP branch.

But Grigsby cared less about ruffling the feathers of the local branch or the national office of the NAACP. He had already accused some white judges of abusing their popularity with blacks and the NAACP by playing "friends in our National Organization to gain the goodwill and at the same time deny Negroes the right of employment under [their] jurisdiction."[38]

This kind of outspokenness paved the way for Grigsby's forced retirement from the CRC several months later. The chairman rarely minced words in criticizing anything or anyone he believed contributed to racial discrimination. Both liberal whites and black community leaders felt his sting. He strongly believed in and expressed the view that black physicians who owned and operated hospitals for only black patients contributed to racial segregation.[39] This view turned off those black physicians struggling to survive professionally as well as attempting to address pressing black health problems. No doubt many black physicians angered by Grigsby's criticisms were only too glad to see him forced into retirement.

The CRC did not waste time just criticizing liberal white judges and black physicians who owned and operated private hospitals. Too much still remained to be done. In October 1938, the CRC attacked white firemen for banning recently hired black firemen from using the station washroom. Early the next year, the Committee issued a statement charging the fire fighters association with discrimination for refusing to accept two black firemen as members. The CRC lectured them on how their racism contributed to the defeat of their proposed 72-hour week charter. "The unions will soon learn," Grigsby pointed out, "that it is better to line up and get the Negro's support, rather than have colored voters go out and help defeat amendments when such amendments are based on color.[40] By spring 1939, Grigsby and the CRC were gearing up to take on one of their greatest challenges: obtaining more jobs for blacks with public utility companies in Detroit, particularly Detroit Edison.

Although Grigsby and the CRC played a leading role in the 1939 campaign to obtain jobs for blacks at Detroit Edison, between 35 and 135 organizations became involved in the protest before it ended. It all started when a dissatisfied city employee in another city informed the CRC that Detroit Edison employed only 40 blacks out of its total workforce of 8,000 employees. Grigsby began researching the situation. The CRC paid high-school students a penny for every light bill they collected from black consumers. They went door to door and announced the protest in black churches. Some student workers ran into trouble when they asked blacks for light bills. Black housewives felt the students wanted to pry into their personal affairs.[41] So the CRC devised a way around this obstacle by providing the students with a short speech especially worded for the concerned, socially aware black mothers:

> Has a Negro ever been to your home to read the meter? Has a Negro girl even been behind the counter or to enter it in the ledger book that you paid your bill? Has the thought ever occurred to you that all Negroes cannot be lawyers and doctors or nurses or school teachers? We have to have some office employees. Now you have a child there. There might be a job for him.[42]

This struck a responsive chord in black housewives. Soon after, blacks began mailing their electric bills to the CRC. Some brought the bills to church. All together the bills numbered between 61,000 and 64,000. They were then tabulated and the results made public.[43] Over 60,000 meters were in black homes and businesses out of a total number of 650,000 meters throughout the city. Blacks made up 8.7 percent of the total population and used 9.4 percent of the meters. Blacks, therefore, should have had about 800 jobs instead of a mere forty. The average black light bill was $3.19. Blacks using 61,000 meters put $194,000 a month and $6,460 a day into the pockets of the Detroit Edison Company.[44] Based upon this research, the CRC and other interested groups were ready to challenge Detroit Edison.

The campaign to increase black jobs at Detroit Edison began in mid-April in typical traditional black protest style—in a church overflowing with leading supporters, well-wishers, and spectators. After Grigsby revealed his research findings, a visiting pastor from New York started things rolling with a scathing attack on Detroit Edison, with warnings about the soft-speaking, "swivel-chair sitters" who are not concerned about black people. He also read a letter from the president of Detroit Edison in which the chief executive implied that racial considerations were secondary to other issues—such as competence. The speaker told how a similar campaign for jobs in New York worked out successfully. Other black leaders who participated in the program included the Reverend William H. Peck, pastor of Bethel AME Church, founder of the BTWTA, and one of the founders of the CRC; Dr. James J. McClendon, president of the Detroit branch of the NAACP; and Louis C. Blount, general manager of the Great Lakes Insurance Company.[45]

It is worth noting that this campaign had features of earlier self-help and protest strategies where blacks from various cities shared strategies in economic ventures and protest. The speaker from New York shared the successes of his organization in that city as had the speaker from Washington, D.C., who shared his organization's successes against police brutality.[46] Similarly, the BTWTA and HWLD also exchanged strategies, successes, and failures with their counterparts in other urban centers. These mutual exchanges and sharing of strategies of self-help and protest greatly enhanced the effectiveness of black struggles in individual cities.

After the mass meeting in April, the CRC and representatives from other organizations held several meetings with officials of Detroit Edison. At one of these meetings in late May, a committee composed of Louis C. Blount as spokesman, the Reverend Charles Hill, Malcolm C. Dade, Dr. James J. McClendon, Wilbur C. Woodson, Margaret McCall, Bernice Johnson, Snow F. Grigsby, among others, met with these officials to find a mutually satisfactory solution to the problem. The management of the employment department at Detroit Edison explained to the committee that he was giving the problem "a great deal of study." He informed the committee that he and the other Detroit Edison officials believed that employing blacks in higher positions might cause racial friction, unless, he cautioned, the committee handled it diplomatically.[47]

At this stage, Detroit Edison officials were trying to impose their game plans on the committee by placing the onus of solving the problem on them. But the committee did not accept their argument or the bait. The committee informed the officials that no such racial friction had occurred at other companies in which blacks were hired into upper bracket positions. Shifting the onus back to the company official, one committee member reminded them that if Detroit Edison's management enforced the rules, no racial friction would occur.[48]

With the ball back in its court, the officials agreed to continue interviewing blacks for jobs in higher positions, emphasizing the fact they were not responding to public pressure and were committed to carrying out what they had promised.[49]

Several weeks later, the CRC assumed the leadership of the larger committee and sent a letter to the Detroit Edison employment manager outlining the policy the company should adopt in increasing its black workforce. Realizing the difficulty for the company to suddenly increase its black workforce, the CRC recommended that qualified blacks be absorbed throughout the entire company in all departments and that an office be set up near the westside black community. The Detroit Edison Company increased its black workforce, but the war between blacks and the company was far from over.[50]

By fall 1939, Snow Grigsby no longer chaired the CRC. Post Office officials forced him to resign under the provision of the recently passed Hatch Bill, which banned "pernicious political activity" by federal employees. Turner Ross, a lesser-known black leader at the time and chairman of the West Side Human Relations Council, was also forced to resign. Both men had been involved in protests before their forced resignations, giving the impression that the postal officials' actions stemmed from partisan concerns. Grigsby had been trying to purchase some property through the federal Home Owners' Loan Corporation (HOLC) and was turned down. The HOLC policy of grading residential areas by occupation, class, and ethnicity, using such terms as "infiltration" and "encroachment" to describe the percentage of such populations in a given residential area, hindered blacks from purchasing property in a given area. For example, if HOLC described an area as "alien and negro encorachment [*sic*] from the East and South," or as an area that "will slowly decline," or as an area in which "the mixed population (Negroes and Polish) precludes the area from a better rating," then blacks would most probably be turned down for a loan in the only areas in which they were allowed to purchase property or owned homes. Evidently some blacks in Detroit and elsewhere felt that the HOLC discriminated against them; so after Grigsby's rejection, a group of black organizations lodged a protest in Washington. This protest, according to some blacks, led to the forced resignation of Grigsby. Ross's forced resignation seemed to have been connected to his organization's involvement in boycotting a white theater because of its hiring practices.[51]

Many blacks complained bitterly over these forced resignations of black protest leaders. They were especially upset over the role of certain blacks in the community who had aided the postal officials in forcing Grigsby and Ross to resign from their respective protest organizations. Speaking in November 1939 before a mass meeting organized to protest the forced resignations, the same visiting preacher from New York who several months earlier had harsh words for Detroit Edison attacked those blacks who had "betrayed the race." He accused them of being "a separate segment that carries on a guerrilla war against blacks." Hill joined in the verbal blasting of those responsible for the forced resignations by including a Michigan congressman and several U.S. senators, who, according to Hill, had refused to answer letters regarding the situation. Protests, however, did little to alter the state of affairs. Snow Grigsby never chaired the CRC again. But he continued to struggle against racial discrimination and to share his strategies for achieving employment opportunities for blacks in city government.[52]

BLACK WORKERS AND THE EXPANSION AND TRANSFORMATION OF PROTEST WITHIN THE COMMUNITY BUILDING PROCESS

Unionization of the black industrial working class played a key role in the expansion and transformation of protest as one of several strategies of community building. Between 1939 and 1941, unionization situated key segments of the black working class, mainly auto workers, within the center of the conflict between capital and labor in industrial Detroit. Unionization also situated black workers into the center of the black protest tradition within the community building process (see chapter 8).

During the 1930s and early 1940s, a series of strikes by black workers set in motion the expansion and transformation of traditional black protest. Many black workers were members of the NAACP and would join in great numbers as the traditional protest agenda of the NAACP merged with the black trade-unionist agenda. They still remained tied to the traditionl race-advancement agenda, however, contrary to the interpretation of black working-class protest articulated by historians Robert Korstad and Nelson Lichtenstein. These authors give the impression that black working-class protest represented a quantum change in the character of black protest, or at least a sharp break with traditional forms of black protest.[53]

During the 1930s, black hotel maids in Detroit were among the first black and women workers to protest bad working conditions. In February 1939, black maids, who had joined Local 705 of the Hotel and Restaurant Workers Union of the AFL just a few years earlier, walked out of the Reid Hotel and left stranded two hundred guests because the management refused to raise their wages to $60 a month minimum.[54] Such a demonstration of defiance and empowerment by black hotel maids, considered by many as humble and powerless, could not but have impressed both the traditional black leadership and the powerful white hotel industry. In 1943 and 1944, black industrial workers engaged in several so-called wildcat strikes as protests against various forms of racial discrimination against blacks in the plants. In March 1943, 600 black male workers walked out of the Chrysler Highland Park plant to protest the working conditions of black women. One worker complained: "We are tired of seeing our women pushed around."[55] This protest, however, came on the heels of two years of conflicts between management and black male workers concerning racial discrimination affecting the men. The black women issue was the proverbial straw that broke the camel's back. According to the testimony of the black women workers, the protest was triggered by the following conditions:

> We are not given the same opportunities for promotions that white women are given. In the first place, . . . the superintendent has stated that we have got to do the hard work, such as pulling steel, running jitneys and heavy mopping. Many of us were hired as elevator operators but have never run an elevator at the plant because the men on the elevators refuse to transfer to work we are doing. They say the work is too hard for them. We have taken our complaints to the union—to the proper sources—but there has been no action. . . .
>
> Many of us have trained for skilled jobs, hired as matrons but our jobs soon developed into common labor in the shop-labor for which the company is unable to hire men. White girls turn these jobs down and are given other

work, but Negro women are told . . . they must do these jobs or ring their cards and go home. I was fired from my job because I wanted to change my clothes before going out to sweep around the building at 6 a.m. on a cold morning. I had been working in a hot place all night and would have been exposed to catching a severe cold.[56]

The second black woman was fired but "after much persuasion" was given her job back. Black women suffered even more humiliation. They were not allowed to eat in the lunchroom. Instead, they were forced to eat in the toilet. Some black women refused to accept these conditions:

> We are constantly being intimidated because we insist on eating in the regular places. When we first went to the plant they gave us separate toilets— far from our work—and we were told that we would have to eat our lunch in these restrooms. There is nothing but two benches and a low table in them. We don't know what they were used for before we were hired. Once when a colored girl changed her clothes in a white girl's restroom, she went back and found out that the buttons had been cut off her coat and her galoshes cut into shreds. We complained to the plant committeeman about this but have not heard anything from him.[57]

Several weeks later, black male workers at the Jefferson Avenue plant walked out in protest of similar working conditions faced by black women. The women were hired mainly to sweep floors and for related light janitorial jobs. After several days at these jobs, the black women were shifted to mopping floors and lifting and dumping containers weighing up to 125 pounds. The black male workers complained that these jobs should not be assigned to women. The women also protested the heavy work. The majority of black men walked off the job and talked to management. The women were then taken off the jobs. But the next day, three other black women were assigned to the same heavy work, which triggered two walk outs by black men before the women were discharged.[58]

After a series of strikes by black workers at the Rouge plant of the Ford Motor Company during this same period, which the company claimed were incited by "irresponsible jitterbugs," the editorial in the *Michigan Chronicle,* the prolabor black newspaper, explained the institutional racist practices behind the series of black working-class protests:

> It is extremely significant that all of the so-called "Negro wild-cat strikes" in the local war plants have arisen in departments in which the Negro workers are jim-crowed and isolated because of their color. Rather than integrate the workers, the companies insist in most cases in creating separate racial gangs in the factory. They claim that this procedure eliminates trouble, yet the facts reveal that wherever workers are so segregated, the separate groups invariably pit themselves against each other and violence follows the slightest provocation. To the normal problem of general worker relations the companies add the second problem of racial relations.[59]

Posing the key question behind the practices of the companies to segregate black workers, the paper was blunt:

> Why then do companies persist in creating a setting in which violence between the races is promoted? Here we must face an ugly fact. The record reveals that many companies deliberately seek to divide the workers in order to destroy a united front in the unions. As long as workers stick together, management must play fair in the matter of wages, hours and working conditions. This divisive technique was used to forestall the unionization of the auto industry and it is being used in some quarters today to weaken the union now established. The record speaks for itself. It takes a long time for a leopard to change its spots and some say it never does. We, however, are still hopeful.[60]

The companies' role in creating racial conflicts in the plants, which triggered strikes and walkouts by black workers, cannot be disputed, but white workers also played a major role in triggering protests by black workers.

In November 1944, 3,000 black workers at the Packard Motor Company went on strike to protest the walkout of white workers protesting the upgrading of four black workers. After a meeting with management and union officials involving in part a promise to address pressing racial problems, the black workers returned.[61]

By 1943, black workers within the NAACP had formed their own labor committee, which staged a major demonstration in April to draw attention to the grievances of black workers, both men and women.[62] The *Michigan Chronicle* called upon the entire black community to support the workers and explained why:

> Next Sunday, April 11, war workers and friends of Democracy will stage a great demonstration in Cadillac Square under the leadership of the Labor Committee of N.A.A.C.P. The rally will be proceeded by an impressive parade in which all Negroes of the community are being asked to participate. Some have asked what does the Labor Committee hope to achieve by this mammoth demonstration.
>
> The time has come when we must let the world know of the grievances which are threatening the morale of our group and the barriers which are jeopardizing the best interests of the nation. . . . In this arsenal of democracy, the Negro worker is being forced to fight in order to make his contribution to the war effort. Our women are jobless which production is menaced by a shortage of labor. These facts must be broadcast in order that we might win the support of all citizens who believe that the preservation of democracy and the safety of this nation is vastly more important that the perpetuation of prejudices against our group. You can help by joining in this important rally.[63]

Strikes, walkouts, and mass demonstrations led by black workers greatly expanded and transformed the traditional role of black protest. Korstad and Lictenstein have correctly pointed out that "mass unionization transformed the character of the black community's traditional race advancement organizations." Accorded to them, "Under pressure from Local 600 leaders like Tappes, Horace Sheffield, . . . the NAACP and the Urban League became more militant and active. Black community leadership still came largely from traditional strata: lawyers, ministers, doctors, and teachers, but the union upsurge reshaped the protest agenda and opened the door to new forms of mass struggle."[64]

This interpretation tends to underestimate the role of key members of the traditional black leadership that established and sustained the tradition of black protest from which many black working-class militants received their first lessons in mass struggle. It also plays down the role of traditional black leadership in paving the way for more radical and militant grassroots struggle. For example, the NAACP's role in the Sweet trial in 1925 educated an entire generation of black people on the techniques of community mobilization (see chapter 5). During the early stages of the union drives in the black community, progressive members of the traditional black leadership, such as Horace White and others, endorsed and supported unionization against the corporate-supported black leaders. Black workers received support from the prolabor *Michigan Chronicle* as well as from a coalition of traditional and nontraditional leaders and organizations, which provided tremendous levers for their labor agenda. Black trade unionism might have been killed in its cradle had not prounion traditional leaders opened their churches and used their influence to nurse it until it could survive somewhat on its own (see Chapter 8).

The young black militant trade unions did not emerge full-blown within the labor movement. Decades of black protracted struggle by traditional black organizations—including the often maligned Urban League—rocked the cradle of one age and produced the militant black trade unionists of another age. Korstad and Lichtenstein and the historical works on which their interpretation is based are on target when they argue:

> The NAACP itself underwent a remarkable transformation. In the successful effort to keep the Sojourner Truth Housing Project open to blacks, NAACP officials had for the first time worked closely with the UAW militants who organized the demonstrations and protests. . . . That mobilization in turn energized the local NAACP, as almost twenty thousand new members joined, making the Detroit branch by far the largest in the nation. Black workers poured in from the region's recently unionized foundries, tire plants, and converted auto / aircraft facilities, and from city government, streetcar lines, restaurants, and retail stores.[65]

No wonder, then, that by 1943, "the Detroit NAACP was one of the most working-class chapters in the country," boasting a labor committee which was "the largest and most active group in the branch, [which] served as a forum for black workers to air their grievances and as a pressure group urging companies and the government to advance black job rights."[66]

While Korstad and Lichtenstein have highlighted the key role of the black working class within the "reshaped" NAACP, the fact remains that their class emphasis ignores the organic, communal ties inherent in the larger community building process. They vastly overemphasized the significance of the working-class character of the "reshaped" NAACP and the fact that the labor committee was "the largest and most active in the branch"—as if there were a major class struggle going on within the black community at the time. Black workers formed the largest and most active group simply because they were, in fact, the largest group in the community and they had been, within the larger black community, the group most directly affected by unionization. The fact that black workers by the thousands joined the traditional NAACP speaks volumes for their faith in a traditionally middle-class organization. They joined and formed a labor committee within this traditional black protest group because the NAACP had rocked their cradle and fought their battles long before the white-dominated labor movement had any use for them. In short, black working-class protest, while expanding and transforming traditional protest and "reshaping" some aspects of the traditional black protest agenda, did so within the larger historical process of black community building.

OTHER FORMS OF PROTEST

Black protests were not limited to the local NAACP and the CRC. Countless black individuals protested in their own unique ways against the countless indignities they faced in their daily lives. As blacks in Detroit grew more self-conscious and proud of themselves as a people who had survived slavery and southern racism, they grew increasingly intolerant of all forms of white racism. At an earlier time or in a different place, white department stores in Detroit might have gotten away with racist advertisements in white newspapers. But in 1941, when Kerns department store placed a full-page ad celebrating its 58th founder's day sale which pictured two black boys gambling, a local black newspaper took them to task. When alerted to this "objectionable new trend in white advertising," Kerns department stores apologized and removed the advertisement.[67] The *Detroit Tribune* also forced the Shell Oil Company to remove an ad featuring a common white racial stereotype of a black boy eating watermelon. In a protest letter to Shell officials in New York during the fall of 1941, the *Detroit Tribune* informed the company that they were writing the letter to "voice the protest of colored citizens in metropolitan Detroit, the Canadian border cities, and the Great Lakes area in general against the policies by your advertising department in featuring pickaninny pictures in Shell Oil Company's outdoor advertising." A current issue of the *Detroit Tribune* was enclosed with a reproduction of the advertisement. The letter went on to say that the ad, and another one showing a black boy being chased by an alligator (with the caption "Off with a jump") might "appeal to white motorists, but will hardly tend to increase Shell's sales among self-respecting Negroes. No racial group likes to be held up to public ridicule, especially by business institutions with whom that race spends its money." The protest and the decline of sales of Shell products to black motorists had the desired effect upon the Shell officials. A week later, Shell began removing the racist advertisements from streets in Detroit. As a result of black protest and loss of sales in Indianapolis, Shell also removed these same ads. The same pressure from blacks forced the Atlantic and Pacific (A&P) grocery stores to recall a brand of shoe polish called "Nigger Head."[68]

Protesting against such racial insults not only put the more racist whites on notice, but it also sent a signal to those whites considering using racist advertisements that any form of racism, no matter how seemingly benign or innocent, would be vigorously protested by the black community. It goes without saying that this aggressive position enhanced the social consciousness of the more lethargic blacks in the community who, without such protests, might well have shrugged their shoulders at these racist advertisements, content with allowing such insults against the race to go unchallenged.

The effects of these black protests against the white business community's use of racist advertisements stemmed directly from the fact that the black population represented a sizable consumer group whose dollars wielded enormous power and influence in the market place. Just as white public officials learned that their manner of handling police brutality could cost them black votes and their jobs, white business firms in Detroit discovered that racist advertisements and other related practices could cost them the loss of black dollars. By the 1930s, large food chain stores such as the A&P had opened stores in black neighborhoods but had refused to hire blacks as managers. The *Detroit Tribune* reminded its black readers that "without Negro patronage, the white-managed stores would be forced to close their doors. Stores that are dependent upon Negroes for support should give us jobs as managers [sic] clerks in those concerns."[69]

Some white chain stores had already recognized the power of black consumer dollars, as well as the justice of black protest, and had hired black managers in their stores located in black neighborhoods. The *Detroit Tribune* applauded these stores for contributing to economic justice and went on to say that "in the spirit of economic justice and self-preservation, we feel entirely justified in asking and demanding the same kind of square deal from them [other white] business firms that depend upon our people for support."[70]

The spirit of black protest extended to areas outside Detroit. When black students faced racial discrimination at the University of Michigan (U of M) in Ann Arbor in 1934, blacks in Detroit made their feelings known.

Both the NAACP and the CRC protested when a black girl was barred from the Martha Cook dormitory on U of M's campus. But the biggest protest from Detroit blacks was triggered in the fall of 1934 when U of M barred Willie Ward, its famous black football player, from participating in the Georgia Tech game. Even the traditionally low profile Detroit Urban League protested this action against one of black Detroit's favorite sons, which was a case of the U of M giving in to southern racism. In the end, Willie Ward decided not to pursue the issue.[71] He later obtained a job with the Ford Motor Company and years later became a black judge in Detroit.

During World War II, blacks not only protested discrimination in housing and war industries, as we have already seen, but they also protested against the treatment of their fathers, sons, brothers, and uncles in uniform, thus fighting a war not only against fascism and racism abroad but also against white racism at home. In August 1941 several thousand blacks held a mass protest at Bethel AME Church to protest the racist treatment of black soldiers.[72]

In early 1943 the *Michigan Chronicle* received a report of racial segregation of black officers at the officers club on Selfridge Air Force Base in Mount Clement, west of Detroit. A white superior officer ordered black officers out of the club, which apparently had been segregated. When the matter came before the commanding officer of the base, he informed the black officers that they did have the right to use the club but that they were not welcome and that he would do all he could to keep them out. He warned them that if they insisted on asserting their rights, he would court martial them for attempting to incite a race riot. The report went on to say that black officers were living in crowded barracks because they were excluded from the officers quarters. Although the *Michigan Chronicle* continued to investigate, rumors persisted. By May 1944, the War Department found itself in the position of explaining why black troops at Selfridge had been transferred, denying that the transfer was related to the race riot the previous summer.[73]

Officials at the War Department realized, as did many white officials and leaders on all levels of government, that blacks in Detroit were not about to slow down their drive for equal rights, not even during the war. When Adam Clayton Powell visited Detroit in the spring of 1943 to support local blacks in their struggle against racism, he exclaimed: "We can't whip Hitler abroad and let fascism run up and down the streets of Detroit." A month later, black workers at the Packard automobile plant walked out to protest the firing of three black machinists. That summer, the NAACP held its national annual meeting in Detroit as a war-emergency conference, and NAACP delegates from 39 states severely criticized the United States for its racial policies.[74]

Black protests in Detroit continued throughout the war years, resisting the temptation of succumbing to accusations of some whites that blacks were disloyal for protesting racism while America was at war. As the war moved to a close in the summer of 1945 and delegates to the San Francisco World Conference had already drawn up a World Charter, the Detroit Council of the National Negro Congress held a conference with the audacious title "Plan for Victory and Peace." One-hundred-twelve delegates attended the conference. Among them were representatives from labor, church, women's, youth, civic, and social organizations from around the city. The main speaker, Congressman Hugh Delacy of the state of Washington, informed the delegates that the World Charter just drafted in San Francisco would have little or no meaning to blacks and others if the necessary machinery was not adequately established. "Negroes," he emphasized, "must become more aware of their power potentialities through the use of individual political actions."[75]

Black and white civic and labor leaders attending the conference focused upon several areas of major concern to black citizens of Detroit. George F. Addes, secretary-treasurer of the United Automobile Workers of America, explained how postwar problems in Detroit industries would affect black employment. Only full employment, he argued, could solve the black employment problem in particular and employment in general. Even seniority for black workers, Addes pointed out, would not solve blacks' employment problem because most black industrial workers had no seniority.[76]

Shelton Tappes, a major black labor leader who played a leading role in the unions struggle of the 1930s and 1940s and was destined to leave his mark on Detroit area labor history in the decades ahead (see Chapter 8), addressed the issue of black attitudes toward compulsory military service. He suggested that blacks could not take any positions on compulsory training "until the foreign policy of the United States has been determined and the reason for a peace time army set forth."[77]

Black war veterans at the conference expressed the unanimous position that they could not back any plan for postwar military service unless all forms of racial segregation in the armed forces were abolished. And an interracial panel on Detroit municipal elections pointed out the advantages of the "united strengths of labor and the Negro people at the ballot box."[78]

The conference passed a number of resolutions involving fair employment practices, the poll tax, the GI Bill, voter registration, black workers, and cutbacks and full employment. The final resolutions captured the spirit of the conference as well as the hope and aspirations of thousands of blacks and their organizations still struggling to overcome racism:

> Be it resolved that the 4th Congress of the Detroit Council of the National Negro Congress go on record as urging all Negro organizations and leaders together with progressive and liberal white organizations and leaders, to join with the National Negro Congress in efforts to realize the results of the programs launched by the deliberation of this Conference, that within their own churches, lodges, civic organizations, labor unions, and so forth,

committees be set up to facilitate this cooperation between the National Negro Congress and themselves.[79]

BLACK POLITICAL DEVELOPMENT

Politics provided blacks in Detroit with another approach to community building. Less than a decade after the first large-scale black migration from the South, blacks in the Motor City were beginning to flex their political muscles. Although black participation in Detroit dates back to the late nineteenth century, southern black migration during and after World War I paved the way for political modernization in the Detroit black community. This process of political modernization also occurred in other northern black communities during the same period.[80] A key stage in this process involved what one scholar described as clientage, or patron-client, politics where a small number of blacks "fashioned personalized links with influential whites," becoming their clients "for a variety of sociopolitical purposes."[81]

As the black population increased, providing black politicians with a mass political base, they no longer had to go hat-in-hand to white party bosses. Instead, white political leaders, fully cognizant of the growing significance of the black vote, often found themselves only too happy to kiss a few black babies and attend a few black social gatherings to obtain the precious black votes that often decided close elections.

Developing political power in Detroit in the 1920s and 1930s posed certain problems for blacks. The structure of Detroit politics simply did not offer the political leverage to blacks as did cities blessed with different governmental structures, such as Chicago and Cleveland. Under a different form of city government, Detroit's increasing black population would have easily translated into increased black political power. In Detroit, however, ethnic and racial political potential was hobbled by the lack of single-member districts, citywide representation on the common council, non-partisan structure of city government, and the nonexistence of a party organization which a minority could eventually control or influence. Furthermore, the expanding black community lacked an agency to educate them in politics.[82]

The structure of the senatorial districts in Detroit placed another obstacle in the path of black political development. The 1925 Reapportionment Act divided the state into 32 senatorial districts. Detroit had three state senatorial districts and shared parts of four other districts, with each district electing one senator. The state legislature was required by law to redraw senatorial districts every decade and not change them for another ten years. But in 1939 the change was four years overdue. Within this setup, black voters wielded real political power only in the third senatorial district, where they had been confined by racial segregation.[83]

Black apathy and Congressional redistricting also hobbled black political development. Between 1915 and 1930, the vast majority of southern blacks arriving in Detroit settled in the east-side wards of the city. By 1930, close to 90,000 blacks were packed in the First Congressional District. Blacks were also heavily concentrated in several other congressional districts within the city. But in the First Congressional District, with the largest number of blacks, blacks failed to exert their political influence until 1932. In fact, not one black in the district attempted to get the nomination from either party; nor did blacks in the area "exert any noticeable influence in the election of the Congressmen until 1932."[84]

Finally, under a new district reapportionment, a black republican, Charles Mahoney, entered the Republican primary. He received the nomination, but it was too late. The boundaries of the district had been changed a year earlier, resulting in the loss of 18,666 potential black voters. Mahoney was defeated in the regular elections by a Polish Democrat.[85] Blacks could do little at the time to control the method of district apportionment. But they could do something about the black political apathy retarding black political progress in the city.

In 1923, a few black political leaders led by Mahoney held a mass meeting at a local church where they formed the United Civic League with the motto "Every Negro vote in every election." Doctors, lawyers, and ministers dominated the executive committee of this organization, suggesting that some members of the black professional class were becoming aware of the growing potential of the black vote in Detroit. The organization's goals included encouraging black to vote; "to convince every Negro that it is his duty to vote in every election"; to consolidate black voting power and "cast it in the direction which will bring us the greatest benefits"; to stimulate community interest in the study of contemporary events related to civic affairs; and to familiarize blacks with the records of city and state public officials "in order that we shall be fully prepared when elections come to separate the dross from the gold."[86]

The United Civic League voiced concern that out of about 65,000 blacks in Detroit only a small percent actually took "an active interest in politics for our civic betterment." Only through the regular and intelligent use of the ballot, the league advised, would blacks be able to obtain fair representation. The big problem, according to the league, was the lack of a central organization to consolidate black political strength.[87]

While the league did not achieve any great political breakthrough, it did manage to unify smaller black political organizations, to counter political hustlers, and to register many blacks who had never shown much interest in politics. The organization provided transportation to voting places and replaced the old habit of last minute mass political meetings with regular well-attended meetings.[88]

A year after its founding in 1924, the league led a membership drive around the issue of blacks on the police force and in the fire department.

The league's work probably contributed to the first large-scale black voter registration drive organized by black Republican Charles A. Roxborough in support of Mayor John W. Smith.[89] Both black Republicans and Democrats spent years politically educating the black community before many blacks in Detroit took voting seriously. The vast majority of blacks in Detroit in the 1920s had come from southern states where blacks had long ago lost the right to vote. Furthermore, most had come to Detroit to work not to vote. Although many placed great value on the privilege of casting a ballot, others had to be educated to see the vote as a tool for community empowerment.

Between World War I and the Great Depression, the expanding black community took on increasingly political importance in the eyes of local white politicians. Gaining control of the black vote was crucial in Detroit where, as already mentioned, citywide representation on the common council and in the nonpartisan structure of city government nullified ethnic and partisan politics. White politicians, eager enough to get a sizable share of the black vote, were able to expand their citywide political base. Consequently, as the black population expanded, individual white politicians began scheming on how they could get their share of the black vote.

White politicians soon realized that the shorter route to the heart of the black voters was through the black church. As the core social institution in the black community, the church had regular access to the largest number of blacks. The church also had authority among the recently settled southern migrants; and in the minds of these newcomers, the minister presided over both the temporal and spiritual worlds. When blacks became numerous enough to influence local politics, black ministers found themselves thrust into the political arena.[90]

Some black ministers failed to see politics as a high priority for blacks. According to them, blacks needed first to adjust to urban life before they became involved in politics. But the pressure mounted, and these ministers soon succumbed to the political game. Black churches and black ministers stood at the center of the scramble for black votes, and white candidates saw the black church as a necessary stepping stone up the political ladder.[91]

In the 1920s, white politicians had little or no past experience with southern blacks. Their political talks in black churches contained all the racial paternalistic stereotypes they thought would appeal to blacks just up from the South. They trotted out Abraham Lincoln, the Great Emancipator, and waved the American flag, and forgot blacks after they won elections.[92]

White politicians were not alone in exploiting the black vote. Some black political leaders matched them in every area of political hustle. Fully aware that white candidates depended upon the black vote but could not get it by themselves, these black leaders set up a system to sell the black votes to white candidates for cash ranging from twenty-five to one-hundred dollars. Certain black ministers also became involved in this very profitable business of fleecing white political candidates.[93]

Local politics had a tendency to corrupt black churches once a minister started accepting cash donations to the church in exchange for votes. Donations included the paying of coal, gas, light bills, and repairs for churches.[94] This dependency upon white politicians seriously undermined the spiritual leadership and credibility of black ministers within the black community. But even more was at stake. Sometimes the minister supported one candidate and only allowed him to speak to the congregation while the officers of the church supported another candidate.[95] Thus churches found themselved divided over issues that bore no relation to their traditional purpose in the community.

Black voters, therefore, needed political education to protect themselves from both friend and foe alike. During the 1920s, blacks in Detroit discovered their political potential and how it could be used and abused. They learned that they could make or break white politicians, and they learned that they needed to vote more often and more wisely.

Throughout the 1930s, the political education of blacks continued. The *Detroit Tribune*, the longest running local black newspaper, carried on a constant campaign to educate black Detroiters about the vital necessity of voting. In the summer of 1933, the newspaper warned blacks to "hang together or hang separately on voting" in the approaching primary.[96]

To its credit, the newspaper attempted to be as nonpartisan as possible. It encouraged blacks to "arouse themselves to the situations and lose no time in becoming affiliated with one or all of the accredited political organizations conducted by and for the Negro citizens of our commonwealth." The paper cautioned blacks not to scatter their votes nor to work separately through small political organizations. Instead, they should unite for the common good of the black community and the larger Detroit community. "The times in which we now live," the paper stressed, "are too serious, and the political and economic issues involved are too vital, to warrant . . . dividing our efforts and scattering our votes at election time. As a people, we must hang together, or we shall hang separately."[97] This nonpartisanship, however, did not last. In the fall of 1934, the newspaper urged black Detroiters to vote the straight Republican ticket to protect their ballots from being thrown out "for improper marking."[98]

A month before the municipal elections in 1933, the *Detroit Tribune* again encouraged blacks to vote. The paper reminded those who had changed their residence since the last registration that they would be disqualified from voting in the upcoming elections if they did not register at city hall. The *Tribune* also warned blacks to "choose with utmost care and prayerful consideration the candidates" for whom they cast their ballot.[99]

In the fall of 1938, the *Detroit Tribune* had not let up raising the political consciousness of Detroit blacks, instructing them to make their vote count and to be aware of the "self-seeking politicians and self-appointed leaders" in the black community whom the paper claimed were doing blacks great harm.[100]

By 1940, the *Detroit Tribune* felt confident enough about the growing political strengths of the black community that it informed its readers that black voters had reached the point where they could decide close elections. While guarding against extravagant claims or overemphasizing the strength of the black vote, the paper wanted both black and white Detroiters to know the power of the black vote in Michigan.[101]

In the early 1940s Detroit blacks began entering into political coalitions with labor, representing a new stage in both black political awareness and development and black community building process in Detroit. Prior to 1943, blacks in Detroit routinely opposed labor in municipal elections because of the widespread racism within the labor movement. For example, in the 1937 mayoralty election, blacks opposed the labor candidate for mayor and supported the nonlabor candidate because he met their traditional criterion of being "a friend of the Negro."[102]

But by 1945, politically aware blacks could see the benefits of entering into a political coalition with labor. In March of that year, a local black newspaper explained to black readers that a coalition was needed because it would be the first step of the liberal majority of blacks and whites in the city to "combat the reactionary elements in the common council and nominate and elect new members to that body who will more nearly represent the liberal elements of the city."[103]

As a result, the 1945 primary election in Detroit became the litmus test for the newly emerging black-labor coalition. Organized labor geared up for its third attempt to elect a mayor while the black community rallied behind a black minister named Charles A. Hill, for councilman. The black community knew that Hill's only chance to win the election was through a coalition of liberal whites and blacks. Unlike the ward system of city government in Chicago and other cities with single member districts which allowed minority groups representation and leverage, Detroit's city council was based upon citywide representation. In short, until blacks constituted the vast majority of the city's total population or forged an effective coalition containing a sufficient number of whites, no black candidate could win a seat on the Detroit Common Council. So blacks and labor made a deal. Blacks agreed to support any labor candidate except Mayor Jeffries (they considered him a racist) and the UAW-CIO agreed to give blacks four labor representatives and four offices in black neighborhoods to campaign for Hill.[104]

Both labor and blacks lost their respective primary contests but the experience of working together to achieve similar political ends strengthened the alliance between them. Hill's primary defeat could have discouraged blacks, but because of his great showing in the running, blacks continued the political struggle for more action. In fact, this primary was the first time in Detroit's political history that a black candidate demonstrated such an excellent chance of winning a council seat by finishing the race among the first nine candidates. In his first try as politician, Hill not only ran ninth throughout the Detroit area but also ran first in predominantly black areas, which attested to the effectivenss of the political candidate. As a result of the alliance with labor, Hill also ran surprisingly well in white working class precincts.[105]

BLACK REPUBLICANS: POLITICAL PIONEERS

By 1945, black Democrats had progressed much further than their Republican counterparts along the path of black political development. But black Republicans had initiated the process. In the 1890s, black Republicans won important elections which placed them in political positions from which they contributed to the larger black community stock of political experience. In 1892, D. Augustus Straker was elected circuit court commissioner. That same year another black Republican, W. W. Ferguson, was elected a state representative. He was also reelected. James W. Ames became the last of this group of black Republicans from Detroit to be elected to the state legislature, becoming a member of the 1901 body of state law makers.[106]

The above black Republicans obtained their political positions through nomination by party bosses in convention. Party voters then elected them on election day. Blacks also held appointive offices under the Republicans. Both the elective and the appointive positions, however, were gifts from the party bosses granted to the black community or an individual for services rendered to the party.[107] Benjamin B. Pelham was the most famous and powerful of all these Republican appointed blacks.

Born in Detroit in 1862, Pelham attended Everett Grammar School and old Central High School. As a newsboy for the *Detroit Post Tribune,* he received a scholarship from James R. Stone, the owner of the newspaper. This scholarship enabled him to study accounting at the Bryand and Stratton Business College. In 1883, he, his brother Robert, and two friends organized a black newspaper, the *Plain Dealer.* Unfortunately, the paper folded ten years later just at the time when it had become "politically influential but financially broke." Pelham sadly conceded that the black population in Detroit could not support the publication.[108]

In 1895, Republicans appointed Pelham to a clerical position under the county treasurer. He left that position in 1903 to work for the register of deeds. In 1908, he made another move to the board of county auditors as an accountant. As county accountant and committee clerk of the Wayne County Board of Supervisors, Pelham dominated Wayne County government as had few blacks or white public officials, past or present. When he retired in 1942 at the age of eighty, he had held three of the most important positions in county government: county accountant, clerk to the board of auditors, and committee clerk of the board of supervisors. Among his many great achievements was his success in guiding Wayne County through the financial crisis of the Great Depression without missing a single payroll.[109] Former fellow office holders and the press considered him the "single most powerful man in the county government."[110]

Ben Pelham was the last of his political type. The direct-primary law passed in 1905 effectively ended the political practice of party bosses nominating blacks to public offices. As a result, no black in Detroit obtained an elected office, except for ward constable, until 1930. That year, Charles Roxborough, one of Detroit's leading black Republicans, succeeded in gaining a seat in the state senate without the aid of clientage politics. He became the first black in Detroit and Michigan to be elected to the office as an elected representative of a predominately black district in Detroit, marking a new stage in black political development in the city and the state. Blacks no longer had to rely on white party leaders to grant them political positions as gifts or rewards for work on their behalf.[111]

As already mentioned, Roxborough had organized the first large-scale black voter registration drive in support of Mayor John A. Smith in 1925. Four years later, Detroit blacks again supported Smith. Blacks considered Smith a friend because he provided them with jobs in the Post Office and the Sanitary Division of the Public Works Department. On the other hand, blacks voted against Judge Charles Bowles, a candidate supported by the local KKK. By the 1930s, white politicians knew that blacks had learned the valuable political lesson of rewarding friends and punishing enemies.[112]

The election of Roxborough marked the end of one form of black political dependency, when black political leaders obtained political favors and positions from white political leaders in exchange for votes. But black political and economic dependency upon members of the white industrial elite such as Henry Ford, a Republican, remained unchanged. The reason for their continuation of black dependency was due to the contrivances of certain blacks "graced" with token jobs within the Ford establishment.

In the 1930s, two leading black Republicans—Donald Marshall, the "Negro-relations" man at the Ford Company between 1923 until his death in 1944; and his second-in-command, Willis Ward, the former University of Michigan football star—routinely used their power and influence at Ford to intimidate blacks into voting Republican. When Henry Ford expressed disappointment with voting returns from black districts where blacks had voted overwhelmingly for the Democrats, Marshall saw to it that blacks in those districts paid the price in lost jobs. Ward reinforced this policy when he let it be known that any blacks sent to him by Democrats would not be hired. Such political intimidation by black Republicans worked wonders and partially explains why in 1931, when Marshall supported a black Republican named Harold H. Emmons, the majority of blacks followed like sheep.[113]

In the late 1930s, Marshall and Ward encouraged the establishment of a black Republican organization, the Wayne County District Voters Association, to recoup the losses that the Republicans had suffered among black voters since 1932. The association was under the control of a "silent board" made up of Marshall, Ward, and Mahoney. Although Marshall and Ward refused to admit their influence over the organizations, they did give jobs to some members. Few black workers, therefore, had any doubt as to who pulled the strings in the organization.[114]

Marshall and Ward used the association as a political machine that at times resembled the Tammany Hall system in New York where local bosses controlled small political areas within the city. Membership cost 25 cents, and any black could join. Before long, the association evolved into the most powerful black political organization in Detroit. Word spread throughout the black community that membership in the association would assist one in obtaining employment as well as security against layoffs. While not all blacks who joined the association received employment or avoided layoffs, the association did achieve some results.[115]

In the end, the black Republicans' game plan failed. Nothing that they could do, even with the weight of Henry Ford on their side, could stop or slow down the Democratic Party's steamroller within the black community. Black Republicans, like their white counterparts, were situated on the wrong side of political history. Blacks might join the association to get and keep their jobs, but as one astute black Republican conceded: "I get the impression a lot of them [blacks] are saying they are all for the party but when they get in the polls, they vote Democratic. They like Roosevelt too much for that."[116]

The black Republicans' machine got behind Marshall when he ran on the Republican ticket for Congress in the First District in May of 1940. He lost in the primaries. Blacks were steadily voting Democratic in county, state, and national elections. And black Republicans were steadily losing out. Not even the popularity of heavyweight boxing champion Joe Louis, who campaigned for black Republicans, could halt their political decline in the black community.[117]

Joe Louis and Charles Roxborough started campaigning together on behalf of the Republican Party in the 1936 national elections. Louis and Roxborough traveled throughout Detroit and Wayne County promoting the Republican ticket, which included the candidacy of Roxborough then running as a representative in Congress of the First Congressional District. They repeated their political performance in 1938.[118] In the 1940 national election, Joe Louis traveled by plane to major cities with large black populations where he spoke to thousands of blacks on behalf of the Republican presidential nominee, Wendell Willkie. Louis's popularity produced larger black crowds in every city he visited than were ever accomplished by any black leader in a political campaign. But, even Louis's popularity as the first black heavyweight champion since Jack Johnson could not convince blacks to abandon Roosevelt. In fact, Louis's campaign for Willkie in 1940 created a storm of controversy in Detroit barber shops, poolrooms, and other places where blacks congregated to discuss racial and political issues.[119]

After the Republicans lost again in 1940, Joe Louis still had not figured out why so many of his people had voted for Roosevelt and the Democrats. As he informed his political mentor, Charles Roxborough: "If my people are as bad off for jobs four years from now as they are today, I will be ready to go with you again to help elect a Republican candidate."[120]

Black Republicans did not allow these political defeats to destroy their determination to try again in 1944. A month after the 1940 national election and Roosevelt's third victory, a local black political writer informed his readers that Republicans were not dead or dying. According to him, they were preparing for 1944 by searching for a "live issue" to attract black voters.[121]

Black Republicans on the national and local levels knew time was running out for them to find this live issue. As early as 1936, black Republicans on the national level began contacting local black leaders in Detroit for advice on how to attract blacks back into the Rebublican fold.

Since the 1920s, the Republican Party had been using Dancy to mobilize the Detroit blacks for "the party." In August 1928, Albon Hosley, secretary of the Colored Voters Division of the Republican National Committee invited Dancy to serve on the first committee of the Division. Another Detroiter, Mrs. Sarah Pelham of the Pelham Family, also served on this committee, which was attached to the Republican Party headquarters in Washington D.C. Evidently Dancy accepted, because a month later, a member of the committee informed him of their goals, which included lining up on the Republican side "all young voters and first voters among men and women and the customary stay-at-home voter who has never taken an interest in political campaigns before."[122]

The Division realized Dancy's tremendous influence among such segments of the black community and desired to get to them via him. As one black Republican woman working for The Organization of Colored Women made clear in her letter to Dancy in September of 1928: "I am trying to sell Herbert Hoover to the voters of the Western division. Knowing that you are a leader in your community, I am asking the privilege of mailing you a blank sheet for names and addresses, to be filled out and returned to me. If you can arrange for meetings, this Headquarters will be pleased to furnish speakers at our expense. Anything that you might do to promote the progress of the Campaign will be appreciated."[123]

In July 1936, Ralph B. Steward, a black medical doctor working on behalf of the National Allied Republican Council in Washington, D.C., wrote John C. Dancy for information on the political tendencies of blacks in the city: "I am informed that the tendency of our group tend to lean toward the New Deal in your city and state," Steward began. "If that is so, can you tell me why and what, if anything, can be done to change their views?" Steward opposed the New Deal and accused the Roosevelt Administration of practicing "mass discrimination" against blacks. Realizing the supposedly nonpartisan nature of the Detroit Urban League, he asked Dancy to share with him his personal opinions on the matter.[124]

In Dancy's response to Steward, he seemed a bit annoyed that the latter criticized the New Deal. "I was happy to have your letter even if it was a protestation of the present New Deal Administration." He proceeded to give Steward his views of black politics in Detroit. Blacks in Detroit are "essentially Republican," but many are becoming Democrats, Dancy explained. Blacks in Detroit have been able to obtain political jobs through the Democratic Party which the Republicans denied them. These jobs, Dancy continued, were the bait that snared blacks. "Recognition has been given several Negroes in the inner council of the Democratic Party," Dancy explained, "and that has helped in this section."[125]

Dancy had no information to convey to Steward on the exact number of black Democrats in Detroit. He did, however, inform Steward that out of 60,000 registered blacks in the Motor City, 5,000 were potentially Democrats. Then he injected a cautionary note: Frank Murphy, who was running for governor on the Democratic ticket, was one of the most popular people among blacks. "He will pull quite a vote from Negro circles."[126]

Dancy might not have told all he knew or suspected about the potential black Democratic vote in Detroit. He obviously knew the Democrats were offering blacks in Detroit more than just jobs as political bait to get them to support the party. His extensive experience working among the poorest blacks in the city provided him with rare insight into black political attitudes and behavior. As director of the Detroit Urban League during two Republican administrations, he witnessed their lack of concern for urban blacks—not that the Democrats had been any better.

The Democratic victories on the state and national levels in the fall of 1936 forced black Republicans in Detroit to confront the hard and bitter fact that they had lost touch with the black masses. Sara Pelham Speaks, a member of the prominent black Pelham family, refused to accept this fact. In March 1938 in Chicago, she told a gathering of Republicans, including black members of the Program Committee of the Republican National Committee, that the view that black votes had been "lost to the Republican Party forever" was untrue. She accused many people in the audience of sharing such a view. Blacks, she argued, are like other disaffected groups within the Republican Party and will return to the Party as soon as the Party demonstrates it understands the need of blacks.[127]

Blacks are not enslaved by the Roosevelt myth, Speaks added. They know that Roosevelt's lack of support led to the defeat of the antilynching bill and the New Deal will "perpetuate for them an inferior status in American life." Blacks would abandon the Democratic Party and return to the fold if the Republican Party made some radical changes. In short, Speaks informed the Republican gathering that if the Republican Party wanted blacks to return to the fold, they "should make radical changes wherever needed to meet the desperate present day necessities of the Negro."[128]

Unlike some black Republicans who merely lamented the loss of black votes to the Democrats, ignoring the root causes, Speaks concentrated on what the Republican must do to regain black political loyalty: They must protect the lives of blacks from mob rule; business leaders should hire blacks in areas in which they have been barred; and child labor should be abolished. Furthermore, she pointed out: "It is important that the Republican Party recognize the fact that because of his most distressing social and economic situation, the Negro will no longer accept the sentimental appeal to Reconstruction days as the basis for supporting a party." Black Republicans, she said, must "urge the Party to reestablish ideals that have made the Republican Party a great party in the past, to unequivocally and with complete courage, dedicate itself to those principles. If the Republican Party deserves to win, it will win with the Negro voters of America helping."[129]

Black Republicans and the Republican Party had two more years to apply Speaks's advice. But the 1940 national elections demonstrated once again that most blacks in Detroit and around the country, as well as the majority of Americans, still preferred Roosevelt.

In December 1940, Dr. Emmett Scott, one of the highest ranking black Republicans in the country, contacted Roxborough, the local black Republican leader. Once again reporting the black Republican dilemma, Scott requested Roxborough's advice on how to win blacks back to the Republican Party: "I am writing to ask if you will be good enough at your earliest convenience to send as full a statement as possible of your evaluation of the political situation as it effects us as a Race, and dealing more particularly with the problems which face us if we are to win our "folk" back to the Republican Party."[130]

Whatever Roxborough told Scott, it did not work. The popular Roosevelt won again in 1944 against the Republican nominee, New York Governor Thomas E. Dewey. Black voters in Michigan gave Roosevelt the state. Detroit blacks gave Roosevelt 41,739 and Dewey 10,683. Statewide, Roosevelt beat Dewey by 20,000 votes, which was sufficient to win Michigan's 19 electoral votes; and many of these votes came from the poorer sections of black Detroit located in 7th, 3rd, and 5th wards on the east side of the city. Blacks in cities around the country voted similarly.[131]

This spelled the end for black Republicans in the city, state, and the nation. Sara Pelham Speaks had been wrong. The black vote was lost to the Republican Party *almost* forever. They have yet to gain the political influence and power in the black community that they had once enjoyed. But this decline did not result from their unwillingness to serve black needs. Rather, the Republican Party lacked a political and economic program containing a "live issue" attractive to hard-pressed urban blacks. Black Republicans in Detroit and the nation had seen the handwriting on the wall as far back as 1932, but many local black Republicans had simply refused to abandon the Republican Party.

Even Sara Pelham Speaks's criticism of Roosevelt in 1938 came to nothing because of the inability of her politically influential family and local black Republicans to address the pressing economic problems in the black community. Black Republicans had contributed their share to the political empowerment of blacks in Detroit, but in the 1930s and 1940s, they followed the ideology of their party instead of rallying behind the vision of their people. As a result, they were relegated to the dust bin of black political history.

BLACK DEMOCRATS: POLITICAL REFORMERS

Before 1932, it was not only considered a disgrace for a black in Detroit to be a Democrat but also, considering the influence of Henry Ford and black Republicans like Marshall and Ward, being a Democrat constituted an economic death wish. Not even Judge Frank Murphy, in whose court Dr. Sweet and his ten companions were acquitted in 1925 and whom Detroit blacks considered their friend, would escape the onus associated with being a Democrat in the minds of the black community. When Murphy ran for mayor in 1931, the major black newspaper could find few legitimate reasons to oppose him except that he was a Democrat.[132]

In the early 1930s, the Democratic Party began forging a new alliance of labor, urban ethnic groups, and blacks. In April 1932, a committee of three black Detroit politicians, Harold Bledsoe, Charles Diggs, and Joseph Craigen, asked for and received permission from the Democratic county chairman to marshal the black vote for the Democratic Party.[133]

During the summer of 1932 an organization of black women called the "Democratic Whip" began working with the Michigan Democratic League, Inc., the official organization of the Democrats. Harold E. Bledsoe was chairman of the League. This was the year that Roosevelt won by a landslide and in the process convinced many blacks in Detroit and elsewhere that voting Democratic was not so terrible after all. Roosevelt's landslide in 1932 put fear in the hearts of black Republicans in Detroit when one of their state senators in the third district was defeated by a Polish Democrat.[134]

From 1932 on the Democrats began building a political base in the Detroit black community. The party elected blacks as delegates to the county convention which also qualified them to be members of the county committee. The Democratic Party also elected blacks to positions as division chairman, congressional district vice chairman, chairmen of congressional district delegations to the state conventions, members of the state central committee, and as delegates and alternates to national conventions. In 1936, the Democrats honored Harold Bledsoe by electing him presidential elector with more votes than the well-known and popular Frank Murphy. Bledsoe became the first black presidential elector in Michigan history.[135]

The Democrats received only a trickle of black votes in 1932 and 1934. Detroit blacks, however, made a dramatic shift from the Republicans to the Democrats between the 1934 and 1936 gubernatorial elections. This shift indicated a carryover effect on the growing black support for President Roosevelt and helped other Democratic state candidates. The 1936 election marked the first time that major black districts in Detroit voted for the Democrats in a national and state election.[136]

Although many local black Republicans deliberately chose to ignore the obvious reasons behind the shifting Detroit black vote to the Democratic Party, the reasons were everywhere apparent. The vast majority of blacks who voted for President Roosevelt and other Democrats had no ideological axe to grind. They lived in the east-side ghetto, where blight, poverty, and crime ravaged their lives. Seventy thousand blacks lived and died in this infamous ghetto that would have been almost unnoticed unless elevated to public attention by folk heroes like Joe Louis or sensationalistic crimes routinely published in both black and white local newspapers.

In this often forgotten center of black poverty and despair, Mrs. Roosevelt walked dirty alleys and streets and stood before fifty-thousand poor blacks holding a black child. Notwithstanding the politics of the times, blacks in the east-side ghetto never forgot that visit.[137]

However, poor blacks in the east-side districts did not vote for Roosevelt because his wife visited their hellhole. They voted for Roosevelt because his New Deal programs made life in that hellhole a little more bearable, something that no Republican had done.

Blacks on the west side of Detroit were much better off than their east-side brethren. Most of them voted for the Republicans. While there was not a clear-cut class division in the Detroit black community, class did exert some influence on black voting patterns.[138]

Several important black businessmen in Detroit supported Roosevelt because his New Deal programs provided jobs for the blacks upon whom they depended for their economic survival and progress. Among these businessmen were such notables as Louis C. Blount, of the Great Lakes Mutual Insurance Company, and Fred Allen, owner and operator of a successful laundry.[139]

According to these black businessmen, New Deal programs benefited black businesses in Detroit by providing employment for blacks displaced by industrial layoffs. Allen, for example, believed that President Roosevelt was "the greatest friend of the Negro businessman. By employing employable men who the factories refused to employ . . . he was able to make it possible that they support themselves and their families, and by so doing, the money they made as wages . . . flowed into the pockets of small businessmen which enabled them to carry on."[140]

Allen went on to point out that federal projects in Detroit helped blacks. He explained that blacks did not want to be on the public dole but had no choice since federal jobs were the only jobs available to those laid off from other industries.[141] This was a major point of difference between the black Democrats and black Republicans. The latter believed that blacks did not need the "dole," but they failed to offer any program to address the serious problem of black poverty.

After the 1936 elections, black Democrats dominated black political power in Detroit and the state. Black Republicans continued to try and turn the tide, but their efforts proved futile. Black Democrats were in power to stay; and no one demonstrated this fact better than the newly-elected Democratic state senator, Charles C. Diggs.

CHARLES C. DIGGS: SYMBOL OF AN AGE

The black votes that swept a host of Democrats into office in 1936 also swept Diggs into office as the first black Democrat to be elected to the Michigan Senate. Diggs represented a district composed of both black and Polish people who had been represented by Roxborough in 1931.[142]

Diggs was born in Tallula, Mississippi, on January 2, 1894. His mother taught school in rural Mississippi and Louisiana. His father was a minister who also spent time as a missionary in Africa. Diggs graduated from Alcorn Mechanical and Industrial College in Mississippi. After college, he decided to seek his fortune in industrial Detroit. He arrived in the Motor City in 1913, on the eve of the large southern black migration wave composed of the various people who several decades later would provide the foundation for his economic and political success.[143]

After settling down, Diggs decided to start a shoe-repair shop. From the profits, he saved enough money to go into a more lucrative career. He went to Philadelphia where he studied embalming at the Eckle's Embalming School. He then returned to Detroit where he opened his own funeral home in 1921. Soon his business grew into the largest black funeral establishment in the city and one of the most financially successful black undertaking businesses in the nation.[144]

Like many of his black political contemporaries, Diggs was an active Republican in the 1920s. He ran for the Detroit Common Council in 1930 and lost. He switched to the Democratic Party in 1932, the year of Roosevelt's landslide. By that time, he had become a leader in Democratic ward politics in Detroit.[145]

Diggs's election in 1936 held far more significance than just an historical first for black Democrats. It opened a new era in northern urban politics based upon the emergence of a new political coalition made up of labor, white ethnics, liberal Democrats, and blacks. And Diggs, in one sense, was one of the chief architects of this coalition because he not only supported civil rights, a traditional black issue, he also supported and championed New Deal reforms and the CIO.[146]

Diggs, therefore, not only switched to the Democratic Party, he became a symbol and a model of progressive black political leadership unprecedented in Detroit's black political history. During his tenure as state senator, he sponsored bills related to strengthening the state's Civil Rights Law in the area of discrimination in public places, regulating hours of work and improving sanitary conditions on the job, increasing welfare and hospital appropriations, reducing the minimum age for old age from 70 to 65 years, and increasing amounts of unemployment compensation, among others.[147]

The black state senator from Detroit often found himself facing walls of resistance as he battled against entrenched racist practices. In 1937, he took on the State Liquor Control Commission for their alleged discrimination against the hiring of blacks. Diggs accused the head of the commission of racism and called him a "self-styled czar" who had "taken it upon himself to keep the Lansing Liquor Control Office lily white."[148]

Obtaining a job in the offices of the State Liquor Control Commission was minor, however, compared to the problem black businessmen in Detroit had in obtaining liquor licenses. The Detroit police department issued these licenses and were accused by black businessmen of discriminating against them. Diggs became involved in this fight on both the local and state level.[149]

Housing conditions in Diggs's district were among the worst in the city, so he fought for better housing. He also mounted a crusade against landlords who were constantly raising rents.[150]

Black workers who faced discrimination on the job could count on Senator Diggs to go to bat on their behalf, and white employers who discriminated against blacks could count on Senator Diggs's relentless fight against their racial practices. For example, in 1939, five black workers were denied employment on a suburban Public Works Administration (PWA) construction project because of their race. They complained to Senator Diggs, who in turn reported the incident to the PWA Commissioner in Washington, D.C. As a result, the employer suffered a large deduction in his WPA grant.[151]

Unions could always count on Senator Diggs to support their struggles for better working conditions and the right to organize, but he in turn expected them to respect and support the same rights of black workers. When they did not, he quickly reprimanded them for their shortcomings and demanded that they put their own house in order, as he did in the spring of 1939 when the Detroit Fire Fighters Association requested his support for a bill reducing their working hours.[152]

The constant struggle against racism consumed much of Senator Diggs's time and energy. And while he won many battles, he never won the war. He suffered many defeats. In 1943, his Anti-Discrimination Bill, designed to put "teeth" in the state's Fair Employment Practice laws, passed unanimously in the state senate, only to go down to defeat in the house. The person responsible for the defeat had ties to the Michigan Manufacturer's Association.[153] But the defeated bill did not put out Diggs's fire. He continued to labor on.

In the 1940 elections, black Democrats in Detroit won big again. Diggs returned to the Michigan State Senate for the third time, having decisively defeated his Republican challenger, Robert L. Ward, by more than four to one. The black Democrats also gained another historical "first" when the Reverend Horace A. White became the first black to be elected to the State House of Representatives by the Democratic Party. White's lead over the nearest Republican was an impressive 100,000 votes. In addition to being the first black Democrat in the house, White also became the fourth black in the state's history to serve in the house. The other three were black Republicans elected in 1900.[154]

By 1940, the black Democrats in Detroit had achieved impressive political victories. They had the majority of blacks behind them and a sophisticated political organization, the Michigan Federation of Democratic Clubs (MFDC), under the leadership of Senator Diggs. Diggs purchased and equipped a large building to function as the permanent headquarters for the MFDC. It had an assembly hall, office and committee rooms, and a place for entertainment. One contemporary observer commented that the MFDC headquarters building was "the best mark made by a political organization in Michigan among our group."[155]

With all of his political accomplishments, Diggs continued to push out into other political fields that had relevance for black political progress. In the fall of 1941, he entered the council race. Although he lost, he achieved a new high for black candidates who had been running for the position since 1927.

Compared to the earlier common council election, in which he also ran in 1931, Diggs received 50 percent more votes than George Green, the black candidate who ran for the common council in 1927. Compared to the number of votes he received in 1931, Diggs's 1941 votes were three times higher. He tripled the number of votes received by William Sherrill, the black who ran for the common council in 1939. Blacks would have to wait sixteen years before one of their own would be finally elected to the Detroit Common Council.[156]

By the spring of 1943, Senator Diggs had become a political legend. In 1943, his friends honored him with a testimonial commemorating his four terms as a state senator. The theme of the ceremony was "Reverence for the living rather than for the dead." At this time, Senator Diggs held the rank of Michigan's senior Democratic leader. But he represented much more to blacks. To them, he was a political institution.[157]

Major figures in the Democratic Party attended the ceremony. Diggs's old friend, Harold E. Bledsoe, with whom he and another friend had first begun recruiting blacks for the Democratic Party back in 1932, reviewed Diggs's impressive record of public service. Bledsoe told the large audience of the work Diggs had done in and out of the legislature. Other speakers paid equal tribute to Senator Diggs. When Diggs finally rose to speak, he thanked all those who had come to pay tribute to him.[158] Few among his admirers at this testimonial dinner, perhaps not even the senator himself, realized that in less than six months, his political career and personal reputation would be in serious disarray.

In the fall of 1943, Senator Diggs, along with another state senator, was charged with attempted bribery in return for votes on the Anti–Branch Chain Bank Bill two years earlier. A Detroit bank controller accused Diggs of soliciting a campaign contribution in return for votes for the bill. Several months later, Diggs was again accused of wrongdoing by a legislative grand jury. This time he and 26 other law makers (mostly Detroit Democrats) stood accused of conspiring to push for an enactment of three bills in 1939 in exchange for money.[159]

In a prepared statement to the press Diggs denied any such wrong doing:

> I have voted on over four thousand Bills and Amendments to Michigan laws. In each case, I have made an honest effort to help pass legislation for the best interest of the people of the State of Michigan. My independent actions as a lawmaker has not been to the liking of certain interests, especially in the City of Detroit, who would like to control the Negro vote through me.
>
> A minority leader, of any elected body, in order to gain support and following to pass legislation that will best help the group he represents, must, at times, support legislation sponsored by other members of the legislature. In my case, I represent the Negro and labor. That I have succeeded in gaining the support and goodwill of other members of the Legislature is a matter of public record.
>
> I have been indeed fortunate since I have been in the Legislature, in that I have gotten most of the important legislation I sponsored, through both Houses, and I feel one of the secrets of my success has been that I have helped other members with legislation they desired to pass. Although I am a member of the minority party (Democrat) I have the support and goodwill of the Republican members.
>
> If it is as it appears on the face of the indictment returned by the Grand Jury, a plan to embarrass or discredit the Democratic Party, it does not reflect itself in the Legislature, in that, as I said before, I have always gotten the support of the Republican members as well as the Democrats.
>
> Prior to the convening of the grand jury I had told some of my close friends that I would not run for a fifth term as State Senator. I have now changed

my mind because I have never been accused (and I am too old to start now) of running away from a fight. I like a good fight and especially when I know I am right and my conscience is clear. When a person in public life is as active as I am and does as much as I do for his constituents and his people, there are bound to be complications arising and, as usual, I will take mine standing up.

I wish to take this opportunity to thank scores of friends who have called to offer their help and express their confidence in me. I wish to thank the law firms of Lewis, Rowlette and Brown, and Loomis, Jones, Piper and Colden and Bledsoe and Simmons, for their support.[160]

In August of 1944, Diggs and 17 other defendants were convicted of graft. He received three to five years in prison for his part in the alleged bribery of state lawmakers in 1939. Diggs appealed the convictions but lost. In 1948 he began serving time in Jackson Prison.[161]

After his release in 1950, Diggs once again entered politics. In November 1950, he again won election to the state senate. But in January 1951, the Michigan Senate, led by a majority of Republicans, voted 22 to 6 to refuse Diggs his seat. They even went so far as to adopt a resolution barring ex-convicts seats in that body.[162]

This ended a great era in black political history dominated in large part by the political visions of Charles C. Diggs. But this was only the beginning of another era. Charles Diggs, Jr., took his father's place. And in April 1951, Charles Diggs won elections to the seat that was refused to his father.[163]

As forms of community empowerment, protest and politics provided blacks with additional means of building their community. Each protest against racial discrimination galvanized blacks by raising their social consciousness, which in turn prepared them for participation in the political process. The local NAACP led the struggle against racial discrimination in Detroit up to the 1930s, when Snow F. Grigby's Detroit Civic Rights Committee joined the struggle. From 1933 to 1945, Grigby and the committee blazed a new trail in the black struggle against racial discrimination in Detroit. As always, in every time and place in America where blacks lived and the means existed, black newspapers fought relentlessly against racial discrimination. Both the *Detroit Tribune* and the *Michigan Chronicle* publicized racist advertisements placed in white newspapers and on bill boards. These papers maintained a close vigilance over all forms of racism in the Detroit area and kept the black community on its toes.

As the black community expanded, political empowerment became an increasingly vital form of community building. By 1925, black Republicans had already begun capitalizing on large concentrations of blacks in key wards. Led by Charles Roxborough, the black Republicans marshaled an impressive number of black votes for mayor John A. Smith in 1925. Less than a decade later, however, the masses of black voters in Detroit, like their counterparts in other northern cities, shifted to the Democratic party.

The black Democrats, led by Charles C. Diggs, the first black to be elected as a Democrat to the state legislature, took over the reins of black political empowerment in 1932. Diggs became the symbol of an age in black Detroit. He fought racial discrimination wherever he found it and used every opportunity at his disposal to build the black community. Unfortunately, in August of 1944, Senator Diggs, along with 17 others, was convicted of graft and received three to five years in prison. Thus ended a major era in black political empowerment. Notwithstanding, the black community was much further ahead politically at the end of this period of community building than at the beginning.

Eight

Conflicting Strategies of Black Community Building: Unionization vs. Ford Corporate Paternalism, 1936–1941

Within the last two years—
something has happened in
Detroit—something nobody
expected. Labor in this
capital of the motor industry
has waked up. And what is
even more surprising, Negro
labor has waked up.

Horace A. White,
February 9, 1938.

A PERIOD OF DIFFICULT CHOICES

By the Great Depression, there could be no questioning the fact that ties between corporate Detroit and the black community had contributed greatly to the community building process. As far back as 1916, Forrester B. Washington, the first director of the DUL, had sought out and received valuable assistance from the white business community. During the early years of Dancy's tenure as director, he built upon and expanded these ties as he continued the arduous task of servicing the needs of the migrant community. As a result of carefully nurtured ties, the Employers Association of Detroit financed the major portion of the DUL operations during the critical early years. Dancy also used his connections to the white business and civic communities to marshal support for many of his programs such as Green Pastures Camp.

Other black leaders also used their ties to powerful whites to leverage their resources on behalf of the larger black community. The Reverend Robert Bradby and Father Everand W. Daniel greatly valued their ties to the Ford family which enabled them to dictate the nature of community building.

While these black leaders might not have enjoyed the ingratiation inherent in their ties to powerful whites, they often welcomed and deliberately nurtured such ties as the only real option for building a strong and prosperous community.

At a time when blacks in Detroit, as elsewhere, had few friends and more than enough enemies, black leaders could not afford the luxury of being choosey. However, as the black community passed through the various stages of community building, the more perceptive black leaders came to the realization that dependency upon the white corporate elite, while vital to the community building process during earlier periods, now constituted a barrier to that same process. They also realized that just as the ministers, the DUL, the black business and professional groups, the NAACP, the black politicians, and the other segments of the black community had played the key roles at various stages of the community building process, black industrial workers once again were about to play a key role in that process via industrial unionism.

By the middle of the 1930s, the black community had already abandoned a political tradition in the shift from the party of the Great Emancipator to the party of Roosevelt that promised them jobs. The shift took great courage. Now they were about to experience an even more dramatic shift from the comforting dependency on one of corporate America's most powerful men—Henry Ford—to the camp of a yet unproven ally, the United Auto Workers of America. This stage of community building involved the coming of age of the black industrial working class, which had played the key role in the process several decades earlier.

Between 1936 and 1941, two major segments of the black community embracing two diametrically opposed philosophies and strategies of community building competed for the support of the black autoworkers. One segment advocated continual dependency upon Ford, a proven friend and supporter of the black community. The other segment advocated a leap of faith on behalf of a social movement composed of working class people.

THE ORIGINS OF FORD CORPORATE PATERNALISM AND BLACK COMMUNITY DEPENDENCY

The major black churches tended to be traditional. They identified with the Republican party and the antiunion biases of Henry Ford. Opposing them were the more radical segments of Detroit's rising black middle class, including some young black ministers and black union officials.

To understand the historical dynamics of these competing philosophies, we must first understand how the traditional approach exemplified by certain prominent black churches in the city evolved and why.

As already mentioned, the community building in the urban industrial north placed unprecedented demands upon the black church. The migration of thousands of southern blacks to Detroit taxed the meager resources of black churches. Though they did their best, it was insufficient. They needed more help.

The Detroit Urban League (DUL) performed near miracles, yet it too required assistance. In due time, both institutions found themselves dependent upon the largess of powerful white industrialists in Detroit.[1]

Since Henry Ford employed more black workers than any other company in the area, certain black churches drifted into Ford's sphere of influence. With so many black workers Ford managers needed assistance in controlling racial conflicts in the plants. And what originally began as a request for assistance gradually developed into a strategy of corporate paternalism grounded in black community dependency.

It all started one day in 1918 when Charles E. Sorenson, the plant manager of Ford Motor Company, invited Mr. Bradby to his office. Sorenson showed Bradby a number of knives and other weapons taken from black and white workers and asked him to help manage the racial conflicts in the plant and to recommend "good Negro workers" to the Ford employment office.[2] By granting Bradby the power to recommend "good Negro workers," Sorenson strengthened Bradby's and the Second Baptist Church's influence and power in the black community. As a result, Bradby and the Second Baptist Church became the gates to the kingdom of Ford. The power to recommend workers assured great status, a greatly sought after prize, coveted by less favored churches. If blacks wanted a job at Ford—and just about everybody did—they had to go to one of the black churches which Ford had blessed with the privilege of the recommendation system. Any church outside this system has little chance of matching the growth and prosperity of Ford-supported churches. As we have seen, in the hands of Marshall and Ward, this recommendation system became a powerful weapon of political intimidation and coercion.

For the next 23 years Mr. Bradby was an inseparable part of Ford's black employee-relations program. His tasks included assisting blacks to become steady and responsible workers at a time when many southern migrants were having difficulty maintaining stable work habits, often walking off the job after payday. Bradby saw himself as an extension of the Ford Motor Company and throughout the years ingratiated himself to Henry Ford and Charles Sorenson for special favors such as requests for concert tickets and other favors.[3]

By 1923, Sorenson discovered the Ford Motor Company's racial problem was too large for a single black minister. Sorenson approached Father Everand W. Daniel, the newly appointed pastor of St. Matthew's Episcopal

Church to assist in the management of the problems. Father Daniel was
an interesting choice, more educated and suave than Bradby and the darling
of the black elite. Most of the black intelligentsia, better paid workmen,
and businessmen sought membership in his church. His social status and
success in catering to the social elites, combined with his ability to obtain
endorsements from the Ford establishment, made him Detroit's chief black
spokesman until his death in 1939.[4]

The Ford establishment's introduction of Daniel into their strategy of
race-relations management created conflict between the two ministers.
Although Bradby remained influential with the Ford establishment until
his death in 1941, during the middle 1920s, Father Daniel surged ahead
"in the race for Ford's power."[5] Top black leaders visiting Detroit were
introduced to high officials by Daniel. The Ford people asked him to
represent the company at formal ceremonies.[6] Both men seemed almost
oblivious to the extent to which Ford's paternalism and their own dependency had eroded their mutual effectiveness in promoting the well-being
of the black community.

The Detroit Community looked upon Henry Ford as "the Negro's friend"
and the Ford Motor Company as "a haven in an otherwise unfriendly
industrial world."[7] Black workers enjoyed more equality at Ford than in
any other Detroit plant. Although most blacks worked in the foundry,
black workers were widely distributed throughout the plant. They worked
on assembly lines, in drafting rooms, as bricklayers and crane operators,
mechanics, electricians, and tool-and-die workers. At a time when few
blacks could gain entry to apprentice schools in Detroit and other cities,
Ford welcomed them. Not even the accepted custom of racial segregation
in employment prevented Henry Ford from integrating black and white
workers on the job. Only at Ford could a black man like James C. Price,
who became Ford's first salaried employee in 1924, rise to the level of
company purchasing agent of abrasives and industrial diamonds. And only
at Ford could one find more black foremen than in the entire industry.
Black foremen, incidentally, often supervised interracial work crews.[8]

Henry Ford's policy regarding black workers reflected his overall policy
of hiring diverse racial and nationality groups. For many years Ford followed a policy of maintaining at the Rouge Plant the same percentage of
blacks living in the Detroit area. Ford exceeded this quota policy of blacks
by 1940 when the percentage of black workers at Rouge reached 10 to 12
percent compared to the 8 percent black population in the Detroit area.[9]

No one knew exactly why Ford developed this policy. One source claimed
that at the beginning of the 1921 depression, representatives of the black
community, fearing that black workers would be laid off first, met with
Henry Ford to discuss the problem. Ford assured them that there would
be no discrimination in layoff policies. To implement this policy Ford
officials placed two black officials, Donald Marshall, a member of Daniel's
church, and Willie Ward, a famous University of Michigan football star,

in the Ford employment office. As already mentioned, their jobs involved handling all issues related to black employees.[10]

This Ford brand of corporate paternalism went even further. The Ford family developed limited social ties with the black community, which greatly enhanced black loyalty to the larger Ford establishment and encouraged even more black dependency. The Ford family frequently entertained black women's and black church groups at the family mansion. George Washington Carver, the black scientist, became a familiar face at the Ford estate. Black vocalists Marion Anderson and Dorothy Maynor appeared many times on the Ford Sunday Evening Hour. Henry Ford and Mrs. Ford also visited St. Matthew's once a year and made large contributions to the church. Henry Ford even put a black in charge of the Ford exhibits at the 1933 Chicago World's Fair, demonstrating to the world his respect for his black workers—or so most blacks and many whites believed. If there were any doubts about the growing reciprocity between Henry Ford and the Detroit black community, they were promptly dispelled as the Ford Dixie Eight, a glee club composed of black Ford employees, gained popularity in the local black community.[11]

Among all the contributions Ford made to the social and economic well-being of the black community, nothing excelled his assistance to blacks in Inkster during the Great Depression. In the 1930s Inkster was a small village located near Dearborn, Michigan. According to one scholar, it was "the most extreme example of Ford paternalism, . . . the closest approximation to a company town known in the automobile industry."[12]

Founded in the middle 1920s, Inkster soon had a predominately black community containing about 1,000 black workers. The majority worked for Ford. A few years into the Great Depression, black workers began losing their jobs to the point that black unemployment in Inkster became almost universal. Township welfare funds hit rock bottom. A desperate black community turned to Henry Ford for help. Ford came to their rescue with a welfare project that not only kept the black community afloat but also drew it further into the orbit of Ford's influence.[13]

First, Ford set up a commissary to provide food to the unemployed workers. Where jobs existed at the Rouge plant, they were given to as many Inkster black workers as possible. Ford then paid remaining unemployed workers a dollar a day to cut weeds and do general cleanup work. He rebuilt some of the houses in the community, took over debts, and paid pressing bills such as fuel, electricity, taxes, insurance, and clothing.[14]

To avoid fostering too much dependency, families obtaining these benefits were required to grant the Ford Motor Company the legal right to administer all property in their possession. Debts taken over by the company were deducted from the workers' pay after they returned to work. Workers also were required to pay their regular bills once they returned to work. Ford built two schools in the black community during this period. He also provided a doctor and a nurse, and he set up a free clinic which provided health care twice a month for the children. Every day except Sundays a company truck collected garbage and rubbish from the community. At Christmas, the company gave a tree and presents to the children of the community. Henry Ford visited the project on many occasions and was always "mobbed" by the black children.[15]

Can there be any wonder that blacks in Detroit and Inkster greatly admired and even loved Henry Ford and his company? Notwithstanding the obvious dangers of the black community and its key leaders' increasing dependency upon Henry Ford, Ford was still one of the major benefactors of black people in twentieth-century America.

By the 1930s, the recommendation system had evolved into a powerful device in the hands of key black leaders. Few black workers could obtain work at Ford without knowing somebody close to the company. And black ministers could build their congregations through the recommendation system. Father Daniel had no qualms about using this system to economically strengthen his own congregation. No doubt many blacks joined Daniel's church just to obtain work and once having obtained it, abandoned him. Strangely enough, such behavior often disappointed Daniel.[16]

Bradby, Daniel, Marshall and Ward became Henry Ford's representatives in the Black community, and they labored hard and long to link the black community's interests to Ford's social and political tastes. We have already discussed how these two blacks used their position at Ford to influence black political behavior.[17]

In all fairness to Bradby, Daniel, Marshall, and Ward—who at times assumed roles resembling pawns in the company's game to control the political and economic direction of the black community—history will no doubt view them as desperate black leaders doing their best "in the complex search for empowerment." At worst, this strategy was merely an outmoded approach pursued by honest but shortsighted men.

A decade before the rise of industrial unionism in the mid 1930s, Henry Ford, through two of black Detroit's most influential ministers and their churches, had drawn the larger black community into a state of economic and political dependency. This state of dependency, sort of a pact with the devil, was constantly reinforced by the infamous recommendation system. A system that, one scholar argued, "was relatively innocuous except for the element of personal favoritism. It was exploited, however, to force the Negro population to conform to the economic and political philosophy of Henry Ford," and Willis Ward and Donald Marshall "were the instruments by which this policy was effected, and job control constituted the power enabling them to keep the Negro community in line."[18]

For over two decades, black dependency upon Ford constituted the dominant strategy of economic survival and progress for many segments of the black community. From a small beginning the Ford power gradually integrated these segments within the structure of corporate paternalism and control. Increasingly few black organizations and institutions could exist, much less grow and develop, outside the orbit of Henry Ford's immense power and influence. Black churches, fraternal organizations, and professional and business people, to the extent that they derived their incomes from black Ford workers, were dependent upon Ford and his black puppets.[19]

Although I disagree with Zunz's view that compared with the history of white ethnic groups in Detroit, "Blacks lived history in reverse," he is correct in the context of the black-Ford relationship that blacks either had to "escape the oppressive system of the ghetto or learn to live in it."[20] Given the alternatives, black leaders adopted the most prudent and creative strategy of community building by aligning themselves to Ford. But, by the mid-1930s, the strategy had reached the point of diminishing returns to the community building process.

Thus, we see how the black community became dependent upon Ford's corporate paternalism. With the rise of industrial unionism, the black community faced hard choices: whether to join a major movement for social justice for working-class people or stay within the bosom of Henry Ford, who opposed such a movement. Whatever path they chose, great risks were involved.

INDUSTRIAL UNIONISM AND BLACK DETROIT

Conflicts seemed inevitable in the industrialization of the black working class in Detroit. Industrialization created the dependency relationship between key black leaders and Henry Ford; it also positioned black workers in the mass-production industries, particularly auto, destined to undergo unionization. Few contemporary black observers realized how much these developments would force segments of the black community to adopt divergent and contradictory strategies perceived to be in the best long-term interest of the larger black community. The local branch of the Urban League, key black churches, and some black Republicans, embraced a more conservative strategy of community building, while the NAACP, black Democrats, an assortment of black radicals, a few brave churches, and black trade unionists adopted a more radical approach to the same end. Of all of these strategies, black trade unionism triggered the worst conflict because, by its very nature, it challenged the powerful hold Henry Ford and his chosen black churches, ministers, and leaders had on the black community.

Trade unionism was not new to black workers in Detroit. In the 1920s, blacks held union membership in at least a dozen unions. For example, numerous black employees belonged to unions: stewards, laundry workers, laborers, bricklayers, plaster and cement mixers, carpenters, streetcar men, moulders, hoist and portable engineers, garment workers, typographers, and garbage truck drivers and helpers. The garbage truck drivers and helpers union, the steward's union, the laundry workers union (all women), and the brick layers union had the most black members.[21]

However, crucial differences existed between the two periods of black trade unionism. The vast majority of blacks were struggling just to survive in the new environment during the years 1918–20 when the Union of Carriage, Wagon and Automobile Workers was active. But even had black workers been prepared to join this industrial union, it showed little interest in recruiting them. A few years later, after the Communist Party took it over and renamed it the Auto Workers Union, a few blacks joined. The union itself, however, remained unknown to most black workers. Black trade unionism remained static in 1926 when the AFL made abortive attempts to revive unionism in the automobile industry. Black workers might have shown some interest had the AFL's segregated union made some attempt to enroll blacks. The failure to do so stemmed in part from the AFL's concentration on skilled workers.[22] Therefore, most black workers, who were unskilled, were excluded on both counts.

The level of class consciousness among automobile workers as well as the overwhelming antiunion, open-shop sentiment pervading the automobile industry at the time also retarded black trade unionism. Trade unionism was alien to the vast majority of automobile workers. Consequently before 1935, trade unionism was not a viable strategy for survival and progress in the eyes of most black and white automobile workers.[23] But times were changing, and in a few short years these same workers would view unionization as key to this process of community building.

In October 1935, Lester Granger of the National Urban League's Industrial Relations Department arrived in Detroit with the express purpose of setting up a Negro Workers Council in the Motor City. This effort stemmed from the National Urban League's nationwide program to educate black workers in trade unionism, increase black membership in unions, and instruct black workers on how "to advance their interests as members of the labor movement." Soon after Granger arrived and prepared to outline his project at the meeting scheduled to take place at the black YMCA, the YMCA secretary abruptly cancelled the meeting and refused to allow the building to be used for such purposes. Everyone present knew that outside pressure had been brought upon the secretary. The meeting was then switched to the black YWCA.[24]

The meeting took place but only a handful of blacks attended. Yet, it looked as if unionism had a chance. Those present did not spend much time discussing the organization of black automobile workers, but everyone understood that any successful worker council would undoubtedly influence black workers in the automobile industry. Afterward, interested parties organized a Negro Workers Council, but it fell apart in less than a year. Another attempt to resurrect the council with new officers failed. Most observers attributed these failures to the general antiunion attitudes of black workers, longtime victims of racist unions. But the death blow to the Negro Workers Council bore the mark of the heavy hand of the black Ford interests that dominated the leadership of the black community.[25]

By 1936, the groundswell of industrial unionism was underway. In Pittsburgh, Gary, Chicago, Toledo, and Milwaukee, black workers were paying serious attention to the unionizing drives. In Detroit, black workers moved cautiously. Few black workers participated in the UAW sit-down strikes in Detroit in 1936 and 1937, yet the issue of trade unionism was being hotly debated. Black workers with trade union experience helped pave the way for the recruiting drives in the black community. Many veteran black trade unionists had experienced years of racial and class discrimination in the AFL and other unions. When they discovered that the UAW had a policy of nondiscrimination, they shifted over.[26]

For example, in the spring of 1937, a black local of the International Moulder Union shifted over to the United Auto Workers (UAW) because its members resented how the union catered to the craft workers, leaving the "leftovers" to the unskilled workers. Therefore, in May 1937, assisted by the subcommittee for the Organization of Negro Workers of the UAW, these black foundry workers set up headquarters of their new local in the middle of the black community to recruit black foundry workers.[27]

Before long, the benefits of unionization became apparent to blacks. Prior to the UAW-CIO organizing drive among blacks, they were making 50 to 56 cents an hour. After joining the union their wages increased from 75 to 85 cents an hour. And no more speedups.[28] Of course these benefits were only possible in plants which had contracts with the UAW. But of all the benefits, racial equality on the job was most important.

The UAW-CIO's policy of racial equality gave it a great advantage over the AFL and other unions. The UAW-CIO started off recruiting black organizers and supported them in elevating themselves. The union's policy on racial equality was unequivocally stated by Jack B. Kennedy speaking at a mass meeting at Union Hall in June of 1937. As a UAW organizer assisting in the supervision of the Ford unionization drive, he outlined the policy of the union toward black workers as one of complete equality with white workers. "No contract can be made by the UAW that shuts out the Negro," he said. "Negroes have been assured their rights by their inclusion on all important committees of the union," he went on to point out that "in any bargaining involving a number of Negro workers, Negroes will be placed on the negotiating committee."[29]

Someone asked what would be done if a white union member refused to work next to or on the same job with a black union member. Kennedy stated that the man would be suspended or fined and that if he still continued to be prejudiced, he would be expelled from the union. This was indeed radical talk coming from a white organizer, particularly at a time in Michigan when the racist Klan-like organization, the Black Legion, was attempting to turn native white workers against labor unions, Jews, Catholics, and blacks.[30] It was also a vast improvement over the racial policy of the AFL.

Fighting racism proved to be the acid test of the UAW's commitment to black equality. If blacks were expected to abandon Henry Ford for the UAW, they needed hard evidence that the union could protect their best interests. Racism had to be attacked head-on.

White working-class racism posed a serious problem because it threatened to split the ranks of the budding UAW-CIO during its upcoming confrontations with the big auto plants. It also threatened to disrupt the newly-established alliance among powerful black national organizations like the NAACP, The National Negro Congress, and the UAW-CIO. Moreover, white working-class racism gave credence to the old paternalistic line that capitalists were more interested in black workers than were white workers within the UAW-CIO. The problem had to be addressed because every racial incident drove a wedge between black and white workers. Organized labor, therefore, had to be on constant guard against diversive racial occurrences.

Building a strong labor union depended on promoting racial integration throughout the union structure, including the locals. This posed a problem in UAW locals. White workers perceived their locals not only as labor organizations but also as social clubs. Blacks could attend labor meetings at locals, but most white workers balked at admitting blacks to social functions held at the locals. The problem came to a head just at the time when top UAW union officials were involved in organizing and integrating newly organized blacks into previously all white locals.

In October 1937, the Welfare Committee of Chevrolet Local 235 gave several black members tickets to sell to the local's first Annual Harvest Ball. When black workers who purchased the tickets arrived, a white worker informed them that hotel policy barred interracial dancing. The hotel denied it, placing the blame back in the laps of the white members of the local. A local black paper picked it up and printed big headlines: "UAW JIM CROWS WORKERS." Blacks held several protest meetings. Even pro-UAW black organizations like the Michigan branch of the National Negro Congress protested. After a stormy session the executive committee of the local issued a statement:

> In answer to the situation which occurred at the Book Cadillac Hotel . . . which was not approved by the executive board of Local 235, the following solution was agreed upon between the colored committee and the executive board: this union is organized on one principle. There will be no discrimination whatsoever, regardless of religion, race, creed, color, political affiliation or nationality. The executive board of Local 235 will follow this principle to the limit.[31]

This incident could have wrecked what racial progress the UAW had made in the black community over the past two years. It put black UAW organizers, as well as top UAW officials, in an embarrassing position. Black UAW organizers warned white workers that their attitudes could harm the labor movement and that their enemies would use such incidents to divide them.

The UAW had its hands full trying to organize and unite black and white workers. White workers had to be constantly reminded of the divide-and-rule tactic of the Ford Motor Company. As one writer for the UAW paper explained:

> Divide and rule! This is the scheme that has been used by the Ford Motor Company for years to keep its workers in a turmoil of conflict among themselves. Nationality, religion and color prejudices—that old boss racket—is shrewdly promoted by the Ford management . . . Henry Ford has you figured out for a sap; Henry wants to keep you 'burned out' over the Negro workers to prevent you from uniting with them into the UAW and ending Ford's industrial slavery. . . . How long will you let Henry play you for a sucker? Henry hates all workers—white and black, native and foreign.[32]

According to the UAW writer, the responsibility for eliminating racism from within the ranks rested squarely upon the shoulders of white workers. "It is the responsibility of the white worker to take the largest step in this direction, since it is the white race that is the offender in this matter." Furthermore, the writer continued, "the white worker must demonstrate his sincerity not by words but by his actions."[33]

The cause of working-class unity suffered when unions within the CIO did not live up to the ideals of racial equality as constantly proclaimed by the leadership. Rank-and-file white workers would have to be dragged kicking and screaming into union fellowship with black workers, because many white locals refused to fight the latter's battles. For example, in May 1938, the CIO Union, United Dairy Workers, Local 83, refused to aid a black milkman who was fired when the milk company he worked for sold the route to another company. As a result the NAACP criticized the union.[34] Blacks within and outside organized labor probably wondered if they should just depend on their already established national and local civil-rights groups instead of hassling with whites in the union.

The problems of racism, then, compounded the problems of labor organizing among blacks and prompted UAW officials to take aggressive position against racism. In 1936, the UAW stated its position on such racist groups as the Black Legion. UAW head Homer Martin asked for a federal investigation of the organization because of its vicious racist and fascist nature.[35] Two years later these problems remained. Another racist organization, the Pioneer League of Michigan, distributed raucous circulars, petitions, and chain letters in Detroit. One such petition circulated during the summer of 1938 stated: "In Michigan, black and white can marry, black and white children cannot be segregated, white teachers teach black children, black teachers teach white children, blacks are the same under law, Michigan law permits interracial housing, public employment is overrun with blacks."[36]

The petition urged whites to protect their families. The next month, the Pioneer League presented an antiblack petition to the Michigan Legislature. The *Detroit Tribune* warned its readers to wake up to the dangers of this white racist group.[37]

The UAW leadership recognized racism as a major problem and realized its potential for dividing the working class. The white president of UAW Local 212, Emil Mazey, wondered if blacks in America would become like the Jews in Germany:

> The Negro worker in America today is facing many of the conditions recently imposed upon the Jewish people in Germany. . . . The entire working class should vigorously protest the persecution of the Jewish people in Germany . . . but what about eliminating persecution and discrimination in America! Many fascist organizations are growing rapidly in America today. . . . The Ku Klux Klan and the Black Legion are avowed enemies of the Negro people . . . why have the public officials ignored the Nego problem? Can it be that the industrialists in America are waiting to play the Negro in a similar role as the fascists in Germany are using the Jewish people?[38]

He referred to the Nazis' persecution of the Jews principally to divert the attention of the German working class from the solution of their economic and social problems.[39]

During a labor speech on Detroit radio station WJR on December 10, 1938, Homer Martin devoted a major portion of his time analyzing the antilabor nature of racism. He also emphasized how organized labor in Germany and the benefits which it had brought to German workers had been destroyed by anti-Semitism and compared it with racism in America.[40]

Both the UAW and progressive black leaders were on guard against such an occurrence arising in America. Blacks made it a point to keep the topic on the minds of the UAW leaders, particularly as regarded the significance of blacks to the UAW drives. As a member of the Michigan Negro Congress said: "Ford will be organized when the Negro workers join the union. They will join when the union effectively takes up the main problem of the Negro, the acute discrimination practiced against his race."[41]

Fortunately, for all concerned, that is exactly what the UAW attempted to do. During a mass rally held in April 1938 to secure passage of an antilynching bill, Martin shared the platform with black leader Lester B. Granger of New York, secretary of the Workers' Bureau of the National Urban League.[42] This public stand taken by the UAW on lynching added to their credibility among Detroit blacks.

The UAW-CIO was first in line to support a civil-rights bill when it was introduced in the states of Michigan and Ohio. The UAW supported a range of antiracist efforts from encouraging black and white workers to attend plays dramatizing the racial problems, to urging them to come out and march together in Labor Day parades.[43]

At their second annual convention in Milwaukee in July of 1938, the UAW adopted a resolution that in part said that special efforts should be made to bring black autoworkers into their ranks by hiring more workers who are acquainted with the special problems of blacks. The resolution included the elimination of all discrimination in hiring, promotion, job layoffs, and education.[44]

By August of that year they could boast of $300,000 in wage increases that had been paid to their 20,000 black members. Nonunion black workers shared in wage increases secured by the union, bringing the total of wage increases for both groups to $450,000.[45]

The UAW learned a lot about recruiting black workers from the failures of the AFL and the problems of the United Mine Workers and the International Ladies Garment Workers, both of which had done "pioneering work in the field" of black labor organizing. As one labor writer put it:

> The United Automobile Workers occupy a pivotal position in approaching the problems of working class race relations. This is due to the tremendous influx of new members into the organization during the past year and the general tendency of automobile executives to "skeletonize" the industry with an appreciable number of Negroes. Here, the problem must be approached with a greater degree of determination and foresight than the past approach of either the United Mine Workers or the International Ladies Garment Workers. . . . [46]

One of the first steps of the UAW in that direction was the appointment of Walter Hardin of Pontiac in August 1937 both to be the general international organizer of black autoworkers and to assist Paul Kirk in carrying through the Negro Industrial Conference coming up later that month. The UAW showed foresight in selecting black organizers and in attending black prounion meetings and events in the black community.[47] They developed more than an expedient strategy, then so commonly employed by white politicians and resented by blacks. They apparently misunderstood the growing desire among black workers to have input into the decision-making process of the union and they responded to it.

In their efforts to recruit black workers the UAW engaged in a sophisticated campaign designed to address certain problems in the black community. They publicized the fact that the majority of black workers in the auto industry were concentrated in the heaviest, dirtiest, and most dangerous jobs, often called "Negro jobs." Such jobs as the shakeout and coremaking, had maimed and killed many black workers.[48]

Black workers could not end these conditions by themselves, the UAW argued. And they could not turn to the AFL. Compared to their role in the AFL, the paper pointed out, blacks are "a part of the United Automobile Workers Union and not a tool in it."[49] The UAW has done more in little over a year, the paper added, than the AFL had in fifty-one years for blacks.[50] While indulging a bit of hyperbole in stating their core, the UAW had gone far beyond the AFL in supporting the rights of black workers.

The UAW missed few opportunities to woo black workers. Nothing that related to the black community's political, economic, or social life was considered too trivial. While the UAW paper could not compete with the local black weeklies, it did give more coverage to black labor problems and utilized black labor writers. Noteworthy items of special interest to the black community were conspicuously integrated with other news. When Jesse Owens, the famous black track star at the 1936 Olympics, broke and made world records, the UAW paper remarked under a big caption, "Non-Aryan Shocks Hitlerites," how "Jesse Owens . . . gave Hitlerite spectators at the Nazi Olympics many uncomfortable moments."[51]

They also seemed especially pleased over any example of working-class unity between blacks and whites. For example, in Cicero, Illinois, in 1937, where black workers at the National Malleable Steel Company comprised about 50 percent of Local 433, two blacks held the highest posts on the Local's executive committee[52] and provided the UAW with invaluable evidence in their campaign propaganda to win other skeptical black workers. But they would have to do more.

Fully aware of Ford's influence in the black community, the UAW embarked upon a campaign to expose every harmful situation and event that happened to black workers in the company. They focused on Ford's employment of blacks in its foundry department, which was known for speedups, lack of safety equipment, poor ventilation, and deaths of hundreds of black workers who died as a result of working in that department. When a black parking attendant was hospitalized for two days after he was beaten by Harry Bennett's thugs in June 1937, the UAW paper emphasized the fact that they got off with a light fine because they were defended by an attorney who was the son of Henry Ford's personal lawyer. Later that same month the paper also reported an attempt by Bennett's men to drive into a crew of UAW members who were under the direction of Paul Kirk, a black organizer of the UAW.[53]

The UAW campaign would eventually pay off, but in the summer of 1937, most black workers had not given much indication that they wanted to join the union. Ford workers still clung to the "old man." They firmly believed that Henry Ford had been more than fair to them. In contrast to other companies in the city, they were right. Henry Ford's aid to Inkster was not easily forgotten nor could it be sidetracked. One black worker, writing in one of the local black weeklys, defended Ford because of his aid to Inkster and his policy of employing blacks in significant numbers in those departments which were closed to them in union shops: "There are more Negroes employed by the Ford Motor Company by percentage than any union shop in the automobile industry. Mr. Ford is not a god, but he has been a savior to thousands of Negroes by giving them employment according to their ability when union shops were closed to them. He kept thousands off the relief bills, thereby saving their moral respect and the city and the state thousands of dollars."[54]

He was correct. Ford had aided Inkster, but people are still speculating about his motives. Ford also had the most progressive policy towards black workers in the industry at a time when blacks in Detroit were in need of every helping hand they could get.

Another black worker defended Ford in the same black weekly, rejecting the views that the majority of blacks were in the foundry, pointing out that Ford distributed blacks through all departments: "Can this be said of any shop now controlled by the UAW? Can the gentleman who wishes to defend the UAW thereby encourage the Negro Ford workers to join same, point out one union shop where Negroes are trained and given employment as tool makers, bricklayers, mill wrights, head of the abrasive material department, laboratory technician, and other departments. These are some of the opportunities given the Negro by the Ford Motor Company."[55] He went on to say that if the labor man can name a closed shop giving blacks such a variety of employment and give the UAW credit for bringing about such conditions, then he will concede the UAW has something to offer black workers.[56]

This worker obviously reflected the sentiments of many other black workers. He posed perhaps the most difficult arguments for the UAW. Having inherited some of the racist legacy of the AFL, the UAW was suspect, notwithstanding radical pronouncements and some very real concrete benefits that had accrued to black workers who had joined their ranks.

It was probably impossible for a "labor man" at that time to point out a union shop's giving blacks a variety of employment as a result of the UAW. The UAW had just started in Detroit. Ford had been employing blacks in increasing numbers and in various departments since 1919. So the antiunion worker could always trot out the achievements of Ford over the past two decades to disarm the prounion workers, as one argued:

> I do not deny that I have been contaminated by Fordism. I have an opportunity to advance according to my ability. I do not have to pay Mr. Ford a fee for the privilege of working or be forced out of work on a strike at the will of the union whether I wanted to work or not, simply because the big union bosses in Washington or in the Hoffman Building in Detroit said so.[57]

He then asked prounion blacks to tell him the difference between the organization methods used by the CIO and those used by the AFL, remarking that they "did not welcome the Negro until they had sufficient strength to dominate their crafts and then replace him with whites?"[58] The worker then defended Don Marshall and Henry Ford and accused the UAW of using false propaganda.

If black UAW organizers and other prounion workers expected to capture the majority of black auto workers at Ford, they would have to quickly prove the merits of the union.

About two weeks earlier, an article in the UAW paper attacked the notion that blacks at Ford were satisfied. The paper called all such statements lies. The writer of the article claimed black workers at Ford were "cowed," and that one out of every 15 or 20 men in the plant were spies, paid to "betray any worker who exerts the right given to him by the United States Constitution and the Wagner Labor Act to join the union of his choice." Black workers, he argued, were made to believe that Ford had "given them a special right to work like slaves because he hired them when other motor companies didn't. 'Ford stuck by us' they say, 'and we'll stick by him.'"[59] He called Don Marshall a "high salaried spy master" who had just selected a handpicked group of black thugs no doubt to help "convince" black workers to appreciate Ford's generosity throughout the years. The only satisfied blacks at Ford, the writer claimed, were the foremen, selected skilled workers, and, of course, Marshall and "his thugs." But the thousands of black workers, he continued, "who slave their youth away on his [Ford's] hot lines, in his blast furnaces, in his coke ovens, and on the heaviest jobs in the assembly line, are not satisfied."[60] He then attacked the argument that blacks owed Ford their loyalty:

> Negro workers working at Ford's don't owe Henry Ford one thing. Each penny they get they earn with the sweat of their brow. Ford found them good workers and gave them jobs because they did the job well. Negroes do the bulk of the hard work done at Ford's. Do the thousands of workers of other nationalities owe him anything? Only the Negro is supposed to feel such—a debt of gratitude to 'Uncle Henry' that he is asked to fight against the union, the only movement by which he stands to gain a great deal. Ford expects his black workers to be slaves, unprotesting, cowardly, lest he give their jobs to white workers.[61]

These conflicts over whether blacks should join the union or remain loyal to Ford would soon embroil other segments of the black community. At this crucial stage in their history, Detroit blacks found themselves struggling with both their past and their future. Their past instructed them to remain loyal to Henry Ford, their benefactor during troubled times; but their future promised more independence from white father figures such as Ford. More importantly, the future promised greater growth and development as part of a movement of working-class people. As already mentioned, black workers in other industrial cities were also being affected by the spirit of industrial unionism. So Detroit blacks were not standing alone at this historical crossroad.

CONFLICTING STRATEGIES OF COMMUNITY BUILDING: INDUSTRIAL
UNIONISM VS. FORD CORPORATE PATERNALISM

In 1937, the NAACP could not have selected a better place to hold their
Twenty-Eighth Annual Conference than Detroit. Few black communities
in America had so much to gain and lose in the next few years. No one
doubted that the labor question would dominate the conference. Some
attendees probably secretly hoped for a peaceful solution of such a disruptive issue. Much was at stake. Would the conference support labor or
capital?

The composition of the conference practically guaranteed conflicts. Predictably, Daniel and Bradby threatened to boycott the conference if Homer
Martin, the president of the UAW, spoke. They made a bad move! Martin
not only spoke, but the discussions on labor had the largest attendance
of the conference.[62]

The large attendance at the labor discussion did not mean everyone
present supported unions. Both John P. Davis, president of the Negro
Congress, and Homer Martin, president of the UAW, the top prounion
speakers at the conference, drew considerable flak over their speeches.
Many in the audience did not agree with them. William Pickens, branch
director of the New York NAACP, jumped to his feet in the course of the
discussion and demanded to know just what grievance, if any, black workers had against Henry Ford.[63]

Everything was going well with Homer Martin as he discussed the racial
policies of the CIO, blacks acquiring seniority rights, black CIO organizers,
and predominately white UAW locals with black officers—but then he blew
it! "I come representing the poor, the oppressed and exploited people, both
colored and white. Jesus also represented the poor, the oppressed, and the
exploited at that time."[64]

That one statement, perhaps said in all innocence, projected Martin as
an egotist, providing critics of labor more grist for their propaganda mills.
The Sunday after the conference, Father Daniel could not pass up the
opportunity to jump on Martin's statement. "It is commonplace to assert
that there has never been a teacher comparable to Jesus. Of course many
have claimed to be his equal. No less a person than Homer Martin lays
claim to this distinction."[65] William Pickens also attacked Martin as a
"suave big shot, all dressed up and . . . trying to explain that he and Jesus
are birds of a feather; that both of them were trying to help the poor, the
helpless and the oppressed."[66]

The opposition helped to focus attention on Martin's unwise statement.
Antilabor people needed an opportunity to criticize labor unions, and
Martin, unfortunately, gave it to them.

Black UAW workers focused on more pertinent aspects of the conference.

One worker noticed that the NAACP had criticized the AFL for neglecting to send organizers among black workers but failed to strongly endorse the CIO, which was sending black and white organizers to recruit blacks. Another worker attacked the Resolution Committee of the conference for hesitating to endorse the CIO by name as well as the NAACP for wishing to "hesitate and let this vital question stay in the studying stage."[67]

The resolution referred to was the one discussed and fought over for two days and nights concerning the endorsement of the CIO by name. It stated in part that black workers should not go blindly into any labor organization. They should first examine the motives and practices of all labor unions "and . . . bear their full share of activity and responsibility . . . in building a more just, and more intelligent labor union movement."[68]

Another view of the conference expressed by a black worker highlighted the tension between the NAACP and certain black members of the UAW. He cautioned the UAW to "depend less on the ready-made, bandwagon-conscious Negro national and community leaders" and instead to "develop and put greater dependence on an intelligent leadership of Negro automobile workers, who after all really know what they want" and what has to be done to get it.[69] He warned the UAW that if they continued to depend on black leaders of nonlabor organizations, they would be "doomed to many more surprises similar to the recent NAACP resolution."[70]

Black UAW members who held this view probably interpreted the UAW's wooing of the traditional black leadership—in this case the NAACP—as a slight to the emerging black working-class leadership in Detroit. According to this view, black workers did not need nonlabor black leaders speaking for them and certainly not making discussion for them. As the worker said, black workers know what they want and how to get it. This view suggested a repudiation of traditional black leadership, what the above worker called "bandwagon-conscious Negro national and community leaders."

The NAACP was not trying to usurp the rights of black workers, nor was the UAW depending on the NAACP to the exclusion of black workers. Rather, the national office of the NAACP, out of years of experience with the labor movement, was only proceeding cautiously in this battle between capital and labor. The UAW had to woo the NAACP because of its influence in the Detroit black community.

Several months after the NAACP conference, the battle for the minds and hearts of black working-class Detroit took a new turn. The national office of the NAACP was obviously angry over the boycotting of the conference by Detroit's two leading ministers. Roy Wilkins, the national secretary of the NAACP, took them to task in a scathing editorial in August:

> In Detroit at least two ministers of the Gospel, one an influential Episcopalian and the other a leading Baptist, were so aroused over the fact . . . the Committee for Industrial Organizations was on the program of the

NAACP that they preached on the inequity of the NAACP and its leaders and the evil men at the head of the CIO. . . . [T]heir argument boiled down to a defense of the Ford Motor Company (which was not mentioned on the NAACP program). . . . If the two greatly disturbed Divines in Detroit feel called upon to attack their one great national organization because of their love for what Mr. Ford has done for Negroes in Detroit, we invite them to Mr. Ford's plants in Edgewater, New Jersey; Chester, Pennsylvania; Atlanta, Georgia; Kansas City, Missouri; and St. Paul, Minnesota, and ask them if they will find anything in those places to cause them to don the garments of the Lord and preach a holy defense of the 800 million-dollar Ford Motor Company.

The spectacle of poor preachers, ministering to the needs of poor people whose lot from birth to death is to labor for a pittance, rising to frenzied, name-calling defense of a billionaire manufacturer, is enough to make the savior himself weep.[71]

Such harsh criticism of two of black Detroit's major leaders greatly undermined their credibility in the black community. That same month, A. Phillip Randolph, speaking at the Second Annual Michigan Negro Economic and Industrial Conference, attacked the Ford Motor Company and told the gathering "the time has come when the Negro has to decide between organized labor and organized capital."[72]

Father Daniel still clung to Henry Ford as the best path for blacks. In one of his Sunday sermons, he challenged anyone to show him any industrialists who had done more for black labor than Henry Ford. "We must not," he said, "follow blind leadership. The NAACP is an organization, not for all the people, but for some of the people." Angered particularly by Wilkins's scalding editorials, Daniel said:

I don't think anybody can sit in a swivel chair in New York and know work conditions in Detroit. You can't tell a man whom to employ and whom not to employ. He might close down on you, and then where would you be? I had prayed that I would not have to fight anymore, but I just must fight for some things. . . . I will not stand for the crucifixion of our boys and girls who are coming up. The doors of opportunity must be kept open to them.[73]

Daniel concluded with a criticism of the local NAACP for permitting the New York office of the NAACP to make such a program. The next Sunday, Don Marshall spoke from the same church. He had been a member since the early 1920s. Speaking to a capacity congregation, he told his listeners that the vast majority of the Ford Motor Company employees did not want to be interfered with and did not desire any agitation: "The vast majority of the Ford Motor Company employees feel that they are being fairly treated. They do not want the CIO monster in their plant. They want to be left alone."[74]

Discussing the UAW, Marshall trotted out the time-worn argument of Ford's contribution to the black community:

> The UAW boast of their extensive power and control but let them show me anything to compare with these things Henry Ford has done for us and let them abolish the segregated meeting places for the colored members of the One Grand Union and then let them get rid of the Moscow-sponsored black and white agitators whose only stock and trade is devilment, denunciation and vilification accompanied by direct attacks upon the characters of those whose lives and work have been devoted to the betterment of mankind in general.[75]

Marshall told the congregation that Henry Ford had done more for blacks than CIO President John L. Lewis. According to Marshall, Ford put approximately $62,021.60 a day or $310,108 a week in the pockets of black workers. He repeated what everyone already knew: that blacks worked throughout the plant and black youths attended the Ford apprentice school. Roy Wilkins also got some licks from Marshall for the *Crisis* editorial, which neither he nor Daniel ever effectively answered.[76]

Daniel was getting old and tired, but Marshall still had a lot of fight left in him. Until a few years before, both men had gone virtually unchallenged in the Detroit black community. Now the prolabor black leaders were gaining ground in the black community, chipping away at the foundation of traditional black leadership. Daniel, the leading apologist of the Ford-minister alliance, had obviously lost some ground from the salvo of Roy Wilkins. As a result, his credibility was breaking down in black intellectual circles. One editor of the two major black newspapers already supported trade unions. The Reverend Horace A. White, one of the greatest allies of the UAW black workers, was a constant thorn in Daniel's side. Marshall, called at one time "the mayor of Detroit Negro Harlem," was also losing some power and prestige among the black workers.

Eager to recoup his losses in the black community, Marshall spoke at several black churches to what amounted to captive audiences of loyal black Ford workers. In fact, he began these talks just at the time of the founding of the Loyal Worker's Club of the Ford plant. Supposedly interested parties formed the club as an educational society to better the condition of the black workers of the Ford Motor Company. But the club was obviously set up to counter the organizing drives of the UAW in the black community. In September 1937, this club sponsored a public meeting at Ebenezer AME Church, one of the largest black churches in Detroit, at which Marshall spoke. Black Ford workers and a few white union observers made up most of the audience. One observer noticed that the audience seemed unresponsive, concluding that the majority of the black workers probably came out of fear of losing their jobs.[77] Marshall attacked Roosevelt and claimed the Wagner Labor Relations Act hurt employers. He conceded that he could not solve acute problems of blacks being laid off indiscriminately without regard for length of time employed.[78]

Evidently, Marshall's talk did not go as well as he and the Loyal Worker's Club had hoped. He received little applause and only that much because, according to a UAW writer, several officers of the Club were positioned throughout the church, "and every time Marshall opened his mouth they applauded."[79]

Even considering the bias of the UAW observer, Marshall and his people were certainly quite capable of packing the church with Ford supporters as well as intimidating the Ford workers to act as if they did support the party line.

In November, Marshall spoke again to a standing-room-only crowd at St. John's Church in River Rouge, a suburb of Detroit with a sizable black population. This time he shared the platform with the president of the River Rouge branch of the Loyal Worker's Club of the Ford Plant.[80]

Meanwhile, the UAW was winning and losing some battles. The union had made some inroads into the black community and had set up a black organizing committee, but it ended the year with a political defeat when blacks supported Richard Reading for mayor against the CIO candidate, Patrick O'Brien. This defeat partly led a top official of the Detroit Civic Rights Federation to complain about the apathy of many black Negro workers towards the CIO and the UAW.[81]

This political defeat was evidence enough that the UAW had much more work to do in the black community. Many blacks still resisted unionism. Hardly had the new year begun when the battle between the prounion and the antiunion forces in the black community reached fever pitch. Walter Hardin, black UAW organizer, stepped up the attack on the Ford myth of being nice to black workers, remarking that most were in the foundries and the few in the good jobs acted as a smoke screen. In January 1938, Mr. White, one of the UAW's most articulate supporters, was not allowed to deliver the Emancipation Day address at the Tabernacle Baptist Church in West Detroit. The Reverend Robert H. Pittman and other church leaders justified their action on the grounds that prounion and members of the church working for Ford might be fired.[82]

In those cases where black organizations and institutions chose to challenge or ignore the wishes of the pro-Ford group, retribution was often swift and harsh. For example, A. Phillip Randolph spoke in Detroit during this period. The sponsors asked for and received permission to use the facilities of Bethel AME Church, then the largest such facility in the black community. Before Randolph arrived, Ford's black officials got wind of it and immediately sent word that if Randolph spoke, members of Bethel working at Ford would face early layoffs and the preacher would lose his recommendation privileges. Yet the church held firm, and Randolph spoke. Predictably, some of the church members, after being told why, were fired by the black Ford officials.[83]

This brave black church decided to stand up to Ford's power on another occasion, but this time church leaders were forced to capitulate. Dr. Mordecai Johnson, president of Howard University, spoke several times at the church on the sensitive issue of unions in which he advised black workers to join unions. Church members working at Ford were understandably afraid. They had already seen the awesome power of Ford. Several of their former coworkers were already walking the streets looking for work as a consequence of the church bucking Henry Ford. Therefore, when some of the church's remaining black Ford workers complained to the church's board that they would lose their jobs if Johnson spoke, the board had no other alternative but to refuse Johnson's sponsors further use of the church's facilities. Johnson spoke later to a capacity crowd of influential black and white citizens at a less vulnerable place. And although he praised Henry Ford, he took the position that "if Negro workers feel that union organization will benefit them they should organize."[84]

The church was so cowed by Ford's power, or more correctly by the use of Ford's power via Donald Marshall and Willie Ward, that when it was later approached by the Detroit Scottsboro Defense Committee for the use of facilities, permission was denied. The reason, the church explained was that "the Committee was regarded as a left-wing organization and hence unacceptable to the Ford interest."[85]

As expected, Johnson's advice to black workers to organize if they felt unionization would benefit them angered Father Daniel. He retorted in his Sunday sermon that "one loses patience with one who is expected to know, but comes with some half-baked ideas. . . . I do not expect the head of organizations to allow themselves to be used as propagandists. If any people criticize Ford, it should not be blacks. They ought to get up and bless his name." "The thing that provokes me," he continued, "is that there are not more to stand up and talk the way I do." He went on to attack Johnson and John L. Lewis for not helping blacks earlier and said that he had been fighting for seventeen years. One could only speculate on whether Daniel would have been so protective had he known that some years ago on Ford's first visit to a black church, Ford wrote on a little scrap of paper, "we are going out in society to a nigger church."[86]

As the labor issue continued to heat up in the black community, most blacks knew Ford and his black supporters were using the black church and other black organizations against the better interests of the larger black community. In fact, several black churches and organizations put up little resistance against being used as instruments through which Ford controlled the black community.

In 1939, the West Side Improvement Association (WSIA), a black organization working to improve the economic and political status of blacks, needed some place to hold its New Year's Day program. It was customary to enlist the aid of black churches for such programs simply because they usually were the only institution in the black community with sufficient space for large gatherings. The WSIA approached a black church and as was consistent with the custom received permission to use the facilities. But as we have seen, the custom of many black churches in Detroit to offer their facilities to certain black groups and organizations during this period was conditional upon approval by the Ford interests. Therefore, when the minister of the church discovered that the speaker for the program was prounion, he quickly informed the association that the program could not be held in his church. Here again the reason was that members of his congregation would lose their jobs and that he as minister would lose his "Ford patronage." When the association asked other black churches in the community, they all responded the same.[87]

Even when prounion blacks sought assistance from seemingly less Ford-dependent black groups and organizations they could not avoid the pervasive power of Ford. In 1940, the Conference of Negro Trade Unionists, a local umbrella organization composed of black trade unionists, was denied permission by the black branch of the YMCA to use its facilities because the black branch secretary feared retribution from Ford's black officials. "I'm in favor of unions but I couldn't let them hold that meeting here," the secretary later confessed to an interviewer. "If I had, the next day Ward and Marshall would have been down here to know why. That would have meant that I couldn't recommend any more men to Ford." In terms of what he perceived as a question of sheer black survival, the secretary conceded: "I've got to do what is best for the largest number."[88]

The pro-Ford faction continued to intimidate the black community. The death in 1939 of the premier Ford supporter, Father Daniel, did not diminish their support for Ford. In December 1940, Donald Marshall pulled out all the stops when he threatened the Reverend Charles Hill that he would fire every black in the neighborhood if he allowed a UAW sponsored meeting at his church. Hill stood fast but, unfortunately, he and a few other brave prounion leaders stood almost alone. In January 1941, Donald Marshall and Willis Ward organized a pro-Ford banquet which was attended by three hundred religious and civic leaders including just about all the black ministers in the Detroit area. John Dancy and the Reverend Robert Bradby spoke glowingly about Ford, and Marshall issued a veiled threat to black ministers that their future was tied to Ford's victory over the union.[89]

The campaign to prevent free discussions of an important issue facing the black community was rooted both in an arrogance of power and in a legitimate fear and apprehension about the future survival and progress of blacks in Detroit. Donald Marshall was described by one contemporary as "a high salaried spy master" who employed unethical methods to keep black workers loyal to Henry Ford. But Mr. Bradby and Fr. Daniel were sincerely perplexed black leaders out of touch with the times. They had been good shepherds and had fashioned a strategy of black community building that to them made good sense. This strategy had been based on the belief that the interests of blacks were best served by depending upon powerful whites. Both the local Urban League and major black churches fostered this belief in theory and practice. Few blacks questioned this strategy until the rise of industrial unionism, which conflicted with capitalists such as Henry Ford. Gradually, some blacks began to realize that the black church was not fulfilling its traditional role of leadership in the community. Instead it was selling out to the wielders of capital. People began wondering: Who indeed "owns the Negro church?" industrialists such as Henry Ford or blacks?

In an article published in *The Christian Century* in February 1938, Mr. White posed such a question: "[W]ho owns the Negro church."[90] White explained that in the last two years something important had happened in Detroit which no one had expected, namely the awakening of labor. But what was even more unexpected was the fact that black labor had also awakened. Black ministers, however, White explained, were not prepared to give leadership to the awakened black worker. "Such a development is new and alarming to the Negro preacher. Has he not preached all his life that the hope of the Negro rests in the generosity of the rich people?" Workers are beginning to "believe in the reality of human brotherhood, especially if the brothers are workers. [They] no longer believe that the crumbs from the table of the controllers of industry are better than a man's place in the line of the march of American workers, with head high and shoulders back in the struggle for economic justice."[91]

White accused the black church in Detroit of having failed black workers. Yet, black workers still depend upon the church for leadership because "it is the one institution which he has been taught to think of his own" but, White asked again "who owns the church? Negroes have always supposed that they do. But do they?" Politicians have exploited the black church and industrialists, White added, are doing the same thing: "In Detroit the people interested to see to it that the Negro stays anti-labor starts with the preachers. The methods used are very subtle, and in most cases the Negro preacher himself does not detest them."[92]

White then described how Ford through Marshall throttled free and open debate of labor and other issues by controlling the black church: "The one organization through which the Negro ought to feel free to express his hopes and to work out his economic salvation cannot help him because the Negro does not own it—it belongs to the same people who own the factories. Therefore, the effort to make the Negro worker labor-conscious is going to prove one of the most difficult jobs of our generation."[93]

White's prolabor position was really a move to get on the winning side before the lines became too clearly drawn. There was, indeed, a bit of the self-preservation motive in White's and other black ministers' prolabor positions. Why should they go down with a sinking ship? Although Detroit industrialists seemed stronger in early 1938, organized labor was by no means getting weaker. White was attempting to preserve the black church's leadership role in the black community by severing it from the influence of the industrialists. He recognized, as did the national and some local leaders of the NAACP and the Urban League, that in all the major urban centers a new black leadership was emerging, the black trade unionist. A. Phillip Randolph represented the best example of this new black leadership on a national level. Similar changes had already occurred in the composition of black leadership in Detroit. By 1938, black trade unionists such as Horace Sheffield, John Conyers, and Shelton Tappes were already assuming the mantle of leadership in the black struggle for social and economic justice.[94]

As if the *Crisis* editorial of Roy Wilkins and Horace A. White's exposé in *The Christian Century* were not sufficient to destroy the credibility of Ford's black supporters, George S. Schuyler, famous black editor and writer, pursued the issue the following month in an article in the UAW paper: "Mr. Ford wishes to continue to run an industrial plantation, well-regimented and policed by 1938 editions of Simon Legree; a modern version of *Uncle Tom's Cabin.*" Obviously referring to Ford, Don Marshall, Daniel, and his fellow ministers, Schuyler continued that "since every Uncle Tom's cabin must of course have an Uncle Tom, it need occasion no surprise that there are any number of Uncle Toms in the Ford setup. Nor is it surprising that these Uncle Toms are to a large degree gentlemen who are eager to sell out their people for filthy lucre." He criticized the arguments used by Ford supporters: "They carefully report, parrot-like, all the so-called arguments of the Ford propaganda machine, all the hoary lies against unionization of workers. They, in their zeal to serve their master, are quite willing to do anything that will antagonize white and colored workers."[95]

Schuyler went beyond the criticism of Wilkins and White by cautioning blacks who opposed trade unionism of the consequences of black workers' being left out of a working-class movement destined to succeed. "One can imagine what this will lead to when all the white workers are organized, as they soon will be, and the Negro workers are not. Antagonism between these two groups may permit the Ford Company to continue being run like a Georgia plantation but it will not help race relations."[96]

According to Schuyler, these consequences went even further. What if labor comes to dominate politics in Detroit? "Since the majority of the Detroit workers are organized, and since labor is becoming increasingly alert to its interests in politics, the time may not be too far in the distance when labor will govern Detroit. Would it not be a bad thing if Negro workers were not included while everybody else was organized?"[97]

Hammering away at the black Ford-supporters' major argument that the black worker owes Ford something because he gave them employment when others did not, Schuyler repeated much of what Wilkins had said: "Black spokesmen for Mr. Ford assert that he loves Negroes because he has given them much and diversified labor. But is it not singular that he employs Negroes only in Detroit. Why must love for the Negro stop at the outskirts of Detroit?"[98]

With a final word on the leaders and what direction workers should go, Schuyler left no doubt in anyone's mind: "Mr. Ford does not love the

Negroes. He loves himself, his profits and his social irresponsibility. Those who are classed as Negro leaders and who seek to thwart the legitimate effort of their people for a price, deserve the bitter condemnation of all men and women who think . . . Black Ford workers who . . . have not been thrown into the street to starve must once and for all let it be known to the world that they are not Henry Ford's Negroes, but free men who insist upon looking out for their interest in their own way—masters of their own fate. The labor union, the UAW is the only agency through which they can bring this about."[99]

Wilkins, White, and Schuyler helped win the intellectual war against blacks who supported Ford. Many blacks continued to support Ford, Marshall, Bradby, and Daniel, but their intellectual defense of Ford no longer seemed so formidable. Ford still remained the greatest benefactor of Detroit blacks but less of the god his supporters wanted to make him. Horace White's article went to the heart of the whole matter of whether or not blacks should join the union. As already mentioned, the article was a proclamation for black ministers in Detroit either to act or to lose the leadership of the black masses. It called upon black ministers to place the black church at the heart of the ongoing black struggle and to shift traditional strategies of community building from dependence upon corporate paternalism to an alliance with organized labor. And several black ministers rose to the occasion. Both during the back-to-work movement at Chrysler in 1939 and the pivotal Ford strike in 1941, a small but devoted core of black ministers—such as the Reverend Charles Hill, the longtime pastor of Hartford Avenue Baptist Church, who began his career as Bradby's assistant pastor; and Malcolm Dade, the rector of St. Cyprian's Episcopal Church; and, of course, the Reverend Horace White—joined forces with the other prolabor black leaders in support of organized labor. This little core of prolabor ministers riding the wave of the future would expand, first dragging and then gently guiding their churches into a new age in which the black church would willingly ally itself with the struggle against race and class oppression. And in the process, the black church would share in the shaping of a new strategy for continuing the process of community building.

In 1939, black UAW members still had to contend with powerful forces operating against them within the community. Ford-backed black ministers and Don Marshall still controlled the black churches. Prounion ministers like Rev. Horace White and Rev. Charles Hill were still in the minority. Don Marshall and Daniel were tireless and relentless foes. Notwithstanding the attacks from the National NAACP, these two remained in the driver's seat, and their power and influence still pervaded the Detroit black community. They controlled the majority of black autoworkers in the city, those at the Ford Motor Company. Both men realized they had to maintain control over these Ford workers if they wanted to control the black community, and the UAW had to win them over if they hoped to upset the Ford power block in the industrial community.

Outside the UAW, other blacks began embracing trade unionism, going on strikes, and assuming leadership roles in the trade union movement. These developments contributed to the rising working-class consciousness of black workers. In February 1939, black maids who had joined Local 705 of the Hotel and Restaurant Workers Union of the AFL a few years earlier, walked out of the Reid Hotel, leaving two hundred guests, because the management refused to raise their wages to $60 a month minimum. That spring the national organizing committee of the United WPA and Unemployed Workers of America named Charles Harrison, a black, to their staff. When 500 black sanitary workers signed up for membership in the AFL, they became the largest all-black local in Michigan. In June, 1,500 blacks joined with 10,000 other workers to storm city hall to protest the provisions of the new Federal Relief Act, which cut wages and increased working hours of those on WPA; and Detroit black railway workers sent delegates to a national conference of Negro railway workers called by Phillip Randolph.[100]

These developments reinforced the UAW's recruitment efforts in the black community, but other developments within the larger trade-union movement in Detroit posed problems for black UAW members. Black sanitary workers in the AFL provided powerful propaganda for their own organizing drives among black autoworkers. The UAW not only had to catch up, but union leaders had to mend their fences. Factionism had disrupted within the UAW, and blacks of the opposing faction accused the former UAW president, Homer Martin, of having sabotaged unity between the races by favoring blacks in the union who agreed to build up his political machines and by telling jokes at press conferences at the expense of blacks. They also accused Martin of pushing certain black labor organizers considered to be "false leaders" and having approved unsatisfactory contracts.[101]

In addition, an earlier meeting of black representatives from all over the state met to discuss problems of blacks in the shops and the unions. The black representatives claimed white union officials did not understand that black problems should be dealt with as such, apart from the regular problems of the whole membership.[102] Pay differentials emerged as their major complaint; however, they also focused on discrimination in opportunity for apprenticeship in the factories and for seniority in all departments. The resolution that came out of this meeting demanded: that more black organizers be added to the organizing staff; that black women be given the right to work in the offices of the locals and the international, as well as in the factories on production work; that blacks be given the same chance to apprenticeship, promotion, and advancement in the factories; that at least one black be put on the executive board of the international; and finally, that a department be set up to deal with the problems of the national minorities.[103] Black UAW leaders were beginning to realize their responsibilities as well as their important place in the UAW. They wanted to make sure that as the union made progress so would black workers, particularly since the larger battles were yet to come.

Some of these concerns could be more easily addressed than others. For example, UAW seniority rules held after the conversion to peacetime. As a result, blacks were able to hold on to gains they had made in semiskilled jobs during the war. On the other hand, white UAW officials rejected granting a black a seat on the executive board, a move they regarded as reverse discrimination.[104]

The biggest and most trying event of 1939 was the Chrysler strike in October and November. It was the acid test of the unity of not only black and white workers but of the few black leaders in Detroit who had sided with organized labor against the Ford–black ministers entente. Twenty-four thousand workers struck the Dodge plant on Detroit's east side, including seventeen hundred black workers. A few blacks crossed the picket line and the word got around that the Chrysler Corporation was using blacks to start a strikebreaking back-to-work movement.[105]

Someone reported that a strikebreaker organizer visited black political clubs in the area to recruit scabs. Some people accused Don Marshall of rounding up black workers to fill the ranks of the back-to-work movement.[106] Black UAW members and their allies quickly sensed the dangers of such a movement. The Detroit Council of the National Negro Congress accused the Chrysler Corporation of using strikebreaking as a tool to divide the black and white workers:

> This movement is being started and backed by forces whose every act and purpose is against the best interest not only of Negro workers but of all the Negro people. The only organization that is struggling to secure for the Negro worker equal opportunities in the automobile factories is the UAW-CIO. . . . Those things will not come from those sinister elements and forces asking you as a Negro worker to forsake your white and Negro brothers who are fighting in this strike to maintain a decent standard of life for all workers.[107]

In late November, the Reverend Horace White called a conference of black and labor leaders in a desperate attempt to avert a race riot. Minor skirmishes had already occurred between black and white workers at the gates. As a result of the conference, appeals were broadcast to Chrysler officials and union officers asking that efforts be made to prevent any fighting between black and white which might easily erupt into a citywide race riot.[108]

An editorial in the *Michigan Chronicle* attacked any idea of blacks being used as scabs and being "maneuvered into a position to draw the fire of organized labor." The editorial clearly pointed out the significance of black labor role in the labor struggle:

The time has come when all the world should know that there is a new Negro in America. You cannot recruit a scab army from among our people and trick them into pulling other people's chestnuts out of the fire. The Negro worker is honest and courageous and he wants and demands a fair share of the opportunities in industry. He knows that he is not the pet of the employer any more than he is the pet of the union. Those forces at work to discredit the Negro worker and which seek to lead him to slaughter should be removed from society.[109]

A group of black leaders distributed a leaflet to black workers signed by Mr. White, Mr. Hill, Senator Diggs, and the editor of the *Michigan Chronicle,* Louis Martin, warning them of the danger of joining a back-to-work movement:

To all Negro workers, it has come to the attention of some leaders . . . that there is an effort to get Negro workers interested in a back-to-work movement [that] contains possibilities of race riots and of race conflicts. Race relations in Detroit have been making definite progress. We do not want to spoil what progress we have made in this direction by having Negroes used as dupes in a back-to-work movement. If Negroes are to have jobs they must have them in cooperation with all workers. Any effort to put Negroes back to work in factories, over the majority of all workers, will spell doom to Negro workers in the factories. Negro workers must not allow themselves to be used by irresponsible leaders.[110]

Another leaflet distributed to black workers (probably by white workers) had a less diplomatic and more threatening tone: "Attention Negro Workers there are only 150,000 in Detroit's 1½ million population. . . . You are outnumbered 10 to 1. Why isolate yourself? Why create trouble for your race?"[111]

The black leaders knew that no actual work could be done even if the strikebreakers were allowed in, because most of the technical and skilled workers were on the picket line. This suggested to them that Chrysler was just interested in dividing the working class at the expense of a terrible race riot.

As the strike continued and tensions increased, Mr. White met 300 black strikebreakers on their way to break the lines and persuaded some to disband and not attempt to enter the plant. The rest continued on. As a last resort, he climbed up to the roof of a building opposite the gates of the plant and, speaking over a public address system, appealed to the 5,000 pickets around the gates to refrain from any violence against the strikebreakers. Over 500 blacks marched through the gates through jeering pickets who mocked them with applause. Handbills were distributed by the thousands urging the workers to keep peaceful and not resort to violence.[112]

The strikebreaking failed, however, because the UAW had enough black

Black UAW organizers at the Ford Motor Company, 1941. (Seated, left to right:
Joseph Billups, Walter Hardin, Veal Clough, Leon Bates, and John Conyers, Sr.
Standing, left to right: Christopher C. Alston and William Bowman.) Courtesy
of the Archives of Labor and Urban Affairs, Wayne State University.

support on the picket lines to support the strike. It warmed the strikers'
hearts to witness the efforts of a few brave black leaders trying to stave
off a possible race riot. Equally warming was the sight of black women
of the Women Auxiliary of Foundry Local 429 from New Haven, Michigan, who travelled over 25 miles to march in the picket lines holding signs
accusing the AFL of "back-to-work scabbery."[113] Of course the AFL denied
it, and one black spokesman accused the UAW-CIO leaders and others of
using "the bogey of race riots to force black workers into line."[114] By this
time, the UAW had already blamed the strikebreaking on both AFL organizers and the Chrylser Corporation.

Most white workers were aware of the race-riot tactic, which probably
explained why they did not do more than just jeer and clap their hands.[115]
Black leaders who aided in cooling things off earned the praises of the
UAW. Workers at the plant, in describing how the strike was won, said
that "invaluable work in defeating the AFL back-to-work movement was
done by Negro civic leaders."[116] The strikers, the majority of whom were
white, also earned some praise:

> Dodge Local 3 and all who were in the picket line Monday and Tuesday
> won the undying admiration of the Negroes in Detroit. Six thousand pickets,
> loyal and militant, obeyed their leader when faced with the most serious

crisis of the day, a soul-stirring sight to behold. We Negroes feel sharply the sting of these scabs going through your lines and we hope you understand how they were misled and misguided by the stooges of the corporation.[117]

The 1939 Chrysler strike provided the best preparation that the pro-union forces could have ever received. It tested their faith in each other under fire. They had held firm. Most importantly their cooperation demonstrated the best example of working-class unity across racial lines. Now they were ready to take on "the old man," Henry Ford.

In the spring of 1941, less than two years after the Chrysler strike, the UAW went on strike against the Ford Motor Company. It looked to be almost a repeat performance of the 1939 Chrysler strike. This was the UAW's last proving ground. As before, but much more so, the balance of the battle was in the hands of the 12,000 black workers at Ford, the largest single aggregate of black workers in the industrial world. The country watched over the shoulder of Detroiters. No wonder Don Marshall tried to head this confrontation off at Chrysler's, trying to break the back of the UAW. Now it had gathered strength and was heading for River Rouge.

A large number of black workers went to the Ford plant that Wednesday morning, the first day of the strike. But the majority of them remained at home discussing the various sides of the strike with friends. Some workers gathered on street corners and talked about how long the strike would last.[118]

Both the UAW-CIO and UAW-AFL had been making a desperate attempt to organize the blacks in the plant. The AFL opened an office in the westside black community and put a black "strong-arm man" in charge. Several back-to-work meetings were being staged by AFL organizers that Wednesday night. One was held at the Forest Club on the famous Hastings Street (known as the "bucket of blood" because of its rough elements) and the other was held farther east in a predominantly black community. More than 2,000 attended the first meeting. Police were stationed at the building to avoid possible trouble. Many of the 5,000 workers who remained in the Ford plant were blacks. Some of them broke through the picket lines to resume work, while still others who were on the night shift remained in the plant. The UAW put out an edition of the paper called "Ford Facts" to explain to the black community the program and policy of the UAW-CIO regarding the strike then in progress at Ford. Black organizers Joseph Billups, Walter Hardin, Christopher Alston, Veal Cloygh, Clarence Bowman, Leon Bates, and John Conyers sprung into action planning a campaign. This was the long awaited day, the battle of battles.[119]

Before the strike was a day old, Louis E. Martin, the editor of the *Michigan Chronicle,* called a meeting of black leaders. They endorsed the UAW and made a public statement opposing black workers being used as strikebreakers. They denounced the back-to-work movement, fearing that it would lead to racial friction and violence. This meeting was in part a response to a leaflet that was circulated in black communities around Detroit that Tuesday night, just prior to the strike, that stated:

> They shall not win
> like all
> law abiding American citizens
> our motto is
> to preserve democracy not
> to destroy it

Continuing on, it said:

> We are the wives of satisfied Ford employees, our husbands having been employed at the Ford Motor Company for 20 years and like the majority of the Ford workers, have never had any misunderstanding and they are ready and willing to stay up and fight to keep the union out of the Ford factory. To you my loyal colored friends, Henry Ford is your best friend showing prejudice toward none. Can this be said of any plant that is controlled by the union? No. If the union has no respect for our president and the laws of the United States, what respect do you think they have for you? Perhaps just a tool to accomplish that which they seek.[120]

Countless efforts had been used to woo black Ford workers away from the UAW. The leaflet was just the latest. Two months prior to the strike, the majority of black foundry workers were wearing UAW-AFL buttons. Black workers in the rolling mill were UAW-CIO people. Big headlines in one black newspaper said: "2 UNIONS FIGHT FOR FORD RACE WORK-ERS," under which was printed the two opposing camps.[121]

As the strike wore on, tensions rose. Walter White rushed to Detroit from the National NAACP office in New York and appealed to blacks in the plant to come out. Some had been injured breaking through the picket line, while others, when assured of safety, left the plant. A sound truck was hired and toured black communities urging black workers not to be strikebreakers. Many had received telegrams and letters ordering them to return to work at once.[122]

The strike broadened the cleavage in the ranks of black ministers in the city. Most black ministers opposed the strike. The Reverend Horace A. White, who had visited the plant several times, and the Reverend Charles Hill were the two most influential pro-UAW ministers. The majority of black ministers, however, belonged to the Interdenominational Ministers Alliance that endorsed Ford in his opposition to the union. They had a powerful hold on the men in the plant, but they were rapidly losing it.[123]

Finally the black workers walked out of the Ford plant. To many, the walk symbolized a break with the past, a decision to stand on their own and not to depend upon Ford to be their guardians. Many of these black workers were also breaking with traditional black leadership as reflected in the black ministers who supported Ford.

Realizing the great risk these black workers had undertaken by walking out and joining the strikers, the top UAW officials issued a statement of appreciation: "The UAW-CIO wishes to express its hearty appreciation of the union solidarity shown by the overwhelming majority of the Negro employees of the Ford Motor Company in going out on strike with the rest of the union members."[124]

Black Ford workers had one more hurdle to jump. They had to vote in the upcoming National Labor Relation Board elections to decide what union—the UAW-CIO or the UAW-AFL—would represent the Ford workers. This would not be an easy hurdle. Both unions geared up for this last decisive battle. The UAW put Walter Hardin, veteran black labor organizer, in charge of organizing black workers for the election. Hardin and his staff played a key role in the debates leading up to the election. As one observer put it, Hardin and his staff "literally argued and debated the opposition into a neutral corner."[125]

Many workers knew the UAW-CIO would win, but the UAW-AFL was determined to fight to the end. Both unions accelerated their efforts to enroll black workers. Blacks took sides and joined in this signing-up campaign. Both the UAW-CIO and the UAW-AFL canvassed black communities in search of Ford workers to sign up. Black workers received the major portions of the attention from both unions. Both unions had brought in national organizers to devote special attention to black workers at Ford. Numerous meetings were held in black communities; appeals in the press and over the radio vied for the attention of black workers. The campaign became so bitter that fights broke out, seriously injuring some workers.[126] Black ministers who had opposed the strike and endorsed Ford but who now sided with the UAW-AFL issued a public statement:

> We believe that the American Federation of Labor is a truly American organization and that it has acted in the best interest of the Negro. . . . Because we know fully well that the American Federation of Labor is solidly behind the national defense program, aid to the allies, and because it is doing everything in its power to aid American workers, we endorse this patriotic organization with all the power at our command.
>
> The Negro people are well aware of the situation at the Ford Motor Company. Many thousands of workers were kept away from their work only because of a radical minority—many of them from other plants and sections— insisted in pulling a minority strike. Many of the colored workers were beaten mercilessly by this same minority group. . . . The American Federation of Labor has never resorted to these discriminative tactics. It does not believe in methods that are unbecoming to true American workers.[127]

The statement was almost incredible in its distortion of fact. Everyone knew that the Ford officials brought in hundreds of strikebreakers. The statement obviously demonstrated the results of a pathetic group of black ministers grabbing for straws. But they were fighting a losing battle. Ernest

Calloway, black labor economist and director of the United Transport Service Employers of America, remarked that "any Negro who does not vote for the United Automobile Workers of the CIO in the election at Ford plant . . . is a traitor to the Negro people." At the big pre-election rally of 60,000 Ford Workers in Cadillac Square in downtown Detroit, Paul Robeson, the famous black baritone, sang "I Will Vote UAW-CIO." On May 21, 1941, 51,866 workers voted for the UAW-CIO in the greatest labor board election in history.[128] The long struggle for unionization had finally come to an end. And black industrial workers had been in the midst of it. Once again, black industrial workers had played a key role in another stage of the process of community building.

THE EMERGING VOICE OF BLACK WORKING-CLASS LEADERSHIP WITHIN
THE COMMUNITY BUILDING PROCESS: SHELTON TAPPES AS A CASE STUDY

Perhaps the most significant development to emerge out of the conflict between the two competing strategies of community building between 1936 and 1945 was the voice of black working-class leaders. The voice of black trade unionism amplified through the UAW-CIO rallied an entire generation of young black workers to the cause of trade unionism. This voice became the dominant expression of black community building during this period. We have heard the voice of the social worker, protest leaders, self-help advocates, politicians and the like, each reflecting the *Zeitgeist* of a stage of black community building; but only in the 1930s and early 1940s would we hear the voice of black labor emerging above the chorus—a loud, clear, and distinctively working-class voice. Some traditional black leaders supported the black workers and occasionally attempted to speak for them, but before long they too realized that the day belonged to black workers, that only they could articulate the manner in which community building would best express itself. They were key voices in the vanguard of the coalition of labor, religious, and civic organizations that supported the black community's struggles for equal rights in employment and housing. As Meier and Rudwick put it: These "black union leaders such as Hardin, Sheffield and Tappes emerged as important community spokesmen in their own right."[129] In short, they were the historical instruments through which the next stage of black community building found its highest expression.

There were many great working-class men and women who guided the black community through the wilderness of competing and often confusing strategies of community building during the unionization period. However, Shelton Tappes rose above the rest in the way in which he assumed the mantle of black working-class leadership. Tappes was born in Omaha, Nebraska, in 1911. He attended the University of Nebraska for a year and planned to become a lawyer, but he dropped out. He moved to Detroit in 1926. Two years laters, he got his first job as an autoworker at the Briggs plant. This was during the preunion days. "The wages were 27 cents an hour, but we were only paid for the time worked, it [*sic*] wasn't unusual to spend ten to twelve hours in the plant, and only get paid for three hours."[130]

By 1929, Tappes was on his way to becoming a major black labor leader in Detroit. That year, he was elected chairman of the Foundry Building as a union representative. This facility had housed the largest group of workers in the plant, of which about 55 percent were blacks. Tappes was elected without opposition. In 1940, Ford fired Tappes for joining the union. A year later, Tappes rebounded with a vengeance. During the drive to unionize Ford, he was appointed to the Ford organizing committee. When he finally returned to work at Ford, union members reelected him as chairman of the Foundry. Tappes remained in this position until the signing of the Ford contract in June of 1942.[131]

Long before he had participated in the famous signing of the Ford contract, Tappes had developed a deep appreciation of the role of the labor movement in the struggle against race and class oppression. This appreciation led him to join the UAW-CIO:

> After working in other shops, then working at the Ford Motor Company, I realized that job security meant a whole lot to a working man. I found that we who worked at Ford's did not have the freedom in the Ford plant that a free man should have who was working for a living. I noticed that Negro and white men who worked in shops that had been organized by the CIO were making from 10 to 25 [cents] an hour more for the same kind of work, working under better conditions and had more security on their jobs. These were the things that I desired, so I joined the CIO.[132]

Unlike many black and white workers who joined the union, Tappes had a broader vision of the role of the union in assisting blacks. He wanted to be involved in the union movement because he could see its potential for uplifting the black community. He was among the first black trade unionists to envision the role of the union movement in the black community building process:

> I wanted to become an active member, because I felt that someone should make a place for other Negroes. Some of them were lax in accepting this organization, yet I felt sure that they would benefit from it some day . . . When I considered . . . the fact that out of the CIO's 42 international unions, all welcome Negro members, there was no doubt in my mind as to which union is better for the Negro Industrial worker.[133]

In January 1942, the members of the Ford Local 600 of UAW-CIO, then the largest local in the world, representing over 87,000 workers, elected Tappes as recording secretary. Tappes was the only black on the slate of officers.[134] The position as recording secretary provided Tappes with a power base from which he could address a range of problems affecting the black community. Along with Horace Sheffield, Tappes represented the voice "of the largest body of black workers in the UAW and functioned in one of its most militant locals."[135]

More importantly, he held a position which allowed him to contribute a black trade-unionist perspective to the community building process. This perspective challenged both labor and some traditional progressive black leadership practices as to what was best for the black community. Such challenges would have been impossible before the emergence of the black trade-unionist connection with the UAW.

Notwithstanding the strong presence of the Labor Committee within the local NAACP branch and its tremendous influence on the larger black community via its ties to the UAW, it still functioned within the largely elite structure of the parent body. Black working-class members increased their numbers but still had to function within a traditional community building framework governed by the black professional and business classes. But Tappes on the other hand, had a powerful all-labor base in Local 600 from which he could apply, within limits, a trade-unionist perspective to black problems.

No one, black or white, was too powerful or influential to be spared Tappes's criticism if he felt they deserved it. Although he had worked closely with the local NAACP and notwithstanding the role of the organization in the long struggle against racial discrimination, Tappes was brutal in his attacks on the 1942 NAACP election that reelected Dr. J. J. McClendon president. Up to this time, few black leaders—and no black working-class leaders—had a sufficient power base to mount such a serious challenge to the NAACP's standing in the black community. Tappes's criticism of the NAACP's election results demanded respect because of his role as recording secretary of Local 600:

> The farce that was held under the auspices of the N.A.A.C.P. . . . has been called an election was a real blow to the principles for which the organization was founded. The people who participated in this high-handed railroading type of conniving are not the true leaders of the Negro mass, but rather representatives of artificial holier than thou untouchables who have established themselves both above, and separate and apart from the common herd. Although the N.A.A.C.P. was founded for the purpose of crusading for the full attainment of the fruit of democracy for the Negro mass, this purpose was actually defeated by the machinations of the so-called "Negro Chamber of Commerce" with its cohorts and stooges, who openly denied the rank and file a fair and just election.[136]

Tappes saw himself as the protector of the black masses against an elite in the black community. According to him, the results of the election were not important; rather, the "manner in which the election meeting was conducted must be termed as rank undemocratic, and a dark stain on the splendid N.A.A.C.P. record book of progressive advancement, and achievement."[137]

"In my opinion, the individuals who took part in the steam rolling tactics . . . have done the N.A.A.C.P. more harm than good," Tappes continued. "In fact, they have simply proved how unscrupulous certain individuals can be when they place the interest of centering the spotlight on themselves, above uplifitng, and advancing the majority."[138]

Tappes's opinions of the NAACP elections reflected the growing audacity of the voice of one major black labor leader who represented a new expression within the black community.

Tappes also went after the white and powerful when he felt they were attacking the interests of black and working-class peoples. In 1942, when Paul V. McNutt, the powerful chairman of the War Manpower Commission (WMC), decided to cancel FEPC railroad hearings, which greatly aroused blacks and their allies around the country, Tappes was a member of the delegation that went to Washington, D.C., to confront the chairman. During the meeting, the WMC deputy chairman, Fowler Harper, defended the chairman's position of shelving the hearings as a response to pressure from the railroads. Tappes's reaction to the deputy chairman gave him a place in local history: "You have the nerve to tell this body that the southern railroads are so powerful they defy the government."[139] Later, a statement by Tappes was published in the local press:

> War Manpower Chairman Paul V. McNutt's cancellation of the FEPC railroad hearing . . . is the most open and alarming indication to date of a policy of appeasement of the Southern Congress bloc and its Republican allies. It is not [merely a threat] to the welfare of Negroes and other races or nationality groups but to all of organized labor and all working people regardless of race and color. Unless such an appeasement be stopped now, the next thing on the agenda for the same kind of scrapping are the wage hour law, the National Labor Relations Act, Social Security measure and the other new deal domestic reforms won during the last ten years.[140]

Linking black community interests with those of other classes became a hallmark of black trade unionism. Much like the coalitional strategy of the black Democrats like Diggs, Tappes and other black trade unionists began increasingly voicing concerns with wide class appeals. Tappes's attack on McNutt represented the heady militancy of both contemporary industrial trade unionism and black labor radicalism:

> My experience in interviewing McNutt as a member of the Detroit Citizens' Committee delegate [sic] convinces me that the only thing to which he responds is pressure. His arrogant insulting and patronizing attitude left no room for an appeal to political expedient. . . . [W]e of labor are being challenged to meet and overcome the pressure being brought to bear by the

Southern Railroad and the Southern Congressman for protection of our democratic ideals and their economic gains, it is imperative that we meet the challenge. We can and we will.[141]

WMC Chairman McNutt did not budge from his position, but undoubtedly he felt the wrath of Tappes which he would not soon forget. And Tappes demonstrated once again the role and voice of the militant black trade unionist in the struggle for the rights of minorities.

The militant labor rhetoric of Tappes, due in part to his relationship to the trade-union movement, not only provided him and other black trade unionists with another reference or primary group, such as a church or voluntary association, but it expanded their racial agendas to include class agendas, which added leverage to community building. When Tappes spoke, he more often than not spoke for both the black community and the labor movement. Because of his powerful position as recording secretary of "the largest local in the world" he carried two banners and articulated two agendas: labor and the black community. He also served as key link in the black community-labor coalition which would come to characterize several strategies of black community building.[142]

Like many black leaders within predominantly white institutions, organizations, and movements, Tappes used his powerful labor position to address the most presenting problems of the black community, such as racial discrimination. In 1944, he investigated complaints concerning the racial attitudes of white Checker Taxicab drivers. After an exchange of letters between Tappes and the president of the company, the latter replied: "Discrimination of any kind against anyone as long as they are orderly persons, is not only unlawful but in violation of one of the strictest rules of the company, which subjects any driver, if a complaint of such a sort is substantiated, to immediate dismissal."[143] In still another case involving the Greyhound Bus station, Tappes once again contacted the company to address the issue.[144]

Of all the problems facing blacks during the war years, housing was the most intractable and the one which most taxed the resources of black leaders. And Tappes was no exception. In fact, according to Tappes, it was his strong stand on the housing issue that led to his eventual defeat as recording secretary of Local 600. In a speech he delivered at the Wayne County CIO Housing Conference in March 1944, which was broadcast on the radio several weeks later, Tappes was highly critical of the housing situation in Detroit:

It is a matter of record that the task of providing war housing for occupancy by White workers has now passed the critical stage. As a matter of fact, substantial vacancies exist now in housing projects designated for White workers. It is because of this, plus the undeniable fact that provision of housing for Negro workers has lagged to an extremely dangerous point that I address my remarks specifically to the Negro housing problem.

Tappes then began discussing the heart of an issue that had plagued race relations during the war years:

> It has been the practice in the past to make available to Negroes only such housing as had been discarded for various reasons by White citizens. Generally speaking, the housing, when it was available to Negroes, had already become dilapidated, rundown and obsolescent to the degree that it was no longer desirable or habitable. In other words, Negroes get only the least desirable "left-overs."
>
> In spite of the fact that the Negro population has expanded from 135,000 persons in 1940 to approximately 185,000 in 1944, it can definitely be stated that by no means has the availability of housing been proportionate to this population increase.

These were the problems which triggered the 1942 Sojourner Truth housing riot. Two years later these problems had not changed because of the persistence of institutionalized racism in housing. Tappes was forced, therefore, to focus attention on the various legal practices used to restrict the housing opportunities of black war workers:

> Negro war workers, who have come to Detroit to work in the great industrial plants engaged in production for war, find individually and as a group the greatest obstacles to the solution of their housing problems. These obstacles are mainly due to the fact that in addition to their marginal economic status which places Negroes in a disadvantage position where the purchase of homes is concerned, it is further a matter of legal practice to limit the areas in which Negroes may live. Restrictive ordinance prevent their rental of homes and purchases of land or houses. For instance, there are relatively few areas in Detroit where Negroes can build new homes under FHA insurance. The result of these restrictions means that Negroes must either pay excessive rentals for overcrowded quarters, or that they must live in dilapidated areas so unsafe or unsanitary that they are unfit for human habitation.

Tappes then reviewed the well-known tales of excessive rents and proposed housing policies that, when combined, placed more burdens upon black workers and their families:

> Added to this is another proposed postwar project for which plans are being made and again apparently without regard to rehousing the many thousands of Negroes who will be displaced by its development. The reference is made to the proposed Medical Center which is to be located in an area on the East Side where thousands of Negroes are housed.

These and other housing issues put forward by Tappes led him to propose the following steps to address the housing needs of black war workers. As he explained:

> Steps should be taken at once to meet the needs of Detroit's Negro war

workers and their families and everything possible should be done to implement such a program. As to a program, the following suggestions are made and of course subject to any changes desired:

1. Programming and construction of at least 18,000 public war housing units to relieve the immediate problem;
2. Immediately make available to eligible Negro workers vacant units in public war housing projects in Wayne and Willow Run areas and priority be given to eligible Negro war workers wherever vacancies exist in public housing projects over resident war workers.
3. That no action be taken by any government agency or official thereof to displace Negroes from their homes in developing postwar projects until such time as other housing is available to these occupants.
4. An immediate investigation by the Detroit Congressional representatives as to the reasons for this completely uncalled for delay in providing these vital war workers for housing in the face of such dire necessity and knowing full well the detrimental effects the lack of shelter has had on war production effort.[145]

This housing speech by Tappes represented one of the best contemporary analyses of the housing problems of black war workers. It placed Tappes on par with the traditional black leaders from the business and professional ranks, those who had not only dominated the leadership positions but had also dominated the intelligentsia that formulated what the larger black community was or should be thinking. Tappes became one of the first black trade-union leaders to gain respect not only for his militant race and labor position but also for his intellectual ability. He gave the voice of black labor credibility for their thinking as well as for their brawn. Black workers had in Tappes more than just a militant leader who could shout at the right time at the right people; he was an articulate strategist who could speak for them. While they still supported traditional black leadership drawn from such organizations as the Urban League and the NAACP, most of whom were from the business and professional classes within the black community, most black workers recognized that Tappes was their man, a man of labor.

Tappes's concern for the housing needs of black war workers tied directly to what the black community needed in this stage of community building. Housing determined the quality of the entire process of building and sustaining a healthy community. As recording secretary of Local 600, Tappes was able to use the local's powerful position to support his housing position. But he paid the price. In the spring of 1945, he was defeated for his fourth term as recording secretary of Ford Local 600. In explaining his defeat, Tappes pointed to the housing issue:

The stand taken by Local 600 Executive Board and General Council on the question of housing and other matters is a recognizable contributing factor toward the lack of success of my candidacy for a fourth term as recording secretary. The reaction to that stand placed our opponent in a position of advantage, because the officers of the local were the brunt of all attacks from the outside.[146]

Tappes and his supporters within Local 600 had run up against Mayor Orville Hubbard, one of the greatest architects and supporters of suburban racism in 20th century urban America.[147] The mayor used correspondence between the local and the city council to ferment misrepresentation of the housing issue. He was able to use Tappes's signature on Local 600's letter to incite racial fears that the local was attempting to challenge housing in Dearborn.[148] Housing was not the only issue that led to the ouster of Tappes as recording secretary of Local 600, but it was by far the key factor. However, he left his post on a grand note:

> I have served Local 600 as recording secretary for three consecutive terms and I look with pride upon the accomplishments of the great organization which I was permitted to help build and administer to in an executive capacity. It is with a sense of gratification that I note that none of those who opposed me have been able to point out any deficiencies in my work or in the manner in which I conducted the duties of my office. . . . To have been a part of the gigantic Ford local which brought benefits to so many through the contract which I was privileged to assist in drafting and negotiating in 1941 has in itself been a real pleasure.[149]

Up to this point in his labor career, Tappes had earned the respect of both labor and nonlabor groups in the larger community. He received many honors for his work on behalf of the black community and the labor movement. In November 1942, he was selected as that year's recipient of the annual award of the Detroit Athletic Association "for meritorious achievement on behalf of Negroes." In January 1943, he was honored in the Michigan Chronicle's "WE HONOR" column. And in November 1944, at the annual UAW Convention, his nomination for vice president of the UAW received an ovation from the entire delegation. He declined the nomination.[150]

Tappes had certainly contributed his share to both the black community and the labor movement, and he would do more.

As Tappes ended his role as recording secretary of the largest Local in the world, from which he had leveraged power and influence to address the needs of the black community and facilitate community building, he, along with other black UAW members, continued a struggle dating back to 1939 of getting a black on the executive board of the UAW. As one of the major leaders in this effort in 1945, Tappes explained that "power politics played in the UAW [would] not permit a Negro regardless of his qualifications to be elected to the UAW National Board at this time."[151] Tappes understood only too well how the election machinery of the union operated against the election of a black to the executive board. This machinery ". . . calls for elections on a regional basis. No one region contains enough progressive votes to elect a Negro."[152] Black UAW members would continue to push for a black representative on the executive board.[153]

Tappes's role as one of the leading black trade unionists continued for decades, complementing the cooperative roles of the UAW and the NAACP in the struggle against racism.[154]

As one of the crucial links between the most powerful unions in industrial Detroit and the black community, Tappes more than demonstrated the vital role of a black working-class leader in the black community building process.

Epilogue

By the end of World War II, the black community in Detroit had progressed to another stage in its long struggle to build a community. Old-Timers looking back to the years of World War I could count many blessings and victories. Of course they could also count the bad times that punctuated three decades of community building. But no one could deny, even as the scars of the 1943 race riots slowly healed, that the black community of 1945 was not a much larger, stronger, and confident community than the one that existed three decades earlier.

Not only had the black community survived, but it had sustained a vision of community building. The migrants who stumbled into Detroit during the Great War, with nothing but their courage and willingness to hew a community out of the chaos of an industrializing city, shared this vision. On the backs of these southern rural black migrants, a community slowly and painfully arose, sometimes with the help of outsiders, but most often without even the faintest encouragement.

The migrants who labored in the factories and mills and in that process became industrial workers stimulated still another process—community building. As they worked and persevered, many returning but most remaining, they formed a foundation steady enough to support community institutions such as churches, hospitals, newspapers, and black business and professional classes. The emergence and stability of the industrial working class, therefore, constituted the key factor in the early stages of the community building process in Detroit.

Building on the foundation provided by the black industrial working class (mainly males) and domestic workers (mainly females), black social workers, reformers, newspaper publishers, teachers, politicians, inventors, lawyers, labor leaders, preachers, and a host of white friends all contributed to the often uneven process of black community building. John C. Dancy and the Detroit Urban League led the way through the worst of times, joined by black business and professional classes.

The worst of times brought racism in employment and public accommodations, police brutality, high rents for substandard living quarters, crime, violence, and an appallingly high death rate. Yet, the majority of blacks—encouraged by the DUL, NAACP, BTWTA, HWLD, the black newspapers, and by the examples of steadfastness of the Sweets and the support of white friends—kept their shoulders to the wheel. These worst of times both generated a sense of community among the most diverse of blacks and clarified their common vision of their purpose as a people barely beyond the shadow of slavery.

As their social consciousness grew, so did their need to exercise more independence as a community. The 1930s brought them face-to-face with new challenges as a community. They met the first challenge by abandoning their ties to the Republican Party, and they survived the second challenge by severing their ties to the Ford establishment in favor of industrial union-ism. In the process of severing their ties to their traditional allies of earlier stages of community building, they matured as a people. With greater confidence, they fought for their rights to war jobs and housing, thus continuing the process of community building.

HOLDING ON TO SLIPPERY GAINS: 1945–55

Standing on the threshold of the post World War II period, the black community faced many old and new problems. The postwar period was in some ways a variation of the community building theme over the last three decades. As one writer put it: "The end of World War II did not bring social stability to Detroit any more than it brought peace to the world." Racial friction persisted, and "for Negroes [it] was a decade of resistance; a continual struggle against discrimination in employment, in housing, in the use of public facilities, in [racist] treatment by the police."[1]

The postwar period found blacks still engaged in the struggle to gain decent housing. This time, however, they were attempting to get the city to pass a fair-employment-practices measure to insure jobs for black work-ers. Sadly, their efforts proved abortive.[2] This defeat did not deter the black community for long. They still had powerful allies in labor and scattered throughout local and state government. Therefore, they were able to make some inroads in less resistance areas. But racism remained a barrier to further community building. "The hardest problem faced by the Negro citizen of Detroit in the decade following the riot of 1943," one observer commented, was the "attitude of the majority group which ascribed Negroes to a secondary role in the community."[3] Yet, compared to the pre-1943 days, the end of World War II brought in the era of "enlightened tolerance" of minorities.

Much of the racial tolerance of this period had been forced upon Detroit by the 1943 race riot as well as by the powerful new alliances forged by the black community. These alliances included the Democratic Party, the UAW-CIO, and a host of civic and liberal organizations which worked throughout the 1950s to elect blacks to state and city political and judicial positions.[4]

Black workers not only insisted on hanging on to the slippery gains obtained during World War II, but they moved into white collar jobs, often to the chagrin of whites. Increasingly, blacks found white-collar jobs in downtown offices due to the changing employment policies of the government, which employed thousands of young black clerks and office workers and gave them jobs in areas where blacks previously had been excluded. A spin-off of this rise of blacks in white-collar jobs in the downtown area was the breakdown of discrimination in restaurants and other places of public accommodation which had refused to serve blacks in the 1930s and 1940s. Michigan Bell Telephone Company and other utility companies also aided this process of desegregating downtown by dramatically increasing their black employment in the period from 1943 to 1953. However, as late as 1953, the average black shopper still had to pick his places carefully if he wanted to have lunch in downtown Detroit.[5]

The black community continued to expand, and many whites continued to respond in predictable ways. Far too many white teachers and administrators could not adjust to the changing racial climate and simply did not respond positively to the needs of the expanding black community.

Instead of developing supportive programs for obvious social and economic deficiencies, they lowered the curriculum standards to the point where blacks were taking courses in schools which did not prepare them for admittance to schools of higher learning. This created and institutionalized a vicious cycle which started from the poor family, was formalized in the school, and ended up in either low-wage jobs or no jobs at all.[6]

Most white churches during this period failed abysmally to contribute to solving the problems of race relations in Detroit. Instead of preparing their congregations for living, working, and worshipping in a racially and culturally diverse society, they were right on the heels of their congregations fleeing the expanding black community.[7] At a time when enlightened leadership was needed, they failed themselves and eroded the prospects for better race relations in Detroit.

The YMCA and the Boy Scouts also failed to play a meaningful role in race relations during this period. Their "white-only policies" laid a "foundation in many instances for less powerful groups to do the same." White hospitals' racist policies added to the barriers facing the black community during this period. In 1953, one could not determine how many hospital beds were available for black patients in Detroit because "there [were] almost as many policies for handling Negro patients as there [were] hospitals."[8] Only black owned-and-operated hospitals would admit black patients at any time and under any circumstances. A few black doctors and nurses had been accepted at white hospitals during this period but "nothing to indicate that the pattern of segregation in medical care had been breached in Detroit."[9]

One of the few rays of hope during this so-called enlightened era was the work of the Public Library. From 1943 to 1953, it addressed the problems of shifting racial populations by courageously serving new communities. In fact, it not only continued providing services in the branches but went out into the communities to encourage reading and the use of the libraries.[10] Such services undoubtedly contributed to the literacy of the black community.

Housing problems continued to plague blacks and adversely affected the quality of black community building. Between 1940 and 1948, no other problem dominated the political and social life of Detroit as did the issue of providing decent housing for blacks. White citizens assisted by white politicians and city government struggled to find solutions "along the time-worn lines of segregation." The expanding black population, due in large part to the increase of black workers during World War II, rendered it impossible to find solutions without triggering serious economic and social controversies. The need for more housing for the black population demanded an increase in the public-housing program. Other cities also faced this problem of providing housing for their expanding black populations.[11]

From 1943 to 1953, blacks in Detroit attempted to solve their housing problems through both public and private housing. Both of these options, however, generated political conflicts. From 1943 to 1948, the political conflict centered around segregated public housing versus integrated public housing, the use of vacant land sites on the outlying areas, and temporary versus permanent housing developments. Complicating all this was the constant pressure from private interests to slow down, and stop if possible, all public housing.[12]

During this period, there was a total of 441,454 housing units in Detroit, of which 166,933 were owner-occupied. Black owners numbered 5,121. Out of 258,614 rental units, blacks occupied 29,751. The housing plight of blacks was far worse on the building front. From 1940 to 1946, there were 42,121 houses built for white buyers but 860 for black buyers. In 1940 there were only 1,000 family units available for blacks in public housing. These inequities forced the larger community after 1943 to search for answers to the housing problems for blacks. The pressures from the white community were so great that the city was blocked every time it attempted to plan housing for blacks outside of already densely populated black areas. As already mentioned, Mayor Jeffries decided to resolve the conflict by accepting the position of the Detroit Common Council and the Housing Commission that the city would not change racial characteristics of any neighborhood. This policy stood until 1952 when the Housing Commission lifted the restriction on occupancy in the Jeffries projects on the west side of Detroit.[13]

Blacks continued moving out of congested black areas into bordering white areas in the midst of the housing controversy. But this gradual black population shift was not large enough to prevent overcrowded schools and recreational facilities. As more blacks sought less crowded living and playing space for their families in areas outside of traditional black areas, they encountered traditional white resistance. As a result, this period witnessed local disturbances, court fights over violations of restrictive covenants, and racial conflicts. All this was further complicated by the Federal Housing Authority, which published model restrictive covenants in the manual designed to show white home owners how to draw them up. Meanwhile, the black population continued to increase.[14]

The Supreme Court ruled against the enforceability of restrictive covenants in private housing in 1948. Detroit lagged behind after the ruling, but housing segregationists no longer had any legal backing to support their position. The decision opened the way for the private housing market in Detroit to provide some relief for blacks confined to densely populated black areas. Two years later, changes in the housing patterns became noticeable. In 1950, out of 522,430 units in Detroit of which 276,313 were owner-occupied, blacks owned 21,606. Out of the 236,101 tenant-occupied houses, blacks made up 42,828. The total units occupied by blacks were 64,439, representing an increase of 29,562 over 1940 and a percentage increase of 84.7.[15]

Changes also occurred in new housing construction. From 1946 to 1952, 44,928 units were built for white buyers and 1,025 for black buyers. During this period, public housing, the cause of so much racial conflict in the 1940s, actually had only 4,000 units. Ten years after the riot, private housing had taken over the lead and had become the major approach for solving housing problems for blacks.[16]

Housing patterns shifted but the ghetto continued to expand, giving rise to white fears and needs to impose social controls upon the black population. White police embodied these fears and often exercised heavy-handed means to intimidate and control blacks. As a result, white policemen were not infrequently the source of many of the racial problems in Detroit between 1945 and 1955. The police department had clearly shown its racism in the 1942 Sojourner Truth riot and the 1943 race riot when they killed 17 blacks but no whites and injured and arrested scores of others. Operating much like foreign soldiers occupying colonies, they appeared to many—not all of them radical or black—as being concerned only with protecting "the rights of the majority against the Negro Minority." In the decade of 1943–53 police brutality "became the symbol of everything that was wrong with Detroit." Relations between the black community and the police became so bad that the NAACP along with other groups "spent most of their time processing complaints against the police department." The black community found itself using the courts to clarify the use of firearms by white policemen in apprehending persons suspected of crime. Unfortunately, the problem continued for several decades until Mayor Coleman Young's election in 1973 finally put a stop to it. In short, it took black political power to end what at times amounted to white police intimidation of the black community in Detroit.[17]

Much of the racism that existed in the police department during this period reflected the social mores of a predominantly white male department. Black and white policemen did not walk beats together nor ride together in squad cars. Black policemen did not belong to the motorcycle squad, the arson squad, or the homicide squad. The department assigned white policemen to black and white districts but assigned black policemen only to predominantly black districts to "do a job with Negroes." In 1953, out of a department of 4,200 policemen, only 101 were black. Out of that number, there were only four uniform sergeants and one detective lieutenant. No black policemen worked in administration at central headquarters or were assigned to any precinct "except on special duty west of Woodward."[18] Most blacks lived east of Woodward.

The first serious attempt to develop a sound policy of race relations between blacks and the police was the appointment of John Ballenger as police commissioner in 1943. He introduced intercultural courses in the police academy, promoted the first uniformed black sergeant, and initiated a general campaign against police brutality. He also created a policy-study commission with members from the black community, unprecedented in the history of Detroit race relations. Sadly, Ballenger was the last police commissioner between 1943 and 1953 to attend a meeting of the Detroit Interracial Committee, a committee in which all police commissioners held membership as a function of their office.[19]

Evidently, most white police officials as well as the white rank and file thought little of efforts to improve race relations in Detroit. Given the fact that the racial policies of city hall were not much better at the time, the police department could not but reflect the racial prejudices of the local governmental unit. In short, the police department was really an extension of the racial policies of city hall, the enforcement arm of a sometimes subtle policy of racial containment and control. The tragic point of it all is that for years it worked very effectively through the thick and thin of black protest, sapping the strength needed for sustaining the community building process.

Fortunately for the black community, the local NAACP continued to struggle against all forms of racial discrimination. If the commuity building process was to go forward, all remaining racial barriers had to be challenged and eliminated. Between 1946 and 1949, under the leadership of Edward M. Swan, its executive secretary, the NAACP carried out successful fights against racial restrictive covenants and the racial policies of the Bob-Lo Excursion Company. The company operated ferry boats from Detroit to its amusement park on Bob-Lo Island. It banned blacks from using the ferry boats and from using the park. The company based its policy on the argument that since the island was in Canadian waters, the Michigan Civil Rights Laws did not apply to it. The local NAACP won the case against the Bob-Lo company in the lower courts. The company appealed several times, and the case was finally decided by the United States Supreme Court on the side of the NAACP.[20]

We have already mentioned the role of the NAACP in the long struggle against undue use of deadly force by white police. Its efforts finally led to the establishment of the first Civilian Complaints Board in the history of the Detroit Police Department. In June, 1950, the NAACP launched a much needed and long awaited legal attack on the racial segregation in the Detroit public housing system. That battle was also won when, in October, 1954, the United States circuit court of appeals in Cincinnati went along with a federal district court opinion banning racial discrimination in public housing projects. The Detroit NAACP provided the leadership in the campaign that eventually led to the passage of the State Fair Employment Practices Law in 1956. One of the Detroit NAACP's major contributions to black community building strategies was its pioneering effort in special fund raising. In 1956, it put on a $100 per plate dinner which grew into an annual affair up to the present day and was picked up by the national office of the NAACP in New York, which held its first national $100 dinner in November 1957.[21]

Between 1943 and 1953, black workers engaged in two major struggles which directly affected the postwar community building process. One was the struggle of black blue-collar workers for seniority and upgrading in the plants. The other was the struggle of black white-collar workers to obtain jobs outside of the factories. The latter group was successful only in finding such jobs in the black community or in government. Black white-collar workers received more jobs in governmental civil-service and technical positions "than in comparable positions in private business." This meant that while there did exist a pool of blacks trained and prepared for such jobs, "private employers [were] far more selective on a racial basis than [the] government." During this period the Detroit Urban League worked hard "and for the most part silently" to open up jobs for blacks."[22]

Black blue-collar workers had to struggle just to hold on to "slippery gains" won during World War II and the Korean War. Black women in the factories were dismissed in wholesale fashion after 1945 while black men managed to hold on to some gains made during the war. Despite much effort, the CIO had a hard time making racial equality a fact. Many AFL unions in Detroit did not even pretend to work on behalf of black workers. As late as 1953, they still barred blacks from some unions and were only then beginning to look at the black skilled worker as a "possible union man." In the large downtown department stores, blacks were still confined to jobs as elevator operators, doormen, maids, janitors, and stock handlers. In 1953, these stores had yet to hire black sales clerks. The same pattern characterized business offices, where blacks remained confined to traditional jobs as janitors, messengers, and maintenance men. Black drivers were unknown in the common-carrier trucking industry and in private bus transportation. They were "conspicuous by their absence from the licensed business trade." In short, the traditional pattern of economic racism had altered only in very select employment situations. "Negroes appear prominently in trades traditionally allocated to them," one black editor commented, "[in] the lowest group in our society."[23]

As small as these gains were, they influenced other developments which directly and indirectly contributed to the community building process. As black workers held on to their jobs in the plants and consolidated their base within the trade union movement, they became a major force in all phases of the community building process. They moved up the job ladder and purchased homes and in the process stabilized black communities. Home ownership among black factory workers and professionals attracted the attention of a black editor who pointed to "hundreds of . . . well-kept substantial houses" which "attest to the economic progress which has been made by factory workers, white collar employees and professionals in the Negro community." These black workers and professionals in turn supported ten black insurance companies that provided insurance coverage, mortgage financing, and other community-sustaining services necessary for larger black community building. In fact, their support extended to other black owned-and-operated businesses which, at the time, were the only avenues through which many black youth could obtain training and employment in the business world.[24]

Of the approximately 15 billion dollars earned and spent by blacks nationally during this period, black workers and housewives in Detroit were estimated to have handled about 1.5 percent of this national income. No wonder then that in the 1950s, the black community in Detroit was hailed across the country as "the home of more Negro owned-and-operated businesses than in any other city."[25] Despite remaining racial barriers, black Detroit was still pushing forward in its effort to build and sustain a community.

NOTES

PREFACE

1. Richard W. Thomas, "From Peasant to Proletarian: The Formation and Organization of the Black Industrial Working Class in Detroit, 1915–45," Ph.D. diss., University of Michigan, 1976.
2. Joe William Trotter, Jr., *Black Milwaukee: The Making of an Industrial Proletariat, 1915–45* (Urbana: University of Illinois Press, 1985) p. 276.
3. Vincent Harding. *There Is A River: The Black Struggle for Freedom in America* (New York: Harcourt Brace Jovanovich, 1981) p. xxi.
4. Trotter, p. 277.
5. Kenneth E. Boulding, *Human Betterment* (Beverly Hills: Sage Publications, 1985).
6. Richard W. Thomas, "The First Urban Guardian: The Detroit Urban League, 1916–30," *Michigan History* (Winter 1976): pp. 315–38; "The Black Experience in Detroit: 1916–1967," *Blacks and Chicanos in Urban Michigan,* ed. Homer C. Hawkins and Richard W. Thomas, *Blacks and Chicanos in Urban Michigan* (Lansing: Michigan Historical Commission, 1979) pp. 56–80; "Unemployment, Employment and Training in Michigan," *The State of Black Michigan 1984* (East Lansing, Urban Affairs Programs, Michigan State University, 1984); "Black Self-help in Michigan" (Ibid., 1986) pp. 27–37; *The State of Black Detroit: Building From Strength* (Detroit: The Detroit Urban League, 1987); Coauthored with Joe Darden, Richard Child Hill, and June M. Thomas, *Detroit: Race and Uneven Development* (Philadelphia: Temple University Press, 1987); One of the community projects in Detroit with which I am presently associated as a cofounder is Fathers Inc., set up to work with black urban youth.

I. EARLY STRUGGLES AND COMMUNITY BUILDING

1. George B. Catlin, *The Story of Detroit* (Detroit: *Detroit News,* 1926) p. 542; David M. Katzman, *Before the Ghetto: Black Detroit in the Nineteenth Century* (Chicago: University of Illinois Press, 1973).
2. Catlin, p. 543.
3. Dorothy Emmer, "The Civil and Political Status of the Negro in Michigan and the Northwest before 1870," M.A. thes., Department of History, Wayne State University, 1935, p. 45.
4. Katzman, pp. 8–11.
5. Ibid., p. 13.
6. Ibid., pp. 19, 23, 29–32.
7. Ibid., pp. 18–19.
8. Ibid.
9. E. Franklin Frazier, *The Negro Church in America* (New York: Schocken, 1964) pp. 27–28. Ira Berlin, *Slaves without Masters: The Free Negro in the Antebellum South* (Oxford: Oxford University Press, 1974) pp. 71–73; W. E. B.

DuBois, *The Philadelphia Negro: A Social Study* (New York: Schocken, 1967) pp. 197–201; Leonard P. Curry, *The Free Black in Urban America, 1800–1850* (Chicago: The University of Chicago Press, 1981) pp. 175–95; James Oliver Horton and Lois E. Horton, *Black Bostonians: Family Life and Community Struggle in the Antebellum North* (New York: Holmes and Meier, 1979) pp. 39–40.

10. Katzman, p. 23; Leonard P. Curry, *The Free Black in Urban America, 1800–1850* (Chicago: The University of Chicago Press, 1981) p. 199.

11. Howard Holman Bell, *A Survey of Negro Convention Movements: 1830–1861* (New York: Arno Press and *The New York Times,* 1969) p. 8.

12. Philip S. Foner and George E. Walker, *Proceedings of the Black State Conventions* (Philadelphia: Temple University Press, 1979) p. 80. Pre–Civil War northern blacks were split over the question of staying in America and fighting for a chance to integrate into white America or emigrating to another country. For details, see Martin R. Delaney, *The Condition, Elevation, Emigration and Destiny of the Colored People of the United States* (New York: Arno and *The New York Times,* 1969) p. 7; Howard H. Bell, "The Negro Emigration Movement, 1844–1854, A Phase of Negro Nationalism," *Phylon* 1959: p. 135.

13. The black press was especially important to black survival in northern cities as Dann points out:

> The black press provided one of the most potent arenas in which the battle for self-definition could be fought and won. By stressing the primacy of racial pride and thus forging ethnic solidarity, the black press became, along with the church, a central institution in the black community. Black editors and their correspondents, as leaders in the community, not only were able to communicate information vital to the community and necessary for its cohesion, but also were often the only educational resources available. Indeed, black papers were usually the only source of information about the repression of the black community since white papers rarely printed such information. See Martin Dann, *The Black Press, 1827–1890* (New York, Putnam, 1971) p. 13.

14. Fred Landon, "The Negro Migration to Canada after 1850," *Journal of Negro History* 5 (January 1920): p. 22. For more on slave fugitive fleeing to Canada, see Robin W. Winks, *The Blacks in Canada* (New Haven: Yale University Press, 1971) pp. 142–77.

15. Emmer, p. 45.

16. Benjamin Quarles, *Black Abolitionists* (New York: Oxford University Press, 1969) p. 200.

17. Ibid., p. 150.

18. Ibid., p. 153.

19. June B. Woodson, "A Century with the Negroes of Detroit: 1830–1930," M.A. thes., Department of History, Wayne State University, 1949, p. 18; Katherine DuPre Lumpkin, "'The General Plan Was Freedom': A Negro Secret Order on the Underground Railroad," *Phylon* 25.1 (Spring 1967): pp. 63–77.

20. *Detroit Daily Post,* February 7, 1870.

21. Ronald P. Formisano, "The Edge of Caste: Colored Suffrage in Michigan, 1827–1861," *Michigan History* 56 (Spring 1972): pp. 29–30.

22. *Detroit Daily Post,* February 7, 1870.

23. "The Great Detroit Riot of 1860," *Detroit Daily Post,* January 1, 1870; *A Thrilling Narrative from the Lips of the Sufferers of the Late Detroit Riot, March 6, 1863* (reprinted Hattiesburg, Miss., 1945).

24. *Anti-Negro Riots in the North, 1863* (New York: Arno Press and *New York Times,* 1969) pp. i–iii; Albon P. Man, Jr., "Labor Competition and the New York

Draft Riots of 1863," *Journal of Negro History* (October 1951): pp. 375–405. Leonard P. Curry, *The Black in Urban America, 1800–1850: The Shadow of the Dream* (Chicago: The University of Chicago Press, 1981) pp. 96–111; Gary B. Nash, *Forging Freedom: The Formation of Philadelphia's Black Community, 1720–1840* (Cambridge: Harvard University Press, 1988) pp. 273–74.

25. Woodson, p. 43; Norman McRae, *Negroes in Michigan during the Civil War* (Lansing, Michigan, Michigan Civil War Centennial Observance Commission, 1966) p. 56.

26. *Detroit Advertiser,* January 2, 1863; *Detroit Tribune,* January 2, 1863.

27. Ibid., January 7, 1863.

28. Willis F. Dunbar and William G. Shade, "The Black Man Gains the Vote: The Centennial of 'Impartial Suffrage' in Michigan," *Michigan History* 56 (Spring 1972): p. 55.

29. William W. Stephensen, "The Colored Schools of Detroit: 1839–1869" student pap. University of Michigan, 1959.

30. *Detroit Free Press,* March 10, 11, 30, 1875.

31. *Detroit Free Press,* August 3, 1852; Benjamin Quarles, "Historic Afro-American Holidays," *Negro Digest* (February 1967): pp. 14–15.

32. Quarles, p. 15.

33. Ibid.

34. *Detroit Free Press,* August 8, 1851. The British Emancipation Day celebrations contributed to building communities on both sides of the border; they represented the cultural building blocks of the North American black community. See Daniel G. Hill, *The Freedom Seekers: Blacks in Early Canada* (Agincourt, Canada: The Book Society of Canada, 1981) pp. 182–84.

35. *Detroit Post,* August 5, 1869.

36. Quarles, pp. 16–17.

37. Ibid., p. 17.

38. *Detroit Tribune,* January 4, 1871.

39. Quarles, p. 18.

40. *Detroit Post,* August 5, 1869.

41. *Detroit Post,* August 3, 1869.

42. Katzman, pp. 162–64.

43. Ibid., pp. 154, 159; Kenneth L. Kusmer, *A Ghetto Takes Shape: Black Cleveland, 1870–1930* (Urbana: University of Illinois Press, 1976) pp. 99–103; Allan H. Spear, *Black Chicago: The Making of A Negro Ghetto, 1890–1920* (Chicago: The University of Chicago Press, 1967) p. 56.

44. Katzman, pp. 162–63.

45. Ibid., p. 164.

46. Ibid., pp. 162, 177

47. Allan Spear, "The Origins of the Urban Ghetto, 1870–1915," *Key Issues in the Afro-American Experience,* ed. Nathan I. Huggins, Martin Kilson, and Daniel M. Fox (New York: Harcourt Brace Jovanovich, 1971) p. 165.

48. Katzman, p. 198.

49. Ibid., p. 199.

50. *Plain Dealer,* October 11, 1889.

51. Katzman, p. 205.

52. Quoted in Ibid., pp. 121–22.

53. Ibid., p. 128.

54. Ibid., p. 28.

55. Ibid., p. 105.

56. Ibid., pp. 100, 116.

57. Ibid., pp. 164–65.

58. Ibid., pp. 130, 166.

59. Ibid., p. 130.

60. Ibid., pp. 131–32.

61. Ibid., p. 156.

62. August Meier, *Negro Thought in America, 1880–1915: Racial Ideologies in the Age of Booker T. Washington* (Ann Arbor: The University of Michigan Press, 1963) pp. 124–35.

63. Donald R. Deskins, Jr., *Residential Mobility of Negroes in Detroit, 1837–1965* (Ann Arbor: Department of Geography, University of Michigan, 1972) pp. 100–01.

64. Deskins, pp. 102–03.

65. Francis H. Warren, *Michigan Manual of Freedmen's Progress* (Detroit, Michigan: Freedmen's Progress Commission, 1915) pp. 40–79.

66. Oliver Zunz, *The Changing Face of Inequality: Urbanization, Industrial Development, and Immigrants in Detroit, 1800–1970* (Chicago: The University of Chicago Press, 1982) p. 6.

67. Katzman, p. 207.

2. THE DEMAND FOR BLACK LABOR, MIGRATION, AND THE EMERGING BLACK INDUSTRIAL WORKING CLASS, 1915–1930

1. See Trotter's discussion of these works, Trotter, p. 276.

2. Richard W. Thomas, "From Peasant to Proletarian: The Formation and Organization of the Black Industrial Working Class in Detroit, 1915–1945," Ph.D. diss. University of Michigan, 1976, p. 4; Trotter, p. 276.

3. Trotter, p. 276.

4. Charles Johnson, "Substitution of Negro for European Immigrant Labor," *National Conference of Social Work Proceedings* (May–June 1926) pp. 319–20; Harold M. Baron, *The Demand for Black Labor: Historical Notes on the Political Economy of Racism* (Cambridge, Mass.: Radical America, 1971) pp. 19–21; Sterling D. Spero and Abram L. Harris, *The Black Worker* (New York: Columbia University Press, 1931) pp. 149–81.

5. Peter Gottlieb, *Making Their Own Way: Southern Blacks' Migration to Pittsburgh, 1916–1930* (Urbana: University of Illinois, Press, 1987) p. 4.

6. Kenneth L. Kusner, *A Ghetto Takes Shape, Black Cleveland, 1870–1930,* (Chicago: University of Illinois Press, 1976) pp. 192–93; Allan H. Spear, *Black Chicago: The Making of a Negro Ghetto* (Chicago: The University of Chicago Press, 1967) pp. 181–87; Homer C. Hawkins and Richard W. Thomas, eds., *Blacks and Chicanos in Urban Michigan* (Lansing: Michigan History Division, 1979) pp. 64–65; Gottlieb, p. 4.

7. Florete Henri, *Black Migration Movement North, 1900–1920* (New York: Doubleday, 1976) p. 79; Gavin Wright, *Old South, New South* (New York: Basic Books, Inc., 1986) pp. 177–81; Paul B. Worthman, "Black Workers and Labor Unions in Birmingham, Alabama, 1897–1904," *Black Labor in America,* ed. Milton Cantor (Westport, Conn.: Negro Universities Press, 1969) pp. 55–58.

8. Emmett J. Scott, *Negro Migration During the War* (Oxford University Press, 1920) p. 26.

9. Ibid.

10. James R. Grossman, *Land of Hope: Chicago, Black Southerns, and the Great Migration* (Chicago: University of Chicago Press, 1989) pp. 66–67.

11. Quoted in W. E. B. DuBois, "Migration of Negroes," *Crisis* 14 (June 1917): p. 66.

12. Scott, pp. 72–85; Ethel Erickson, "Escaping Slaves," *Crisis* 13 (November 1916): p. 23. For a more comprehensive examination of legal and other means

southern states used to restrict black migration, see Leo A. Lilumas, "Statutory Means of Impeding Emigration of the Negro," *Journal of Negro History* 22 (April 1937): pp. 148–62; Gottlieb, p. 55; Tuttle, pp. 77–78.

13. R. H. Leavell, "Negro Migration from Mississippi," in J. H. Dillard, *Negro Migration in 1916–1917* (Washington: Department of Labor, Government Printing Office, 1919) p. 34.

14. George W. Grohn, *The Black Migration: The Journey to Urban America* (New York: Weybright and Talley, 1972) p. 53.

15. Ibid.

16. Martin Kilson, "Political Change in the Negro Ghetto, 1900–1940s," in *Key Issues,* ed. Huggin, Kilson and Fox, p. 168.

17. Willis F. Dunbar, "The Speeding Tempo of Urbanization," *Michigan History* 35 (September 1951): p. 294; Melvin Holli, "The Impact of Automobile Manufacturing upon Detroit," *Detroit in Perspective: A Journal of Regional History* 2 (Spring 1976): p. 177.

18. Dunbar, p. 295.

19. Ibid.

20. Louise Ranklin, "Detroit Nationality Groups," *Michigan History* 22 (Spring 1939): pp. 131–90.

21. Ibid., pp. 156, 174, 176–188, 189; Zunz, pp. 100–01.

22. Holli, p. 79.

23. U.S. Department of Commerce, Bureau of the Census (Washington, D.C.): *Twelfth Census of the United States, 1900: Manufacturers, II; Thirteenth Census of the United States, 1910: Manufacturers, VIII,* p. 84; *Fourteenth Census of the United States, 1920: Manufacturers, VIII,* p. 19. *Detroit Directory* (Detroit: R. L. Polk and Co., 1916) pp. 7–9.

24. *Detroit City Directory:* 1921–22, p. 41; 1922–23, pp. 31–32; 1930–31, pp. 1–9.

25. Sidney Glazer, *Detroit: A Study in Urban Development* (New York: Bookman Associates, Inc., 1965) p. 79.

26. "Population," *The Negro in Detroit* (Detroit: Bureau of Governmental Research, 1926) p. 6; George E. Haynes, *The Negro at Work During the War and Reconstruction* (Washington, D.C.: Government Printing Office, 1921) p. 77; "Population," *The Negro in Detroit,* p. 6.

27. Glen E. Carlson, "The Negro in the Industries of Detroit," Ph.D. diss., University of Michigan, 1929, pp. 52–53, 59–60; typewritten memo, "The Negro in Detroit Industry, January, 1921," Detroit Urban League Papers, Michigan Historical Commission, Ann Arbor, Mich. (hereafter cited as, DULP-MHC), Executive Secretary general file 1921–22; box 1; Report of the Urban League for October 14, 1920, box 11, folder 2; John C. Dancy, Jr., typewritten speech, "Unemployment, 1921," box 11.

28. For an example of an employer's bringing blacks into Detroit, see letter from Boyd Fisher to Mr. Clarke, June 27, 1916, DULP-MHC, Executive Secretary general file, box 1, folder 1916, and "Conditions Among Newcomers in Detroit," DUL Report, Spring 1918, box 1. Letters reflecting refusal and reluctance are scattered throughout this folder. For employers' stationing labor agents in neighboring cities, see Lloyd H. Bailer, "Negro Labor in the Automobile Industry," Ph.D. diss., University of Michigan, 1943, p. 31.

29. "Publicity," in Annual Report of Director, 1917, DULP-MHC, box 11.

30. Ibid.

31. Report of Director to monthly meeting of joint committee, Detroit League on Urban Conditions among Negroes [DLUCM], January 19, 1917, DULP-MHC, box 11, folder [11-0]; Report of Director, September 18, 1919, box 11, folder 1919.

32. Forrester B. Washington, *The Negro in Detroit: A Survey of the Condition of a Negro Group in a Northern Industrial Center During the World Prosperity Period* (Detroit: Research Bureau, Associated Charities of Detroit, 1920) pp. 1–2.
33. Ibid.
34. Katzman, p. 121.
35. Washington, p. 2.
36. David L. Lewis, "History of Negro Employment in Detroit Area Plants of Ford Motor Company, 1914–1941," seminar paper, University of Detroit, 1954, pp. 7–9.
37. Ibid., p. 7.
38. Washington, p. 9; These four plants were only part of a larger sample that did not respond to the study, so there might well have been others with similar racial compositions.
39. The major cities with large black urban forces were New York, Philadelphia, Chicago, Detroit, Pittsburgh, Cleveland, and Cincinnati; see Louise Venable Kennedy, *The Negro Peasant Turns Cityward: Effects of Recent Migrations to Northern Centers* (New York: Columbia University Press, 1930) p. 74.
40. Washington, p. 16. *Thirteenth Census of the United States, 1910: Occupations, IV,* p. 554; *Fourteenth Census of the United States, 1920: Occupations, IV,* p. 1102.
41. According to the classification made by the employment managers of Detroit plants, a skilled job took a year or two to learn, a semiskilled job took from two weeks to six months, and for an unskilled job, "you merely tell the man how to do it and he can do it" (Carlson, p. 105).
42. Some farm labor in the South received about 26.5 cents per hour compared to the 24 to 47 cents received in domestic and personal services. These figures were taken from interviews of a sample of Detroit migrants; see Washington, p. 23. Another researcher said farm labor in the South rarely received more than 75 cents a day; see Lorenzo J. Greene and Carter G. Woodson, *The Negro Wage-Earner* (Washington, D.C.: The Association for the Study of Negro Life and History, Inc., 1930) p. 208.
43. Berry Gordy, Sr., *Movin' Up.* (New York: Harper and Row, 1979) p. 86.
44. Ibid., pp. 86–87.
45. Washington, p. 23.
46. Ibid.
47. "Population," *The Negro in Detroit,* p. 18.
48. Report of Director to monthly meeting of joint committee, Detroit League on Urban Conditions among Negroes, January 19, 1917. DULP-MHC, box 11, folder [11-0]; "Detroit Negroes in Industry", March 1, 1926, box 1, folder January–March 1, 1926.
49. Ibid.
50. Ibid.
51. These percentages were computed from *Thirteenth Census of the United States, 1910: Occupations, IV,* pp. 554–55; *Fourteenth Census of the United States, 1930: Occupations, IV,* p. 805; *Sixteenth Census of the United States, 1940: Occupations, The Labor Force, III.*
52. Report of Director, February 8, 1917; regular monthly meeting of joint committee, November 9, 1916; Report of Director, April 12, 1917: DULP-MHC, box 11, folder [11-0].
53. DUL Report from October 9 to November 13, 1919, DULP-MHC, box 11, folder 1919; "Industry", *The Negro in Detroit,* p. 17.
54. "For Newspapers," general file 1919; director's report, March 10, 1921; Director's Report for March, 1922; Board of Directors' Report, 1922: DULP-MHC, box 11.

55. David M. Katzman, *Seven Days A Week: Women and Domestic Service in Industrializing America* (New York: Oxford University Press, 1978) pp. 226–80; Gottlieb, p. 104.

56. "Industry," *The Negro in Detroit,* p. 27.

57. Annual Report of the Detroit Urban League for 1929, January 30, 1930, DULP-MHC, box 11, folder [11-11].

58. Lewis, p. 8.

59. Gottlieb, p. 124.

60. Trotter, p. 62.

61. Gottlieb, p. 124.

62. Washington, p. 154.

63. Washington, pp. 55–56; see Henderson H. Donald, "The Negro Migration of 1916–1918," *Journal of Negro History* 6 (October 1921): p. 451.

64. Washington, pp. 56–57.

65. Ibid., p. 157.

66. Report of Director, September 18 to October 19, 1919; Report of Director, October 19, 1919: DULP-MHC, box 11, folder 1919. Report for October–November 13, 1910, box 11.

67. Letter, T. Arnold Hill to John C. Dancy, April 3, 1926. DULP-MHC, box 1, folder April–June 1926.

68. Minutes of Urban League Board meeting, June 8, 1922, DULP-MHC, box 11.

69. Minutes of the meeting of the Urban League Board, September 16, 1920; Minutes of the meeting of the Urban League Board, May 13, 1920: DULP-MHC, box 11, folder 1920.

70. Report of Director, September 18, 1919, DULP-MHC, box 11, folder 1919; Gottlieb, 206.

71. Report, Department of Labor, Office of the Secretary, Washington, D.C., March 9, 1925, DULP-MHC, box 11, folder Jan–June 1925.

72. Minutes of the Urban League Board meeting for May 11, 1922; Urban League Minutes of January 13, 1921: DULP-MHC, box 11.

73. Minutes of the Urban League Board meeting for September 1922, DULP-MHC, box 11, folder 1972; Minutes of The Urban League Board meeting of April 12, 1923, box 11, folder 1923.

74. Report 1930, DULP-MHC, folder gen. file 1930; DUL Report, Spring 1918, "Conditions Among Newcomers in Detroit," box 1, folder 1918.

75. "Industry," *The Negro in Detroit,* p. 18.

76. Ibid.

77. Carlson, p. 148.

78. Ibid., p. 139–140.

79. Washington, pp. 18–19.

80. Ibid.

81. Ibid.

82. Ibid.

83. Carlson, p. 140.

84. For the influence of America's wars in black economic development see, Sidney Willhelm, *Who Needs the Negro* (Cambridge, Mass.: Schemk, 1970).

85. Carlson, p. 140.

86. It is important that this process of unskilled and semiskilled substitution be understood in order to determine the extent of both absolute and relative black economic progress.

87. Although blacks had a larger percentage of their total work force in transportation in 1910 than whites (see table 2), the majority were in the unskilled categories of dragmen, teamsters, and expressmen; see *Thirteenth Census of the United States, 1910: Occupations, IV,* p. 554.

88. John C. Dancy, Jr., "The Negro in Detroit Industry, January, 1921," type-written memo, DULP-MHC, Executive Secretary general file 1921–22, box 1.

89. Report of the Urban League for October 14, 1920, DULP-MHC, box 11, folder 2.

90. Ibid. John C. Dancy, Jr., "Unemployment, 1921," typewritten speech.

91. Ibid.

92. William Jennifer, "Back to the Farm in Michigan," *Detroit Independent,* June 10, 1927, p. 4.

93. Carlson, pp. 99–101.

94. Report of the Director, November 11, 1920, DULP-MHC, box 11, folder 2; Minutes of the committee of the Urban League for March 11, 1921, box 11, folder 2; Board of Directors' Minutes and Reports, January 19, 1922, box 11, folder 4.

95. "Education, Recreation, Employment, 1919," Typewritten Memorandum, DULP-MHC, Executive Secretary general file, box 1, folder 10.

96. Carlson, p. 100.

97. Ibid., p. 101.

98. Ibid., p. 90.

99. See chap. 4.

3. THE ROLE OF THE DETROIT URBAN LEAGUE IN THE COMMUNITY
BUILDING PROCESS, 1916–1945

1. William M. Tuttle, Jr., *Race Riot: Chicago in the Red Summer of 1919* (New York: Atheneum, 1972); Elliott Rudwick, *Race Riot at East St. Louis July 12, 1917* (New York: Atheneum, 1972).

2. Letter from Robert R. Moton, James H. Dillard, L. Hollingsworth Wood, John R. Shillady, Eugene Kinckle Jones, and Thomas Jessie Jones to William R. Wilson, February 12, 1918, chief clerk files, record group 174, National Archives, Washington, D.C.

3. Ibid.

4. Ibid.

5. "Appointment and Function of the Director of Negro Economics, United States Department of Labor," *Monthly Labor Review* 7 (September 1918): p. 37.

6. George E. Haynes, *The Negro At Work During the World War and Recon-struction* (Washington, D.C.: Government Printing Office, 1921) p. 12.

7. Ibid., pp. 13–14, 114, 139.

8. Ibid., p. 15

9. Ibid., pp. 14–15.

10. Nancy J. Weiss, *The National Urban League: 1910–1940* (New York: Oxford University Press, 1974) pp. 41–46.

11. Ibid.; L. Hollingsworth Wood, "The Urban League Movement," *Journal of Negro History* 9 (April 1924): pp. 119–20.

12. Sterling D. Spero and Abram L. Harris, *The Black Worker* (New York: Columbia University Press, 1931) p. 141.

13. John M. T. Chavis and William McNitt, *A Brief History of the Detroit Urban League* (Ann Arbor: Michigan Historical Collection, 1971) p. 8.

14. Joseph J. Boris, ed., *Who's Who in Colored America: 1928–1924* (New York, 1929) pp. 384–85.

15. See Boyd Fisher letters to various manufacturers, June 27, 1916; Margail B. Munn to Forrester B. Washington, June 13, 1916; Cora W. Northup to Forrester

B. Washington, June 28, 1916: DULP-MHC, Executive Secretary general file, box 1, folder 1916.

16. Ibid.

17. JoEllen McNergney Vinyard, "The Inter-Dependence of a City and its Residents: Nineteenth Century Detroit," *Detroit in Perspective: A Journal of Regional History* 1.1 (Autumn 1972): p. 48.

18. Ibid.

19. Forrester B. Washington, Report of Director, October 16, 1916, Associated Charities of Detroit Collection, box 12, folder 41, Archives of Labor and Urban Affairs, Wayne State University, Detroit, Michigan (hereafter cited as ALUA-WSU).

20. Ibid.

21. Forrester B. Washington, Report of Director, December 12, 1916, Associated Charities of Detroit Collections, box 12, folder 41, ALUA-WSU.

22. Ibid.

23. Ibid.

24. Guichard Parris and Lester Brooks, *Blacks in the City: A History of the National Urban League* (Boston: Little, Brown, and Company, 1971) pp. 89–90.

25. Forrester B. Washington, Report of the Director, October 16, 1916, Associated Charities of Detroit Collection, box 12, folder 41, ALUA-WSU.

26. Ibid.

27. Untitled pamphlet, DULP-MHC, the Detroit Urban League 19, box 1, folder 9, pp. 2–3.

28. David Allen Levine, *Internal Combustion: The Races in Detroit, 1915–1926* (Westport, Conn.: Greenwood Press, 1976) p. 54.

29. Forrester B. Washington, Report of the Director, October 16, 1916, and November 9, 1916, Associated Charities of Detroit Collection, box 12, folder 41, ALUA-WSU.

30. Parris and Brooks, p. 91.

31. Ibid.

32. Forrester B. Washington, Report of Director, December 12, 1916, Associated Charities of Detroit Collection, box 12, folder 41, ALUA-WSU; Report of Director to monthly meeting of joint committee, Detroit League on Urban Conditions among Negroes, March 8, 1917, Associated Charities of Detroit Collection, box 12, folder 41, ALUA-WSU.

33. Report of Director, March 8, 1917.

34. Eugene Kinckle Jones to Miss L. Green, January 29, 1917, Associated Charitites of Detroit Collection, box 12, folder 40, ALUA-WSU.

35. Edith L. Spurlock to Miss L. Green, January 29, 1917; J. Byre Deacon to Lee Greenwood, March 26, 1917; W. M. Cross to Lee Greenwood, March 28, 1917; Associated Charities of Detroit Collection, box 12, folder 40, ALUA-WSU.

36. Forrester B. Washington, Efficiency Speech at St. Mark's Brotherhood Church, May 20, 1917, DULP-MHC, Executive Secretary file, box 1, folder 3.

37. Forrester B. Washington, "A Program of Work for The Assimilation of Negro Immigrants in Northern Cities," in Proceedings of the Forty-Fourth Annual Session of the National Conference of Social Work, Pittsburgh, 1917, pp. 497–99.

38. Ibid.

39. John C. Dancy, Jr., *Sands Against the Winds: The Memoirs of John C. Dancy* (Detroit: Wayne State University Press, 1966) pp. 71–81; Boris, *Who's Who in Colored America: 1928–29,* p. 97.

40. Memorandum, 1919, DULP-MHC, Executive Secretary general file, box 1.

41. See the director's monthly reports on employment and annual reports of Detroit Urban League, 1919–1945, DULP-MHC, box 11.

42. Report of Director, September 18, 1919, December 18, 1919; see monthly reports, 1921–30: DULP-MHC, box 11.

43. Urban League Board Meeting Report, May 13, 1920, DULP-MHC, box 11.

44. Urban League Board Meeting Report, January 13, 1921; Urban League Report for February 10, 1921; Minutes of the Urban League Committee, April 14, 1921: DULP-MHC, box 11.

45. Director's Report, June 8, 1922, DULP-MHC, box 11.

46. Urban League Report for April 1922, DULP-MHC, box 11.

47. Director's Report for September–October 1921; Urban League Report for December 1921. DULP-MHC, box 11.

48. Ibid. Minutes of Minsterial Conference, March 17, 1919; "Education, Recreation, Employment, 1919," typewritten memorandum: DULP-MHC, Executive Secretary general file, box 1, folder 10. David M. Katzman, *Seven Days a Week: Women and Domestic Service in Industrial America* (New York: Oxford University Press, 1978) p. 245.

49. Urban League Board Report, September 14, 1922, DULP-MHC, box 11.

50. Director's Report, January 17; April, 1923: DULP-MHC, box 11.

51. Annual Urban League Report, January 10, 1924; Director's Report for June 12, 1924; Urban League Board Meeting Report for September 1924: DULP-MHC.

52. Annual Report of Director for year 1924, DULP-MHC.

53. Annual Report for 1928, DULP-MHC, box 11.

54. Board of Directors' Report, March 20, 1930, DULP-MHC.

55. Urban League Report, November 6, 1931, DULP-MHC, box 11.

56. Minutes of the Urban League Board of Trustees, May 12, 1938, DULP-MHC, box 11.

57. Résumé of year's activities, Detroit Urban League, 1940, DULP-MHC, box 11. For discussion on discrimination in defense industries in Detroit, see chap. 6.

58. Annual Report of the Detroit Urban League for year 1941, DULP-MHC.

59. Detroit Urban League Annual Report, 1945, p. 4, DULP-MHC.

60. Ibid.

61. Ibid., p. 5.

62. Typewritten account of blacks in Detroit, DULP-MHC, general file 1930, box 1.

63. Minutes of Urban League Meeting, June 12, 1919; Annual Report of Director for year 1924: DULP-MHC, box 11.

64. Memorandum of Detroit Urban League Community Center, 1919; Reports and Minutes of the Community Center Board Meeting, 1919–1923, DULP-MHC, Executive Secretary general file; minutes of settlement house meeting, July 31, 1919, Detroit Urban League Center, folder 1918–20, box 8.

65. "Four Hundred Children Taken on Urban League Outing," DULP-MHC, general file 1919, box 1.

66. Columbia Community Center Minutes of Board Meeting, September 25, 1919, DULP-MHC, folder community center, box 8.

67. Report of the Detroit Urban League, September 18–October 19, 1919, DULP-MHC, box 11.

68. Director's Report for March 11, 1920, DULP-MHC, box 11.

69. Director's Report, November 1920, DULP-MHC, box 11.

70. Report of the Columbia Commuity Center Board for May–October, 1920, DULP-MHC, box 11.

71. Columbia Community Center Report, January 27, 1921, Detroit Urban League Community folder 1921–25; Community Center Committee Report, February 24, 1924, topical file 1918–1960, Detroit Community Center; Minutes of the committee of the Urban League for March 11, 1921, folder Detroit Urban League Community Center 1921–25: DULP-MHC, box 8.

72. Minutes, Detroit Urban League Board, May 14, 1929; Annual Report for 1929: DULP-MHC, box 11.

73. Minutes of the Urban League Board, October 26, 1928; Detroit Urban League Board of Directors' Report, May 17, 1929: DULP-MHC, box 11.

74. Detroit Urban League Annual Report, 1944; Detroit Urban League Annual Report, 1945: DULP-MHC, box 11, folder 1940–45.

75. Report of Director to Monthly Meeting of Joint Committee of Detroit League on Urban Conditions Among Negroes, February 8, 1917, DULP-MHC, box 11.

76. Ibid.

77. Detroit Urban League Board Meeting, January 8, 1920; Director's Report for September 1921: DULP-MHC, box 11.

78. Annual Report of Director for the Year, 1924; Annual report of Detroit Urban League, January 14, 1926: DULP-MHC, box 11.

79. Director's Report, April 8, 1920; Urban League Board Notice for September 13, 1923; Minutes of the September Meeting, September 21, 1927: DULP-MHC, box 11.

80. Forrester B. Washington, "Deluxe Summer Camp for Colored Children," *Opportunity* 9 (October 1931): pp. 305–06.

81. Ibid., pp. 304–05.

82. Keri Bancroft, "Snapshots of Heaven: Michigan's Green Pasture Camp," *Michigan History* (September-October 1985): p. 29; Washington, p. 303; Guide to The Microfilm Edition of The Detroit Urban League Papers (Michigan Historical Collections, Bently Historical Library, University of Michigan, 1974) p. 5. Dancy, *Sand Against the Wind,* p. 161–62.

83. Bancroft, p. 33; Washington, pp. 303–05.

84. Ibid., pp. 34–35.

85. Ibid., pp. 35–36

86. Ibid., p. 36.

87. Ibid., p. 37.

88. Ibid., p, p. 36; Dancy, pp. 162–63.

89. Ibid., p. 37.

90. Ibid., pp. 37–8.

91. Washington, "A Program of Work" pp. 305–06; Bancroft, p. 38.

92. Dancy, p. 164.

93. Report of Director to monthly meeting of joint committee, October 16, 1916, DULP-MHC, box 11.

94. Ibid., p. 7.

95. Ibid.; Report of Director to monthly meeting of joint committee, Detroit Urban League on Urban Conditions Among Negroes, March 8, 1917, DULP-MHC, box 12.

96. "Health", *The Negro In Detroit,* p. 1; letter from Albertus Cleage, M.D., and Frank P. Raiford, M.D. to various ministers, April 2, 1923, DULP-MHC, Executive Secretary general file, box 1.

97. Chavis and McNitt, pp. 18–19. See Chapter 4.

98. Detroit Urban League Annual Report, 1945, DULP-MHC, box 11. See also Chapters 6 and 7.

99. Brief History of Detroit Urban League, p. 7.

100. Letters, Alonzo C. Thayer to John C. Dancy, June 3, 1927, November 26, 1927, July 2, 1928, DULP-MHC, general file, box 1, folders July–December 1927 and July–September 1928; Letter, Samuel A. Allen to John C. Dancy, November 26, 1926, general file, box 1, folder July–December 1926.

101. Letter, Wm V. Kelly to John C. Dancy, February 26, 1930; Letter, Mr. Crawford to John C. Dancy, December 11; Letter, Forrester B. Washington to John C. Dancy, October 12, 1926: DULP-MHC, box 1.

332 Notes for pages 85–92

102. Letter, Samuel A. Allen to John C. Dancy, August 23, 1923; Letter, Nimrod B. Allen to John C. Dancy, October 27, 1926; Letter, A. L. Foster to John C. Dancy, July 26, 1926; Letter, J. Harvey Kerns to John C. Dancy, August 4, November 5, 1928; Letter, Evelyn Crawford to John C. Dancy, September 23, 1926; Letter, Wm. V. Kelly to John C. Dancy, July 9, 1928; Letter, Carter G. Woodson to John C. Dancy, August 31, 1931; E. Franklin Frazier to John C. Dancy, January 17, 1930: DULP-MHC, box 1.

103. Director's Report for April 1925, DULP-MHC, box 11.

104. Letters, Forrester B. Washington to John C. Dancy, November 12, 1928, January 26, 1929, DULP-MHC, box 1.

105. Letter, Forrester B. Washington to John C. Dancy, August 9, 1929, DULP-MHC, box 1.

106. Letter, Forrester B. Washington to John C. Dancy, November 9, 1928, DULP-MHC, box 1.

107. Detroit Annual Report, 1945, DULP-MHC, box 11.

4. WEATHERING THE STORM

1. Charles Denby, *Indignant Heart: A Black Workers' Journal* (Boston: South End Press, 1978) p. 27.

2. Haynes, p. 10.

3. *The New York Times,* May 25, 1916, p. 19.

4. John Ihlder, "Blooming Detroit," *The Survey* 26 (July 1916): pp. 449–50.

5. Publicity article no. 5., n.d., "U.S. Homes Registration Service cooperate with other agencies." U.S. Housing Corporation Homes Registration Section, National Archives, Washington, D.C. (hereafter cited as USHC-HRID), reference file, box 303, R.G. 3.

6. Letter, James Ford (USHC Manager, Homes Registration and Information Division) to Miss Louise Osburne Rowe, Commissioner, Department of Public Welfare, Chicago, Illinois, May 22, 1919. Correspondence with Field Agents and Committees, USHC-HRID, box 307, R.G. 3.

7. Letter, Edward L. Schaul to Dr. James Ford, April 16, 1919; Letter, James Ford to Mayor James Couzens, May 6, 1919: Correspondence with Field Agents and Committees, USHC-HRID, box 307, R.G. 3.

8. Memorandum, Director of Negro Economics to Dr. James Ford, U.S. Housing Corporation, October 31, 1918, Correspondence with Field Agents and Committees, USHC-HRID, box 307, R.G. 3. Letter, Chief Field Agent, Middle Central West, U.S. Home Registration Service, to S. W. Smith, Chicago, June 18, 1919, Correspondence with Field Agents and Committees, USHC-HRID, box 307, R.G. 3.

9. Washington, "Environment," p. 107 (see chap. 2, n. 32)

10. Ibid.

11. Haynes, p. 9; *Detroit Times,* January 4, 1934; *Detroit News* January 3, 1934; *Detroit News,* February 2, 1946.

12. Washington, p. 107; Haynes, p. 23.

13. Haynes, p. 21.

14. Ibid.

15. Ibid., p. 22–23. The family sizes were: 18 families of one person; 169 families of 2; 108 families of 3; 51 families of 4; 28 families of 5; 19 families of 6; 10 families of 7; 3 families of 8; and one family of 9 persons, excluding lodgers.

16. Ibid.

17. "Housing," *The Negro in Detroit,* pp. 1–2.

18. George F. Haynes, "Negro Migration—Its Effects on Family and Community Life in the North," National Conference of Social Work, Proceedings of the Fifty-first Annual Session, Toronto, Ontario, 1924, p. 69.

19. "Housing," p. 1; Kusmer, p. 227; Trotter, p. 71; Clyde Vernon Kiser, *Sea Island to City* (New York: Athenevy 1969).

20. Florette Henri, *Black Migration, Movement North, 1900–1920* (New York: Anchor Books, 1976), p. 102.

21. Ibid.; pp. 102–03.

22. "Housing," *The Negro in Detroit,* pp. 2–3.

23. Washington, p. 145.

24. Ibid.

25. Ibid., p. 146.

26. Ibid., p. 144.

27. Ibid., p. 146.

28. Ibid.

29. *Detroit Tribune,* October 4, 1941.

30. Ibid.

31. Ibid.

32. Ibid.

33. *Detroit Tribune,* May 31, 1941.

34. Ibid.

35. *Detroit Tribune,* November 8, 1941.

36. Interview, Joseph Billups, October 27, 1967, transcript, Archives of Labor History and Urban Affairs, p. 5.

37. *Detroit Tribune,* November 5, 1937.

38. Ibid.

39. *Detroit Tribune,* May 24, 1941.

40. Ibid.

41. Washington, 126.

42. Ibid., p. 136.

43. Ibid., p. 138.

44. Ibid., p. 137–38.

45. *Detroit City Directory, 1923–1924,* p. 33.

46. "Housing," *The Negro in Detroit,* pp. 12–18.

47. Ibid., p. 53.

48. Ibid., p. 59.

49. Ibid.

50. *Detroit Saturday Night,* December 10, 1927, p. 3.

51. Washington, pp. 127, 134; "Housing," *The Negro in Detroit,* p. 12; *Detroit Times,* January 4, 1934.

52. *Detroit Times,* January 4, 1934.

53. Ibid.

54. *Detroit News,* January 3, 1934.

55. Boykin, p. 55.

56. "Summary of economic, real estate and mortgage survey area descriptions of greater Detroit, Michigan," Home Owners Loan Corporation City Survey, USHC-HRID, file 1935–40, box 0018, R. G. 195.

57. "Health," *The Negro in Detroit,* p. 1.

58. Board of Directors Minutes and Reports, January 1924, DULP-MHC.

59. "Health," *The Negro in Detroit,* pp. 3–4.

60. Ibid., pp. 1–9.

61. Ibid., pp. 1–9; Boykin, pp. 59–60.

62. Henri, p. 109.

63. Henri, p. 113; United States Department of Commerce, *Birth, Stillbirth, and Infant Mortality Statistics: Tenth Annual Report, 1924* (Washington, D.C.: U.S. Government Printing Office, 1926) p. 32.

64. United States Department of Commerce, *Birth, Stillbirth, and Infant Mortality Statistics: Seventeenth Annual Report, 1931* (Washington, D.C.: U.S. Government printing Office, 1934) p. 27; United States Department of Commerce, *Vital Statistics of the United States, 1940* (Washington, D.C.: U.S. Government Printing Office, 1943) p. 86.

65. "Health," *The Negro in Detroit*, pp. 18–19. See the excellent work of Loudell F. Snow, "Folk Medical Beliefs and Their Implications for Care of Patients: A Review Based on Studies Among Black Americans," *Annals of Internal Medicine* 81, no. 1 (July 1974): pp. 82–96; "Ethnicity and Clinical Care: American Blacks," *Physician assistant 8 Health Practitioner* (July 1980): pp. 50–54, 58.

66. Eugene Genovese, *Roll, Jordan, Roll* (New York: Vintage Books, 1972) p. 227.

67. "Health," *The Negro in Detroit*, pp. 6–8.

68. Snow, "Folk Medical Beliefs," p. 82–96, "Ethnicity and Clinical Care," pp. 50–54, 58.

69. "Health," *The Negro in Detroit*, pp. 6–8.

70. Carlson, p. 21.

71. Ibid.

72. *United Auto Workers*, June 19, 1937, p. 7.

73. Ibid.

74. Denby, pp. 30–31.

75. Ibid.

76. Ibid.

77. *United Auto Workers*, June 19, 1937, p. 7; "Health," *The Negro in Detroit*, pp. 1–9.

78. Morris Davis, "Black Workers and Occupational Hazard," *Science for the People* (March/April 1980).

79. Carlson, pp. 139–40.

80. Ibid., p. 123.

81. Denby, p. 31.

82. Carlson, p. 89.

83. Rose Toomer Brunson, "Socialization Experiences and Socio-Economic Characteristics of Urban Negroes as Related to Use of Selected Southern Foods and Medical Remedies," Ph.D. dissertation, Michigan State University, 1962, p. 55.

84. Ibid., p. 51.

85. Ibid., p. 64.

86. *Detroit News*, July 15, 1917.

87. Ibid.

88. Quoted in *Detroit Saturday Night*, December 24, 1927.

89. Ibid.

90. Ibid.

91. Ibid.

92. Ibid.

93. Roger Lane, *Roots of Violence in Black Philadelphia, 1860–1900.* (Cambridge: Harvard University Press, 1986) p. 134.

94. For vivid accounts of these race riots, see Elliott Rudwick, *Race Riot at East St. Louis, July 2, 1917* (New York: Atheneum, 1972); William M. Tuttle, Jr., *Race Riot: Chicago in the Red Summer of 1919* (New York: Atheneum, 1972).

95. "Crime," *The Negro In Detroit*, p. 5.

96. Ibid.

97. Letter, James W. Incher to John C. Dancy, November 13, 1920, DULP-MHC, Secretary general file, box 1, folder 1920.

98. Ibid.

99. Ibid.

100. Letter, John C. Dancy, Jr. to James W. Incher, November 27, 1920, DULP-MHC, Executive Secretary general file, box 1, folder 1920.

101. Ibid.

102. *Detroit News,* July 15, 1917.

103. Many blacks survived during the 1930s by working in black-controlled numbers racket, one of the pillars of the black underground economy in Detroit; see Gustov G. Carlson, "Number Gambling: A Study of a Culture Complex," Ph.D. diss., University of Michigan, 1940.

104. "Crime," *The Negro in Detroit,* p. 16; *Sixty Fifth Annual Report of the Detroit Police Department, 1930,* p. 25; *Seventieth Annual Report of Detroit Police Department, 1935,* p. 54. See the *Detroit Independent* for examples of black crime in the 1920s. For the 1930s, particularly between 1933 and 1939 and 1936 and 1939, see the *Detroit Tribune* and the *Michigan Chronicle,* respectively.

105. "Crime," *The Negro in Detroit,* p. 16.

106. Ibid., pp. 7, 13.

107. For representative examples of black-on-black crime which occured throughout this period, see the *Detroit Tribune:* May 24, 1934; October 9, 1937; January 1, 1938; March 5, 1938, November 5, 1938, November 26, 1938, July 9, 1939, January 4, 1941; July 12, 1941; and May 7, 1942.

108. "Crime," *The Negro in Detroit,* p. 18.

109. *Sixty-fifth Annual Report of the Detroit Police Department, 1930,* p. 25; *Seventieth Annual Report of the Detroit Police Department, 1935,* p. 54; *Seventy-fifth Annual Report of the Detroit Police Department, 1940,* p. 68; *Eightieth Annual Report of the Detroit Police Department, 1945,* p. 64.

110. "Crime," *The Negro in Detroit,* pp. 10, 14, 17; *Annual Reports of the Detroit Police Department, 1930,* p. 25; *1940,* p. 68; *1944,* p. 64.

111. *Detroit Tribune,* April 14, 1933.

112. Ibid., December 28, 1940.

113. Ibid., January 4, 1941.

114. More than likely, most blacks arrested for "gambling" cited in the annual police reports were connected with numbers racket; see above reports.

115. Carlson, *Numbers Gambling,* p. 50.

116. Ibid., p. 46.

117. Ibid., p. 101–13.

118. Ibid., p. 112.

119. Ibid., p. 113.

120. Ibid., p. 134.

121. Ibid., p. 145.

122. Ibid., p. 148.

123. Ibid., pp. 145–46.

124. Ibid.

125. Ibid., pp. 153–54. Number gambling had the same influence in other northern black communities such as Chicago. See "Business Under a Cloud," vol. 2, chap. 17, in St. Clair Drake and Horace R. Cayton, *Black Metropolis: A Study of Negro Life in a Northern City* (New York: Harper and Row, 1962).

126. Carlson, p. 154.

127. *Detroit Tribune,* July 5, 1941.

128. *Detroit Tribune,* November 1, 1941; Jitterbugging was one of the dances developed or "invented" by southern blacks after they migrated to northern cities. Usually done to big band swing music of the time, jitterbugging typified a black

dance craze that included the Lindy Hop, Suzi-Q, Camel Walk, and Truckin'. See Clarence Major, *Dictionary of Afro-American Slang* (New York: International Publishers, 1970) p. 71; Lynne Fauley Emery, *Black Dance in the United States from 1619 to 1970* (Palo Alto, Calif.: National Press Books, 1972) p. 221.

129. Ibid.
130. Ibid.
131. Ibid.
132. *Detroit Tribune,* September 27, 1941.
133. *Detroit Tribune,* November 1, 1941.
134. Ibid.
135. Ibid.
136. Ibid.
137. *Detroit Tribune,* May 2, 1941.
138. Ibid.
139. *Detroit News,* October 5, 1942.
140. Ibid.
141. *Detroit News,* February 11, 1946.

5. RACIAL DISCRIMINATION IN INDUSTRIAL DETROIT

1. Joseph Boskin, *Urban Racial Violence in the Twentieth Century* (London: Collier MacMillan Publishers, 1976) pp. 39–76.

2. Boskin, pp. 39–54; Hollis R. Lynch, *The Black Urban Condition* (New York: Thomas Y. Crowell Co., 1973) pp. 186–87; 346.

3. Elliot M. Rudwick, *Race Riot at East St. Louis,* (Carbondale: Southern Illinois University Press, 1964); William M. Tuttle, Jr., *Race Riot: Chicago in the Red Summer of 1919* (New York: Atheneum, 1970).

4. *Detroit News,* July 15, 1917.

5. Ibid.

6. Ibid.

7. See *Report of the National Advisory Commission on Civil Disorders* (New York: Bantam Books, 1968) p. 2; Louis L. Knowles and Kenneth Prewitt, eds., *Institutional Racism in America* (Englewood Cliffs, N.J.: Prentice-Hall, 1969).

8. Lewis H. Carlson and George A. Colborn, eds., *In Their Place: White America Defines Her Minorities, 1850–1950* (New York: John Wiley and Sons, 1972), pp. 72–115.

9. Carlson, p. 140.

10. *Detroit Contender,* November 13, 1920. *Detroit Tribune,* December 17, 1933; May 27, 1933; February 23, 1935; March 9, 1935; April 6, 1935.

11. *Detroit Tribune,* December 14, 1940; August 5, 1941, September 6, 1941.

12. Katzman, *Before the Ghetto,* p. 94.

13. *Detroit Tribune,* May 27, 1933.

14. Katzman, p. 93.

15. Ibid., p. 96.

16. Ibid., p. 93.

17. Ibid.

18. *Detroit Contender,* November 13, 1920.

19. Ibid.

20. Ibid.

21. *Detroit Tribune,* June 17, 1933.

22. Oral interview of Arthur McPhail by Norman McRae, April 5, 1970,

Archives of Labor History and Urban Affairs, Wayne State University, Detroit, Michigan (hereafter cited as ALHUA-WSA).

23. *Detroit Tribune,* May 5, 1934.

24. *Detroit Tribune,* June 2, 1934.

25. *Detroit Tribune,* August 11, 1934.

26. *Journal of the Senate of the State of Michigan, Regular Session, 1937,* p. 17.

27. *Detroit Tribune,* March 1928.

28. Ibid.; *Detroit Tribune,* March 26, 1938.

29. *Detroit Tribune,* October 1, 1938.

30. *Detroit Tribune,* October 29, 1938.

31. *Detroit Tribune,* September 6, 1941.

32. *Detroit Tribune,* December 6, 1941.

33. *Michigan Chronicle,* March 14, 1953.

34. "Recreation," *The Negro in Detroit,* p. 13.

35. Ibid., p. 16.

36. Ibid., 10.

37. Ibid., p. 12.

38. *Fifth Annual Report of the Detroit NAACP, 1914,* p. 14.

39. *Detroit Tribune,* May 27, 1933.

40. *Detroit Tribune,* April 20, 1935.

41. *Detroit Tribune,* August 10, 1935.

42. *Detroit Tribune,* February 12, 1938.

43. *Detroit Tribune,* June 9, 1934; June 30, 1934.

44. *Detroit Tribune,* June 30, 1934.

45. "Recreation," *The Negro in Detroit,* p. 10; Snow Grigsby, *White Hypocrisy and Black Lethargy* (Detroit: Snow Grigsby, 1937) p. 26.

46. "Recreation," *The Negro in Detroit,* p. 20.

47. "Health," *The Negro in Detroit,* p. 14; Boykins, p. 49.

48. *Michigan Chronicle,* March 14, 1953.

49. "Health," *The Negro in Detroit,* p. 15.

50. Ibid.

51. Ibid., p. 16; Grigsby, p. 34.

52. *Detroit Tribune,* April 9, 1938.

53. Harold Black, "Restrictive Covenants in Relation to Segregated Negro Housing in Detroit," M.S. thes., Wayne State University, 1947, p. 6.

54. Clement E. Vose, *Caucasians Only: The Supreme Court, The NAACP and the Restrictive Covenant Case* (Berkeley and Los Angeles: University of California Press, 1967) pp. 122–23.

55. *Detroit Free Press,* June 24, 1925.

56. *Detroit Free Press,* July 10, 1925.

57. *Detroit Free Press,* July 12, 1925.

58. Ibid; September, 13, 1925; *New York Times,* July 12, 1925.

59. Sidney Fine and Frank Murphy, *The Detroit Years* (Ann Arbor: The University of Michigan, 1975) pp. 147–48; Kenneth G. Weinberg, *A Man's Home, A Man's Castle* (New York: The McCall Publishing Company, 1971).

60. *Detroit Free Press,* May 8, 1926.

61. *Detroit Free Press,* September 11, 1926; Fine, p. 150.

62. *Baltimore Afro-American,* October 31, 1925.

63. Quoted in the *Baltimore Afro-American,* October 24, 1925.

64. *Baltimore Afro-American,* October 24, 31; November 14, 21, 28; December 5, 26, 1925; January 2; March 27; May 8, 1926; *Pittsburgh Courier,* September 19; November 7, 14, 28; December 8, 1925; January 9, 23; March 27; April 24;

May 1, 8, 15, 22, 1926; *New York Times,* November 28, 1925; January 4, 1926; *Detroit Free Press,* 1925; *Messenger* 7 (December 1925): p. 388.

65. Fine, pp. 150–70; *Detroit Free Press,* May 14, 1926; *Baltimore Afro-American,* December 5, 1926.

66. *Detroit Free Press,* May 14, 1926; Fine, pp. 166–67.

67. Four representative examples of this white resistance during the period, see: *Detroit Tribune,* July 22, 1939; August 26, 1939; March 16, 1940; May 17, 1941; August 31, 1941.

68. *Detroit Tribune,* March 23, 1940.

69. Ibid.

70. *Detroit Tribune,* August 17, 1940.

71. *Detroit Tribune,* August 10, 1940.

72. Ibid.

73. Ibid.

74. Ibid.

75. *Detroit Tribune,* August 17, 1941.

76. *Detroit Tribune,* June 14, 1941.

77. *Detroit Tribune,* August 9, 1941.

78. *Detroit Tribune,* March 23, 1940.

79. *Detroit Tribune,* July 5, 1941.

80. *Detroit Tribune,* August 2, 1941.

81. *Detroit Tribune,* August 31, 1940.

82. Ibid.

83. *Michigan Chronicle,* February 7, 1942; "Summary of Sojourner Truth Homes, Detroit, Michigan, March 6, 1942," NAACP Papers, general office files 1940–55, R.G. 11, box A-234, Library of Congress.

84. Bette Smith Jenkins, "The Racial Policies of the Detroit Housing Commission and Their Administration." M. A. Thes. Wayne State University, 1950, p. 30.

85. Robert Conot, *American Odyssey* (New York: William Morrow, 1974) p. 465.

86. *Michigan Chronicle,* February 7, 1942.

87. *Detroit Free Press,* January 16, 1942.

88. August Meier and Elliot Rudwick, *Black Detroit and the Rise of the UAW* (New York: Oxford University Press) p. 178.

89. Quotes in Ibid.

90. Letter, Lester B. Granger to John C. Dancy, January 13, 1942, DULP-MHC, Executive Secretary general files, box 4, folder January–March 1942.

91. Telegram, Lester B. Granger to Baird Snyder, January 14, 1942; Telegram, Lester B. Granger to Mrs. Franklin D. Roosevelt, January 14, 1942; Telegram, Lester B. Granger to the Honorable Franklin D. Roosevelt, January 14, 1942; DULP-MHC, Executive Secretary general files, box 4, folder January–March 1942.

92. Ibid.

93. *Detroit Free Press,* January 18, 1942.

94. *Detroit Free Press,* January 19–21, 26, 28, 1942; *Michigan Chronicle,* January 31, 1942; Meier and Rudwick, pp. 180–81.

95. *Tribune,* February 14, 1942, quoted in Dominic J. Capeci, Jr., *Race Relations in Wartime Detroit: The Sojourner Truth Housing Controversy of 1942* (Philadelphia: Temple University Press, 1984).

96. *Detroit Free Press,* February 3–4, 1942; *Michigan Chronicle,* February 7, 1942.

97. Meier and Rudwick, p. 181.

98. B. J. Widick, *Detroit: City of Race and Class Violence* (Chicago: Quadrangle Books, 1972) pp. 95–96.

99. *Michigan Chronicle,* March 14, 1942.

100. Meier and Rudwick, p. 183.

101. *Michigan Chronicle,* March 28, 1942.

102. Ulysses W. Boykin, *A Handbook on the Detroit Negro* (Detroit, Michigan: The Minority Study Associate, 1943) p. 57.

103. Lester Velie, "Housing, Detroit's Time Bomb," *Collier's* (November 23, 1946.)

104. See chap. 3.

105. Ibid., p. 42.

106. Industrial codes were minimum-wage standards established for particular occupations based on the theory that increased wages would expand total purchasing power, which in turn would aid in stimulating economic recovery. See Raymond Wolters, *Negroes and the Great Depression* (Westport, Conn.: Greenwood Publishing Corporation, 1970) p. 85.

107. Wolters, pp. 115–16.

108. *Detroit Tribune,* December 2, 1933.

109. *Detroit Tribune,* June 17, 1933.

110. Ibid.

111. Ibid.

112. Grigsby, pp. 17, 41.

113. Ibid., p. 26.

114. Ibid., p. 25.

115. *Detroit Tribune,* March 17, 1934.

116. *Detroit Tribune,* August 6, 1938.

117. Ibid.

118. Ibid.

119. Ibid.

120. Ibid.; *Detroit Tribune,* October 29, 1938; December 6, 1941. As a result of a century of racial discrimination, racial problems in the Detroit Fire Department were still being "worked out" in 1984; see *New York Times,* December 14, 1984.

121. Robert C. Weaver, *Negro Labor: A National Problem* (New York: Harcourt, Brace and World, 1946), p. 15.

122. Ibid., p. 46.

123. Ibid., p. 49.

124. *Michigan State Conference on Employment Problems of the Negro: Findings, Reports and Recommendations,* Detroit, October 8, 1940, United States Employment Service, R.G. 183, National Archives.

125. Ibid.

126. Robert Shogan and Tom Craig, *The Detroit Race Riot: A Study in Violence* (Philadelphia and New York: Chilton Books, 1964) p. 32.

127. The War Manpower Commission (WMC) was established by Executive Order 9139 of April 18, 1942, to "formulate plans and programs and establish basic national policies to assure the most effective mobilization and maximum utilization of the nation's manpower in the prosecution of the war." Charles Zaid, *Inventory of the Records of the War Manpower Commission* (Washington, D.C.: National Archives and Record Service, General Services Administration, 1973) p. 1.

128. "Labor Market Problems on Selected Firms Manufacturing Radio and Radar and Radar Equipment, January 11, 1943," *Industry Labor Market Report, Records of the Analysis Division,* War Manpower Commission, box 650, R.G. 211, National Archives.

129. Ibid.

130. Past production methods had never required so many trained workers, and the depression had depleted the country's supply of skilled labor and almost

curtailed the training of young people. In order to meet the pressing need for skilled workers, the government resorted to two major programs: breaking down skilled operations, and starting mass training for industrial workers (defense training). The first was designed to facilitate the use of a large number of workers who knew only one or two operations of a skill, and the second was designed to prepare millions for such operations in a short space of time; see Weaver, p. 18.

131. "Labor Market Problems in the Metal-Working Machinery Industry, September 10, 1942," *Industry Labor Market Report, Records of the Analysis Division*, War Manpower Commission, box 649, R.G. 211, National Archives.

132. "Labor Market Problems of the Cotton Textile Industry, March 1943," *Industry Labor Market Report.*

133. "Urgent Need for Unskilled labor in the Forge and Foundry Industries in This Area, 1944," Report, Detroit-Willow Run, Committee for Congested Production Areas, central file, box 52, R.G. 212, National Archives.

134. Ibid.

135. Weaver, p. 19; Letter, Ernest T. Marshall to John C. Dancy, April 24, 1941; "Employment Opportunities for Negroes in Michigan Industries," DULP-MHC, Executive Secretary general file, box 4, folder January–June, 1941.

136. Weaver, p. 19.

137. Ibid., p. 17.

138. "National Defense Chronology for the Year 1941," *The Negro Handbook*, ed. Florence Murray (New York: Wendell Mailliet and Company, 1942), pp. 77–76; Louis Ruchames, *Race, Jobs and Politics: The Story of FEPC* (New York: Columbia University Press, 1953) pp. 20–21.

139. Robert C. Weaver, "Detroit and Negro Skill," *Phylon 4* (April–June 1943): p. 133.

140. Ibid.

141. Ibid.

142. Ibid.; Herbert R. Northrup, *Organized Labor and the Negro* (New York: Harper and Brothers Publishers, 1944) p. 199.

143. Newspaper clipping, Active Case File of Ford Motor Company, Detroit, Michigan, August 1941 to May 1942, Records of the Committee on Fair Employment Practices, box 2, R.G. 228, National Archives.

144. Ibid.

145. Ibid.

146. Ibid.

147. Weaver, "Detroit and Negro Skill," p. 136; Northrup, pp. 197–98.

148. Weaver, "Detroit and Negro Skill," p. 136.

149. Ibid., p. 134.

150. Ibid., pp. 136–37.

151. Ibid.

152. Ibid., p. 137.

153. Ibid.

154. Ibid.

155. Ibid., p. 39.

156. Lloyd H. Bailer, "The Negro Automobile Worker," *The Journal of Political Economy* 51 (October 1943): p. 425; *The Michigan Chronicle*, May 1, 1943.

157. Weaver, "Detroit and Negro Skill," pp. 138–139.

158. Ibid., p. 139.

159. *Michigan CIO News*, June 11, 1943; p. 4; Weaver, *Negro Labor*, p. 77.

160. Weaver, *Negro Labor*, p. 17.

161. Ibid.

162. Bailer, "The Negro Automobile Worker," p. 426.

163. Ibid.

164. Ibid., p. 426.

165. *Michigan Chronicle,* February 20, 1943.

166. Bailer, "The Negro Automobile Worker," p. 422.

167. Meier and Rudwick, pp. 134–55; Richard W. Thomas, "From Peasant to Proletarian: The Formation and Organization of the Black Industrial Working Class in Detroit," Ph.D. Dissertation, University of Michigan, 1976, pp. 234–66.

168. Jack Kresnak, "City Police: A Port of Racism," *Blacks in Detroit* (Detroit, Michigan: Detroit Free Press, 1980) pp. 70–73.

169. *Report of the Mayor's Committee on Race Relations* (Detroit: Detroit Bureau of Governmental Research, 1926) p. 7.

170. Ibid., p. 8.

171. *Detroit Tribune,* September 30, 1933; June 15, 1935; August 24, 1935.

172. Ibid.

173. Ibid.

174. Kresnak, p. 72.

175. Ibid., p. 74.

176. Widick, p. 100.

177. Ibid., p. 101.

178. *Michigan Chronicle,* June 7, 1943, p. 1.

179. Widick, p. 100.

180. Alfred McClung Lee and Norman Daymond Humphrey, *Race Riot* (New York: Dryden Press, 1943) pp. 20–21.

181. Shogan and Craig, p. 43.

182. Widick, pp. 102–03.

183. Widick, p. 108; *CIO News,* June 28, 1943, p. 3.

184. Lee and Humphrey, p. 46.

185. Ibid.

186. Shogan and Craig, p. 87.

187. Widick, pp. 110–11.

188. "Speech of William Dowling, Prosecutor, before the Kiwanis Club regarding the Race Riot, June 17, 1944," NAACP Papers, general office files 1940–55, R.G. 11, box A-496, Library of Congress.

189. Ibid.

190. *CIO News,* June 28, 1943.

191. Ibid.

192. Ibid.

193. Ibid.

194. *CIO News,* July 12, 1943, p. 1.

195. *CIO News,* July 19, 1943, p. 1.

196. *CIO News,* August 21, 1943, p. 8.

197. "Report of Survey of Race Relations in Detroit, Michigan, Made by Field Consultant during the Period Beginning August 26, 1943, and Ending September, 1943," from field consultant Loring B. Moore to Civilian War Services, September 11, 1943, NAACP Papers, general office files 1940–55, R.G. 11, box A-496, Library of Congress.

198. *CIO News,* August 30, 1943, p. 8.

199. Walter White. "What Caused the Detroit Riots." NAACP Papers, general office files 1940–55, R.G. 11, box A-496, Library of Congress.

200. "Report of Thurgood Marshall, NAACP, Concerning Activities of the Detroit, Michigan Police during the Riots of June 21 and 22, 1943, July 26, 1943," NAACP Papers, general office files 1940–55, R.G. 11, box A-496, Library of Congress.

201. *Michigan Chronicle,* August 13, 1943, p. 1.

202. *The National Urban League's Report of the Detroit Race Riot and Rec-*

ommendations for a Program of Community Action, p. 617, June 28, 1943, DULP-MHC, Executive Secretary file, box 5, folder June–July 1943.

6. SOCIAL CONSCIOUSNESS AND SELF-HELP

1. *Detroit Contender,* May 7, 1921.
2. Ibid.
3. Boykin, p. 32.
4. "Religion," *The Negro in Detroit,* pp. 10–11.
5. *Second Baptist Advocate,* Anniversay Edition, April 1961, p. 30; Edith Davis Gamble, "Down Memory Lane: 131 years of Church History"; Ibid., June 1966, p. 20; Ibid., June 1967, p. 36.
6. *An Historical Sketch: Eightieth Anniversary of Bethel AME Church, Detroit Michigan, 1841–1921* (Detroit, Bethel AME, 1941) p. 7.
7. Ibid., p. 2.
8. Ibid., p. 33.
9. Ibid., p. 42.
10. Ibid., p. 54.
11. Katzman, *Before the Ghetto,* p. 137 (see chap. 1, n. 1).
12. *St. Matthew's Episcopal Church Centennial Celebration 1846–1946* (Detroit: St. Matthew's Episcopal Church, 1946).
13. Ibid.
14. Ibid.
15. Ibid.
16. Ibid.
17. Katzman, p. 136.
18. Ibid., p. 137.
19. Ibid., p. 135–36.
20. "Religion," *The Negro in Detroit,* p. 8.
21. Ibid.
22. Ibid., p. 9.
23. Boykin, p. 49.
24. Ibid., p. 50.
25. Ibid.; *The Detroit Tribune,* November 6, 1937.
26. Ibid.
27. Compiled from *Thirteenth Census of the United States 1910: Occupations,* IV, pp. 553–55; *Fourteenth Census of the United States, 1930: Occupations,* IV, pp. 1101–04; *Fifteenth Census of the United States, 1930: Occupations,* IV, pp. 803–05; *Sixteenth Census of the United States, 1940: The Labor Force,* III, pp. 612–13.
28. Boykin, p. 50.
29. Parkside Hospital, 1933–1950, DULP-MHC, Executive Secretary topical file, January 17, 1934.
30. Minutes of the Board of Trustees of Parkside Hospital, December 28, 1933, DULP-MHC.
31. Minutes of the Board of Directors of Parkside Hospital, March 1, 1934.
32. See Chapter 3.
33. Boykin, p. 51.
34. Grigsby, p. 35.
35. Ibid., pp. 35–36.
36. "Thrift and Business," *The Negro in Detroit,* pp. 9–10.
37. Grigsby, pp. 43–44.
38. "Thrift and Business," *The Negro in Detroit,* p. 7.

39. Ibid., p. 11.
40. Boykin, p. 108.
41. *Detroit Tribune,* February 19, 1938.
42. *Detroit Tribune,* April 26, 1941; Boykin, p. 108.
43. Boykin, p. 109; "Thrift and Business," *The Negro in Detroit,* p. 3.
44. Letter, C. Henri Lewis, Jr. to John C. Dancy, March 13, 1933, Michigan People's Finance Company 1928–1938, DULP-MHC, Executive Secretary topical file.
45. Boykin, pp. 109–10.
46. Ibid.; *Bethel African Methodist Church, 140th Anniversary: 1841–1981,* (Detroit: Bethel African Methodist, 1981) p. 65.
47. Ibid.
48. Ibid.
49. Ibid., p. 112.
50. Ibid.
51. Elaine Leaphart, "Historical Overview of *The Detroit Tribune,*" student pap., Department of Journalism, The University of Michigan, MHC, 1977, pp. 11–15.
52. Ibid., p. 15.
53. Ibid., p. 11; much if not all of this "promotional" spirit was the result of the black economic nationalism set in motion by the Booker T. Washington Trade Association and its sister organization, the Housewives League, which we will discuss later.
54. Ibid., pp. 13–15; see various issues between 1933 and 1945.
55. See the *Detroit Tribune* for these years.
56. *Detroit Tribune,* December 14, 1935; August 19, 1933.
57. *Detroit Tribune,* January 17, 1942.
58. *Detroit Tribune,* September 20, 1941.
59. Ibid.
60. Meier and Rudwick, p. 33.
61. *Michigan Chronicle,* January 14, 1939.
62. Meier and Rudwick, p. 33.
63. Ibid.
64. *Michigan Chronicle,* April 22, 1939.
65. *Michigan Chronicle,* January 21, 1939.
66. *Michigan Chronicle,* January 4, 1941.
67. *Michigan Chronicle,* April 10, 1943.
68. *Michigan Chronicle,* December 30, 1944.
69. For example, see: the *Detroit Tribune,* September 30, 1939; June 7, 1941; July 5, 1941; the *Michigan Chronicle,* February 3, 1945.
70. *Detroit Tribune,* June 7, 1941; *Michigan Chronicle,* October 25, 1941; February 3, 1945.
71. *Detroit Tribune,* September 27, 1941; *Michigan Chronicle,* February 3, 1945.
72. A quick scan of the society page of both newspapers would verify this observation. For a few representative examples see: the *Detroit Tribune,* September 23, 1939; October 14, 1939; January 11, 1941; February 22, 1941; the *Michigan Chronicle,* April 7, 1945.
73. Judith Stein, *The World of Marcus Garvey: Race and Class in Modern Society* (Baton Rouge: Louisiana State University Press, 1986) pp. 275–76.
74. Letter, Bishop C. S. Smith to A. Mitchell Palmer, Attorney General, June 25, 1919, in vol. 1, *The Marcus Garvey and Universal Improvement Association Papers,* ed. Robert A. Hill (Berkeley: University of California Press, 1983) p. 446.
75. Hill, vol. 1, p. 413.

76. "John Charles Zampty," 1974 interview; in *Marcus Garvey's Footsoldiers of the Universal Improvement Association,* ed. Jeannette Smith-Ibuin (Trenton, New Jersey: African World Press, Inc., 1989) p. 41.

77. Ibid., pp. 46–47.

78. Hill, vol. 4, p. 570.

79. Stein, pp. 231, 233; Hill, vol. 5, pp. 510, 629, 694.

80. Stein, pp. 230–31.

81. Smith-Ibuin, pp. 41–42.

82. Tony Martin, *The Pan-African Connection: From Slavery to Garvey and Beyond* (Dover, Mass: The Majority Press, 1985) p. 64.

83. Smith-Ibuin, p. 48.

84. Ibid., p. 47.

85. Ibid., p. 49.

86. E. David Cronon, *Black Moses: The Story of Marcus Garvey and the UNIA* (Madison: The University of Wisconsin Press, 1955) p. 139.

87. Blacks in Detroit compared favorably with blacks from other cities in contributing to the Parent body's fund; see the *Negro World,* July 31, 1926.

88. Quoted in Hill, vol. 6, p. 552.

89. Ibid.

90. Stein, p. 234.

91. Ibid., p. 232.

92. Katzman, pp. 115–16.

93. Ibid.

94. Ibid., pp. 132–33.

95. *Detroit Contender,* November 13, 1920; Arthur Turner and Earl R. Moses, *Colored Detroit* (Detroit: Turner and Moses, 1924) p. 16.

96. Turner and Moses, p. 21; Carter G. Woodson, *The Negro in Our History* (Washington, D.C.: The Associated Publishers, Inc.) p. 461.

97. "Thrift and Business," *The Negro in Detroit,* pp. 25–26.

98. Ibid., pp. 24–25.

99. Ibid., p. 25.

100. Turner and Moses, p. 24; Hoyt W. Fuller and Frank Seymour, "Courage and Five Hundreds Built a Chain of Stores," *Inside Michigan* 2 (March 1952): pp. 48–56.

101. *Detroit Tribune,* January 26, 1935.

102. Ibid.

103. *Michigan Chronicle,* October 23, 1943.

104. Ibid.

105. "Hotel Gotham: Detroit's 200 Room Hostelry is Finest in Negro America," *Ebony* (August 1947): pp. 28–31.

106. Ibid., p. 31.

107. "Thrift and Business," *The Negro in Detroit,* pp. 4, 7, 21; *Detroit Contender,* November 13, 1920; See Chapter 6.

108. *Detroit Tribune,* November 2, 1935; August 14, 1937; March 5, 1938; August 26, 1939; July 6, 1940; July 27, 1940.

109. Amber Cooley Neumann, "Twenty-five Years of Negro Activity in Detroit, 1910–1935," M.A. Thesis, University of Detroit, 1935, p. 20.

110. John Hope Franklin, *From Slavery to Freedom,* 4th ed. (New York: Alfred A. Knopf, 1974), p. 174.

111. Ibid.

112. For the tremendous impact this movement had on urban black communities, see Abram L. Harris, *The Negro as Capitalist* (Philadelphia: American Academy of Political and Social Science, 1936); J. H. Harman, Jr., Arnett G. Lindsay and Carter G. Woodson, *The Negro as Businessman* (Washington, D.C.: Association

for the Study of Negro History as Life, 1929); Allan Spear, *Black Chicago: The Making of a Negro Ghetto, 1890–1920* (Chicago: The University of Chicago Press, 1967) pp. 73–80 passim, pp. 86–87; Gilbert Osofsky, Harlem: *The Making of a Ghetto* (New York: Harper Torchbooks, 1963) pp. 62–104.

113. "Thrift and Business," *The Negro in Detroit,* p. 26.

114. Ibid., pp. 26–27.

115. *Detroit Tribune,* March 5, 1938; July 27, 1940; April 3, June 22, 1943; Robert L. Gill, "The Booker T. Washington Trade Association," seminar paper, 1939, DULP-MHC; "History," Housewives League of Detroit Papers, box 1, folder "History," Burton Historical Collection, Detroit Public Library, Detroit, Michigan, (hereafter cited as HLDP-BHC).

116. *Constitution and By-Laws of Housewives League of Detroit Declaration of Principles of the Constitution and By-Laws of the Booker T. Washington Trade Association 1937,* box 1, folder "Constitution and By-Laws," HLDP-BHC.

117. Ibid.

118. Ibid.

119. Gill, p. 20; *Program: The Booker T. Washington Trade Association and the Housewives League of Detroit,* 1935, box 3, folder "Printed Materials, 1934–1968," HLDP-BHC.

120. *Detroit Tribune,* April 15, 1934.

121. *Detroit Tribune,* April 29, 1933.

122. *Detroit Tribune,* February 5, 1938; June 11, 1938; September 17, 1938; April 15, 1939.

123. *Detroit Tribune,* August 17, 1940; August 31, 1940.

124. *Detroit Tribune,* December 14, 1935.

125. Bulletin, "Housewives Page," May 1, 1934.

126. Quoted in Gill, pp. 25, 37.

127. Ibid.

128. Ibid., p. 48.

129. Ibid., p. 25; "History," box 1, folder "History," HLDP-BHC.

130. "Housewives Page," May 1, 1934.

131. "History," box 1, folder "History," HLDP-BHC.

132. Gill, p. 50.

133. Ibid., pp. 51–53.

134. Robin S. Peebles, "Detroit's Black Women's Clubs," Michigan History 70 (January–February, 1986): p. 48.

135. Ibid.

136. E. Davis, *Lifting As We Climb* (Chicago: NACWC, 1933) pp. 319–320.

137. Peebles, p. 48; "Biography of Rosa Lee Slade Gragg," Rosa L. Slade Gragg Papers, Folder, Biographical information, Burton Historical Collection, Detroit Public Library; Detroit News, September 5, 1946.

138. Lewis College of Business (1982–1983 Self-Study Report), (Detroit, 1983), p. 4.

139. Ibid; pp. 6–7; Lewis College of Business (Brochure).

140. *Detroit Free Press,* April 28, 1940.

141. *Detroit Tribune,* May 4, 1940.

142. Ibid.

143. *Detroit Tribune,* May 11, 1940.

144. Ibid.

145. *Detroit Tribune,* May 4, 1940; *Michigan Chronicle,* February 3, 1940; *Detroit Tribune,* March 23, 1940.

146. *Detroit Tribune,* May 11, 1940.

147. *Michigan Chronicle,* February 17, 1940.

148. *Detroit Tribune,* May 18, 1940.

149. *Detroit Tribune,* May 4, 11, 18, 25, 1940.

150. *Detroit Tribune,* May 11, 1940.

151. *Detroit Tribune,* May 25, 1940.

152. *Detroit Free Press,* May 9, 1940, quoted in *Detroit Tribune,* May 18, 1940.

7. PROTEST AND POLITICS

1. See chap. 5; Arthur L. Johnson, *A Brief Account of the Detroit Branch of the NAACP,* 1958 NAACP Detroit Branch Collection, box 8, folder "History of Detroit Branch NAACP," ALUA-WSU.

2. Arthur L. Johnson, "The Fight Against Discrimination in Detroit," *The Negro History Bulletin* (October 1962): p. 19; *The Fifth Annual Report of the Detroit NAACP, 1914,* p. 4.; *Eighth and Ninth Annual Report of the Detroit NAACP, 1917–1918,* p. 62.

3. Johnson, p. 19.

4. Ibid.

5. *Detroit Tribune,* July 23, 1938; August 6, 1938.

6. *Detroit Tribune,* February 11, 1939.

7. Ibid.

8. *Detroit Tribune,* April 8, 1939; April 22, 1939.

9. *Detroit Tribune,* July 15, 1939.

10. *Detroit Tribune,* July 29, 1939.

11. *Michigan Chronicle,* July 29, 1939; *Detroit Tribune,* September 2, 1939; *Michigan Chronicle,* September 2, 1937.

12. *Detroit Tribune,* January 24, 1939.

13. *Detroit Tribune,* November 11, 1939; November 16, 1940.

14. *Detroit Tribune,* June 18, 1935; May 14, 1938. See Chapter 4. *Forward with Action: Annual Report, 1943* (Detroit NAACP), p. 27.

15. *Forward with Action: Annual Report, 1943,* p. 16.

16. Ibid., p. 26.

17. Ibid., p. 26.

18. Oral interview, Arthur McPhaul, April 5, 1970, p. 8; oral interview, Mrs. Geraldine Bledsoe, 1970, p.4; oral interview, Jack Raskin, 1970, p. 7; oral interview, Beulah Whitby, September 16, 1967, n. pag.: ALUA-WSU.

19. *Detroit Tribune,* December 23, 1933.

20. Ibid.

21. Oral interview, Snow Grigsby, March 12, 1967, p. 5, ALUA-WSU.

22. Grigsby, *White Hypocrisy and Black Lethargy.*

23. Ibid.

24. Oral interview, Grigsby, p. 2.

25. *The Detroit Free Press,* February 11, 1981.

26. Oral interview, Grigsby, p. 2.

27. Ibid.

28. Julius Jacobsen, ed., *The Negro and the American Labor Movement* (Garden City, N.J.: Anchor Books, 1968) pp. 232–85; David M. Gordon, *Theories of Poverty and Unemployment: Orthodox, Radical, and Dual Labor Market Perspectives* (Lexington: D. C. Heath and Company, 1972).

29. *Detroit Tribune,* June 30, 1934; oral interview, Grigsby, p. 2.

30. Oral interview, Grigsby, p. 2.

31. Ibid.

32. Ibid.

33. Grigsby, *White Hypocrisy and Black Lethargy,* p. 25.

34. *Detroit Tribune,* February 16, 1935.

35. Ibid.

36. Grigsby, *White Hypocrisy and Black Lethargy,* p. 23; *Detroit Tribune,* April 1, 1939.

37. *Detroit Tribune,* April 15, 1939.

38. Grigsby, *White Hypocrisy and Black Lethargy,* p. 23.

39. Ibid., p. 35.

40. *Detroit Tribune,* October 29, 1938; February 11, 1939.

41. *Detroit Free Press,* February 11, 1981; oral interview, Snow Grigsby, p. 5.

42. Oral interview, Grigsby, p. 5.

43. There is some discrepancy in these two accounts of the number of light bills collected from blacks. The 1967 interview says the CRC collected 61,000. A higher figure, 64,000, is quoted in the 1981 interview. For the latter figure, see the *Detroit Free Press,* February 11, 1981.

44. Oral interview, Grigsby, p. 5.

45. *Detroit Tribune,* April 22, 1939.

46. Ibid.

47. *Detroit Tribune,* May 27, 1939.

48. Ibid.

49. Ibid.

50. *Detroit Tribune,* June 10, 1939, September 23, 1939; October 14, 1939.

51. *Detroit Tribune,* September 23, 1939; October 14, 1939; "Summary of Economic, Real Estate and Mortgage Survey Area Descriptions of Greater Detroit, Michigan." Home Owners Loan Corporation City Survey, file 1935–40, areas C-50 and D-57, box 0018, National Archives.

52. *Detroit Tribune,* November 4, 1939; November 11, 1939; January 25, 1941.

53. Robert Korstad and Nelson Lichtenstein, "Opportunities Found and Lost: Labor, Radicals and the Early Civil Rights Movement," *Journal of American History* 75, no. 3 (December 1988): p. 798.

54. *Michigan Chronicle,* February 25, 1939.

55. *Michigan Chronicle,* March 27 and April 3, 1943.

56. *Michigan Chronicle,* March 27, 1943.

57. Ibid.

58. *Michigan Chronicle,* April 3, 1943.

59. *Michigan Chronicle,* May 8, 1943.

60. Ibid.

61. *Michigan Chronicle,* November 18, 1944.

62. *Detroit Free Press,* April 12, 1943.

63. *Michigan Chronicle,* April 10, 1943.

64. Korstad and Lichtenstein, p. 789.

65. Ibid.

66. Ibid.

67. *Detroit Tribune,* July 5 and September 6, 1941.

68. *Detroit Tribune,* September 20, 1941.

69. *Detroit Tribune,* August 12, 1933.

70. Ibid.

71. *Detroit Tribune,* September 1, 15, 29, 1934; October 27, 1934.

72. *Detroit Tribune,* August 30, 1941.

73. *Michigan Chronicle,* January 21, 1943; May 13, 1944.

74. *Detroit Tribune,* April 10, 1943; May 29, 1943; June 5, 12, 1943.

75. "Fourth Congress of the Detroit Council of the National Negro Congress," June 30, 1945, vertical file, ALUA-WSU.

76. Ibid.

77. Ibid.

78. Ibid.

79. Ibid.

80. Martin Kilson, "Political Change in the Negro Ghetto," vol. 11, *Key Issues in the Afro-American Experience,* ed. Nathan L. Huggins, Martin Kilson, and Daniel M. Fox (New York: Harcourt Brace Jovanovich, 1971) pp. 167–92.

81. Ibid., p. 171.

82. Soloman, p. 57.

83. Ibid., p. 22.

84. Ibid., p. 25.

85. Soloman, p. 26.

86. Turner and Moses, p. 47.

87. Ibid.

88. Ibid.

89. Ibid.

90. Soloman, p. 61.

91. Ibid.

92. Ibid.

93. Ibid.

94. Ibid.

95. Ibid.

96. *Detroit Tribune,* July 1, 1933.

97. Ibid.

98. *Detroit Tribune,* November 10, 1934.

99. *Detroit Tribune,* September 2, 1933.

100. *Detroit Tribune,* September 3, 1938.

101. *Detroit Tribune,* November 16, 1940.

102. Gloster B. Current, "Negro Participation in the August 7, 1945 Primary in Detroit," M.A. Thesis, Wayne State University, 1946, p. 5.

103. *Michigan Chronicle,* March 31, 1945.

104. Current, p. 43.

105. Ibid.

106. Soloman, p. 49.

107. Ibid., p. 50.

108. Rea McCain, Aris A. Mallas, Jr., and Margaret K. Hedden, *40 Years in Politics: The Story of Ben Pelham* (Detroit: Wayne State University Press, 1957) pp. 38, 81.

109. Ibid., pp. 81–82.

110. Wade H. McCree, Jr., "The Negro Renaissance in Michigan Politics," *Negro History Bulletin* 26 (October 1962): p. 7.

111. Ralph J. Bunche, *The Political Status of the Negro in the Age of FDR* (Chicago: The University of Chicago Prss, 1973) p. 50.

112. Soloman, pp. 123–24; Boykin, p. 85.

113. Bailer, p. 164; Lewis, p. 38.

114. Bailer, p. 168.

115. Ibid., p. 169.

116. Ibid., p. 171.

117. Ibid.; *Detroit Tribune,* November 28, 1940.

118. *Detroit Tribune,* November 28, 1940.

119. Ibid.

120. Ibid.

121. *Detroit Tribune,* December 14, 1940.

122. Letter, Albon L. Holsey to John C. Dancy, August 9, 1928; Letter, Mareen P. Alexander to John C. Dancy, September 20, 1928, DULP-MHC, general file, box 1, folder July–September 1928.

123. Letter, Lethia C. Fleming to John C. Dancy, September 12, 1928, DULP-MHC, general file, box 1, folder July–September 1928.

124. Letter, Ralph B. Steward to John C. Dancy, July 22, 1936, DULP-MHC, Executive Secretary's file, box 3.

125. Ibid.

126. Ibid.

127. *Detroit Tribune,* March 5, 1938.

128. Ibid.

129. Ibid.

130. *Detroit Tribune,* December 14, 1940.

131. *Michigan Chronicle,* November 18, 1944.

132. Soloman, p. 55.

133. Ibid.

134. Ibid., p. 57.

135. Ibid., pp. 56–57.

136. Soloman, p. 138.

137. *Detroit Tribune,* November 16, 1940.

138. Soloman, p. 141–42; *Detroit Tribune,* November 16, 1940.

139. *Detroit Tribune,* October 26, 1940.

140. Ibid.

141. Ibid.

142. Bunch, p. 50; *Detroit Free Press,* April 26, 1967.

143. *Detroit Free Press,* April 27, 1967; *Michigan Manual 1941* (Lansing: Secretary of State, 1941) p. 664.

144. Ibid.

145. Ibid., Meier and Rudwick, pp. 32–33.

146. Meier and Rudwick, pp. 32–33.

147. *Michigan Journal of the Senate,* regular sessions: January 25, 1937, p. 79; March 25, 1937, p. 388; May 14, 1937, p. 914; Boykins, p. 126.

148. *Detroit Tribune,* August 14, 1937.

149. *Detroit Tribune,* February 5, 1938; March 5, 1938.

150. *Detroit Tribune,* May 27, 1939; December 30, 1939; October 12, 1940.

151. *Detroit Tribune,* December 16, 1939.

152. *Detroit Tribune,* April 22, 1939.

153. *Detroit Tribune,* March 20, 1943, April 3, 1943.

154. *Detroit Tribune,* November 9, 1940.

155. *Detroit Tribune,* October 19, 1940.

156. *Detroit Tribune,* November 8, 1941; McCree, p. 8.

157. *Michigan Chronicle,* April 10, 1943.

158. Ibid.

159. *Michigan Chronicle,* October 2, 1943; January 29, 1944; March 11, 1944.

160. *Michigan Chronicle,* January 29, 1944.

161. *Detroit Free Press,* April 26, 1967; *Michigan Chronicle,* August 19, 1944.

162. *Detroit Free Press,* April 26, 1967; McCree, pp. 7–8.

163. Ibid.

8. CONFLICTING STRATEGIES OF BLACK COMMUNITY BUILDING

1. See chap. 5.

2. Lewis, p. 17.

3. Letter, R. L. Bradby to C. E. Sorenson, June 7, 1929; Letter, R. L. Bradby

to C. E. Sorenson, October 14, 1937; Letter, C. E. Sorenson to R. L. Bradby, October 15, 1937, accession 38, box 125, Ford Archives, Dearborn, Michigan.

4. Ibid; Lewis, p. 17.
5. Lewis, p. 20.
6. Ibid.
7. Bailer, p. 176.
8. Ibid., p. 175; Meier and Rudwick, pp. 8–9.
9. Bailer, pp. 138–40.
10. Ibid.
11. Ibid., p. 177.
12. Ibid., pp. 155–56.
13. Ibid., p. 156.
14. Ibid.
15. Ibid.
16. Boykin, p. 85.
17. See chap. 6.
18. Bailer, p. 161.
19. Ibid., p. 166.
20. Zunz, p. 398.
21. "Industry," *The Negro in Detroit,* p. 22.
22. Bailer, pp. 190–92.
23. Ibid., p. 191.
24. Ibid., p. 193.
25. Ibid.
26. Horace R. Cayton and George S. Mitchell, *Black Workers and the New Unions* (College Park, Md.: McGrath Publishing Company, 1939) pp. 159–224; Herbert R. Northrop, *Organized Labor and the Negro* (New York and London: Harper and Brothers, 1944) chapters 5–9 passim; Meier and Rudwick, p. 34; Trotter, p. 163.
27. *Detroit Tribune,* June 5, 1937.
28. *UAW,* June 12, 1937.
29. Ibid.
30. *UAW,* July 7, 1936; Widick, p. 66.
31. *Detroit Tribune,* October 30, 1937.
32. *UAW,* November 13, 1937.
33. Ibid.
34. *Detroit Tribune,* May 14, 1938.
35. *UAW,* July 7, 1936.
36. *Detroit Tribune,* July 30, 1938, p. 10.
37. Ibid.
38. *UAW,* December 24, 1938.
39. Ibid.
40. *UAW,* December 17, 1938.
41. *UAW,* July 23, 1938.
42. *UAW,* April 9, 16, 1938.
43. *UAW,* October 15, 1938; August 30, 1939.
44. *UAW,* July 2, 1938; United Automobile Workers of America, *Proceedings of Second Annual Convention,* (Milwaukee, Wisconsin, 1937), p. 241.
45. *UAW,* August 21, 1938.
46. *UAW,* October 9, 1939.
47. *Detroit Tribune,* August 1937.
48. *UAW,* June 19, 1937.
49. Ibid.
50. *UAW,* June 5, 1937; June 19, 1937. For the racial practices of the AFL, see

"The Negro and the AFL," chap. 2, in Ray Marshall, *The Negro and Organized Labor* (New York: John Wiley & Sons, 1965) pp. 15–33.

51. *UAW,* August 1936.
52. *UAW,* June 26, 1937.
53. *UAW,* June 5, 1937; June 19, 1937; June 27, 1937.
54. *Detroit Tribune,* June 12, 1937.
55. *Detroit Tribune,* July 17, 1937.
56. Ibid.
57. *Detroit Tribune,* July 17, 1937.
58. Ibid.
59. *UAW,* June 30, 1937.
60. Ibid.
61. Ibid.
62. *Detroit Tribune,* July 31, 1937.
63. *Detroit Tribune,* July 3, 1937.
64. *Detroit Tribune,* July 10, 1937.
65. Ibid.
66. *Detroit Tribune,* July 31, 1937.
67. Ibid.
68. "Detroit Conference Largest in History," *Crisis* (August 1937): pp. 242, 244–46.
69. *UAW,* October 9, 1937.
70. Ibid.
71. "Editorial," *Crisis* 44 (August 1937).
72. *Detroit Tribune,* August 14, 1937.
73. *Detroit Tribune,* August 21, 1937.
74. *Detroit Tribune,* August 28, 1937, p. 1.
75. Ibid.
76. Ibid.
77. *UAW,* September 25, 1937.
78. Ibid.
79. Ibid.
80. *Detroit Tribune,* November 6, 1937.
81. *Detroit Tribune,* December 4, 1937.
82. *Detroit Tribune,* January 8, 1938.
83. Bailer, p. 166.
84. *Detroit Tribune,* January 8, 1938; January 29, 1938; Bailer, p. 166.
85. Bailer, p. 166.
86. *Detroit Tribune,* February 5, 1938; Personal notes of Henry Ford, accession 23, box 14, Ford Archives. This was first cited in Lewis's unpublished paper.
87. Bailer, p. 167.
88. Ibid.
89. Meier and Rudwick, p. 85.
90. Horace A. White, "Who Owns the Negro Churches," *The Christian Century* (February 9, 1938): pp. 176–77.
91. Ibid.
92. Ibid.
93. Ibid.
94. Meier and Rudwick, pp. 80–84, 106–07.
95. *UAW,* March 5, 1938.
96. Ibid.
97. Ibid.
98. Ibid.
99. Ibid.

100. *Michigan Chronicle,* February 25, 1939; April 8, 1939; April 15, 1939; July 15, 1939; June 3, 1939.

101. *UAW,* March 11, 1939.

102. *Michigan Chronicle,* March 4, 1939.

103. Ibid.

104. Meier and Rudwick, p. 210.

105. *UAW,* November 29, 1939.

106. *UAW,* December 2, 1939.

107. *Michigan Chronicle,* December 2, 1939.

108. Ibid.

109. Ibid.

110. *UAW,* November 29, 1939.

111. Leaflet, "Attention Negro Workers," 1939, Joe Brown Collection, folder 3, ALUA-WSU.

112. *Michigan Chronicle,* December 2, 1939, p. 1.

113. *UAW,* December 6, 1939, p. 5.

114. *Michigan Chronicle,* December 1939, p. 12.

115. *Dodge Bulletin,* Local No. 3, UAW-CIO, November 28, 1939, Joe Brown Collection, folder 3, ALUA-WSU.

116. *UAW,* December 6, 1939, pp. 1–2.

117. Ibid., p. 3.

118. *Detroit Tribune,* April 5, 1941.

119. Ibid.; "Ford Facts," April 5, 1941.

120. *Detroit Tribune,* April 5, 1941.

121. Ibid.

122. *Detroit Tribune,* April 12, 1941.

123. Ibid.

124. *UAW,* "Local 7 Edition," April 15, 1941.

125. Louis Emanuel Martin, "The Ford Contract: An Opportunity," *Crisis* (September 1941): p. 285.

126. *Detroit Tribune,* April 19, 1941; April 26, 1941; May 2, 1941.

127. *Detroit Tribune,* April 26, 1941.

128. *UAW,* "Ford Facts," May 20, 1941; *UAW,* June 1, 1941.

129. Meier and Rudwick, p. 113–14.

130. Interview, Shelton Tappes by Herbert Hill, October 27, 1967, p. 1, ALUA-WSU.

131. *Michigan Chronicle,* January 23, 1943; Meier and Rudwick, p. 113–14.

132. "Why We Chose the CIO," ca. 1941, UAW Organizing Committee, file "Miscellaneous Publications," ALUA-WSU.

133. Ibid.

134. *Michigan Chronicle,* January 23, 1943.

135. Meier and Rudwick, p. 117.

136. *Michigan Chronicle,* December 19, 1942.

137. Ibid.

138. Ibid.

139. Meier and Rudwick, p. 159.

140. *Michigan Chronicle,* January 30, 1945.

141. Ibid.

142. For some history on how black community-labor coalitions contributed to the community building process, see: Philip S. Foner, *Organized Labor and the Black Workers, 1619–1973* (New York: International Publisher, 1976) pp. 215–36, 332–98; Meier and Rudwick, pp. 175–206.

143. *Michigan Chronicle,* August 5, 1944.

144. Ibid.

145. Shelton Tappes, "Detroit's Negro Housing Problem," pp. 2–5, Speech given at Wayne County CIO Housing Conference, March 31, 1944, file, "Miscellaneous Publications," ALUA-WSU.

146. *Michigan Chronicle,* April 21, 1945.

147. For Mayor Orville Hubbard's role in preventing blacks from moving into Dearborn, see Joe Darden, Richard C. Hill, June M. Thomas, and Richard W. Thomas, *Detroit: Race and Uneven Development* (Philadelphia: Temple University Press, 1987), pp. 119–25.

148. *Michigan Chronicle,* April 4, 1945.

149. Ibid.; *Michigan Chronicle,* November 1, 1944.

150. *UAW,* "Ford Facts," November 15, 1942; *Michigan Chronicle,* January 23, 1943.

151. *Michigan Chronicle,* June 23, 1945.

152. Ibid.

153. Meier and Rudwick, p. 212.

154. Meier and Rudwick, 117; *UAW,* "Ford Facts," December 30, 1950; *Detroit Free Press,* April 2, 1980.

EPILOGUE

1. Widick, p. 113.

2. *Michigan Chronicle,* 1949–1953 passim.

3. *Michigan Chronicle,* "Detroit, Ten Years After," March 14, 1953.

4. For more information on the history of this alliance, see Meier and Rudwick, pp. 175–206; Wade H. McCree, Jr., "The Negro Renaissance in Michigan Politics," *Negro History Bulletin* 26 (October 1962): pp. 7–8; Victor G. Reuther, *The Brothers Reuther* (Boston: Houghton Mifflin Company, 1979), pp. 237–40; Philip S. Foner, *Organized Labor and the Black Workers, 1619–1973* (New York: International Publishers, 1974) pp. 258–59.

5. *Michigan Chronicle,* March 14, 1953. During the 1950s, white restaurants around some auto plants also discriminated against black workers; see, Denby, p. 149.

6. *Michigan Chronicle,* March 14, 1953.

7. Ibid.

8. Ibid.

9. Ibid.

10. Ibid.

11. *Michigan Chronicle,* February 28, 1953; Robert Conot, *American Odyssey* (New York: William Morrow, 1974) p. 517; Arnold R. Hirsch, *Making the Second Ghetto: Race and Housing in Chicago, 1940–1960* (New York: Cambridge University Press, 1983), pp. 1–41; Karl E. Taeuber and Alma F. Taeuber, *Negroes in Cities: Residential Segregation and Neighborhood Change* (New York: Atheneum, 1972) p. 196; Harold X. Connolly, *A Ghetto Grows in Brooklyn* (New York: New York University Press, 1977) p. 196.

12. *Michigan Chronicle,* February 28, 1953. For a more detailed discussion of the policies and politics surrounding the housing problems for blacks, see Joe T. Darden, Richard Child Hill, June Thomas, and Richard W. Thomas, *Detroit: Race and Uneven Development* (Philadelphia, Temple University Press, 1987) pp. 158–67.

13. *Michigan Chronicle,* February 28, 1953.

14. Ibid.

15. Ibid.

16. Ibid.

17. *Michigan Chronicle,* March 21, 1953; Patrick James Ashton, "Race, Class and Black Politics: The Implications of the Election of a Black Mayor for the Police and Policing in Detroit," Ph.D. dissertation, Michigan State University, 1981, pp. 368–69; *Detroit Free Press,* May 11, 1973.

18. *Michigan Chronicle,* March 21, 1953. Other impressions of the racial practices of The Detroit Police Department during this period can be found in Jack Kresnak, "City Police: A past of racism," *Blacks in Detroit* (Detroit, *Detroit Free Press,* 1980) pp. 70–74. In 1966, in his book, John C. Dancy commented on the insulting manner in which white police in Detroit addressed blacks. See Dancy, p. 232. Less than a year later, the unresolved conflicts between the white police and the black community triggered the 1967 black rebellion. See *Report of The National Advisory Commission on Civil Disorder* (New York: *New York Times,* 1968) pp. 84–107.

19. *Michigan Chronicle,* March 21, 1953.

20. Arthur L. Johnson, "The Fight Against Discrimination in Detroit," *The Negro History Bulletin* 26 (October 1962): p. 19.

21. Johnson, p. 29.

22. *Michigan Chronicle,* March 7, 1953.

23. *Michigan Chronicle,* March 7, 1953. Structural factors in the regional and local economies compounded the racial problems facing black workers. Few cities in the 1950s experienced "the severe dislocations which were the lot of Detroit." In spite of the high production and success in the auto industry (which also led to the mistaken belief that whatever was happening in the auto industry was also happening in the city), the city of Detroit was steadily deteriorating. Chronic unemployment existed among autoworkers, particularly black workers, due to the impact of postwar recessions, the elimination of small manufacturers, the loss of defense jobs, the impact of automation, and the decentralization of the auto industry, all of which affected the jobs of inner-city black workers. During the winter of 1949–50, sudden layoffs in the auto industry put 127,000 unemployed workers on the streets, many of them black. By 1953–54, a recession hit the auto industry, producing 107,000 unemployed workers. Soon after, Chrysler lost out to Ford for second place in sales, and its share of the market was reduced 2 percent. The company also collapsed. Chrysler's employment during the 1950s fell from 100,000 to 35,000, most of which occurred in Detroit where its major plants were located. This of course added to the woes of the black community. When the auto industry recovered in 1955, auto production was moving with the white flight to the suburbs, and there were still many unemployed black workers on the streets. The urban policies of the federal government also contributed to the decline of Detroit's inner city, which negatively affected the black community. By financing construction of a large highway system and insuring loans for suburban homes, the government stimulated the flight of white workers and businesses to the suburbs. See, Widick, pp. 137–41; Darden, Hill, Thomas and Thomas, pp. 16–17.

24. *Michigan Chronicle,* March 28, 1953.

25. Ibid.

SOURCES

All of the sources used in this book are cited in full in the notes. The sources listed below cover only major archives, key government documents, newspapers, proceedings, magazines, and unpublished sources.

MANUSCRIPT COLLECTIONS

Walter Reuther Labor and Urban Archives, Wayne State University, Detroit, Michigan.
  Associated Charities of Detroit Collections
  Joe Brown Collections
  Detroit Branch of the NAACP Collections
  Vertical File: Detroit Council of the National Negro Congress
  Oral Interviews: Joseph Billups, Geraldine Bledsoe, Snow Grigsby, Arthur McPhaul, Jack Raskin, Shelton Tappes, Beulah Whitley

Burton Historical Collection, Detroit Public Library, Detroit, Michigan
  Housewives League of Detroit Papers
  Rosa L. Slade Gragg Papers
  Report of the Mayor's Committee on Race Relations
  Photographs

Henry Ford Archives, Dearborn, Michigan
  C. E. Sorensen Letters

Library of Congress, Washington, D.C.
  NAACP Papers

Michigan Historical Collections, Bentley Library, Ann Arbor, Michigan
  Detroit Urban League Papers

State of Michigan Archives, Lansing, Michigan
  Photographs

National Archives, Washington, D.C.
  United States Employment Service Records, 1940–1945
  War Manpower Commission Records, 1940–1945
  Records of the Committee on Fair Employment Practices, 1940–1945
  Records of the U.S. Housing Corporation, 1918–1940
  Records of the Federal Home Loan Bank System, 1935–1940
  General Records of the Department of Labor, 1918–1925

UNPUBLISHED DOCUMENTS

Bailer, Lloyd H., "Negro Labor in the Automobile Industry." Ph.D. dissertation, University of Michigan, 1929.
Black, Harold, "Restrictive Covenants in Relation to Segregated Negro Housing in Detroit." M.S. thesis, Wayne State University.
Carlson, Glen E., "The Negro in the Industries of Detroit." Ph.D. dissertation, University of Michigan, 1929.

Carlson, Gustav G., "Number Gambling: A Study of a Culture Complex." Ph.D. dissertation, University of Michigan, 1940.

Current, Gloster B., "Negro Participation in the August 7, 1945 Primary in Detroit." M.A. thesis, Wayne State University, 1946.

Emmer, Dorothy, "The Civil and Political Status of the Negro in Michigan and the Northwest." M.A. thesis, Wayne State University, 1935.

Gill, Robert L., "The Booker T. Washington Trade Association." Student seminar paper, 1939. Michigan Historical Collection, Bentley Library, Ann Arbor, Michigan.

Jenkins, Bette Smith, "The Racial Policies of the Detroit Housing Commission and Their Administration." M.A. thesis, Wayne State University, 1950.

Leaphart, Elaine, "Historical Overview of *The Detroit Tribune*." Student paper, University of Michigan, 1977.

Levine, David Allen, "Expecting the Barbarians: Race Relations and Social Control in Detroit, 1915–1925." Ph.D. dissertation, University of Chicago, 1970.

Lewis, David. "History of Negro Employment in Detroit Area Plants of Ford Motor Company, 1914–1941." Seminar paper, University of Detroit, 1954.

Neumann, Amber C., "Twenty-Five Years of Negro Activity in Detroit, 1910–1933." M.A. thesis, University of Detroit, 1935.

Soloman, Thomas S., "Participation of Negroes in Detroit Elections." Ph.D. dissertation, University of Michigan, 1937.

Stephensen, William W., "The Colored Schools of Detroit: 1839–1869." Student paper, University of Michigan, 1959.

Woodson, June B., "A Century with the Negroes of Detroit: 1830–1930." M.A. thesis, Wayne State University, 1949.

NEWSPAPERS, MAGAZINES, AND JOURNALS, PROCEEDINGS AND REPORTS

Newspapers
  Detroit Contender
  Detroit Free Press
  Detroit Tribune [White]
  Detroit Tribune [Black]
  Detroit News
  Detroit Times
  Detroit Independent
  Detroit Advertiser
  Detroit Saturday Night
  Detroit Daily Post
  Michigan C.I.O. News
  Michigan Chronicle
  United Automobile Worker
  Plain Dealer
  Pittsburgh Courier
  New York Times
  Baltimore Afro-American
  Christian Century

Magazines and Journals
  Crisis
  Detroit In Perspective: A Journal of Regional History
  Ebony
  Journal of Negro History
  Journal of Political Economy
  Messenger
  Michigan Journal of The Senate

Michigan History
Monthly Labor Review
Negro History Bulletin
Survey
Phylon

Proceedings and Reports
Annual Reports of The Detroit NAACP
National Conference of Social Workers Proceedings
United Automobile Workers of America Proceedings
Detroit City Directories
Report of the Mayor's Committee on Race Relations

GOVERNMENT DOCUMENTS

National (U.S. Department of Commerce and Bureau of the Census)
Twelfth Census of the United States, 1900: Manufacturers
Thirteenth Census of the United States, 1910: Manufacturers
Fourteenth Census of the United States, 1920: Manufacturers
Thirteenth Census of the United States, 1910: Occupations
Fourteenth Census of the United States, 1920: Occupations
Fifteenth Census of the United States, 1930: Occupations
Sixteenth Census of the United States, 1940: The Labor Forces
Sixteenth Census of the United States, 1940: Classified Index of Occupations
Mortality Statistics: Thirty-First Annual Report, 1930
Vital Statistics of the United States, 1940
Birth, Stillbirth, and Infant Mortality Statistics: Tenth Annual Report, 1924
Birth, Stillbirth, and Infant Mortality Statistics: Seventeenth Annual Report, 1931

Local (City of Detroit)
Sixty-Fifth Annual Report of the Detroit Police Department, 1930
Seventieth Annual Report of the Detroit Police Department, 1935
Seventy-Fifth Annual Report of the Detroit Police Department, 1940
Eightieth Annual Report of the Detroit Police Department, 1945
City Directory, 1916–1931.

INDEX

Unless otherwise indicated, black *is a tacit modifier of all demographic and socio-genic entries.*

Abolition movement, 5, 12
AFL (American Federation of Labor), 169, 271–312 passim. *See also* UAW-AFL
African-American Mysteries: The Order of the Men of Oppression, 4
"Afro-American" vis-à-vis "Negro," 11
Agricultural class, transformation of, x, 30, 56–57, 124. *See also* Migrants, southern
Allen, Fred, 205, 264, 265
"Angels of Darkness," 190
Antiunionism. *See* Unionism: resistance to
Apex Film Manufacturing Company, 203
Assimilation versus solidarity, 10–11, 15, 17, 124, 217–18, 272
Associated Charities of Detroit, 53, 54, 57, 59, 81
Atlanta School of Social Work, 53, 85
Automobile industry, 14, 25, 26, 29, 30, 42–43, 45, 156–57, 277–78, 354n.23

Ballenger, John, 318
Bethel African Methodist Episcopal (AME) Church, 2, 176, 177–78, 179, 180; activities of, 177–78
Billups, Joseph, 96
Black history: promoted at Green Pastures Camp, 77–78; and the William H. Peck History Club, 178
Black Legion, 279, 281
Black Muslims. *See* Nation of Islam
Blackburn, Ruth and Thornton, 2
Bledsoe, Harold E., 232, 263–64, 268
Blount, Louis C., 205, 223, 228, 242, 264
Blues singing, 175
Booker T. Washington Trade Association (BTWTA), xiv, 176, 182, 189, 205, 213, 214–21, 227, 228, 241, 242, 313, 343n.53
Boston Massacre, 8
Bradby, Rev. Robert L., 59, 81, 176, 216, 272–73, 276, 287, 293, 296
Brewster Home Project, 192

British West Indies, celebration of emancipation of slaves in, 8, 19
Brown, John, 5, 19
Buffa, Joseph, 144, 146
Buhl Malleable Iron Company, 29, 33
Business class. *See* Professional and business class
Business development, 14, 201–208, 220; and community empowerment, 228, and consumer base, 201; and New Deal programs, 264; and non-black "brothers," 220. *See also* Economic development

Cale, Philip H., 140–41
Calvary Baptist Church, 145, 179–80
Canada: and fugitive slaves, 3–4; joint celebrations with, 9–10
Capitalists: 16, 191
—Black, 16, 191
—White: and business, 220; and workers, 280; as invaluable resource, 52; and southern migration, 50
Cass High School, 70, 74
Celebrations: importance of, 6–10; and race-consciousness, 10–11
Children's Fund of Michigan, 76
Chrysler Motor Corporation: hiring practices of, 157, 163; strikes against, 244, 299–301; and wartime conversion, 160
Churches: as catalyst, 21; as cornerstone of activity, 2–3, 175; domestics as mainstay of, 34; and DUL, 59; Ford-supported, 273–74; and gambling, 116–17; and health concerns, 82, 103, 182; largest, 179; membership, 179; and migration-based expansion, 178–79, 273; and political power, 254–55; and recreation, 69, 180; resources of, xiii, 273; as schools, 7, and self-help, 175–80; and social consciousness, 175–76, 180; and equality, 169; and social services, 176; storefront, 179; and unions, 272, 276, 291–93, 296. *See also specific churches*
CIO (Congress of Industrial Organizations), 147, 162, 169, 233, 266, 271–312 passim. *See also* UAW-CIO
Civil Rights Act (1875), 8, 12, 127

RICHARD W. THOMAS is Associate Professor of History and Urban Affairs Programs at Michigan State University. He has authored and co-authored over two dozen publications in the field of race relations and black history.